THREE NOVELS

Anatole France

THE CRIME OF SYLVESTRE BONNARD

THAIS

THE RED LILY

TABLE OF CONTENTS

From the editor

Jacques Anatole François Thibault (1844-1924) wrote under the pen name Anatole France. France's whole life was connected with books — his father was a bookseller, and bookshelves were the future writer's natural ambience. France, with his admiration of culture and written word, of reason and sensibility, revived the French tradition rooted in the XVIIIth century Enlightenment. His high rationalism was only matched by his irony and skeptical attitude to the mankind.

THE CRIME OF
SYLVESTRE BONNARD

PART I — The Log

December 24, 1849.

I had put on my slippers and my dressing-gown. I wiped away a tear with which the north wind blowing over the quay had obscured my vision. A bright fire was leaping in the chimney of my study. Ice-crystals, shaped like fern-leaves, were sprouting over the windowpanes and concealed from me the Seine with its bridges and the Louvre of the Valois.

I drew up my easy-chair to the hearth, and my table-volante, and took up so much of my place by the fire as Hamilcar deigned to allow me. Hamilcar was lying in front of the andirons, curled up on a cushion, with his nose between his paws. His think find fur rose and fell with his regular breathing. At my coming, he slowly slipped a glance of his agate eyes at me from between his half-opened lids, which he closed again almost at once, thinking to himself, "It is nothing; it is only my friend."

"Hamilcar," I said to him, as I stretched my legs — "Hamilcar, somnolent Prince of the City of Books — thou guardian nocturnal! Like that Divine Cat who combated the impious in Heliopolis — in the night of the great combat — thou dost defend from vile nibblers those books which the old savant acquired at the cost of his slender savings and indefatigable zeal. Sleep, Hamilcar, softly as a sultana, in this library, that shelters thy military virtues; for verily in thy person are united the formidable aspect of a Tatar warrior and the slumbrous grace of a woman of the Orient. Sleep, thou heroic and voluptuous Hamilcar, while awaiting the moonlight hour in which the mice will come forth to dance before the Acta Sanctorum of the learned Bolandists!"

The beginning of this discourse pleased Hamilcar, who accompanied it with a throat-sound like the song of a kettle on

7

the fire. But as my voice waxed louder, Hamilcar notified me by lowering his ears and by wrinkling the striped skin of his brow that it was bad taste on my part so to declaim.

"This old-book man," evidently thought Hamilcar, "talks to no purpose at all while our housekeeper never utters a word which is not full of good sense, full of significance — containing either the announcement of a meal or the promise of a whipping. One knows what she says. But this old man puts together a lot of sounds signifying nothing."

So thought Hamilcar to himself. Leaving him to his reflections, I opened a book, which I began to read with interest; for it was a catalogue of manuscripts. I do not know any reading more easy, more fascinating, more delightful than that of a catalogue. The one which I was reading — edited in 1824 by Mr. Thompson, librarian to Sir Thomas Raleigh — sins, it is true, by excess of brevity, and does not offer that character of exactitude which the archivists of my own generation were the first to introduce into works upon diplomatics and paleography. It leaves a good deal to be desired and to be divined. This is perhaps why I find myself aware, while reading it, of a state of mind which in nature more imaginative than mine might be called reverie. I had allowed myself to drift away this gently upon the current of my thoughts, when my housekeeper announced, in a tone of ill-humor, that Monsieur Coccoz desired to speak with me.

In fact, some one had slipped into the library after her. He was a little man — a poor little man of puny appearance, wearing a thin jacket. He approached me with a number of little bows and smiles. But he was very pale, and, although still young and alert, he looked ill. I thought as I looked at him, of a wounded squirrel. He carried under his arm a green toilette, which he put upon a chair; then unfastening the four corners of the toilette, he uncovered a heap of little yellow books.

"Monsieur," he then said to me, "I have not the honour to be known to you. I am a book-agent, Monsieur. I represent the leading houses of the capital, and in the hope that you will kindly honour me with your confidence, I take the liberty to offer you a few novelties."

Kind gods! just gods! such novelties as the homunculus Coccoz showed me! The first volume that he put in my hand was "L'Histoire de la Tour de Nesle," with the amours of Marguerite de Bourgogne and the Captain Buridan.

"It is a historical book," he said to me, with a smile — "a book of real history."

"In that case," I replied, "it must be very tiresome; for all the historical books which contain no lies are extremely tedious. I write some authentic ones myself; and if you were unlucky enough to carry a copy of any of them from door to door you would run the risk of keeping it all your life in that green baize of yours, without ever finding even a cook foolish enough to buy it from you."

"Certainly Monsieur," the little man answered, out of pure good-nature.

And, all smiling again, he offered me the "Amours d'Heloise et d'Abeilard"; but I made him understand that, at my age, I had no use for love-stories.

Still smiling, he proposed me the "Regle des Jeux de la Societe" — piquet, bezique, ecarte, whist, dice, draughts, and chess.

"Alas!" I said to him, "if you want to make me remember the rules of bezique, give me back my old friend Bignan, with whom I used to play cards every evening before the Five Academies solemnly escorted him to the cemetery; or else bring down to the frivolous level of human amusements the grave intelligence of Hamilcar, whom you see on that cushion, for he is the sole companion of my evenings."

The little man's smile became vague and uneasy.

"Here," he said, "is a new collection of society amusements — jokes and puns — with a receipt for changing a red rose to a white rose."

I told him that I had fallen out with the roses for a long time, and that, as to jokes, I was satisfied with those which I unconsciously permitted myself to make in the course of my scientific labours.

The homunculus offered me his last book, with his last smile. He said to me:

"Here is the Clef des Songes — the 'Key of Dreams' — with the explanation of any dreams that anybody can have; dreams of gold, dreams of robbers, dreams of death, dreams of falling from the top of a tower.... It is exhaustive."

I had taken hold of the tongs, and, brandishing them energetically, I replied to my commercial visitor:

"Yes, my friend; but those dreams and a thousand others, joyous or tragic, are all summed up in one — the Dream of Life; is your little yellow book able to give me the key to that?"

"Yes, Monsieur," answered the homunculus; "the book is complete, and it is not dear — one franc twenty-five centimes, Monsieur."

I called my housekeeper — for there is no bell in my room — and said to her:

"Therese, Monsieur Coccoz — whom I am going to ask you to show out — has a book here which might interest you: the 'Key of Dreams.' I shall be very glad to buy it for you."

My housekeeper responded:

"Monsieur, when one has not even time to dream awake, one has still less time to dream asleep. Thank God, my days are just enough for my work and my work for my days, and I am able to say every night, 'Lord, bless Thou the rest which I am going to take.' I never dream, either on my feet or in bed; and I never mistake my eider-down coverlet for a devil, as my cousin did; and, if you will allow me to give my opinion about it, I think you have books enough here now. Monsieur has thousands and thousands of books, which simply turn his head; and as for me, I have just tow, which are quite enough for all my wants and purposes — my Catholic prayer-book and my Cuisiniere Bourgeoise."

And with those words my housekeeper helped the little man to fasten up his stock again within the green toilette.

The homunculus Coccoz had ceased to smile. His relaxed features took such an expression of suffering that I felt sorry to have made fun of so unhappy a man. I called him back, and told him that I had caught a glimpse of a copy of the "Histoire d'Estelle et de Nemorin," which he had among his books; that I was very fond of shepherds and shepherdesses, and that I would be quite willing to purchase, at a reasonable price, the story of these two perfect lovers.

"I will sell you that book for one franc twenty-five centimes, Monsieur," replied Coccoz, whose face at once beamed with joy. "It is historical; and you will be pleased with it. I know now just what suits you. I see that you are a connoisseur. To-morrow I will bring you the Crimes des Papes. It is a good book. I will bring you the edition d'amateur, with coloured plates."

I begged him not to do anything of the sort, and sent him away happy. When the green toilette and the agent had disappeared in the shadow of the corridor I asked my housekeeper whence this little man had dropped upon us.

"Dropped is the word," she answered; "he dropped on us from the roof, Monsieur, where he lives with his wife."

"You say he has a wife, Therese? That is marvelous! Women are very strange creatures! This one must be a very unfortunate little woman."

"I don't really know what she is," answered Therese; "but every morning I see her trailing a silk dress covered with grease-spots over the stairs. She makes soft eyes at people. And, in the name of common sense! does it become a woman that has been received here out of charity to make eyes and to wear dresses like that? For they allowed the couple to occupy the attic during the time the roof was being repaired, in consideration of the fact that the husband is sick and the wife in an interesting condition. The concierge even says that the pain came on her this morning, and that she is now confined. They must have been very badly off for a child!"

"Therese," I replied, "they had no need of a child, doubtless. But Nature had decided that they should bring one into the world; Nature made them fall into her snare. One must have exceptional prudence to defeat Nature's schemes. Let us be sorry for them and not blame them! As for silk dresses, there is no young woman who does not like them. The daughters of Eve adore adornment. You yourself, Therese — who are so serious and sensible — what a fuss you make when you have no white apron to wait at table in! But, tell me, have they got everything necessary in their attic?"

"How could they have it, Monsieur?" my housekeeper made answer. "The husband, whom you have just seen, used to be a jewellery-peddler — at least, so the concierge tells me — and nobody knows why he stopped selling watches. you have just seen that his is now selling almanacs. That is no way to make an honest living, and I never will believe that God's blessing can come to an almanac-peddler. Between ourselves, the wife looks to me for all the world like a good-for-nothing — a Marie-couche toi-la. I think she would be just as capable of bringing up a child as I should be of playing the guitar. Nobody seems to know where they came from; but I am sure they must have come by Misery's coach from the country of Sans-souci."

"Wherever they have come from, Therese, they are unfortunate; and their attic is cold."

"Pardi! — the roof is broken in several places and the rain comes through in streams. They have neither furniture nor clothing. I don't think cabinet-makers and weavers work much for Christians of that sect!"

"That is very sad, Therese; a Christian woman much less well provided for than this pagan, Hamilcar here! — what does she have to say?"

"Monsieur, I never speak to those people; I don't know what she says or what she sings. But she sings all day long; I hear her from the stairway whenever I am going out or coming in."

"Well! the heir of the Coccoz family will be able to say, like the Egg in the village riddle: Ma mere me fit en chantant. ["My mother sang when she brought me into the world."] The like happened in the case of Henry IV. When Jeanne d'Albret felt herself about to be confined she began to sing an old Bearnaise canticle:

"Notre-Dame du bout du pont,
Venez a mon aide en cette heure!
Priez le Dieu du ciel
Qu'il me delivre vite,
Qu'il me donne un garcon!

"It is certainly unreasonable to bring little unfortunates into the world. But the thing is done every day, my dear Therese and all the philosophers on earth will never be able to reform the silly custom. Madame Coccoz has followed it, and she sings. This is creditable at all events! But, tell me, Therese, have you not put the soup to boil to-day?"

"Yes, Monsieur; and it is time for me to go and skim it."

"Good! but don't forget, Therese, to take a good bowl of soup out of the pot and carry it to Madame Coccoz, our attic neighbor."

My housekeeper was on the point of leaving the room when I added, just in time:

"Therese, before you do anything else, please call your friend the porter, and tell him to take a good bundle of wood out of our stock and carry it up to the attic of those Coccoz folks. See, above all, that he puts a first-class log in the lot — a real Christmas log. As for the homunculus, if he comes back again, do not allow either himself or any of his yellow books to come in here."

Having taken all these little precautions with the refined egotism of an old bachelor, I returned to my catalogue again.

With what surprise, with what emotion, with what anxiety did I therein discover the following mention, which I cannot even now copy without feeling my hand tremble:

"LA LEGENDE DOREE DE JACQUES DE GENES (Jacques de Voragine); — traduction francaise, petit in-4.

"This MS. of the fourteenth century contains, besides the tolerably complete translation of the celebrated work of Jacques de Voragine, I. The Legends of Saints Ferreol, Ferrution,

Germain, Vincent, and Droctoveus; 2. A poem 'On the Miraculous Burial of Monsieur Saint-Germain of Auxerre.' This translation, as well as the legends and the poem, are due to the Clerk Alexander.

"This MS. is written upon vellum. It contains a great number of illuminated letters, and two finely executed miniatures, in a rather imperfect state of preservation: — one represents the Purification of the Virgin, and the other the Coronation of Proserpine."

What a discovery! Perspiration moistened my forehead, and a veil seemed to come before my eyes. I trembled; I flushed; and, without being able to speak, I felt a sudden impulse to cry out at the top of my voice.

What a treasure! For more than forty years I had been making a special study of the history of Christian Gaul, and particularly of that glorious Abbey of Saint-Germain-des-Pres, whence issued forth those King-Monks who founded our national dynasty. Now, despite the culpable insufficiency of the description given, it was evident to me that the MS. of the Clerk Alexander must have come from the great Abbey. Everything proved this fact. All the legends added by the translator related to the pious foundation of the Abbey by King Childebert. Then the legend of Saint-Droctoveus was particularly significant; being the legend of the first abbot of my dear Abbey. The poem in French verse on the burial of Saint-Germain led me actually into the nave of that venerable basilica which was the umbilicus of Christian Gaul.

The "Golden Legend" is in itself a vast and gracious work. Jacques de Voragine, Definitor of the Order of Saint-Dominic, and Archbishop of Genoa, collected in the thirteenth century the various legends of Catholic saints, and formed so rich a compilation that from all the monasteries and castles of the time there arouse the cry: "This is the 'Golden Legend.'" The "Legende Doree" was especially opulent in Roman hagiography. Edited by an Italian monk, it reveals its best merits in the treatment of matters relating to the terrestrial domains of Saint

Peter. Voragine can only perceive the greater saints of the Occident as through a cold mist. For this reason the Aquitanian and Saxon translators of the good legend-writer were careful to add to his recital the lives of their own national saints.

I have read and collated a great many manuscripts of the "Golden Legend." I know all those described by my learned colleague, M. Paulin Paris, in his handsome catalogue of the MSS. of the Biblotheque du Roi. There were two among them which especially drew my attention. One is of the fourteenth century and contains a translation by Jean Belet; the other, younger by a century, presents the version of Jacques Vignay. Both come from the Colbert collection, and were placed on the shelves of that glorious Colbertine library by the Librarian Baluze — whose name I can never pronounce without uncovering my head; for even in the century of the giants of erudition, Baluze astounds by his greatness. I know also a very curious codex in the Bigot collection; I know seventy-four printed editions of the work, commencing with the venerable ancestor of all — the Gothic of Strasburg, begun in 1471, and finished in 1475. But no one of those MSS., no one of those editions, contains the legends of Saints Ferreol, Ferrution, Germain, Vincent, and Droctoveus; no one bears the name of the Clerk Alexander; no one, in find, came from the Abbey of Saint-Germain-des-Pres. Compared with the MS. described by Mr. Thompson, they are only as straw to gold. I have seen with my eyes, I have touched with my fingers, an incontrovertible testimony to the existence of this document. But the document itself — what has become of it? Sir Thomas Raleigh went to end his days by the shores of the Lake of Como, whither he carried with him a part of his literary wealth. Where did the books go after the death of that aristocratic collector? Where could the manuscript of the Clerk Alexander have gone?

"And why," I asked myself, "why should I have learned that this precious book exists, if I am never to possess it — never even to see it? I would go to seek it in the burning heart of Africa, or in the icy regions of the Pole if I knew it were there. But I do not know where it is. I do not know if it be guarded in a triple-locked iron case by some jealous biblomaniac. I do not know if it be growing mouldy in the attic of some ignoramus. I shudder at the thought that perhaps its tore-out leaves may have been used to cover the pickle-jars of some housekeeper."

August 30, 1850

The heavy heat compelled me to walk slowly. I kept close to the walls of the north quays; and, in the lukewarm shade, the shops of the dealers in old books, engravings, and antiquated furniture drew my eyes and appealed to my fancy. Rummaging and idling among these, I hastily enjoyed some verses spiritedly thrown off by a poet of the Pleiad. I examined an elegant Masquerade by Watteau. I felt, with my eye, the weight of a two-handed sword, a steel gorgerin, a morion. What a thick helmet! What a ponderous breastplate — Seigneur! A giant's garb? No — the carapace of an insect. The men of those days were cuirassed like beetles; their weakness was within them. To-day, on the contrary, our strength is interior, and our armed souls dwell in feeble bodies.

...Here is a pastel-portrait of a lady of the old time — the face, vague like a shadow, smiles; and a hand, gloved with an openwork mitten, retains upon her satiny knees a lap-dog, with a ribbon about its neck. That picture fills me with a sort of charming melancholy. Let those who have no half-effaced pastels in their own hearts laugh at me! Like the horse that scents the stable, I hasten my pace as I near my lodgings. There it is — that great human hive, in which I have a cell, for the purpose of therein distilling the somewhat acrid honey of erudition. I climb the stairs with slow effort. Only a few steps more, and I shall be at my own door. But I divine, rather than see, a robe descending with a sound of rustling silk. I stop, and press myself against the balustrade to make room. The lady who is coming down is bareheaded; shi is young; she sings; her eyes and teeth gleam in the shadow, for she laughs with lips and eyes at the same time. She is certainly a neighbor, and a very familiar one. She holds in her arms a pretty child, a little boy — quite naked, like the son of a goddess; he has a medal hung round his neck by a little silver chain. I see him sucking his thumb and looking at me with those big eyes so newly opened on this old universe. The mother simultaneously looks at me in a sly, mysterious way; she stops — I think blushes a little — and holds out the little creature to me. The baby has a pretty wrinkle between wrist and arm, a pretty wrinkle about his neck, and all over him, from head to foot, the daintiest dimples laugh in his rosy flesh.

The mamma shows him to me with pride.

"Monsieur," she says, "don't you think he is very pretty — my little boy?"

She takes one tiny hand, lifts it to the child's own lips, and, drawing out the darling pink fingers again towards me, says,

"Baby, throw the gentleman a kiss."

Then, folding the little being in her arms, she flees away with the agility of a cat, and is lost to sight in a corridor which, judging by the odour, must lead to some kitchen.

I enter my own quarters.

"Therese, who can that young mother be whom I saw bareheaded on the stairs just now, with a pretty little boy?"

And Therese replies that it was Madame Coccoz.

I stare up at the ceiling, as if trying to obtain some further illumination. Therese then recalls to me the little book-peddler who tried to sell me almanacs last year, while his wife was lying in.

"And Coccoz himself?" I asked.

I was answered that I would never see him again. The poor little man had been laid away underground, without my knowledge, and, indeed, with the knowledge of very few people, on a short time after the happy delivery of Madame Coccoz. I leaned that his wife had been able to console herself: I did likewise.

"But, Therese," I asked, "has Madame Coccoz got everything she needs in that attic of hers?"

"You would be a great dupe, Monsieur," replied my housekeeper, "if you should bother yourself about that creature.

17

They gave her notice to quit the attic when the roof was repaired. But she stays there yet — in spite of the proprietor, the agent, the concierge, and the bailiffs. I think she has bewitched every one of them. She will leave the attic when she pleases, Monsieur; but she is going to leave in her own carriage. Let me tell you that!"

Therese reflected for a moment; and then uttered these words:

"A pretty face is a curse from Heaven."

"Then I ought to thank Heaven for having spared me that curse. But here! put my hat and cane away. I am going to amuse myself with a few pages of Moreri. If I can trust my old fox-nose, we are going to have a nicely flavoured pullet for dinner. Look after that estimable fowl, my girl, and spare your neighbors, so that you and your old master may be spared by them in turn."

Having thus spoken, I proceeded to follow out the tufted ramifications of a princely genealogy.

May 7, 1851

I have passed the winter according to the ideal of the sages, in angello cum libello; and now the swallows of the Quai Malaquais find me on their return about as when they left me. He who lives little, changes little; and it is scarcely living at all to use up one's days over old texts.

Yet I feel myself to-day a little more deeply impregnated than ever before with that vague melancholy which life distils. The economy of my intelligence (I dare scarcely confess it to myself!) has remained disturbed ever since that momentous hour in which the existence of the manuscript of the Clerk Alexander was first revealed to me.

It is strange that I should have lost my rest simply on account of a few old sheets of parchment; but it is unquestionably true. The poor man who has no desires possesses the greatest of riches; he possesses himself. The rich man who desires something is only a wretched slave. I am just such a slave. The sweetest pleasures — those of converse with some one of a delicate and well-balanced mind, or dining out with a friend — are insufficient to enable me to forget the manuscript which I know that I want, and have been wanting from the moment I knew of its existence. I feel the want of it by day and by night: I feel the want of it in all my joys and pains; I feel the want of it while at work or asleep.

I recall my desires as a child. How well I can now comprehend the intense wishes of my early years!

I can see once more, with astonishing vividness, a certain doll which, when I was eight years old, used to be displayed in the window of an ugly little shop of the Rue de Seine. I cannot tell how it happened that this doll attracted me. I was very proud of being a boy; I despised little girls; and I longed impatiently for the day (which alas! has come) when a strong beard should bristle on my chin. I played at being a soldier; and, under the pretext of obtaining forage for my rocking-horse, I used to make sad havoc among the plants my poor mother delighted to keep on her window-sill. Manly amusements those, I should say! And, nevertheless, I was consumed with longing for a doll. Characters like Hercules have such weaknesses occasionally. Was the one I had fallen in love with at all beautiful? No. I can see her now. She had a splotch of vermilion on either cheek, short soft arms, horrible wooden hands, and long sprawling legs. Her flowered petticoat was fastened at the waist with two pins. Even now I cans see the balck heads of those two pins. It was a decidedly vulgar doll — smelt of the faubourg. I remember perfectly well that, child as I was then, before I had put on my first pair of trousers, I was quite conscious in my own way that this doll lacked grace and style — that she was gross, that she was course. But I loved her in spite of that; I loved her just for that; I loved her only; I wanted her. My soldiers and my drums had become as nothing in my eyes, I ceased to stick sprigs of heliotrope and veronica into the mouth of my rocking-horse. That doll was all the world to me. I invented ruses worthy of a savage to oblige Virginie, my nurse, to take me by the little shop in the Rue de Seine. I would press my nose against the window until my nurse had to take my arm and drag me away. "Monsieur Sylvestre, it is late, and your mamma will scold you." Monsieur Sylvestre in those days made very little of either scoldings or whippings. But his nurse lifted him up like a feather, and Monsieur Sylvestre yielded to force. In after-years, with age, he degenerated, and sometimes yielded to fear. But at that time he used to fear nothing.

I was unhappy. An unreasoning but irresistible shame prevented me from telling my mother about the object of my love. Thence all my sufferings. For many days that doll, incessantly present in fancy, danced before my eyes, stared at me fixedly, opened her arms to me, assuming in my imagination a sort of life which made her appear at once mysterious and weird, and thereby all the more charming and desirable.

Finally, one day — a day I shall never forget — my nurse took me to see my uncle, Captain Victor, who had invited me to lunch. I admired my uncle a great deal, as much because he had fired the last French cartridge at Waterloo, as because he used to prepare with his own hands, at my mother's table, certain chapons-a-l'ail [Crust on which garlic has been rubbed], which he afterwards put in the chicory salad. I thought that was very fine! My Uncle Victor also inspired me with much respect by his frogged coat, and still more by his way of turning the whole house upside down from the moment he came into it. Even now I cannot tell just how he managed it, but I can affirm that whenever my Uncle Victor found himself in any assembly of twenty persons, it was impossible to see or to hear anybody but him. My excellent father, I have reason to believe, never shared my admiration for Uncle Victor, who used to sicken him with his pipe, give him great thumps in the back by way of friendliness, and accuse him of lacking energy. My mother, though always showing a sister's indulgence to the Captain, sometimes advised him to fold the brandy-bottle a little less frequently. But I had no part either in these repugnances or these reproaches, and Uncle Victor inspired me with the purest enthusiasm. It was therefore with a feeling of pride that I entered into the little lodging he occupied in the Rue Guenegaud. The entire lunch, served on a small table close to the fireplace, consisted of cold meats and confectionery.

The Captain stuffed me with cakes and undiluted wine. He told me of numberless injustices to which he had been a victim. He complained particularly of the Bourbons; and as he neglected to tell me who the Bourbons were, I got the idea — I can't tell how — that the Bourbons were horse-dealers established at Waterloo. The Captain, who never interrupted his talk except for the purpose of pouring out wine, furthermore made charges against a number of dirty scoundrels, blackguards, and good-for-nothings whom I did not know anything about, but whom I hated from the bottom of my heart. At dessert I thought I heard the Captain say my father was a man who could be led anywhere by the nose; but I am not quite sure that I understood him. I had a buzzing in my ears; and it seemed to me that the table was dancing.

My uncle put on his frogged coat, took his bell shaped hat, and we descended to the street, which seemed to me singularly changed. It looked to me as if I had not been in it before for ever so long a time. Nevertheless, when we came to the Rue de Seine, the idea of my doll suddenly returned to my mind and excited me in an extraordinary way. My head was on fire. I resolved upon a desperate expedient. We were passing before the window. She was there, behind the glass — with her red checks, and her flowered petticoat, and her long legs.

"Uncle," I said, with a great effort, "will you buy that doll for me?"

And I waited.

"Buy a doll for a boy — sacrebleu!" cried my uncle, in a voice of thunder. "Do you wish to dishonour yourself? And it is that old Mag there that you want! Well, I must compliment you, my young fellow! If you grow up with such tastes as that, you will never have any pleasure in life; and your comrades will call you a precious ninny. If you asked me for a sword or a gun, my boy, I would buy them for you with the last silver crown of my pension. But to buy a doll for you — by all that's holy! — to disgrace you!

21

Never in the world! Why, if I were ever to see you playing with a puppet rigged out like that, Monsieur, my sister's son, I would disown you for my nephew!"

On hearing these words, I felt my heart so wrung that nothing but pride — a diabolical pride — kept me from crying.

My uncle, suddenly calming down, returned to his ideas about the Bourbons; but I, still smarting under the weight of his indignation, felt an unspeakable shame. My resolve was quickly made. I promised myself never to disgrace myself — I firmly and for ever renounced that red-cheeked doll.

I felt that day, for the first time, the austere sweetness of sacrifice.

Captain, though it be true that all your life you swore like a pagan, smoked like a beadle, and drank like a bell-ringer, be your memory nevertheless honoured — not merely because you were a brave soldier, but also because you revealed to your little nephew in petticoats the sentiment of heroism! Pride and laziness had made you almost insupportable, Uncle Victor! — but a great heart used to beat under those frogs upon your coat. You always used to wear, I now remember, a rose in your button-hole. That rose which you offered so readily to the shop-girls — that large, open-hearted flower, scattering its petals to all the winds, was the symbol of your glorious youth. You despised neither wine nor tobacco; but you despised life. Neither delicacy nor common sense could have been learned from you, Captain; but you taught me, even at an age when my nurse had to wipe my nose, a lesson of honour and self-abrogation that I shall never forget.

You have now been sleeping for many years in the Cemetery of Mont-Parnasse, under a plain slab bearing the epitaph:

CI-GIT

ARISTIDE VICTOR MALDENT,

Capitaine d'Infanterie,

Chevalier de la Legion d'Honneur.

But such, Captain, was not the inscription devised by yourself to be placed above those old bones of yours — knocked about so long on fields of battle and in haunts of pleasure.

22

Among your papers was found this proud and bitter epitaph, which, despite your last will none could have ventured to put upon your tomb:

CI-GIT

UN BRIGAND DE LA LOIRE

"Therese, we will get a wreath of immortelles to-morrow, and lay them on the tomb of the Brigand of the Loire." ...

But Therese is not here. And how, indeed, could she be near me, seeing that I am at the rondpoint of the Champs-Elysees? There, at the termination of the avenue, the Arc de Triomphe, which bears under its vaults the names of Uncle Victor's companions-in-arms, opens its giant gate against the sky. The trees of the avenue are unfolding to the sun of spring their first leaves, still all pale and chilly. Beside me the carriages keep rolling by to the Bois de Boulogne. Unconsciously I have wandered into this fashionable avenue on my promenade, and halted, quite stupidly, in front of a booth stocked with gingerbread and decanters of liquorice-water, each topped by a lemon. A miserable little boy, covered with rags, which expose his chapped skin, stares with widely opened eyes at those sumptuous sweets which are not for such as he. With the shamelessness of innocence he betrays his longing. His round, fixed eyes contemplate a certain gingerbread man of lofty stature. It is a general, and it looks a little like Uncle Victor. I take it, I pay for it, and present it to the little pauper, who dares not extend his hand to receive it — for, by reason of precocious experience, he cannot believe in luck; he looks at me, in the same way that certain big dogs do, with the air of one saying, "You are cruel to make fun of me like that!"

"Come, little stupid," I say to him, in that rough tone I am accustomed to use, "take it — take it, and eat it; for you, happier than I was at your age, you can satisfy your tastes without disgracing yourself."...And you, Uncle Victor — you, whose manly figure has been recalled to me by that gingerbread general, come, glorious Shadow, help me to forget my new doll. We remain for ever children, and are always running after new toys.

23

Same day.

In the oddest way that Coccoz family has become associated in my mind with the Clerk Alexander.

"Therese," I said, as I threw myself into my easy-chair, "tell me if the little Coccoz is well, and whether he has got his first teeth yet — and bring me my slippers."

"He ought to have them by this time, Monsieur," replied Therese; "but I never saw them. The very first fine day of spring the mother disappeared with the child, leaving furniture and clothes and everything behind her. They found thirty-eight empty pomade-pots in the attic. It passes all belief! She had visitors latterly; and you may be quite sure she is not now in a convent of nuns. The niece of the concierge says she saw her driving about in a carriage on the boulevards. I always told you she would end badly."

"Therese," I replied, "that young woman has not ended either badly or well as yet. Wait until the term of her life is over before you judge her. And be careful not to talk too much with that concierge. It seemed to me — though I only saw her for a moment on the stairs — that Madame Coccoz was very fond of her child. For that mother's love at least, she deserves credit."

"As far as that goes, Monsieur, certainly the little one never wanted for anything. In all the Quarter one could not have found a child better kept, or better nourished, or more petted and coddled. Every day that God makes she puts a clean bib on him, and sings to him to make him laugh from morning till night."

"Therese, a poet has said, 'That child whose mother has never smiled upon him is worthy neither of the table of the gods nor of the couch of the goddesses.'"

July 8, 1852.

Having been informed that the Chapel of the Virgin at Saint-Germain-des-Pres was being repaved, I entered the church with the hope of discovering some old inscriptions, possibly exposed by the labours of the workmen. I was not disappointed. The architect kindly showed me a stone which he had just had raised up against the wall. I knelt down to look at the inscription engraved upon that stone; and then, half aloud, I read in the shadow of the old apsis these words, which made my heart leap:

"Cy-gist Alexandre, moyne de ceste eglise, qui fist mettre en argent le menton de Saint-Vincent et de Saint-Amant et le pie des Innocens; qui toujours en son vivant fut preud'homme et vayllant. Priez pour l'ame de lui."

I wiped gently away with my handkerchief the dust covering that gravestone; I could have kissed it.

"It is he! it is Alexander!" I cried out; and from the height of the vaults the name fell back upon me with a clang, as if broken.

The silent severity of the beadle, whom I saw advancing towards me, made me ashamed of my enthusiasm; and I fled between the two holy water sprinklers with which tow rival "rats d'eglise" seemed desirous of barring my way.

At all events it was certainly my own Alexander! there could be no more doubt possible; the translator of the "Golden Legend," the author of the saints lives of Saints Germain, Vincent, Ferreol, Ferrution, and Droctoveus was, just as I had supposed, a monk of Saint-Germain-des-Pres. And what a monk, too — pious and generous! He had a silver chin, a silver head, and a silver foot made, that certain precious remains should be covered with an incorruptible envelope! But shall I never be able to view his handiwork? or is this new discovery only destined to increase my regrets?

August 20, 1859.

"I, that please some, try all; both joy and terror Of good and bad; that make and unfold error — Now take upon me, in the name of Time To use my wings. Impute it not a crime To me or my swift passage, that I slide O'er years."

Who speaks thus? 'Tis an old man whom I know too well. It is Time.

Shakespeare, after having terminated the third act of the "Winter's Tale," pauses in order to leave time for little Perdita to grow up in wisdom and in beauty; and when he raises the curtain again he evokes the ancient Scythe-bearer upon the stage to render account to the audience of those many long days which have weighted down upon the head of the jealous Leontes.

Like Shakespeare in his play, I have left in this diary of mine a long interval to oblivion; and after the fashion of the poet, I make Time himself intervene to explain the omission of ten whole years. Ten whole years, indeed, have passed since I wrote one single line in this diary; and now that I take up the pen again, I have not the pleasure, alas! to describe a Perdita "now grown in grace." Youth and beauty are the faithful companions of poets; but those charming phantoms scarcely visit the rest of us, even for the space of a season. We do not know how to retain them with us. If the fair shade of some Perdita should ever, through some inconceivable whim, take a notion to traverse my brain, she would hurt herself horribly against heaps of dog-eared parchments. Happy the poets! — their white hairs never scare away the hovering shades of Helens, Francescas, Juliets, Julias, and Dorotheas! But the nose alone of Sylvestre Bonnard would put to flight the whole swarm of love's heroines.

Yet I, like others, have felt beauty; I have known that mysterious charm which Nature has lent to animate form; and the clay which lives has given to me that shudder of delight which makes the lover and the poet. But I have never known either how to love or how to sing. Now in my memory — all encumbered as it is with the rubbish of old texts — I can discern again, like a miniature forgotten in some attic, a certain bright young face, with violet eyes.... Why, Bonnard, my friend, what an old fool you are becoming! Read that catalogue which a Florentine bookseller sent you this very morning. It is a catalogue of Manuscripts; and he promises you a description of several famous ones, long preserved by the collectors of Italy and Sicily. There is something better suited to you, something more in keeping with your present appearance.

I read; I cry out! Hamilcar, who has assumed with the approach of age an air of gravity that intimidates me, looks at me reproachfully, and seems to ask me whether there is any rest in this world, since he cannot enjoy it beside me, who am old also like himself.

In the sudden joy of my discovery, I need a confidant; and it is to the sceptic Hamilcar that I address myself with all the effusion of a happy man.

"No, Hamilcar! no," I said to him; "there is no rest in this world, and the quietude which you long for is incompatible with the duties of life. And you say that we are old, indeed! Listen to what I read in this catalogue, and then tell me whether this is a time to be reposing:

"'LA LEGENDE DOREE DE JACQUES DE VORAGINE; — trduction francaise du quatorzieme sicle, par le Clerc Alexandre.

"'Superb MS., ornamented with two miniatures, wonderfully executed, and in a perfect state of preservation: — one representing the Purification of the Virgin; the other the Coronation of Proserpine.

"'At the termination of the "Legende Doree" are the Legends of Saints Ferreol, Ferrution, Germain, and Droctoveus (xxxviij pp.) and the Miraculous Sepulture of Monsieur Saint-Germain d'Auxerre (xij pp.).

"'This rare manuscript, which formed part of the collection of Sir Thomas Raleigh, is now in the private study of Signor Michel-Angelo Polizzi, of Girgenti.'"

"You hear that, Hamilcar? The manuscript of the Clerk Alexander is in Sicily, at the house of Michel-Angelo Polizzi. Heaven grant he may be a friend of learned men! I am going to write him!"

Which I did forthwith. In my letter I requested Signor Polizzi to allow me to examine the manuscript of Clerk Alexander, stating on what grounds I ventured to consider myself worthy of so great a favour. I offered at the same time to put at his disposal several unpublished texts in my own possession, not devoid of interest. I begged him to favour me with a prompt reply, and below my signature I wrote down all my honorary titles.

"Monsieur! Monsieur! where are you running like that?" cried Therese, quite alarmed, coming down the stairs in pursuit of me, four steps at a time, with my hat in her hand.

"I am going to post a letter, Therese."

"Good God! is that a way to run out in the street, bareheaded, like a crazy man?"

"I am crazy, I know, Therese. But who is not? Give me my hat, quick!"

"And your gloves, Monsieur! and your umbrella!"

I had reached the bottom of the stairs, but still heard her protesting and lamenting.

October 10, 1859.

I awaited Signor Polizzi's reply with ill-contained impatience. I could not even remain quiet; I would make sudden nervous gestures — open books and violently close them again. One day I happened to upset a book with my elbow — a volume of Moreri. Hamilcar, who was washing himself, suddenly stopped, and looked angrily at me, with his paw over his ear. Was this the tumultuous existence he must expect under my roof? Had there not been a tacit understanding between us that we should live a peaceful life? I had broken the covenant.

"My poor dear comrade," I made answer, "I am the victim of a violent passion, which agitates and masters me. The passions are enemies of peace and quiet, I acknowledge; but without them there would be no arts or industries in the world. Everybody would sleep naked on a dung-heap; and you would not be able, Hamilcar, to repose all day on a silken cushion, in the City of Books."

I expatiated no further to Hamilcar on the theory of the passions, however, because my housekeeper brought me a letter. It bore the postmark of Naples and read as follows:

"Most Illustrious Sir, — I do indeed possess that incomparable manuscript of the 'Golden Legend' which could not escape your keen observation. All-important reasons, however, forbid me, imperiously, tyrannically, to let the manuscript go out of my possession for a single day, for even a single minute. It will be a joy and pride for me to have you examine it in my humble home in Girgenti, which will be embellished and illuminated by your presence. It is with the most anxious expectation of your visit that I presume to sign myself, Seigneur Academician, "Your humble and devoted servant "Michel-Angelo Polizzi, "Wine-merchant and Archaeologist at Girgenti, Sicily."

Well, then! I will go to Sicily:

"Extremum hunc, Arethusa, mihi concede laborem."

October 25, 1859.

My resolve had been taken and my preparations made; it only remained for me to notify my housekeeper. I must acknowledge it was a long time before I could make up my mind to tell her I was going away. I feared her remonstrances, her railleries, her objurgations, her tears. "She is a good, kind girl," I said to myself; "she is attacked to me; she will want to prevent me from going; and the Lord knows that when she has her mind set upon anything, gestures and cries cost her no effort. In this instance she will be sure to call the concierge, the scrubber, the mattress-maker, and the seven sons of the fruit-seller; they will all kneel down in a circle around me; they will begin to cry, and then they will look so ugly that I shall be obliged to yield, so as not to have the pain of seeing them any more."

Such were the awful images, the sick dreams, which fear marshaled before my imagination. Yes, fear — "fecund Fear," as the poet says — gave birth to these monstrosities in my brain. For — I may as well make the confession in these private pages — I am afraid of my housekeeper. I am aware that she knows I am weak; and this fact alone is sufficient to dispel all my courage in any contest with her. Contests are of frequent occurrence; and I invariably succumb.

But for all that, I had to announce my departure to Therese. She came into the library with an armful of wood to make a little fire — "une flambe," she said. For the mornings are chilly. I watched her out of the corner of my eye while she crouched down at the hearth, with her head in the opening of the fireplace. I do not know how I then found the courage to speak, but I did so without much hesitation. I got up, and, walking up and down the room, observed in a careless tone, with that swaggering manner characteristic of cowards,

"By the way, Therese, I am going to Sicily."

Having thus spoken, I awaited the consequence with great anxiety. Therese did not reply. Her head and her vast cap remained buried in the fireplace; and nothing in her person, which I closely watched, betrayed the least emotion. She poked some paper under the wood, and blew up the fire. That was all!

Finally I saw her face again; — it was calm — so calm that it made me vexed. "Surely," I thought to myself, "this old maid has no heart. She lets me go away without saying so much as AH! Can the absence of her old master really affect her so little?"

"Well, then go, Monsieur," she answered at last, "only be back here by six o'clock! There is a dish for dinner to-day which will not wait for anybody."

Naples, November 10, 1859.

"Co tra calle vive, magna, e lave a faccia."

I understand, my friend — for three centimes I can eat, drink, and wash my face, all by means of one of those slices of watermelon you display there on a little table. But Occidental prejudices would prevent me from enjoying that simple pleasure freely and frankly. And how could I suck a watermelon? I have enough to do mereley to keep on my feet in this crowd. What a luminous, noisy night in the Strada di Porto! Mountains of fruit tower up in the shops, illuminated by multicoloured lanterns. Upon charcoal furnaces lighted in the open air water boils and steams, and ragouts are singing in frying-pans. The smell of fried fish and hot meats tickles my nose and makes me sneeze. At this moment I find that my handkerchief has left the pocket of my frock-coat. I am pushed, lifted up, and turned about in every direction by the gayest, the most talkative, the most animated and the most adroit populace possible to imagine; and suddenly a young woman of the people, while I am admiring her magnificent hair, with a single shock of her powerful elastic shoulder, pushes me staggering three paces back at least, without injury, into the arms of a maccaroni-eater, who receives me with a smile.

I am in Naples. How I ever managed to arrive here, with a few mutilated and shapeless remains of baggage, I cannot tell, because I am no longer myself. I have been travelling in a condition of perpetual fright; and I think that I must have looked awhile ago in this bright city like an owl bewildered by sunshine. To-night it is much worse! Wishing to obtain a glimpse of popular manners, I went to the Strada di Porto, where I now am. All about me animated throngs of people crowd and press before the eating-places; and I float like a waif among these living surges, which, even while they submerge you, still caress. For this Neopolitan people has, in its very vivacity, something indescribably gentle and polite. I am not roughly jostled, I am merely swayed about; and I think that by dint of thus rocking me to and fro, these good folks want to lull me asleep on my feet. I admire, as I tread the lava pavements of the strada, those porters and fishermen who move by me chatting, singing, smoking, gesticulating, quarrelling, and embracing each other the next moment with astonishing versatility of mood. They live through all their sense at the same time; and, being philosophers without knowing it, keep the measure of their desires in accordance with the brevity of life. I approach a much-patronised tavern, and see inscribed above the entrance this quatrain in Neopolitan patois:

"Amice, alliegre magnammo e bevimmo
N fin che n'ce stace noglio a la lucerna:
Chi sa s'a l'autro munno n'ce verdimmo?
Chi sa s'a l'autro munno n'ce taverna?"
["Friends, let us merrily eat and drink
as long as oil remains in the lamp:
Who knows if we shall meet again in another world?
Who knows if in the other world there will be a tavern?"]

Even such counsels was Horace wont to give to his friends. You received them, Posthumus; you heard them also, Leuconoe, perverse beauty who wished to know the secrets of the future. That future is now the past, and we know it well. Of a truth you were foolish to worry yourselves about so small a matter; and your friend showed his good sense when he told you to take life wisely and to filter your Greek wines — "Sapias, vina liques." Even thus the sight of a fair land under a spotless sky urges to the pursuit of quiet pleasures. but there are souls for ever harassed by some sublime discontent; those are the noblest. You were of such, Leuconoe; and I, visiting for the first time, in my declining years, that city where your beauty was famed of old, I salute with deep respect your melancholy memory. Those souls of kin to your own who appeared in the age of Chrisitianity were souls of saints; and the "Golden Legend" is full of the miracles they wrought. Your friend Horace left a less noble posterity, and I see one of his descendants in the person of that tavern poet, who at this moment is serving out wine in cups under the epicurean motto of his sign.

And yet life decides in favour of friend Flaccus, and his philosophy is the only one which adapts itself to the course of events. There is a fellow leaning against that trellis-work covered with vine-leaves, and eating an ice, while watching the stars. He would not stoop even to pick up the old manuscript I am going to seek with so much trouble and fatigue. And in truth man is made rather to eat ices than to pore over old texts.

I continued to wander about among the drinkers and the singers. There were lovers biting into beautiful fruit, each with an arm about the other's waist. Man must be naturally bad; for all this strange joy only evoked in me a feeling of uttermost despondency. That thronging populace displayed such artless delight in the simple act of living, that all the shynesses begotten by my old habits as an author awoke and intensified into something like fright. Furthermore, I found myself much discouraged by my inability to understand a word of all the storm of chatter about me. It was a humiliating experience for a philologist. Thus I had begun to feel quite sulky, when I was startled to hear someone behind me observe:

"Dimitri, that old man is certainly a Frenchman. He looks so bewildered that I really fell sorry for him. Shall I speak to him? …He has such a goo-natured look, with that round back of his — do you not think so, Dimitri?"

It was said in French by a woman's voice. For the moment it was disagreeable to hear myself spoken of as an old man. Is a man old at sixty-two? Only the other day, on the Pont des Arts, my colleague Perrot d'Avrignac complimented me on my youthful appearance; and I should think him a better authority about one's age than that young chatterbox who has taken it on herself to make remarks about my back. My back is round, she says. Ah! ah! I had some suspicion myself to that effect, but I am not going now to believe it at all, since it is the opinion of a giddy-headed young woman. Certainly I will not turn my head round to see who it was that spoke; but I am sure it was a pretty woman. Why? Because she talks like a capricious person and like a spoiled child. Ugly women may be naturally quite as capricious as pretty ones; but as they are never petted and spoiled, and as no allowances are made for them, they soon find themselves obliged either to suppress their whims or to hide them. On the other hand, the pretty women can be just as fantastical as they please. My neighbour is evidently one of the latter…. But, after all, coming to think it over, she really did nothing worse than to express, in her own way, a kindly thought about me, for which I ought to feel grateful.

These reflections — include the last and decisive one — passed through my mind in less than a second; and if I have taken a whole minute to tell them, it is characteristic of most philologists. In less than a second, therefore, after the voice had ceased, I did turn round, and saw a pretty little woman — a sprightly brunette.

"Madame," I said, with a bow, "excuse my involuntary indiscretion. I could not help overhearing what you have just said. You would like to be of service to a poor old man. And the wish, Madame, has already been fulfilled — the mere sound of a French voice has given me such pleasure that I must thank you."

I bowed again, and turned to go away; but my foot slipped upon a melon-rind, and I should certainly have embraced the Parthenopean soil had not the young lady put out her hand and caught me.

There is a force in circumstances — even in the very smallest circumstances — against which resistance is vain. I resigned myself to remain the protege of the fair unknown.

"It is late," she said; "do you not wish to go back to your hotel, which must be quite close to ours — unless it be the same one?"

"Madame," I replied, "I do not know what time it is, because somebody has stolen my watch; but I think, as you say, that it must be time to retire; and I shall be very glad to regain my hotel in the company of such courteous compatriots."

So saying, I bowed once more to the young lady, and also saluted her companion, a silent colossus with a gentle and melancholy face.

After having gone a little way with them, I learned, among other matters, that my new acquaintances were the Prince and Princess Trepof, and that they were making a trip round the world for the purpose of finding match-boxes, of which they were making a collection.

We proceeded along a narrow, tortuous vicoletto, lighted only by a single lamp burning in the niche of a Madonna. The purity and transparency of the air gave a celestial softness and clearness to the very darkness itself; and one could find one's way without difficulty under such a limpid night. But in a little while we began to pass through a "venella," or, in Neopolitan parlance, a sottoportico, which led under so many archways and so many far-projecting balconies that no gleam of light from the sky could reach us. My young guide had made us take this route as a short cut, she assured us; but I think she did so quite as much simply in order to show that she felt at home in Naples, and knew the city thoroughly. Indeed, she needed to know it very thoroughly to venture by night into that labyrinth of subterranean alleys and flights of steps. If ever any many showed absolute docility in allowing himself to be guided, that man was myself. Dante never followed the steps of Beatrice with more confidence than I felt in following those of Princess Trepof.

The lady appeared to find some pleasure in my conversation, for she invited me to take a carriage-drive with her on the morrow to visit the grotto of Posilippo and the tomb of Virgil. She declared she had seen me somewhere before; but she could not remember if it had been a Stockholm or at Canton. In the former event I was a very celebrated professor of geology; in the latter, a provision-merchant whose courtesy and kindness had been much appreciated. One thing certain was that she had seen my back somewhere before.

"Excuse me," she added; "we are continually travelling, my husband and I, to collect match-boxes and to change our ennui by changing country. Perhaps it would be more reasonable to content ourselves with a single variety of ennui. But we have made all our preparations and arrangements for travelling: all our plans have been laid out in advance, and it gives us no trouble, whereas it would be very troublesome for us to stop anywhere in particular. I tell you all this so that you many not be surprised if my recollections have become a little mixed up. But from the moment I first saw you at a distance this evening, I felt — in fact I knew — that I had seen you before. Now the question is, 'Where was it that I saw you?' You are not then, either the geologist or the provision-merchant?"

"No, Madame," I replied, "I am neither the one nor the other; and I am sorry for it — since you have had reason to esteem them. There is really nothing about me worthy of your interest. I have spent all my life poring over books, and I have never traveled: you might have known that from my bewilderment, which excited your compassion. I am a member of the Institute."

"You are a member of the Institute! How nice! Will you not write something for me in my album? Do you know Chinese? I would like so much to have you write something in Chinese or Persian in my album. I will introduce you to my friend, Miss

Fergusson, who travels everywhere to see all the famous people in the world. She will be delighted.... Dimitri, did you hear that? — this gentleman is a member of the Institute, and he has passed all his life over books."

The prince nodded approval.

"Monsieur," I said, trying to engage him in our conversation, "it is true that something can be learned from books; but a great deal more can be learned by travelling, and I regret that I have not been able to go round the world like you. I have lived in the same house for thirty years and I scarcely every go out."

"Lived in the same house for thirty years!" cried Madame Trepof; "is it possible?"

"Yes, Madame," I answered. "But you must know the house is situated on the bank of the Seine, and in the very handsomest and most famous part of the world. From my window I can see the Tuileries and the Louvre, the Pont-Neuf, the towers of Notre-Dame, the turrets of the Palais de Justice, and the spire of the Sainte-Chapelle. All those stones speak to me; they tell me stories about the days of Saint-Louis, of the Valois, of Henri IV., and of Louus XIV. I understand them, and I love them all. It is only a very small corner of the world, but honestly, Madame, where is there a more glorious spot?"

At this moment we found ourselves upon a public square — a largo steeped in the soft glow of the night. Madame Trepof looked at me in an uneasy manner; her lifted eyebrows almost touched the black curls about her forehead.

"Where do you live then?" she demanded brusquely.

"On the Quai Malaquais, Madame, and my name is Bonnard. It is not a name very widely known, but I am contented if my friends do not forget it."

This revelation, unimportant as it was, produced an extraordinary effect upon Madame Trepof. She immediately turned her back upon me and caught her husband's arm.

"Come, Dimitri!" she exclaimed, "do walk a little faster. I am horribly tired, and you will not hurry yourself in the least. We shall never get home.... As for you, monsieur, your way lies over there!"

She made a vague gesture in the direction of some dark vicolo, pushed her husband the opposite way, and called to me, without even turning her head.

"Adieu, Monsieur! We shall not go to Posilippo to-morrow, nor the day after, either. I have a frightful headache!... Dimitri, you are unendurable! will you not walk faster?"

I remained for the moment stupefied, vainly trying to think what I could have done to offend Madame Trepof. I had also lost my way, and seemed doomed to wander about all night. In order to ask my way, I would have to see somebody; and it did not seem likely that I should find a single human being who could understand me. In my despair I entered a street at random — a street, or rather a horrible alley that had the look of a murderous place. It proved so in fact, for I had not been two minutes in it before I saw two men fighting with knives. They were attacking each other more fiercely with their tongues than with their weapons; and I concluded from the nature of the abuse they were showering upon each other that it was a love affair. I prudently made my way into a side alley while those two good fellows were still much too busy with their own affairs to think about mine. I wandered hopelessly about for a while, and at last sat down, completely discouraged, on a stone bench, inwardly cursing the strange caprices of Madame Trepof.

"How are you, Signor? Are you back from San Carlo? Did you hear the diva sing? It is only at Naples you can hear singing like hers."

I looked up, and recognised my host. I had seated myself with my back to the facade of my hotel, under the window of my own room.

Monte-Allegro, November 30, 1859.

We were all resting — myself, my guides, and their mules — on a road from Sciacca to Girgenti, at a tavern in the miserable village of Monte-Allegro, whose inhabitants, consumed by the mal aria, continually shiver in the sun. But nevertheless they are Greeks, and their gaiety triumphs over all circumstances. A few gather about the tavern, full of smiling curiosity. One good story would have sufficed, had I known how to tell it to them, to make them forget all the woes of life. They had all a look of intelligence! and their women, although tanned and faded, wore their long black cloaks with much grace.

Before me I could see old ruins whitened by the sea-wind — ruins about which no grass ever grows. The dismal melancholy of deserts prevails over this arid land, whose cracked surface can barely nourish a few shriveled mimosas, cacti, and dwarf palms. Twenty yards away, along the course of a ravine, stones were gleaming whitely like a long line of scattered bones. They told me that was the bed of a stream.

I had been fifteen days in Sicily. On coming into the Bay of Palermo — which opens between the two mighty naked masses of the Pelligrino and the Catalfano, and extends inward along the "Golden Conch" — the view inspired me with such admiration that I resolved to travel a little in this island, so ennobled by historic memories, and rendered so beautiful by the outlines of its hills, which reveal the principles of Greek art. Old pilgrim though I was, grown hoary in the Gothic Occident — I dared to venture upon that classic soil; and, securing a guide, I went from Palermo to Trapani, from Trapani to Selinonte, from Selinonte to Sciacca — which I left this morning to go to Girgenti, where I am to find the MS. of Clerk Alexander. The beautiful things I have seen are still so vivid in my mind that I feel the task of writing them would be a useless fatigue. Why spoil my pleasure-trip by collecting notes? Lovers who love truly do not write down their happiness.

Wholly absorbed by the melancholy of the present and the poetry of the past, my thoughts people with beautiful shapes, and my eyes ever gratified by the pure and harmonious lines of the landscape, I was resting in the tavern at Monte-Allegro, sipping a glass of heavy, fiery wine, when I saw two persons enter the waiting-room, whom, after a moment's hesitation, I recognised as the Prince and Princess Trepof.

This time I saw the princess in the light — and what a light! He who has known that of Sicily can better comprehend the words of Sophocles: "Oh holy light!... Eye of the Golden Day!" Madame Trepof, dressed in a brown-holland and wearing a broad-brimmed straw hat, appeared to me a very pretty woman of about twenty-eight. Her eyes were luminous as a child's; but her slightly plump chin indicated the age of plenitude. She is, I must confess it, quite an attractive person. She is supple and changeful; her mood is like water itself — and, thank Heaven! I am no navigator. I thought I discerned in her manner a sort of ill-humour, which I attributed presently, by reason of some observations she uttered at random, to the fact that she had met no brigands upon her route.

"Such things only happen to us!" she exclaimed, with a gesture of discouragement.

She called for a glass of iced water, which the landlord presented to her with a gesture that recalled to me those scenes of funeral offerings painted upon Greek vases.

I was in no hurry to introduce myself to a lady who had so abruptly dropped my acquaintance in the public square at Naples; but she perceived me in my corner, and her frown notified me very plainly that our accidental meeting was disagreeable to her.

After she had sipper her ice-water for a few moments — whether because her whim had suddenly changed, or because my loneliness aroused her pity, I did not know — she walked directly to me.

"Good-day, Monsieur Bonnard," she said. "How do you do? What strange chance enables us to meet again in this frightful country?"

"This country is not frightful, Madame," I replied. "Beauty is so great and so august a quality that centuries of barbarism cannot efface it so completely that adorable vestiges of it will not always remain. The majesty of the antique Ceres still overshadows these arid valleys; and that Greek Muse who made Arethusa and

Maenalus ring with her divine accents, still sings for my ears upon the barren mountain and in the place of the dried-up spring. Yes, Madame, when our globe, no longer inhabited, shall, like the moon, roll a wan corpse through space, the soil which bears the ruins of Selinonte will still keep the seal of beauty in the midst of universal death; and then, then, at least there will be no frivolous mouth to blaspheme the grandeur of these solitudes."

I knew well enough that my words were beyond the comprehension of the pretty little empty-head which heard them. But an old fellow like myself who has worn out his life over books does not know how to adapt his tone to circumstances. Besides I wished to give Madame Trepof a lesson in politeness. She received it with so much submission, and with such an air of comprehension, that I hastened to add, as good-naturedly as possible,

"As to whether the chance which has enabled me to meet you again be lucky or unlucky, I cannot decide the question until I am sure that my presence be not disagreeable to you. You appeared to become weary of my company very suddenly at Naples the other day. I can only attribute that misfortune to my naturally unpleasant manner — since, on that occasion, I had had the honour of meeting you for the first time in my life."

These words seem to cause her inexplicable joy. She smiled upon me in the most gracious, mischievous way, and said very earnestly, holding out her hand, which I touched with my lips,

"Monsieur Bonnard, do not refuse to accept a seat in my carriage. You can chat with me on the way about antiquity, and that will amuse me ever so much."

"My dear," exclaimed the prince, "you can do just as you please; but you ought to remember that one is horribly cramped in that carriage of yours; and I fear that you are only offering Monsieur Bonnard the chance of getting a frightful attack of lumbago."

Madame Trepof simply shook her head by way of explaining that such considerations had no weight with her whatever; then she untied her hat. The darkness of her black curls descended over her eyes, and bathed them in velvety shadow. She remained a little while quite motionless, and her face assumed a surprising expression of reverie. But all of a sudden she darted at some oranges which the tavern-keeper had brought in a basket, and began to throw them, one by one, into a fold of her dress.

"These will be nice on the road," she said. "We are going just where you are going — to Girgenti. I must tell you all about it. you know that my husband is making a collection of match-boxes. We bought thirteen hundred match-boxes at Marseilles. But we heard there was a factory of them at Girgenti. According to what we were told, it is a very small factory, and its products — which are very ugly — never go outside the city and its suburbs. So we are going to Girgenti just to buy match-boxes. Dimitri has been a collector of all sorts of things; but the only kind of collection which can now interest him is a collection of match-boxes. He has already got five thousand two hundred and fourteen different kinds. Some of them gave us frightful trouble to find. For instance, we knew that at Naples boxes were once made with the portraits of Mazzini and Garibaldi on them; and that the police had seized the plates from which the portraits were printed, and put the manufacturer in gaol. Well, by dint of searching and inquiring for ever so long a while, we found one of those boxes at last for sale at one hundred francs, instead of two sous. It was not really too dear at that price; but we were denounced for buying it. We were taken for conspirators. All our baggage was searched; they could not find the box, because I had hidden it so well; but they found my jewels, and carried them off. They have them still. The incident made quite a sensation, and we were going to get arrested. But the king was displeased about it, and he ordered them to leave us alone. Up to that time, I used to think it was very stupid to collect match-boxes; but when I found that there were risks of losing liberty, and perhaps even life, by doing it, I began to feel a taste for it. Now I am an absolute fanatic on the subject. We are going to Sweden next summer to complete our series.... Are we not, Dimitri?"

I felt — must I confess it? — a thorough sympathy with these intrepid collectors. No doubt I would rather have found Monsieur and Madame Trepof engaged in collecting antique marbles or painted vases in Sicily. I should have like to have found them interested in the ruins of Syracuse, or the poetical traditions of the Eryx. But at all events, they were making some sort of a collection — they belonged to the great confraternity — and I could not possibly make fun of them without making fun of myself. Besides, Madame Trepof had spoken of her collection with such an odd mingling of irony and enthusiasm that I could not help finding the idea a very good one.

We were getting ready to leave the tavern, when we noticed some people coming downstairs from the upper room, carrying carbines under their dark cloaks. to me they had the look of thorough bandits; and after they were gone I told Monsieur Trepof my opinion of them. He answered me, very quietly, that he also thought they were regular bandits; and the guides begged us to apply for an escort of gendarmes, but Madame Trepof besought us not to do anything of the kind. She declared that we must not "spoil her journey."

Then, turning her persuasive eyes upon me, she asked,

"Do you not believe, Monsieur Bonnard, that there is nothing in life worth having except sensations?"

"Why, certainly, Madame," I answered; "but then we must take into consideration the nature of the sensations themselves. Those which a noble memory or a grand spectacle creates within us certainly represent what is best in human life; but those merely resulting from the menace of danger seem to me sensations which one should be very careful to avoid as much as possible. For example, would you think it a very pleasant thing, Madame, while travelling over the mountains at midnight, to find the muzzle of a carbine suddenly pressed against your forehead?"

"Oh, no!" she replied; "the comic-operas have made carbines absolutely ridiculous, and it would be a great misfortune to any young woman to find herself in danger from an absurd weapon. But it would be quite different with a knife — a very cold and very bright knife blade, which makes a cold shudder go right through one's heart."

She shuddered even as she spoke; closed her eyes, and threw her head back. Then she resumed:

"People like you are so happy! You can interest yourselves in all sorts of things!"

She gave a sidelong look at her husband, who was talking with the innkeeper. Then she leaned towards me, and murmured very low:

"You see, Dimitri and I, we are both suffering from ennui! We have still the match-boxes. But at last one gets tired even of match-boxes. Besides, our collection will soon be complete. And then what are we going to do?"

"Oh, Madame!" I exclaimed, touched by the moral unhappiness of this pretty person, "if you only had a son, then you would know what to do. You would then learn the purpose of your life, and your thoughts would become at once more serious and yet more cheerful."

"But I have a son," she replied. "He is a big boy; he is eleven years old, and he suffers from ennui like the rest of us. Yes, my George has ennui, too; he is tired of everything. It is very wretched."

She glanced again towards her husband, who was superintending the harnessing of the mules on the road outside — testing the condition of girths and straps. Then she asked me whether there had been many changes on the Quai Malaquais during the past ten years. She declared she never visited that neighbourhood because it was too far way.

"Too far from Monte Allegro?" I queried.

"Why, no!" she replied. "Too far from the Avenue des Champs Elysees, where we live."

And she murmured over again, as if talking to herself, "Too far! — too far!" in a tone of reverie which I could not possibly account for. All at once she smiled again, and said to me,

"I like you, Monsieur Bonnard! — I like you very, very much!"

43

The mules had been harnessed. The young woman hastily picked up a few oranges which had rolled off her lap; rose up; looked at me, and burst out laughing.

"Oh!" she exclaimed, "how I should like to see you grappling with the brigands! You would say such extraordinary things to them!... Please take my hat, and hold my umbrella for me, Monsieur Bonnard."

"What a strange little mind!" I thought to myself, as I followed her. "It could only have been in a moment of inexcusable thoughtlessness that Nature gave a child to such a giddy little woman!"

Girgenti. Same day.

Her manners had shocked me. I left her to arrange herself in her lettica, and I made myself as comfortable as I could in my own. These vehicles, which have no wheels, are carried by two mules — one before and one behind. This kind of litter, or chaise, is of ancient origin. I had often seen representations of similar ones in the French MSS. of the fourteenth century. I had no idea then that one of those vehicles would be at a future day placed at my own disposal. We must never be too sure of anything.

For three hours the mules sounded their little bells, and thumped the calcined ground with their hoofs. On either hand there slowly defiled by us the barren monstrous shapes of a nature totally African.

Half-way we made a halt to allow our animals to recover breath.

Madame Trepof came to me on the road, took my arm, and drew me a little away from the party. Then, very suddenly, she said to me in a tone of voice I had never heard before:

"Do not think that I am a wicked woman. My George knows that I am a good mother."

We walked side by side for a moment in silence. She looked up, and I saw that she was crying.

44

"Madame," I said to her, "look at this soil which has been burned and cracked by five long months of fiery heat. A little white lily has sprung up from it."

And I pointed with my cane to the frail stalk, tipped by a double blossom.

"Your heart," I said, "however arid it be, bears also its white lily; and that is reason enough why I do not believe that you are what you say — a wicked woman."

"Yes, yes, yes!" she cried, with the obstinacy of a child — "I am a wicked woman. But I am ashamed to appear so before you who are so good — so very, very good."

"You do not know anything at all about it," I said to her.

"I know it! I know all about you, Monsieur Bonnard!" she declared, with a smile.

And she jumped back into her lettica.

Girgenti, November 30, 1859.

I awoke the following morning in the House of Gellias. Gellias was a rich citizen of ancient Agrigentum. He was equally celebrated for his generosity and for his wealth; and he endowed his native city with a great number of free inns. Gellias has been dead for thirteen hundred years; and nowadays there is no gratuitous hospitality among civilised peoples. But the name of Gellias has become that of a hotel in which, by reason of fatigue, I was able to obtain one good night's sleep.

The modern Girgenti lifts its high, narrow, solid streets, dominated by a sombre Spanish cathedral, upon the side of the acropolis of the antique Agrigentum. I can see from my windows, half-way on the hillside towards the sea, the white range of temples partially destroyed. The ruins alone have some aspect of coolness. All the rest is arid. Water and life have forsaken Agrigentine. Water — the divine Nestis of the Agrigentine Empedocles — is so necessary to animated beings that nothing can live far from the rivers and the springs. But the port of Girgenti, situated at a distance of three kilometres from the city, has a great commerce. "And it is in this dismal city," I said to

45

myself, "upon this precipitous rock, that the manuscript of Clerk Alexander is to be found!" I asked my way to the house of Signor Michel-Angelo Polizzi, and proceeded thither.

I found Signor Polizzi, dressed all in white from head to feet, busy cooking sausages in a frying-pan. At the sight of me, he let go the frying-pan, threw up his arms in the air, and uttered shrieks of enthusiasm. He was a little man whose pimply features, aquiline nose, round eyes, and projecting chin formed a very expressive physiognomy.

He called me "Excellence," said he was going to mark the day with a white stone, and made me sit down. The hall in which we were represented the union of the kitchen, reception-room, bedchamber, studio, and wine-cellar. There were charcoal furnaces visible, a bed, paintings, an easel, bottles, strings of onions, and a magnificent lustre of coloured glass pendants. I glanced at the paintings on the wall.

"The arts! the arts!" cried Signor Polizzi, throwing up his arms again to heaven — "the arts! What dignity! what consolation! Excellence, I am a painter!"

And he showed me an unfinished Saint-Francis, which indeed could very well remain unfinished for ever without any loss to religion or to art. Next he showed me some old paintings of a better style, but apparently restored after a decidedly reckless manner.

"I repair," he said — "I repair old paintings. Oh, the Old Masters! What genius, what soul!"

"Why, then," I said to him, "you must be a painter, an archaeologist, and a wine-merchant all in one?"

"At your service, Excellence," he answered. "I have a zucco here at this very moment — a zucco of which every single drop is a pearl of fire. I want your Lordship to taste of it."

"I esteem the wines of Sicily," I responded, "but it was not for the sake of your flagons that I came to see you , Signor Polizzi."

He: "Then you have come to see me about paintings. You are an amateur. It is an immense delight for me to receive amateurs. I am going to show you the chef-d'oeuvre of Monrealese; yes, Excellence, his chef-d'oeuvre! An Adoration of Shepherds! It is the pearl of the whole Sicilian school!"

I: "Later on I will be glad to see the chef-d'oeuvre; but let us first talk about the business which brings me here."

His little quick bright eyes watched my face curiously; and I perceived, with anguish, that he had not the least suspicion of the purpose of my visit.

A cold sweat broke out over my forehead; and in the bewilderment of my anxiety I stammered out something to this effect:

"I have come from Paris expressly to look at a manuscript of the Legende Doree, which you informed me was in your possession."

At these words he threw up his arms, opened his mouth and eyes to the widest possible extent, and betrayed every sign of extreme nervousness.

"Oh! the manuscript of the 'Golden Legend!' A pearl, Excellence! a ruby, a diamond! Two miniatures so perfect that they give one the feeling of glimpses of Paradise! What suavity! Those colours ravished from the corollas of flowers make a honey for the eyes! Even a Sicilian could have done no better!"

"Let me see it, then," I asked; unable to conceal either my anxiety or my hope.

"Let you see it!" cried Polizzi. "But how can I, Excellence? I have not got it any longer! I have not got it!"

And he seemed determined to tear out his hair. He might indeed have pulled every hair in his head out of his hide before I should have tried to prevent him. But he stopped of his own accord, before he had done himself any grievous harm.

"What!" I cried out in anger — "what! you make me come all the way from Paris to Girgenti, by promising to show me a manuscript, and now, when I come, you tell me you have not got it! It is simply infamous, Monsieur! I shall leave your conduct to be judged by all honest men!"

Anybody who could have seen me at that moment would have been able to form a good idea of the aspect of a furious sheep.

"It is infamous! it is infamous!" I repeated, waving my arms, which trembled from anger.

Then Michel-Angelo Polizzi let himself fall into a chair in the attitude of a dying hero. I saw his eyes fill with tears, and his hair — until then flamboyant and erect upon his head — fall down in limp disorder over his brow.

"I am a father, Excellence! I am a father!" he groaned, wringing his hands.

He continued, sobbing:

"My son Rafael — the son of my poor wife, for whose death I have been mourning fifteen years — Rafael, Excellence, wanted to settle at Paris; he hired a shop in the Rue Lafitte for the sale of curiosities. I gave him everything precious which I had — I gave him my finest majolicas; my most beautiful Urbino ware; my masterpieces of art; what paintings, Signor! Even now they dazzle me with I see them only in imagination! And all of them signed! Finally, I gave him the manuscript of the 'Golden Legend'! I would have given him my flesh and my blood! An only son, Signor! the son of my poor saintly wife!"

"So," I said, "while I — relying on your written word, Monsieur — was travelling to the very heart of Sicily to find the manuscript of the Clerk Alexander, the same manuscript was actually exposed for sale in a window in the Rue Lafitte, only fifteen hundred yards from my house?"

"Yes, it was there! that is positively true!" exclaimed Signor Polizzi, suddenly growing calm again; "and it is there still — at least I hope it is, Excellence."

He took a card from a shelf as he spoke, and offered it to me, saying,

"Here is the address of my son. Make it known to your friends, and you will oblige me. Faience and enameled wares; hangings; pictures. He has a complete stock of objects of art — all at the fairest possible prices — and everything authentic, I can

48

vouch for it, upon my honour! Go and see him. He will show you the manuscript of the 'Golden Legend.' Two miniatures miraculously fresh in colour!"

I was feeble enough to take the card he held out to me.

The fellow was taking further advantage of my weakness to make me circulate the name of Rafael Polizzi among the Societies of the learned!

My hand was already on the door-knob, when the Sicilian caught me by the arm; he had a look as of sudden inspiration.

"Ah! Excellence!" he cried, "what a city is this city of ours! It gave birth to Empedocles! Empedocles! What a great man what a great citizen! What audacity of thought! what virtue! what soul! At the port over there is a statue of Empedocles, before which I bare my head each time that I pass by! When Rafael, my son, was going away to found an establishment of antiquities in the Rue Lafitte, at Paris, I took him to the port, and there, at the foot of that statue of Empedocles, I bestowed upon him my paternal benediction! 'Always remember Empedocles!' I said to him. Ah! Signor, what our unhappy country needs to-day is a new Empedocles! Would you not like me to show you the way to his statue, Excellence? I will be your guide among the ruins here. I will show you the temple of Castor and Pollux, the temple of the Olympian Jupiter, the temple of the Lucinian Juno, the antique well, the tomb of Theron, and the Gate of Gold! All the professional guides are asses; but we — we shall make excavations, if you are willing — and we shall discover treasures! I know the science of discovering hidden treasures — the secret art of finding their whereabouts — a gift from Heaven!"

I succeeded in tearing myself away from his grasp. But he ran after me again, stopped me at the foot of the stairs, and said in my ear,

"Listen, Excellence. I will conduct you about the city; I will introduce you to some Girgentines! What a race! what types! what forms! Sicilian girls, Signor! — the antique beauty itself!"

"Go to the devil!" I cried at last, in anger, and rushed into the street, leaving him still writing in the loftiness of his enthusiasm.

When I had got out of his sight, I sank down upon a stone, and began to think, with my face in my hands.

"And it was for this," I said to myself — "it was to hear such propositions as this that I came to Sicily! That Polizzi is simply a scoundrel, and his son another; and they made a plan together to ruin me." But what was their scheme? I could not unravel it. Meanwhile, it may be imagined how discouraged and humiliated I felt.

A merry burst of laughter caused me to turn my head, and I saw Madame Trepof running in advance of her husband, and holding up something which I could not distinguish clearly.

She sat down beside me, and showed me — laughing more merrily all the while — an abominable little paste-board box, on which was printed a red and blue face, which the inscription declared to be the face of Empedocles.

"Yes, Madame," I said, "but that abominable Polizzi, to whom I advise you not to send Monsieur Trepof, has made me fall out for ever with Empedocles; and this portrait is not at all of a nature to make me feel more kindly to the ancient philosopher."

"Oh!" declared Madame Trepof, "it is ugly, but it is rare! These boxes are not exported at all; you can buy them only where they are made. Dimitri has six others just like this in his pocket. We got them so as to exchange with other collectors. You understand? At none o'clock this morning we were at the factory. You see we did not waste our time."

"So I certainly perceive, Madame," I replied, bitterly; "but I have lost mine."

I then saw that she was a naturally good-hearted woman. All her merriment vanished.

"Poor Monsieur Bonnard! poor Monsieur Bonnard!" she murmured.

And, taking my hand in hers, she added:

"Tell me about your troubles."

I told her about them. My story was long; but she was evidently touched by it, for she asked me quite a number of circumstantial questions, which I took for proof of her friendly interest. She wanted to know the exact title of the manuscript, its shape, its appearance, and its age; she asked me for the address of Signor Rafael Polizzi.

And I gave it to her; thus doing (O destiny!) precisely what the abominable Polizzi had told me to do.

It is sometimes difficult to check oneself. I recommenced my plaints and my imprecations. But this time Madame Trepof only burst out laughing.

"Why do you laugh?" I asked her.

"Because I am a wicked woman," she answered.

And she fled away, leaving me all disheartened on my stone.

Paris, December 8, 1859.

My unpacked trunks still encumbered the hall. I was seated at a tabled covered with all those good things which the land of France produces for the delectation of gourmets. I was eating a pate le Chartres, which is alone sufficient to make one love one's country. Therese, standing before me with her hands joined over her white apron, was looking at me with benignity, with anxiety, and with pity. Hamilcar was rubbing himself against my legs, wild with delight.

These words of an old poet came back to my memory:

"Happy is he who, like Ulysses, hath made a goodly journey."

..."Well," I thought to myself, "I travelled to no purpose; I have come back with empty hands; but, like Ulysses, I made a goodly journey."

And having taken my last sip of coffee, I asked Therese for my hat and cane, which she gave me not without dire suspicions; she feared I might be going upon another journey. But I reassured her by telling her to have dinner ready at six o'clock.

It had always been a keen pleasure for me to breathe the air in those Parisian streets whose every paving-slab and every stone I love devotedly. But I had an end in view, and I took my way straight to the Rue Lafitte. I was not long in find the establishment of Signor Rafael Polizzi. It was distinguishable by a great display of old paintings which, although all bearing the signature of some illustrious artist, had a certain family air of resemblance that might have suggested some touching idea about the fraternity of genius, had it not still more forcibly suggested the professional tricks of Polizzi senior. Enriched by these doubtful works of art, the shop was further rendered attractive by various petty curiosities: poniards, drinking-vessels, goblets, figulines, brass guadrons, and Hispano-Arabian wares of metallic lustre.

Upon a Portuguese arm-chair, decorated with an escutcheon, lay a copy of the "Heures" of Simon Vostre, open at the page which has an astrological figure on it; and an old Vitruvius, placed upon a quaint chest, displayed its masterly engravings of caryatides and telamones. This apparent disorder which only masked cunning arrangement, this factitious hazard which had placed the best objects in the most favourable light, would have increased my distrust of the place, but that the distrust which the mere name of Polizzi had already inspired could not have been increased by any circumstances — being already infinite.

Signor Rafael, who sat there as the presiding genius of all these vague and incongruous shapes, impressed me as a phlegmatic young man, with a sort of English character. he betrayed no sign whatever of those transcendent faculties displayed by his father in the arts of mimcry and declamation.

I told him what I had come for; he opened a cabinet and drew from it a manuscript, which he placed on a table that I might examine it at my leisure.

Never in my life did I experience such an emotion — except, indeed, during some few brief months of my youth, months whose memories, though I should live a hundred years, would remain as fresh at my last hour as in the first day they came to me.

It was, indeed, the very manuscript described by the librarian of Sir Thomas Raleigh; it was, indeed, the manuscript of the Clerk Alexander which I saw, which I touched! The work of Voragine himself had been perceptibly abridged; but that made little difference to me. All the inestimable additions of the monk of Saint-Germain-des-Pres were there. That was the main point! I tried to read the Legend of Saint Droctoveus; but I could not — all the lines of the page quivered before my eyes, and there was a sound in my ears like the noise of a windmill in the country at night. Nevertheless, I was able to see that the manuscript offered every evidence of indubitable authenticity. The two drawings of the Purification of the Virgin and the Coronationof Proserpine were meagre in design and vulgar in violence of colouring. Considerably damaged in 1824, as attested by the catalogue of Sir Thomas, they had obtained during the interval a new aspect of freshness. But this miracle did not surprise me at all. And, besides, what did I care about the two miniatures? The legends and the poem of Alexander — those alone formed the treasure I desired. My eyes devoured as much of it as they had the power to absorb.

I affected indifference while asking Signor Polizzi the price of the manuscript; and, while awaiting his reply, I offered up a secret prayer that the price might not exceed the amount of ready money at my disposal — already much diminished by the cost of my expensive voyage. Signor Polizzi, however, informed me that he was not at liberty to dispose of the article, inasmuch as it did not belong to him, and was to be sold at auction shortly, at the Hotel des Ventes, with a number of other MSS. and several incunabula.

This was a severe blow to me. It tried to preserve my calmness, notwithstanding, and replied somewhat to this effect:

"You surprise me, Monsieur! Your father, whom I talked with recently at Girgenti, told me positively that the manuscript was yours. You cannot now attempt to make me discredit your father's word."

"I DID own the manuscript, indeed," answered Signor Rafael with absolute frankness; "but I do not own it any longer. I sold that manuscript — the remarkable interest of which you have not failed to perceive — to an amateur whom I am forbidden to name, and who, for reasons which I am not at liberty to mention, finds himself obliged to sell his collection. I am honoured with the confidence of my customer, and was commissioned by him to draw up the catalogue and manage the sale, which takes place the 24th of December. Now, if you will be kind enough to give me your address, I shall have the pleasure of sending you the catalogue, which is already in the press. you fill find the 'Legende Doree' described in it as 'No. 42.'"

I gave my address, and left the shop.

The polite gravity of the son impressed me quite as disagreeably as the impudent buffoonery of the father. I hated, from the bottom of my heart, the tricks of the vile hagglers! It was perfectly evident that the two rascals had a secret understanding, and had only devised this auction-sale, with the aid of a professional appraiser, to force the bidding on the manuscript I wanted so much up to an outrageous figure. I was completely at their mercy. There is one evil in all passionate desires, even the noblest — namely, that they leave us subject to the will of others, and in so far dependent. This reflection made me suffer cruelly; but it did not conquer my longing to won the work of Clerk Alexander. While I was thus meditating, I heard a coachman swear. And I discovered it was I whom he was swearing at only when I felt the pole of a carriage poke me in the ribs. I started aside, barely in time to save myself from being run over; and whom did I perceive through the windows of the coupe? Madame Trepof, being taken by two beautiful horses, and a coachman all wrapped up in furs like a Russian Boyard, into the very street I had just left. She did not notice me; she was laughing to herself with that artless grace of expression which still preserved for her, at thirty years, all the charm of her early youth.

"Well, well!" I said to myself, "she is laughing! I suppose she must have just found another match-box."

And I made my way back to the Ponts, feeling very miserable.

Nature, eternally indifferent, neither hastened nor hurried the twenty-fourth day of December. I went to the Hotel Bullion, and took my place in Salle No. 4, immediately below the high desk at which the auctioneer Boulouze and the expert Polizzi were to sit. I saw the hall gradually fill with familiar faces. I shook hands with several old booksellers of the quays; but that prudence which any large interest inspires in even the most self-assured caused me to keep silence in regard to the reason of my unaccustomed presence in the halls of the Hotel Bullion. On the other hand, I questioned those gentlemen at the auction sale; and I had teh satisfaction of finding them all interested about matters in no wise related to my affair.

Little by little the hall became thronged with interested or merely curious spectators; and, after half an hour's delay, the auctioneer with his ivory hammer, the clerk with his bundle of memorandum-papers, and the crier, carrying his collection-box fixed to the end of a pole, all took their places on the platform in the most solemn business manner. The attendants ranged themselves at the foot of the desk. The presiding officer having declared the sale open, a partial hush followed.

A commonplace series of Preces dia, with miniatures, were first sold off at mediocre prices. Needless to say, the illuminations of these books were in perfect condition!

The lowness of the bids gave courage to the gathering of second-hand booksellers present, who began to mingle with us, and become more familiar. The dealers in old brass and bric-a-brac pressed forward in their tun, waiting for the doors of an adjoining room to be opened; and the voice of the auctioneer was drowned by the jests of the Auvergnats.

A magnificent codex of the "Guerre des Juifs" revived attention. It was long disputed for. "Five thousand francs! five thousand!" called the crier, while the bric-a-brac dealers remained silent with admiration. Then seven or eight antiphonaries brought us back again to low prices. A fat old woman, in a loose gown, bareheaded — a dealer in second-hand goods — encouraged by the size of the books and the low prices bidden, had one of the antiphonaries knocked down to her for thirty francs.

At last the expert Polizzi announced No. 42: "The 'Golden Legend'; French MS.; unpublished; two superb miniatures, with a starting bid of three thousand francs."

"Three thousand! three thousand bid!" yelled the crier.

"Three thousand!" dryly repeated the auctioneer.

There was a buzzing in my head, and, as through a cloud, I saw a host of curious faces all turning towards the manuscript, which a boy was carrying open through the audience.

"Three thousand and fifty!" I said.

I was frightened by the sound of my own voice, and further confused by seeing, or thinking that I saw, all eyes turned on me.

"Three thousand and fifty on the right!" called the crier, taking up my bid.

"Three thousand one hundred!" responded Signor Polizzi.

Then began a heroic duel between the expert and myself.

"Three thousand five hundred!"

"Six hundred!"

"Seven hundred!"

"Four thousand!"

"Four thousand five hundred."

Then by a sudden bold stroke, Signor Polizzi raised the bid at once to six thousand.

Six thousand francs was all the money I could dispose of. It represented the possible. I risked the impossible.

"Six thousand one hundred!"

Alas! even the impossible did not suffice.

"Six thousand five hundred!" replied Signor Polizzi, with calm.

I bowed my head and sat there stupefied, unable to answer either yes or no to the crier, who called to me:

"Six thousand five hundred, by me — not by you on the right there! — it is my bid — no mistake! Six thousand five hundred!"

"Perfectly understood!" declared the auctioneer. "Six thousand five hundred. Perfectly clear; perfectly plain.... Any more bids? The last bid is six thousand five hundred francs."

A solemn silence prevailed. Suddenly I felt as if my head had burst open. It was the hammer of the officiant, who, with a loud blow on the platform, adjudged No. 42 irrevocably to Signor Polizzi. Forthwith the pen of the clerk, coursing over the papier-timbre, registered that great fact in a single line.

I was absolutely prostrated, and I felt the utmost need of rest and quiet. Nevertheless, I did not leave my seat. My powers of reflection slowly returned. Hope is tenacious. I had one more hope. It occurred to me that the new owner of the "Legende Doree" might be some intelligent and liberal bibliophile who would allow me to examine the MS., and perhaps even to publish the more important parts. And, with this idea, as soon as the sale was over I approached the expert as he was leaving the platform.

"Monsieur," I asked him, "did you buy in No. 42 on your own account, or on commission?"

"On commission. I was instructed not to let it go at any price."

"Can you tell me the name of the purchaser?"

"Monsieur, I regret that I cannot serve you in that respect. I have been strictly forbidden to mention the name."

I went home in despair.

December 30, 1859.

"Therese! don't you hear the bell? Somebody has been ringing at the door for the last quarter of an hour?"

Therese does not answer. She is chattering downstairs with the concierge, for sure. So that is the way you observe your old master's birthday? You desert me even on the eve of Saint-Sylvestre! Alas! if I am to hear any kind wishes to-day, they must come up from the ground; for all who love me have long been buried. I really don't know what I am still living for. There is the bell again!... I get up slowly from my seat at the fire, with my shoulders still bent from stooping over it, and go to the door myself. Whom do I see at the threshold? It is not a dripping love, and I am not an old Anacreon; but it is a very pretty little boy of about ten years old. He is alone; he raises his face to look at me. His cheeks are blushing; but his little pert nose gives one an idea of mischievous pleasantry. He has feathers in his cap, and a great lace-ruff on his jacket. The pretty little fellow! He holds in both arms a bundle as big as himself, and asks me if I am Monsieur Sylvestre Bonnard. I tell him yes; he gives me the bundle, tells me his mamma sent it to me, and then he runs downstairs.

I go down a few steps; I lean over the balustrade, and see the little cap whirling down the spiral of the stairway like a feather in the wind. "Good-bye, my little boy!" I should have liked so much to question him. But what, after all, could I have asked? It is not polite to question children. Besides, the package itself will probably give me more information than the messenger could.

It is a very big bundle, but not very heavy. I take it into my library, and there untie the ribbons and unfasten the paper wrappings; and I see — what? a log! a first-class log! a real Christmas log, but so light that I know it must be hollow. Then I find that it is indeed composed of two separate pieces, opening on hinges, and fastened with hooks. I slip the hooks back, and find myself inundated with violets! Violets! they pour over my table, over my knees, over the carpet. They tumble into my vest, into my sleeves. I am all perfumed with them.

"Therese! Therese! fill me some vases with water, and bring them here, quick! Here are violets sent to us I know not from what country nor by what hand; but it must be from a perfumed country, and by a very gracious hand.... Do you hear me, old crow?"

I have put all the violets on my table — now completely covered by the odorous mass. But there is still something in the log...a book — a manuscript. It is...I cannot believe it, and yet I cannot doubt it.... It is the "Legende Doree"! — It is the manuscript of the Clerk Alexander! Here is the "Purification of the Virgin" and the "Coronation of Proserpine"; — here is the legend of Saint Droctoveus. I contemplate this violet-perfumed relic. I turn the leaves of it — between which the dark rich blossoms have slipped in here and there; and, right opposite the legend of Saint-Cecilia, I find a card bearing this name:

"Princess Trepof."

Princess Trepof! — you who laughed and wept by turns so sweetly under the fair sky of Agrigentum! — you, whom a cross old man believed to be only a foolish little woman! — to-day I am convinced of your rare and beautiful folly; and the old fellow whom you now overwhelm with happiness will go to kiss your hand, and give you back, in another form, this precious manuscript, of which both he and science owe you an exact and sumptuous publication!

Therese entered my study just at that moment; she seemed to be very much excited.

"Monsieur!" she cried, "guess whom I saw just now in a carriage, with a coat-of-arms painted on it, that was stopping before the door?"

"Parbleu! — Madame Trepof," I exclaimed.

"I don't know anything about any Madame Trepof," answered my housekeeper. "The woman I saw just now was dressed like a duchess, and had a little boy with her, with lace-frills all along the seams of his clothes. And it was that same little Madame Coccoz you once sent a log to, when she was lying-in here about eleven years ago. I recognized her at once."

"What!" I exclaimed, "you mean to say it was Madame Coccoz, the widow of the almanac-peddler?"

"Herself, Monsieur! The carriage-door was open for a minute to let her little boy, who had just come from I don't know where, get in. She hasn't changed scarcely at all. Well, why should those women change? — they never worry themselves about anything. Only the Coccoz woman looks a little fatter than she used to be. And the idea of a woman that was taken in here out of pure charity coming to show off her velvets and diamonds in a carriage with a crest painted on it! Isn't it shameful!"

"Therese!" I cried, in a terrible voice, "if you ever speak to me again about that lady except in terms of the deepest respect, you and I will fall out! ...Bring me the Sevres vases to put those violets in, which now give the City of Books a charm it never had before."

While Therese went off with a sigh to get the Sevres vases, I continued to contemplate those beautiful scattered violets, whose odour spread all about me like the perfume of some sweet presence, some charming soul; and I asked myself how it had been possible for me never to recognise Madame Coccoz in the person of the Princess Trepof. But that vision of the young widow, showing me her little child on the stairs, had been a very rapid one. I had much more reason to reproach myself for having passed by a gracious and lovely soul without knowing it.

"Bonnard," I said to myself, "thou knowest how to decipher old texts; but thou dost not know how to read in the Book of Life. That giddy little Madame Trepof, whom thou once believed to possess no more soul than a bird, has expended, in pure gratitude, more zeal and finer tact than thou didst ever show for anybody's sake. Right royally hath she repaid thee for the log-fire of her churching-day!

"Therese! Awhile ago you were a magpie; now you are becoming a tortoise! Come and give some water to these Parmese violets."

PART II — The Daughter of Clementine

Chapter I — The Fairy

When I left the train at the Melun station, night had already spread its peace over the silent country. The soil, heated through all the long day by a strong sun — by a "gros soleil," as the harvesters of the Val de Vire say — still exhaled a warm heavy smell. Lush dense odours of grass passed over the level of the fields. I brushed away the dust of the railway carriage, and joyfully inhaled the pure air. My travelling-bag — filled by my housekeeper wit linen and various small toilet articles, munditiis, seemed so light in my hand that I swung it about just as a schoolboy swings his strapped package of rudimentary books when the class is let out.

Would to Heaven that I were again a little urchin at school! But it is fully fifty years since my good dead mother made me some tartines of bread and preserves, and placed them in a basket of which she slipped the handle over my arm, and then led me, thus prepared, to the school kept by Monsieur Douloir, at a corner of the Passage du Commerce well known to the sparrows, between a court and a garden. The enormous Monsieur Douloir smiled upon us genially, and patted my cheek to show, no doubt, the affectionate interest which my first appearance had inspired. But when my mother had passed out of the court, startling the sparrows as she went, Monsieur Douloir ceased to smile — he showed no more affectionate interest; he appeared, on the contrary, to consider me as a very troublesome little fellow. I discovered, later on, that he entertained the same feelings towards all his pupils. He distributed whacks of his ferule with an agility no one could have expected on the part of so corpulent a person. But his first aspect of tender interest invariably reappeared when he spoke to any of our mothers in our presence; and always at such times, while warmly praising our remarkable aptitudes, he would cast down upon us a look of intense affection. Still, those were happy days which I passed on the benches of the Monsieur Couloir with my little playfellows, who, like myself, cried and laughed by turns with all their might, from morning till evening.

After a whole half-century these souvenirs float up again, fresh and bright as ever, to the surface of memory, under this starry sky, whose face has in no wise changed since then, and whose serene and immutable lights will doubtless see many other schoolboys such as I was slowly turn into grey-headed servants, afflicted with catarrh.

Stars, who have shown down upon each wise or foolish head among all my forgotten ancestors, it is under your soft light that I now feel stir within me a certain poignant regret! I would that I could have a son who might be able to see you when I shall see you no more. How I should love him! Ah! such a son would —

what am I saying? — why, he would be no just twenty years old if you had only been willing, Clementine — you whose cheeks used to look so ruddy under your pink hood! But you are married to that young bank clerk, Noel Alexandre, who made so many millions afterwards! I never met you again after your marriage, Clementine, but I can see you now, with your bright curls and your pink hood.

A looking-glass! a looking-glass! a looking-glass! Really, it would be curious to see what I look like now, with my white hair, sighing Clementine's name to the stars! Still, it is not right to end with sterile irony the thought begun in the spirit of faith and love. No, Clementine, if your name came to my lips by chance this beautiful night, be it for ever blessed, your dear name! and may you ever, as a happy mother, a happy grandmother, enjoy to the very end of life with your rich husband the utmost degree of that happiness which you had the right to believe you could not win with the poor young scholar who loved you! If — though I cannot even now imagine it — if your beautiful hair has become white, Clementine, bear worthily the bundle of keys confided to you by Noel Alexandre, and impart to your grandchildren the knowledge of all domestic virtues!

Ah! beautiful Night! She rules, with such noble repose, over men and animals alike, kindly loosed by her from the yoke of daily toil; and even I feel her beneficent influence, although my habits of sixty years have so changed me that I can feel most things only through the signs which represent them. My world is wholly formed of words — so much of a philologist I have become! Each one dreams the dream of life in his own way. I have dreamed it in my library; and when the hour shall come in which I must leave this world, may it please God to take me from my ladder — from before my shelves of books!...

"Well, well! it is really himself, pardieu! How are you, Monsieur Sylvestre Bonnard? And where have you been travelling to all this time, over the country, while I was waiting for you at the station with my cabriolet? You missed me when the train came in, and I was driving back, quite disappointed, to Lusance.

Give me your valise, and get up here beside me in the carriage. Why, do you know it is fully seven kilometres from here to the chateau?"

Who addresses me thus, at the very top of his voice from the height of his cabriolet? Monsieur Paul de Gabry, nephew and heir of Monsieur Honore de Gabry, peer of France in 1842, who recently died at Monaco. And it was precisely to Monsieur Paul de Gabry's house that I was going with that valise of mine, so carefully strapped by my housekeeper. This excellent young man has just inherited, conjointly with his two brothers-in-law, the property of his uncle, who, belonging to a very ancient family of distinguished lawyers, had accumulated in his chateau at Lusance a library rich in MSS., some dating back to the fourteenth century. It was for the purpose of making an inventory and catalogue of these MSS. that I had come to Lusance at the urgent request of Monsieur Paul de Gabry, whose father, a perfect gentleman and distinguished bibliophile, had maintained the most pleasant relations with me during his lifetime. To tell the truth, Monsieur Paul has not inherited the fine tastes of his father. Monsieur Paul likes sporting; he is a great authority on horses and dogs; and I much fear that of all the sciences capable of satisfying or of duping the inexhaustible curiosity of mankind, those of the stable and the dog-kennel are the only ones thoroughly mastered by him.

I cannot say I was surprised to meet him, since we had made a rendezvous; but I acknowledge that I had become so preoccupied with my own thoughts that I had forgotten all about the Chateau de Lusance and its inhabitants, and that the voice of the gentleman calling out to me as I started to follow the country road winding away before me — "un bon ruban de queue," as they say — had given me quite a start.

I fear my face must have betrayed my incongruous distraction by a certain stupid expression which it is apt to assume in most of my social transactions. My valise was pulled up into the carriage, and I followed my valise. My host pleased me by his straightforward simplicity.

"I don't know anything myself about your old parchments," he said; "but I think you will find some folks to talk to at the house. Besides the cure, who writes books himself, and the doctor, who is a very good fellow — although a radical — you will meet somebody able to keep your company. I mean my wife. She is not a very learned woman, but there are few things which she can't divine pretty well. Then I count upon being able to keep you with us long enough to make you acquainted with Mademoiselle Jeanne, who has the fingers of a magician and the soul of an angel."

"And is this delightfully gifted young lady one of your family?" I asked.

"Not at all," replied Monsieur Paul.

"Then she is just a friend of yours?" I persisted, rather stupidly.

"She has lost both her father and mother," answered Monsieur de Gabry, keeping his eyes fixed upon the ears of his horse, whose hoofs rang loudly over the road blue-tinted by the moonshine. "Her father managed to get us into some very serious trouble; and we did not get off with a fright either!"

Then he shook his head, and changed the subject. He gave me due warning of the ruinous condition in which I should find the chateau and the park; they had been absolutely deserted for thirty-two years.

I learned from him that Monsieur Honore de Gabry, his uncle, had been on very bad terms with some poachers, whom he used to shoot at like rabbits. One of them, a vindictive peasant, who had received a whole charge of shot in his face, lay in wait for the Seigneur one evening behind the trees of the mall, and very nearly succeeded in killing him, for the ball took off the tip of his ear.

"My uncle," Monsieur Paul continued, "tried to discover who had fired the shot; but he could not see any one, and he walked back slowly to the house. The day after he called his steward and ordered him to close up the manor and the park, and allow no living soul to enter. He expressly forbade that anything should be touched, or looked after, or any repairs made on the estate during his absence. He added, between his teeth, that he would return at Easter, or Trinity Sunday, as they say in the song; and, just as the song has it, Trinity Sunday passed without a sign of him. He died last year at Monaco; my brother-in-law and myself were the first to enter the chateau after it had been abandoned for thirty-two years. We found a chestnut-tree growing in the middle of the parlour. As for the park, it was useless trying to visit it, because there were no longer any paths or alleys."

My companion ceased to speak; and only the regular hoof-beat of the trotting horse, and the chirping of insects in the grass, broke the silence. On either hand, the sheaves standing in the fields took, in the vague moonlight, the appearance of tall white women kneeling down; and I abandoned myself awhile to those wonderful childish fancies which the charm of night always suggests. After driving under the heavy shadows of the mall, we turned to the right and rolled up a lordly avenue at the end of which the chateau suddenly rose into view — a black mass, with turrets en poivriere. We followed a sort of causeway, which gave access to the court-of-honor, and which, passing over a moat full of running water, doubtless replaced a long-vanished drawbridge. The loss of that draw-bridge must have been, I think, the first of various humiliations to which the warlike manor had been subjected ere being reduced to that pacific aspect with which it received me. The stars reflected themselves with marvelous clearness in the dark water. Monsieur Paul, like a courteous host, escorted me to my chamber at the very top of the building, at the end of a long corridor; and then, excusing himself for not presenting me at once to his wife by reason of the lateness of the hour, bade me good-night.

My apartment, painted in white and hung with chintz, seemed to keep some traces of the elegant gallantry of the eighteenth century. A heap of still-glowing ashes — which testified to the pains taken to dispel humidity — filled the fireplace, whose marble mantlepiece supported a bust of Marie

Antoinette in bisuit. Attached to the frame of the tarnished and discoloured mirror, two brass hooks, that had once doubtless served the ladies of old-fashioned days to hang their chatelaines on, seemed to offer a very opportune means of suspending my watch, which I took care to wind up beforehand; for, contrary to the opinion of the Thelemites, I hold that man is only master of time, which is Life itself, when he has divided it into hours, minutes and seconds — that is to say, into parts proportioned to the brevity of human existence.

And I thought to myself that life really seems short to us only because we measure it irrationally by our own mad hopes. We have all of us, like the old man in the fable, a new wing to add to our building. I want, for example, before I die, to finish my "History of the Abbots of Saint-Germain-de-Pres." The time God allots to each one of us is like a precious tissue which we embroider as we best know how. I had begun my woof with all sorts of philological illustrations.... So my thoughts wandered on; and at last, as I bound my foulard about my head, the notion of Time led me back to the past; and for the second time within the same round of the dial I thought of you, Clementine — to bless you again in your prosperity, if you have any, before blowing out my candle and falling asleep amid the chanting of the frogs.

Chapter II

During breakfast I had many opportunities to appreciate the good taste, tact, and intelligence of Madame de Gabry, who told me that the chateau had its ghosts, and was especially haunted by the "Lady-with-three-wrinkles-in-her-back," a prisoner during her lifetime, and thereafter a Soul-in-pain. I could never describe how much wit and animation she gave to this old nurse's tale. We took out, coffee on the terrace, whose balusters, clasped and forcibly torn away from their stone coping by a vigorous growth of ivy, remained suspended in the grasp of the amorous plant like bewildered Athenian women in the arms of ravishing Centaurs.

The chateau, shaped something like a four-wheeled wagon, with a turret at each of the four angles, had lost all original character by reason of repeated remodellings. It was merely a fine spacious building, nothing more. It did not appear to me to have suffered much damage during its abandonment of thirty-two years. But when Madame de Gabry conducted me into the great salon of the ground-floor, I saw that the planking was bulged in and out, the plinths rotten, the wainscotings split apart, the paintings of the piers turned black and hanging more than half out of their settings. A chestnut-tree, after forcing up the planks of the floor, had grown tall under the ceiling, and was reaching out its large-leaved branches towards the glassless windows.

This spectacle was not devoid of charm; but I could not look at it without anxiety as I remembered that the rich library of Monsieur Honore de Gabry, in an adjoining apartment, must have been exposed for the same length of time to the same forces of decay. Yet, as I looked at the young chestnut-tree in the salon, I could not but admire the magnificent vigour of Nature, and that resistless power which forces every germ to develop into life. On the other hand I felt saddened to think that, whatever effort we scholars may make to preserve dead things from passing away, we are labouring painfully in vain. Whatever has lived becomes the necessary food of new existences. And the Arab who builds himself a hut out of the marble fragments of a Palmyra temple is really more of a philosopher than all the guardians of museums at London, Munich, or Paris.

August 11.

All day long I have been classifying MSS.... The sun came in through the loft uncurtained windows; and, during my reading, often very interesting, I could hear the languid bumblebees bump heavily against the windows, and the flies intoxicated with light and heat, making their wings hum in circles around my head. So loud became their humming about three o'clock that I looked up from the document I was reading — a document containing very precious materials for the history of Melun in the thirteenth century — to watch the concentric movements of those tiny creatures. "Bestions," Lafontaine calls them: he found this form of the word in the old popular speech, whence also the term, tapisserie-a-bestions, applied to figured tapestry. I was compelled to confess that the effect of heat upon the wings of a fly is totally different from that it exerts upon the brain of a paleographical archivist; for I found it very difficult to think, and a rather pleasant languor weighing upon me, from which I could rouse myself only by a very determined effort. The dinner-bell then startled me in the midst of my labours; and I had barely time to put on my new dress-coat, so as to make a respectable appearance before Madame de Gabry.

The repast, generously served, seemed to prolong itself for my benefit. I am more than a fair judge of wine; and my hostess, who discovered my knowledge in this regard, was friendly enough to open a certain bottle of Chateau-Margaux in my honour. With deep respect I drank of this famous and knightly old wine, which comes from the slopes of Bordeaux, and of which the flavour and exhilarating power are beyond praise. The ardour of it spread gently through my veins, and filled me with an almost juvenile animation. Seated beside Madame de Gabry on the terrace, in the gloaming which gave a charming melancholy to the park, and lent to every object an air of mystery, I took pleasure in communicating my impression of the scene to my hostess. I discoursed with a vivacity quite remarkable on the part of a man so devoid of imagination as I am. I described to her spontaneously, without quoting from an old texts, the caressing melancholy of the evening, and the beauty of that natal earth which feeds us, not only with bread and wine, but also with ideas, sentiments, and beliefs, and which will at last take us all back to her maternal breast again, like so many tired little children at the close of a long day.

"Monsieur," said the kind lady, "you see these old towers, those trees, that sky; is it not quite natural that the personage of the popular tales and folk-songs should have been evoked by such scenes? Why, over there is the very path which Little Red Ridinghood followed when she went to the woods to pick nuts. Across this changeful and always vapoury sky the fairy chariots used to roll; and the north tower might have sheltered under its pointed roof that same old spinning woman whose distaff picked the Sleeping Beauty in the Wood."

I continued to muse upon her pretty fancies, while Monsieur Paul related to me, as he puffed a very strong cigar, the history of some suit he had brought against the commune about a water-right. Madame de Gabry, feeling the chill night air, began to shiver under the shawl her husband had wrapped about her, and left us to go to her room. I then decided, instead of going to my own, to return to the library and continue my examination of the manuscripts. In spite of the protests of Monsieur Paul, I entered what I may call, in old-fashioned phrase, "the book-room," and started to work by the light of a lamp.

After having read fifteen pages, evidently written by some ignorant and careless scribe, for I could scarcely discern their meaning, I plunged my hand into the pocket of my coat to get my snuff-box; but this movement, usually so natural and almost instinctive, this time cost me some effort and even fatigue. Nevertheless, I got out the silver box, and took from it a pinch of the odorous powder, which, somehow or other, I managed to spill all over my shirt-bosom under my baffled nose. I am sure my nose must have expressed its disappointment, for it is a very expressive nose. More than once it has betrayed my secret thoughts, and especially upon a certain occasion at the public library of Coutances, where I discovered, right in front of my colleague Brioux, the "Cartulary of Notre-Dame-des-Anges."

What a delight! My little eyes remained as dull and expressionless as ever behind my spectacles. But at the mere sight of my thick pug-nose, which quivered with joy and pride, Brioux knew that I had found something. He noted the volume I was looking at, observed the place where I put it back, pounced upon it as soon as I turned my heel, copied it secretly, and published in haste, for the sake of playing me a trick. But his edition swarms with errors, and I had the satisfaction of afterwards criticising some of the gross blunders he made.

But to come back to the point at which I left off: I began to suspect that I was getting very sleepy indeed. I was looking at a chart of which the interest may be divined from the fact that it contained mention of a hutch sold to Jehan d'Estonville, priest, in 1312. But although, even then, I could recognise the importance of the document, I did not give it that attention it so strongly invited. My eyes would keep turning, against my will, towards a certain corner of the table where there was nothing whatever interesting to a learned mind. There was only a big German book there, bound in pigskin, with brass studs on the sides, and very thick cording upon the back. It was a find copy of a compilation which has little to recommend it except the wood engravings it contains, and which is known as the "Cosmography of Munster." This volume, with its covers slightly open, was placed upon edge with the back upwards.

I could not say for how long I had been staring causelessly at the sixteenth-century folio, when my eyes were captivated by a sight so extraordinary that even a person as devoid of imagination as I could not but have been greatly astonished by it.

I perceived, all of a sudden, without having noticed her coming into the room, a little creature seated on the back of the book, with one knee bent and one leg hanging down — somewhat in the attitude of the amazons of Hyde Park or the Bois de Boulogne on horseback. She was so small that her swinging foot did not reach the table, over which the trail of her dress extended in a serpentine line. But her face and figure were those of an adult. The fulness of her corsage and the roundness of her waist could leave no doubt of that, even for an old savant like myself. I will venture to add that she was very handsome, with a proud mien; for my iconographic studies have long accustomed me to recognise at once the perfection of a type and the character of a physiognomy. The countenance of this lady who had seated herself inopportunely on the back of "Cosmography of Munster" expressed a mingling of haughtiness and mischievousness. She had the air of a queen, but a capricious queen; and I judged, from the mere expression of her eyes, that she was accustomed to wield great authority somewhere, in a very whimsical manner. Her mouth was imperious and mocking, and those blue eyes of hers seemed to laugh in a disquieting way under her finely arched black eyebrows. I have always heard that black eyebrows are very becoming to blondes; but this lady was very blonde. On the whole, the impression she gave me was one of greatness.

It may seem odd to say that a person who was no taller than a wine-bottle, and who might have been hidden in my coat pocket — but that it would have been very disrespectful to put her in it — gave me precisely an idea of greatness. But in the fine proportions of the lady seated upon the "Cosmography of Munster" there was such a proud elegance, such a harmonious majesty, and she maintained an attitude at once so easy and so noble, that she really seemed to me a very great person. Although my ink-bottle, which she examined with an expression of such mockery as appeared to indicate that she knew in advance every word that would come out of it at the end of my pen, was for her a deep basin in which she would have blackened her gold-clocked pink stockings up to the garter, I can assure you that she was great, and imposing even in her sprightliness.

Her costume, worthy of her face, was extremely magnificent; it consisted of a robe of gold-and-silver brocade, and a mantle of nacarat velvet, lined with vair. Her head-dress was a sort of hennin, with two high points; and pearls of splendid lustre made it bright and luminous as a crescent moon. Her little white hand held a wand. That wand drew my attention very strongly, because my archaeological studies had taught me to recognise with certainty every sign by which the notable personages of legend and of history are distinguished. This knowledge came to my aid during various very queer conjectures with which I was labouring. I examined the wand, and saw that it appeared to have been cut from a branch of hazel.

"Then its a fairy's wand," I said to myself; "consequently the lady who carries it is a fairy."

71

Happy at thus discovering what sort of a person was before me, I tried to collect my mind sufficiently to make her a graceful compliment. It would have given me much satisfaction, I confess, if I could have talked to her about the part taken by her people, not less in the life of the Saxon and Germanic races, than in that of the Latin Occident. Such a dissertation, it appeared to me, would have been an ingenious method of thanking the lady for having thus appeared to an old scholar, contrary to the invariable custom of her kindred, who never show themselves but to innocent children or ignorant village-folk.

Because one happens to be a fairy, one is none the less a woman, I said to myself; and since Madame Recamier, according to what I heard J. J. Ampere say, used to blush with pleasure when the little chimney-sweeps opened their eyes as wide as they could to look at her, surely the supernatural lady seated upon the "Cosmography of Munster" might feel flattered to hear an erudite man discourse learnedly about her, as about a medal, a seal, a fibula, or a token. But such an undertaking, which would have cost my timidity a great deal, became totally out of the question when I observed the Lady of the Cosmography suddenly take from an alms purse hanging at her girdle the very smallest of nuts I had ever seen, crack the shells between her teeth, and throw them at my nose, while she nibbled the kernels with the gravity of a sucking child.

At this conjuncture, I did what the dignity of science demanded of me — I remained silent. But the nut-shells caused such a painful tickling that I put up my hand to my nose, and found, to my great surprise, that my spectacles were straddling the very end of it — so that I was actually looking at the lady, not through my spectacles, but over them. This was incomprehensible, because my eyes, worn out over old texts, cannot ordinarily distinguish anything without glasses — could not tell a melon from a decanter, though the two were placed close up to my nose.

That nose of mine, remarkable for its size, its shape, and its coloration, legitimately attracted the attention of the fairy; for she seized my goose-quill pen, which was sticking up from the ink-bottle like a plume, and she began to pass the feather-end of that pen over my nose. I had had more than once, in company, occasion to suffer cheerfully from the innocent mischief of young ladies, who made me join their games, and would offer me their cheeks to kiss through the back of a chair, or invite me to blow out a candle which they would lift suddenly above the range of my breath. But until that moment no person of the fair sex had ever subjected me to such a whimsical piece of familiarity as that of tickling my nose with my own feather pen. Happily I remembered the maxim of my late grandfather, who was accustomed to say that everything was permissible on the part of ladies, and that whatever they do to us is to be regarded as a grace and a favour. Therefore, as a grace and a favour I received the nutshells and the titillations with my own pen, and I tried to smile. Much more! — I even found speech.

"Madame," I said, with dignified politeness, "you accord the honour of a visit not to a silly child, not to a boor, but to a bibliophile who is very happy to make your acquaintance, and who knows that long ago you used to make elf-knots in the manes of mares at the crib, drink the milk from the skimming-pails, slip graines-a-gratter down the backs of our great-grandmothers, make the hearth sputter in the faces of the old folks, and, in short, fill the house with disorder and gaiety. You can also boast of giving the nicest frights in the world to lovers who stayed out in the woods too late of evenings. But I thought you had vanished out of existence at least three centuries ago. Can it really be, Madame, that you are still to be seen in this age of railways and telegraphs? My concierge, who used to be a nurse in her young days, does not know your story; and my little boy-neighbour, whose nose is still wiped for him by his bonne, declares that you do not exist."

"What do you yourself think about it?" she cried, in a silvery voice, straightening up her royal little figure in a very haughty fashion, and whipping the back of the "Cosmography of Munster" as though it were a hippogriff.

73

"I don't really know," I answered rubbing my eyes.

This reply, indicating a deeply scientific scepticism, had the most deplorable effect upon my questioner.

"Monsieur Sylvestre Bonnard," she said to me, "you are nothing but an old pedant. I always suspected as much. The smallest little ragamuffin who goes along the road with his shirt-tail sticking out through a hole in his pantaloons knows more about me than all the old spectacled folks in your Institutes and your Academies. To know is nothing at all; to imagine is everything. Nothing exists except that which is imagined. I am imaginary. That is what it is to exist, I should think! I am dreamed of, and I appear. Everything is only dream; and as nobody ever dreams about you, Sylvestre Bonnard, it is YOU who do not exist. I charm the world; I am everywhere — on a moon-beam, in the trembling of a hidden spring, in the moving of leaves that murmur, in the white vapours that rise each morning from the hollow meadow, in the thickets of pink brier — everywhere!... I am seen; I am loved. There are sighs uttered, weird thrills of pleasure felt by those who follow the light print of my feet, as I make the dead leaves whisper. I make the little children smile; I give wit to the dullest-minded nurses. Leaning above the cradles, I play, I comfort, I lull to sleep — and you doubt whether I exist! Sylvestre Bonnard, your warm coat covers the hide of an ass!"

She ceased speaking; her delicate nostrils swelled with indignation; and while I admired, despite my vexation, the heroic anger of this little person, hse pushed my pen about in the ink-bottle, backward and forward, like an oar, and then suddenly threw it at my nose, point first.

I rubbed by face, and felt it all covered with ink. She had disappeared. My lamp was extinguished. A ray of moonlight streamed down through a window and descended upon the "Cosmography of Munster." A strong cool wind, which had arisen very suddenly without my knowledge, was blowing my papers, pens, and wafers about. My table was all stained with ink.

I had left my window open during the storm. What an imprudence!

Chapter III

I wrote to my housekeeper, as I promised, that I was safe and sound. But I took good care not to tell her that I had caught a cold from going to sleep in the library at night with the window open; for the good woman would have been as unsparing in her remonstrances to me as parliaments to kings. "At your age, Monsieur," she would have been sure to say, "one ought to have more sense." She is simple enough to believe that sense grows with age. I seem to her an exception to this rule.

Not having any similar motive for concealing my experiences from Madame de Gabry, I told her all about my vision, which she seemed to enjoy very much.

"Why, that was a charming dream of yours," she said; "and one must have real genius to dream such a dream."

"Then I am a real genius when I am asleep," I responded.

"When you dream," she replied; "and you are always dreaming."

I know that Madame de Gabry, in making this remark, only wished to please me; but that intention alone deserves my utmost gratitude; and it is therefore in a spirit of thankfulness and kindliest remembrance that I write down her words, which I will read over and over again until my dying day, and which will never be read by any one save myself.

I passed the next few days in completing the inventory of the manuscripts in the Lusance library. Certain confidential observations dropped by Monsieur Paul de Gabry, however, caused me some painful surprise, and made me decide to pursue the work after a different manner from that in which I had begun it. From those few words I learned that the fortune of Monsieur Honore de Gabry, which had been badly managed for many years, and subsequently swept away to a large extent through the failure of a banker whose name I do not know, had been transmitted to the heirs of the old French nobleman only under the form of mortgaged real estate and irrecoverable assets.

Monsieur Paul, by agreement with his joint heirs, had decided to sell the library, and I was intrusted with the task of making arrangements to have the sale effected upon advantageous terms. But totally ignorant as I was of all the business methods and trade-customs, I thought it best to get the advice of a publisher who was one of my private friends. I wrote him at once to come and join me at Lusance; and while waiting for his arrival I took my hat and cane and made visits to the different churches of the diocese, in several of which I knew there were certain mortuary inscriptions to be found which had never been correctly copied.

So I left my hosts and departed my pilgrimage. Exploring the churches and the cemeteries every day, visiting the parish priests and the village notaries, supping at the public inns with peddlers and cattle-dealers, sleeping at night between sheets scented with lavender, I passed one whole week in the quiet but profound enjoyment of observing the living engaged in their various daily occupations even while I was thinking of the dead. As for the purpose of my researches, I made only a few mediocre discoveries, which caused me only a mediocre joy, and one therefore salubrious and not at all fatiguing. I copied a few interesting epitaphs; and I added to this little collection a few recipes for cooking country dishes, which a certain good priest kindly gave me.

With these riches, I returned to Lusance; and I crossed the court-of-honour with such secret satisfaction as a bourgeois fells on entering his own home. This was the effect of the kindness of my hosts; and the impression I received on crossing their threshold proves, better than any reasoning could do, the excellence of their hospitality.

I entered the great parlour without meeting anybody; and the young chestnut-tree there spreading out its broad leaves seemed to me like an old friend. But the next thing which I saw — on the pier-table — caused me such a shock of surprise that I readjusted my glasses upon my nose with both hands at once, and then felt myself over so as to get at least some superficial proof of my own existence. In less than one second there thronged from my mind twenty different conjectures — the most rational of which was that I had suddenly become crazy. It seemed to me absolutely impossible that what I was looking at could exist; yet it was equally impossible for me not to see it as a thing actually existing. What caused my surprise was resting on the pier-table, above which rose a great dull speckled mirror.

I saw myself in that mirror; and I can say that I saw for once in my life the perfect image of stupefaction. But I made proper allowance for myself; I approved myself for being so stupefied by a really stupefying thing.

The object I was thus examining with a degree of astonishment that all my reasoning power failed to lessen, obtruded itself on my attention though quite motionless. The persistence and fixity of the phenomenon excluded any idea of hallucination. I am totally exempt from all nervous disorders capable of influencing the sense of sight. The cause of such visual disturbance is, I think, generally due to stomach trouble; and, thank God! I have an excellent stomach. Moreover, visual illusions are accompanied with special abnormal conditions which impress the victims of hallucination themselves, and inspire them with a sort of terror. Now, I felt nothing of this kind; the object which I saw, although seemingly impossible in itself, appeared to me under all the natural conditions of reality. I observed that it had three dimensions, and colours, and that it cast a shadow. Ah! how I stared at it! The water came into my eyes so that I had to wipe the glasses of my spectacles.

Finally I found myself obliged to yield to the evidence, and to affirm that I had really before my eyes the Fairy, the very same Fairy I had been dreaming of in the library a few evenings before. It was she, it was her very self, I assure you! She had the same air of child-queen, the same proud supple poise; she held the same hazel wand in her hand; she still wore her double-peaked head-dress, and the train of her long brocade robe undulated about her little feet. Same face, same figure. It was she indeed; and to prevent any possible doubt of it, she was seated on the back of a huge old-fashioned book strongly resembling the "Cosmography of Munster." Her immobility but half reassured me; I was really afraid that she was going to take some more nuts out of her alms-purse and throw the shells at my face.

I was standing there, waving my hands and gaping, when the musical and laughing voice of Madame de Gabry suddenly rang in my ears.

"So you are examining your fairy, Monsieur Bonnard!" said my hostess. "Well, do you think the resemblance good?"

It was very quickly said; but even while hearing it I had time to perceive that my fairy was a statuette in coloured wax, modeled with much taste and spirit by some novice hand. But the phenomenon, even thus reduced by a rational explanation, did not cease to excite my surprise. How, and by whom, had the Lady of the Cosmography been enabled to assume plastic existence? That was what remained for me to learn.

Turning towards Madame de Gabry, I perceived that she was not alone. A young girl dressed in black was standing beside her. She had large intelligent eyes, of a grey as sweet as that of the sky of the Isle of France, and at once artless and characteristic in their expression. At the extremities of her rather thin arms were fidgeting uneasily two slender hands, supple but slightly red, as it becomes the hands of young girls to be. Sheathed in her closely fitting merino robe, she had the slim grace of a young tree; and her large mouth bespoke frankness. I could not describe how much the child pleased me at first sight! She was not beautiful; but the three dimples of her cheeks and chin seemed to laugh, and her whole person, which revealed the awkwardness of innocence, had something in it indescribably good and sincere.

My gaze alternated from the statuette to the young girl; and I saw her blush — so frankly and fully! — the crimson passing over her face as by waves.

"Well," said my hostess, who had become sufficiently accustomed to my distracted moods to put the same question to me twice, "is that the very same lady who came in to see you through the window that you left open? She was very saucy, but then you were quite imprudent! Anyhow, do you recognise her?"

"It is her very self," I replied; "I see her now on that pier-table precisely as I saw her on the table in the library."

"Then, if that be so," replied Madame de Gabry, "you have to blame for it, in the first place, yourself, as a man who, although devoid of all imagination, to use your own words, knew how to depict your dream in such vivid colours; in the second place, me, who was able to remember and repeat faithfully all your dream; and lastly, Mademoiselle Jeanne, whom I now introduce to you, for she herself modeled that wax figure precisely according to my instructions."

Madame de Gabry had taken the young girl's hand as she spoke; but the latter had suddenly broken away from her, and was already running through the park with the speed of a bird.

"Little crazy creature!" Madame de Gabry cried after her. "How can one be so shy? Come back here to be scolded and kissed!"

But it was all of no avail; the frightened child disappeared among the shrubbery. Madame de Gabry seated herself in the only chair remaining in the dilapidated parlour.

"I should be much surprised," she said, "If my husband had not already spoken to you of Jeanne. She is a sweet child, and we both lover her very much. Tell me the plain truth; what do you think of her statuette?"

I replied that the work was full of good taste and spirit, but that it showed some want of study and practice on the author's part; otherwise I had been extremely touched to think that those young fingers should have thus embroidered an old man's rough sketch of fancy, and given form so brilliantly to the dreams of a dotard like myself.

"The reason I ask your opinion," replied Madame de Gabry, seriously, "is that Jeanne is a poor orphan. Do you think she could earn her living by modelling statuettes like this one?"

"As for that, no!" I replied; "and I think there is no reason to regret the fact. You say the girl is affectionate and sensitive; I can well believe you; I could believe it from her face alone. There are excitements in artist-life which impel generous hearts to act out of all rule and measure. This young creature is made to love; keep her for the domestic hearth. There only is real happiness."

"But she has no dowry!" replied Madame de Gabry.

Then, extending her hand to me, she continued:

"You are our friend; I can tell you everything. The father of this child was a banker, and one of our friends. He went into a colossal speculation, and it ruined him. He survived only a few months after his failure, in which, as Paul must have told you, three-fourths of my uncle's fortune were lost, and more than half of our own.

"We had made his acquaintance at Manaco, during the winter we passed there at my uncle's house. He had an adventurous disposition, but such an engaging manner! He deceived himself before ever he deceived others. After all, it is in the ability to deceive oneself that the greatest talent is shown, is it not? Well, we were captured — my husband, my uncle, and I; and we risked much more than a reasonable amount in a very hazardous undertaking. But, bah! as Paul says, since we have no children we need not worry about it. Besides, we have the satisfaction of knowing that the friend in whom we trusted was an honest man.... You must know his name, it was so often in the papers an on public placards — Noel Alexandre. His wife was a very sweet person. I knew her only when she was already past her prime, with traces of having once been very pretty, and a taste for fashionable style and display which seemed quite becoming to her. She was naturally fond of social excitement; but she showed a great deal of courage and dignity after the death of her husband. She died a year after him, leaving Jeanne alone in the world."

"Clementine!" I cried out.

And on thus learning what I had never imagined — the mere idea of which would have set all the forces of my soul in revolt — upon hearing that Clementine was no longer in this world, something like a great silence came upon me; and the feeling which flooded my whole being was not a keen, strong pain, but a quiet and solemn sorrow. Yet I was conscious of some incomprehensible sense of alleviation, and my thought rose suddenly to heights before unknown.

"From wheresoever thou art at this moment, Clementine," I said to myself, "look down upon this old heart now indeed cooled by age, yet whose blood once boiled for thy sake, and say whether it is not reanimated by the mere thought of being able to love all that remains of thee on earth. Everything passes away since thou thyself hast passed away; but Life is immortal; it is that Life we must love in its forms eternally renewed. All the rest is child's play; and I myself, with all my books, am only like a child playing with marbles. The purpose of life — it is thou, Clementine, who has revealed it to me!"...

Madame de Gabry aroused me from my thoughts by murmuring,

"The child is poor."

"The daughter of Clementine is poor!" I exclaimed aloud; "how fortunate that is so! I would not whish that any one by myself should proved for her and dower her! No! the daughter of Clementine must not have her dowry from any one but me."

And, approaching Madame de Gabry as she rose from her chair, I took her right hand; I kissed that hand, and placed it on my arm, and said:

"You will conduct me to the grave of the widow of Noel Alexandre."

And I heard Madame de Gabry asking me:

"Why are you crying?"

Chapter IV — The Little Saint-George

April 16.

Saint Drocoveus and the early abbots of Saint-Germain-des-Pres have been occupying me for the past forty years; but I do not know if I shall be able to write their history before I go to join

81

them. It is already quite a long time since I became an old man. One day last year, on the Pont des Arts, one of my fellow members at the Institute was lamenting before me over the ennui of becoming old.

"Still," Saint-Beuve replied to him, "it is the only way that has yet been found of living a long time."

I have tried this way, and I know just what it is worth. The trouble of it is not that one lasts too long, but that one sees all about him pass away — mother, wife, friends, children. Nature makes and unmakes all these divine treasures with gloomy indifference, and at last we find that we have not loved, we have only been embracing shadows. But how sweet some shadows are! If ever creature glided like a shadow through the life of a man, it was certainly that young girl whom I fell in love with when — incredible though it now seems — I was myself a youth.

A Christian sarcophagus from the catacombs of Rome bears a formula of imprecation, the whole terrible meaning of which I only learned with time. It says: "Whatsoever impious man violates this sepulchre, may he die the last of his own people!" In my capacity of archaeologist, I have opened tombs and disturbed ashes in order to collect the shreds of apparel, metal ornaments, or gems that were mingled with those ashes. But I did it only through that scientific curiosity which does not exclude feelings of reverence and of piety. May that malediction graven by some one of the first followers of the apostles upon a martyr's tomb never fall upon me! I ought not to fear to survive my own people so long as there are men in the world; for there are always some whom one can love.

But the power of love itself weakens and gradually becomes lost with age, like all the other energies of man. Example proves it; and it is this which terrifies me. Am I sure that I have not myself already suffered this great loss? I should surely have felt it, but for the happy meeting which has rejuvenated me. Poets speak of the Fountain of Youth; it does exist; it gushes up from the earth at every step we take. And one passes by without drinking of it!

The young girl I loved, married of her own choice to a rival, passed, all grey-haired, into the eternal rest. I have found her daughter — so that my life, which before seemed to me without utility, now once more finds a purpose and a reason for being.

To-day I "take the sun," as they say in Provence; I take it on the terrace of the Luxembourg, at the foot of the statue of Marguerite de Navarre. It is a spring sun, intoxicating as young wine. I sit and dream. My thoughts escape from my head like the foam from a bottle of beer. They are light, and their fizzing amuses me. I dream; such a pastime is certainly permissible to an old fellow who has published thirty volumes of texts, and contributed to the 'Journal des Savants' for twenty-six years. I have the satisfaction of feeling that I performed my task as well as it was possible for me to do, and that I utilised to their fullest extent those mediocre faculties with which Nature endowed me. My efforts were not all in vain, and I have contributed, in my own modest way, to that renaissance of historical labours which will remain the honour of this restless century. I shall certainly be counted among those ten or twelve who revealed to France her own literary antiquities. My publication of the poetical works of Gautier de Coincy inaugurated a judicious system and fixed a date. It is in the austere calm of old age that I decree to myself this deserved credit, and God, who sees my heart, knows whether pride or vanity have aught to do with this self-award of justice.

But I am tired; my eyes are dim; my hand trembles, and I see an image of myself in those old me of Homer, whose weakness excluded them from the battle, and who, seated upon the ramparts, lifted up their voices like crickets among the leaves.

So my thoughts were wandering when three young men seated themselves near me. I do not know whether each one of them had come in three boats, like the monkey of Lafontaine, but the three certainly displayed themselves over the space of twelve chairs. I took pleasure in watching them, not because they had anything very extraordinary about them, but because I discerned in them that brave joyous manner which is natural to youth. They were from the schools. I was less assured of it by the books they were carrying than by the character of their physiognomy. For all who busy themselves with the things of the mind can be at once recognised by an indescribably something which is common to all of them. I am very fond of young people; and these pleased me, in spite of a certain provoking wild manner which recalled to me my own college days with marvellous vividness. But they did not wear velvet doublets and long hair, as we used to do; they did not walk about, as we used to do, "Hell and malediction!" They were quite properly dressed, and neither their costume nor their language had anything suggestive of the Middle Ages. I must also add that they paid considerable attention to the women passing on the terrace, and expressed their admiration of some of them in very animated language. But their reflections, even on this subject, were not of a character to oblige me to flee from my seat. Besides, so long as youth is studious, I think it has a right to its gaieties.

One of them, having made some gallant pleasantry which I forget, the smallest and darkest of the three exclaimed, with a slight Gascon accent,

"What a thing to say! Only physiologists like us have any right to occupy ourselves about living matter. As for you, Gelis, who only live in the past — like all your fellow archivists and paleographers — you will do better to confine yourself to those stone women over there, who are your contemporaries."

And he pointed to the statues of the Ladies of Ancient France which towered up, all white, in a half-circle under the trees of the terrace. This joke, though in itself trifling, enabled me to know that the young man called Gelis was a student at the Ecole des Chartes. From the conversation which followed I was able to learn that his neighbor, blond and wan almost to diaphaneity, taciturn and sarcastic was Boulmier, a fellow student. Gelis and the future doctor (I hope he will become one some day) discoursed together with much fantasy and spirit. In the midst of the loftiest speculations they would play upon words, and make jokes after the peculiar fashion of really witty persons — that is to say, in a style of enormous absurdity. I need hardly say, I suppose, that they only deigned to maintain the most monstrous kind of paradoxes. They employed all their powers of imagination to make themselves as ludicrous as possible, and all their powers of reasoning to assert the contrary of common sense. All the better for them! I do not like to see young folks too rational.

The student of medicine, after glancing at the title of the book that Boulmier held in his hand, exclaimed,

"What! — you read Michelet — you?"

"Yes," replied Boulmier, very gravely. "I like novels."

Gelis, who dominated both by his fine stature, imperious gestures, and ready wit, took the book, turned over a few pages rapidly, and said,

"Michelet always had a great propensity to emotional tenderness. He wept sweet tears over Maillard, that nice little man introduced la paperasserie into the September massacres. But as emotional tenderness leads to fury, he becomes all at once furious against the victims. There was no help for it. It is the sentimentality of the age. The assassin is pitied, but the victim is considered quite unpardonable. In his later manner Michelet is more Michelet than ever before. There is no common sense in it; it is simply wonderful! Neither art nor science, neither criticism nor narrative; only furies and fainting-spells and epileptic fits over matters which he never deigns to explain. Childish outcries — envies de femme grosse! — and a style, my friends! — not a single finished phrase! It is astounding!"

And he handed the book back to his comrade. "This is amusing madness," I thought to myself, "and not quite so devoid of common sense as it appears. This young man, though only playing has sharply touched the defect in the cuirass."

But the Provencal student declared that history was a thoroughly despicable exercise of rhetoric. According to him, the only true history was the natural history of man. Michelet was in the right path when he came in contact with the fistula of Louis XIV., but he fell back into the old rut almost immediately afterwards.

After this judicious expression of opinion, the young physiologist went to join a party of passing friends. The two archivists, less well acquainted in the neighbourhood of a garden so far from the Rue Paradis-au-Marais, remained together, and began to chat about their studies. Gelis, who had completed his third class-year, was preparing a thesis on the subject of which he expatiated with youthful enthusiasm. Indeed, I thought the subject a very good one, particularly because I had recently thought myself called upon to treat a notable part of it. It was the Monasticon Gallicanum. The young erudite (I give him the name as a presage) wanted to describe all the engravings made about 1690 for the work which Dom Michel Germain would have had printed but for the one irremediable hindrance which is rarely foreseen and never avoided. Dom Michel Germain would have had printed but for the one irremediable hindrance which is rarely foreseen and never avoided. Dom Michel Germain left his manuscript complete, however, and in good order when he died. Shall I be able to do as much with mine? — but that is not the present question. So far as I am able to understand, Monsieur Gelis intends to devote a brief archaeological notice to each of the abbeys pictured by the humble engravers of Dom Michel Germain.

His friend asked him whether he was acquainted with all the manuscripts and printed documents relating to the subject. It was then that I pricked up my ears. They spoke at first of original sources; and I must confess they did so in a satisfactory manner, despite their innumerable and detestable puns. Then they began to speak about contemporary studies on the subject.

"Have you read," asked Boulmier, "the notice of Courajod?"

"Good!" I thought to myself.

"Yes," replied Gelis; "it is accurate."

"Have you read," said Boulmier, "the article of Tamisey de Larroque in the 'Revue des Questions Historiques'?"

"Good!" I thought to myself, for the second time.

"Yes," replied Gelis, "it is full of things."...

"Have you read," said Boulmier, "the 'Tableau des Abbayes Benedictines en 1600,' by Sylvestre Bonnard?"

"Good!" I said to myself, for the third time.

"Mai foi! no!" replied Gelis. "Bonnard is an idiot!" Turning my head, I perceived that the shadow had reached the place where I was sitting. It was growing chilly, and I thought to myself what a fool I was to have remained sitting there, at the risk of getting rheumatism, just to listen to the impertinence of those two young fellows!

"Well! well!" I said to myself as I got up. "Let this prattling fledgling write his thesis and sustain it! He will find my colleague, Quicherat, or some other professor at the school, to show him what an ignoramus he is. I consider him neither more nor less than a rascal; and really, now that I come to think of it, what he said about Michelet awhile ago was quite insufferable, outrageous! To talk in that way about an old master replete with genius! It was simply abominable!"

April 17.

"Therese, give me my new hat, my best frock-coat, and my silver-headed cane."

But Therese is deaf as a sack of charcoal and slow as Justice. Years have made her so. The worst is that she thinks she can hear well and move about well; and, proud of her sixty years of upright domesticity, she serves her old master with the most vigilant despotism.

"What did I tell you?" ...And now she will not give me my silver-headed cane, for fear that I might lose it! It is true that I often forget umbrellas and walking-sticks in the omnibuses and booksellers' shops. But I have a special reason for wanting to take out with me to-day my old cane with the engraved silver head representing Don Quixote charging a windmill, lance in rest, while Sancho Panza, with uplifted arms, vainly conjures him to a stop. That cane is all that came to me from the heritage of my uncle, Captain Victor, who in his lifetime resembled Don Quixote much more than Sancho Panza, and who loved blows quite as much as most people fear them.

For thirty years I have been in the habit of carrying this cane upon all memorable or solemn visits which I make; and those two figures of knight and squire give me inspiration and counsel. I imagine I can hear them speak. Don Quixote says,

"Think well about great things; and know that thought is the only reality in this world. Lift up Nature to thine own stature; and let the whole universe be for thee no more than the reflection of thine own heroic soul. Combat for honour's sake: that alone is worthy of a man! and if it should fall thee to receive wounds, shed thy blood as a beneficent dew, and smile."

And Sancho Panza says to me in his turn,

"Remain just what heaven made thee, comrade! Prefer the bread-crust which has become dry in thy wallet to all the partridges that roast in the kitchen of lords. Obey thy master, whether he by a wise man or a fool, and do not cumber thy brain with too many useless things. Fear blows; 'tis verily tempting God to seek after danger!"

But if the incomparable knight and his matchless squire are imagined only upon this cane of mine, they are realities to my inner conscience. Within every one of us there lives both a Don Quixote and a Sancho Panza to whom we hearken by turns; and though Sancho most persuades us, it is Don Quixote that we find ourselves obliged to admire.... But a truce to this dotage! — and let us go to see Madame de Gabry about some matters more important than the everyday details of life....

Same day.

I found Madame de Gabry dressed in black, just buttoning her gloves.

"I am ready," she said.

Ready! — so I have always found her upon any occasion of doing a kindness.

After some compliments about the good health of her husband, who was taking a walk at the time, we descended the stairs and got into the carriage.

I do not know what secret influence I feared to dissipate by breaking silence, but we followed the great deserted drives without speaking, looking at the crosses, the monumental columns, and the mortuary wreaths awaiting sad purchasers.

The vehicle at last halted at the extreme verge of the land of the living, before the gate upon which words of hope are graven.

"Follow me," said Madame de Gabry, whose tall stature I noticed then for the first time. She first walked down an alley of cypresses, and then took a very narrow path contrived between the tombs. Finally, halting before a plain slab, she said to me,

"It is here."

And she knelt down. I could not help noticing the beautiful and easy manner in which this Christian woman fell upon her knees, leaving the folds of her robe to spread themselves at random about her. I had never before seen any lady kneel down with such frankness and such forgetfulness of self, except two fair Polish exiles, one evening long ago, in a deserted church in Paris.

This image passed like a flash; and I saw only the sloping stone on which was graven the name of Clementine. What I then felt was something so deep and vague that only the sound of some rich music could convey the idea of it. I seemed to hear instruments of celestial sweetness make harmony in my old heart. With the solemn accords of a funeral chant there seemed to mingle the subdued melody of a song of love; for my soul blended into one feeling the grave sadness of the present with the familiar graces of the past.

I cannot tell whether we had remained a long time at the tomb of Clementine before Madame de Gabry arose. We passed through the cemetery again without speaking to each other. Only when we found ourselves among the living once more did I feel able to speak.

"While following you there," I said to Madame de Gabry, "I could not help thinking of those angels with whom we are said to meet on the mysterious confines of life and death. That tomb you led me to, of which I knew nothing — as I know nothing, or scarcely anything, concerning her whom it covers — brought back to me emotions which were unique in my life, and which seem in the dullness of that life like some light gleaming upon a dark road. The light recedes farther and farther away as the journey lengthens; I have now almost reached the bottom of the last slope; and, nevertheless, each time I turn to look back I see the glow as bright as ever.

"You, Madame, who knew Clementine as a young wife and mother after her hair had become grey, you cannot imagine her as I see her still; a young fair girl, all pink and white. Since you have been so kind as to be my guide, dear Madame, I ought to tell you what feelings were awakened in me by the sight of that grave to which you led me. Memories throng back upon me. I feel myself like some old gnarled and mossy oak which awakens a nestling world of birds by shaking its branches. Unfortunately the song my birds sing is old as the world, and can amuse no one but myself."

"Tell me your souvenirs," said Madame de Gabry. "I cannot read your books, because they are written only for scholars; but I like very much to have you talk to me, because you know how to give interest to the most ordinary things in life. And talk to me just as you would talk to an old woman. This morning I found three grey threads in my hair."

"Let them come without regret, Madame," I replied. "Time deals gently only with those who take it gently. And when in some years more you will have a silvery fringe under your black fillet, you will be reclothed with a new beauty, less vivid but more touching than the first; and you will find your husband admiring your grey tresses as much as he did that black curl which you gave him when about to be married, and which he preserves in a locket as a thing sacred.... These boulevards are broad and very quiet. We can talk at our ease as we walk along. I will tell you, to begin with, how I first made the acquaintance of Clementine's father. But you must not expect anything extraordinary, or anything even remarkable; you would be greatly deceived.

"Monsieur de Lessay used to live in the second storey of an old house in the Avenue de l'Observatoire, having a stuccoed front, ornamented with antique busts, and a large unkept garden attached to it. That facade and that garden were the first images my child-eyes perceived; and they will be the last, no doubt, which I still see through my closed eyelids when the Inevitable Day comes. For it was in that house that I was born; it was in that garden I first learned, while playing, to feel and know some particles of this old universe. Magical hours! — sacred hours! — when the soul, all fresh from the making, first discoveries the world, which for its sake seems to assume such caressing brightness, such mysterious charm! And that, Madame, is indeed because the universe itself is only the reflection of our soul.

"My mother was being very happily constituted. She rose with the sun, like the birds; and she herself resembled the birds by her domestic industry, by her maternal instinct, by her perpetual desire to sing, and by a sort of brusque grace, which I could feel the of very well even as a child. She was the soul of the house, which she filled with her systematic and joyous activity. My father was just as slow as she was brisk. I can recall very well that placid face of his, over which at times an ironical smile used to flit. He was fatigued with active life; and he loved his fatigue. Seated beside the fire in his big arm-chair, he used to read from morning till night; and it is from him that I inherit my love of books. I have in my library a Mably and a Raynal, which he annotated with his own hand from beginning to end. But it was utterly useless attempting to interest him in anything practical whatever. When my mother would try, by all kinds of gracious little ruses, to lure him out of his retirement, he would simply shake his head with that inexorable gentleness which is the force of weak characters. He used in this way greatly to worry the poor woman, who could not enter at all into his own sphere of meditative wisdom, and could understand nothing of life except its daily duties and the merry labour of each hour. She thought him sick, and feared he was going to become still more so. But his apathy had a different cause.

"My father, entering the Naval office under Monsieur Decres, in 1801, gave early proof of high administrative talent. There was a great deal of activity in the marine department in those times; and in 1805 my father was appointed chief of the

Second Administrative Division. That same year, the Emperor, whose attention had been called to him by the Minister, ordered him to make a report upon the organisation of the English navy. This work, which reflected a profoundly liberal and philosophic spirit, of which the editor himself was unconscious, was only finished in 1807 — about eighteen months after the defeat of Admiral Villeneuve at Trafalgar. Napoleon, who, from that disastrous day, never wanted to hear the word ship mentioned in his presence, angrily glanced over a few pages of the memoir, and then threw it in the fire, vociferating, 'Words! — words! I said once before that I hated ideologists.' My father was told afterwards that the Emperor's anger was so intense at the moment that he stamped the manuscript down into the fire with his boot-heels. At all events, it was his habit, when very much irritated, to poke down the fire with his boot-soles. My father never fully recovered from this disgrace; and the fruitlessness of all his efforts towards reform was certainly the cause of the apathy which came upon him at a later day. Nevertheless, Napoleon, after his return from Elba, sent for him, and ordered him to prepare some liberal and patriotic bulletins and proclamations for the fleet. After Waterloo, my father, whom the event had rather saddened than surprised, retired into private life, and was not interfered with — except that it was generally averred of him that he was a Jacobin, a buveur-de-sang — one of those men with whom no one could afford to be on intimate terms. My mother's eldest brother, Victor Maldent, and infantry captain — retired on half-pay in 1814, and disbanded in 1815 — aggravated by his bad attitude the situation in which the fall of the Empire had placed my father. Captain Victor used to shout in the cafes and the public balls that the Bourbons had sold France to the Cossacks. He used to show everybody a tricoloured cockade hidden in the lining of his hat; and carried with much ostentation a walking-stick, the handle of which had been so carved that the shadow thrown by it made the silhouette of the Emperor.

"Unless you have seen certain lithographs by Charlet, Madame, you could form no idea of the physiognomy of my

Uncle Victor, when he used to stride about the garden of the Tuileries with a fiercely elegant manner of his own — buttoned up in his frogged coat, with his cross-of-honour upon his breast, and a bouquet of violets in his button-hole.

"Idleness and intemperance greatly intensified the vulgar recklessness of his political passions. He used to insult people whom he happened to see reading the 'Quotidienne,' or the 'Drapeau Blanc,' and compel them to fight with him. In this way he had the pain and the shame of wounding a boy of sixteen in a duel. In short, my Uncle Victor was the very reverse of a well-behaved person; and as he came to lunch and dine at our house every blessed day in the year, his bad reputation became attached to our family. My poor father suffered cruelly from some of his guest's pranks; but being very good-natured, he never made any remarks, and continued to give the freedom of his house to the captain, who only despised him for it.

"All this which I have told you, Madame, was explained to me afterwards. But at the time in question, my uncle the captain filled me with the very enthusiasm of admiration, and I promised myself to try to become some day as like him as possible. So one fine morning, in order to begin the likeness, I put my arms akimbo, and swore like a trooper. My excellent mother at once gave me such a box on the ear that I remained half stupefied for some little while before I could even burst out crying. I can still see the old arm-chair, covered with yellow Utrecht velvet, behind which I wept innumerable tears that day.

"I was a very little fellow then. One morning my father, lifting me upon his knees, as he was in the habit of doing, smiled at me with that slightly ironical smile which gave a certain piquancy to his perpetual gentleness of manner. As I sat on his knee, playing with his long white hair, he told me something which I did not understand very well, but which interested me very much, for the simple reason that it was mysterious to me. I think but am not quite sure, that he related to me that morning the story of the little King of Yvetot, according to the song. All of a sudden we heard a great report; and the windows rattled. My father slipped me down gently on the floor at his feet; he threw up his trembling arms, with a strange gesture; his face became all inert and white, and his eyes seemed enormous. He tried to speak, but his teeth were chattering. At last he murmured, 'They have shot him!' I did not know what he meant, and felt only a vague terror. I knew afterwards, however, that hew was speaking of Marshal Ney, who fell on the 7th of December, 1815, under the wall enclosing some waste ground beside our house.

"About that time I used often to meet on the stairway an old man (or, perhaps, not exactly an old man) with little black eyes which flashed with extraordinary vivacity, and an impassive, swarthy face. He did not seem to me alive — or at least he did not seem to me alive in the same way that other men are alive. I had once seen, at the residence of Monsieur Denon, where my father had taken me with him on a visit, a mummy brought from Egypt; and I believed in good faith that Monsieur Denon's mummy used to get up when no one was looking, leave its gilded case, put on a brown coat and powdered wig, and become transformed into Monsieur de Lessay. And even to-day, dear Madame, while I reject that opinion as being without foundation, I must confess that Monsier de Lessay bore a very strong resemblance to Monsieur Denon's mummy. The fact is enough to explain why this person inspired me with fantastic terror.

"In reality, Monsieur de Lessay was a small gentleman and a great philosopher. As a disciple of Mably and Rousseau, he flattered himself on being a man without any prejudices; and this pretension itself is a very great prejudice.

"He professed to hate fanaticism, yet was himself a fanatic on the topic of toleration. I am telling you, Madame, about a character belonging to an age that is past. I fear I may not be able to make you understand, and I am sure I shall not be able to interest you. It was so long ago! But I will abridge as much as possible: besides, I did not promise you anything interesting; and you could not have expected to hear of remarkable adventures in the life of Sylvestre Bonnard."

Madame de Gabry encouraged me to proceed, and I resumed:

"Monsieur de Lessay was brusque with men and courteous to ladies. He used to kiss the hand of my mother, whom the customs of the Republic and the Empire had not habituated to such gallantry. In him, I touched the age of Louis XVI. Monsieur de Lessay was a geographer; and nobody, I believe, ever showed more pride then he in occupying himself with the face of the earth. Under the Old Regime he had attempted philosophical agriculture, and thus squandered his estates to the very last acre. When he had ceased to own one square foot of ground, he took possession of the whole globe, and prepared an extraordinary number of maps, based upon the narratives of travellers. But as he had been mentally nourished with the very marrow of the "Encyclopedie," he was not satisfied with merely parking off human beings within so many degrees, minutes, and seconds of latitude and longitude. he also occupied himself, alas! with the question of their happiness. It is worthy of remark, Madame, that those who have given themselves the most concern about the happiness of peoples have made their neighbors very miserable. Monsieur de Lessay, who was more of a geometrician than D'Alembert, and more of a philosopher than Jean Jacques, was also more of a royalist than Louis XVIII. But his love for the King was nothing to his hate for the Emperor. He had joined the conspiracy of Georges against the First Consul; but in the framing of the indictment he was not included among the inculpated parties, having been either ignored or despised, and this injury he never could forgive Bonaparte, whom he called the Ogre of Corsica, and to whom he used to say he would never have confided even the command of a regiment, so pitiful a soldier he judged him to be.

"In 1820, Monsieur de Lessay, who had then been a widower for many years, married again, at the age of sixty, a very young woman, whom he pitilessly kept at work preparing maps for him, and who gave him a daughter some years after their marriage, and died in childbed. My mother had nursed her during her brief illness, and had taken care of the child. The name of that child was Clementine.

"It was from the time of that birth and that death that the relations between our family and Monsieur de Lessay began. In the meanwhile I had been growing dull as I began to leave my true childhood behind me. I had lost the charming power of being able to see and feel; and things no longer caused me those delicious surprises which form the enchantment of the more tender age. For the same reason, perhaps, I have no distinct remembrance of the period following the birth of Clementine; I only know that a few months afterwards I had a misfortune, the mere thought of which still wrings my heart. I lost my mother. A great silence, a great coldness, and a great darkness seemed all at once to fill the house.

"I fell into a sort of torpor. My father sent me to the lycee, but I could only arouse myself from my lethargy with the greatest of effort.

"Still, I was not altogether a dullard, and my professors were able to teach me almost everything they wanted, namely, a little Greek and a great deal of Latin. My acquaintances were confined to the ancients. I learned to esteem Miltiades, and to admire Themistocles. I became familiar with Quintus Fabius, as far, at least, as it was possible to become familiar with so great a Consul. Proud of these lofty acquaintances, I scarcely ever condescended to notice little Clementine and her old father, who, in any event, went away to Normandy one fine morning without my having deigned to give a moment's thought to their possible return.

"They came back, however, Madame, they came back! Influences of Heaven, forces of nature, all ye mysterious powers which vouchsafe to man the ability to love, you know how I again beheld Clementine! They re-entered our melancholy home. Monsieur de Lessay no longer wore a wig. Bald, with a few grey locks about his ruddy temples, he had all the aspect of robust old age. But that divine being whom I saw all resplendent, as she leaned upon his arm — she whose presence illuminated the old faded parlour — she was not an apparition! It was Clementine

96

herself! I am speaking the simple truth: her violet eyes seemed to me in that moment supernatural, and even to-day I cannot imagine how those two living jewels could have endured the fatigues of life, or become subjected to the corruption of death.

"She betrayed a little shyness in greeting my father, whom she did not remember. Her complexion was slightly pink, and her half-open lips smiled with that smile which makes one think of the Infinite — perhaps because it betrays no particular thought, and expresses only the joy of living and the bliss of being beautiful. Under a pink hood her face shone like a gem in an open casket; she wore a cashmere scarf over a robe of white muslin plaited at the waist, from beneath which protruded the tip of a little Morocco shoe.... Oh! you must not make fun of me, dear Madame, that was the fashion of the time; and I do not know whether our new fashions have nearly so much simplicity, brightness, and decorous grace.

"Monsieur de Lessay informed us that, in consequence of having undertaken the publication of a historical atlas, he had come back to live in Paris, and that he would be pleased to occupy his former apartment, if it was still vacant. My father asked Mademoiselle de Lessay whether she was pleased to visit the capital. She appeared to be, for her smile blossomed out in reply. She smiled at the windows that looked out upon the green and luminous garden; she smiled at the bronze Marius seated among the ruins of Carthage above the dial of the clock; she smiled a the old yellow-velveted arm-chairs, and at the poor student who was afraid to lift his eyes to look at her. From that day — how I loved her!

"But here we are already a the Rue de Severs, and in a little while we shall be in sight of your windows. I am a very bad story-teller; and if I were — by some impossible chance — to take it into my head to compose a novel, I know I should never succeed. I have been drawing out to tiresome length a narrative which I must finish briefly; for there is a certain delicacy, a certain grace of soul, which an old man could not help offending by an complacent expatiation upon the sentiments of even the purest love. Let us take a short turn on this boulevard, lined with convents; and my recital will be easily finished within the distance separating us from that little spire you see over there....

"Monsieur de Lessay, on finding that I had graduated at the Ecole des Chartes, judged me worthy to assist him in preparing his historical atlas. The plan was to illustrate, by a series of maps, what the old philosopher termed the Vicissitudes of Empires from the time of Noah down to that of Charlemagne. Monsieur de Lessay had stored up in his head all the errors of the eighteenth century in regard to antiquity. I belonged, so far as my historical studies were concerned, to the new school; and I was just at that age when one does not know how to dissemble. The manner in which the old man understood, or, rather, misunderstood, the epoch of the Barbarians — his obstinate determination to find in remote antiquity only ambitious princes, hypocritical and avaricious prelates, virtuous citizens, poet-philosophers, and other personages who never existed outside of the novels of Marmontel, — made me dreadfully unhappy, and at first used to excite me into attempts at argument, — rational enough, but perfectly useless and sometimes dangerous, for Monsieur de Lessay was very irascible, and Clementine was very beautiful. Between her and him I passed many hours of torment and of delight. I was in love; I was a coward, and I granted to him all that he demanded of me in regard to the political and historical aspect which the Earth — that was at a later day to bear Clementine — presented in the time of Abraham, of Menes, and of Deucalion.

"As fast as we drew our maps, Mademoiselle de Lessay tinted them in water-colours. Bending over the table, she held the brush lightly between two fingers; the shadow of her eyelashes descended upon her cheeks, and bather her half-closed eyes in a delicious penumbra. Sometimes she would lift her head, and I would see her lips pout. There was so much expression in her beauty that she could not breathe without seeming to sigh; and her most ordinary poses used to throw me into the deepest ecstasies of admiration. Whenever I gazed at her I fully agreed with Monsieur de Lessay that Jupiter had once reigned as a despot-king over the mountainous regions of Thessaly, and that Orpheus had committed the imprudence of leaving the teaching of philosophy to the clergy. I am not now quite sure whether I was a coward or a hero when I accorded al this to the obstinate old man.

"Mademoiselle de Lessay, I must acknowledge, paid very little attention to me. But this indifference seemed to me so just and so natural that I never even dreamed of thinking I had a right to complain about it; it made me unhappy, but without my knowing that I was unhappy at the time. I was hopeful; — we had then only got as far as the First Assyrian Empire.

"Monsieur de Lessay came every evening to take coffee with my father. I do not know how they became such friends; for it would have been difficult to find two characters more oppositely constituted. My father was a man who admired very few things, but was still capable of excusing a great many. Still, as he grew older, he evinced more and more dislike of everything in the shape of exaggeration. He clothed his ideas with a thousand delicate shades of expression, and never pronounced an opinion without all sorts of reservations. These conversational habits, natural to a finely trained mind, used greatly to irritate the dry, terse old aristocrat, who was never in the least disarmed by the moderation of an adversary — quite the contrary! I always foresaw one danger. That danger was Bonaparte. My father had not himself retained an particular affection for his memory; but, having worked under his direction, he did not like to hear him abused, especially in favour of the Bourbons, against whom he had serious reason to feel resentment. Monsieur de Lessay, more of a Voltairean and a Legitimist than ever, now traced back to Bonaparte the origin of every social, political, and religious evil. Such being the situation, the idea of Uncle Victor made me feel particularly uneasy. This terrible uncle had become absolutely unsufferable now that his sister was no longer there to calm him down. The harp of David was broken, and Saul was wholly delivered over to the spirit of madness. The fall of Charles X. had increased the audacity of the old Napoleonic veteran, who uttered all imaginable bravadoes. He no longer frequented our house, which had become too silent for him. But sometimes, at the dinner-hour, we would see him suddenly make his appearance, all covered with flowers, like a mausoleum. Ordinarily he would sit down to table with an oath, growled out from the very bottom of his chest, and brag, between every two mouthfuls, of his good fortune with the ladies as a vieux brave. Then, when the dinner was over, he would fold up his napkin in the shape of a bishop's mitre, gulp down half a decanter of brandy, and rush away with the hurried air of a man terrified at the mere idea of remaining for any length of time, without drinking, in conversation with an old philosopher and a young scholar. I felt perfectly sure that, if ever he and Monsieur de Lessay should come together, all would be lost. But that day came, Madame!

"The captain was almost hidden by flowers that day, and seemed so much like a monument commemorating the glories of the Empire that one would have liked to pass a garland of immortelles over each of his arms. He was in an extraordinarily good humour; and the first person to profit by that good humour was our cook — for he put his arm around her waist while she was placing the roast on the table.

"After dinner he pushed away the decanter presented to him, observing that he was going to burn some brandy in his coffee later on. I asked him tremblingly whether he would not prefer to have his coffee at once. He was very suspicious, and not at all dull of comprehension — my Uncle Victor. My precipitation seemed to him in very bad taste; for he looked at me in a peculiar way, and said,

"'Patience! my nephew. It isn't the business of the baby of the regiment to sound the retreat! Devil take it! You must be in a great hurry, Master Pedant, to see if I've got spurs on my boots!'

"It was evident the captain had divined that I wanted him to go. And I knew him well enough to be sure that he was going to stay. He stayed. The least circumstances of that evening remain impressed on my memory. My uncle was extremely jovial. The mere idea of being in somebody's way was enough to keep him in good humour. He told us, in regular barrack style, ma foi! a certain story about a monk, a trumpet, and five bottles of Chambertin, which must have been much enjoyed in the garrison society, but which I would not venture to repeat to you, Madame, even if I could remember it. When we passed into the parlour, the captain called attention to the bad condition of our andirons, and learnedly discoursed on the merits of rotten-stone as a brass-polisher. Not a word on the subject of politics. He was husbanding his forces. Eight o'clock sounded from the ruins of Carthage on the mantlepiece. It was Monsieur de Lessay's hour. A few moments later he entered the parlour with his daughter. The ordinary evening chat began. Clementine sat down and began to work on some embroidery beside the lamp, whose shade left her pretty head in a soft shadow, and threw down upon her fingers a radiance that made them seem almost self-luminous. Monsieur de Lessay spoke of a comet announced by the astronomers, and developed some theories in relation to the subject, which, however audacious, betrayed at least a certain degree of intellectual culture. My father, who knew a good deal about astronomy, advanced some sound ideas of his own, which he ended up with his eternal, 'But what do we know about it, after all?' In my turn I cited the opinion of our neighbour of the Observatory — the great Arago. My Uncle Victor declared that comets had a peculiar influence on the quality of wines, and related in support of this view a jolly tavern-story. I was so delighted with the turn the conversation had taken that I did all in my power to maintain it in the same groove, with the help of my most recent studies, by a long exposition of the chemical composition of those nebulous bodies which, although extending over a length of billions of leagues, could be contained in a small bottle. My father, a little surprised at my unusual eloquence, watched me with his peculiar, placid, ironical smile. But one cannot always remain in heaven. I spoke, as I looked at Clementine, of a certain comete of diamonds, which I had been admiring in a jeweller's window the evening before. It was a most unfortunate inspiration of mine.

"'Ah! my nephew,' cried Uncle Victor, that "comete" of yours was nothing to the one which the Empress Josephine wore in her hair when she came to Strasburg to distribute crosses to the army.'

"'That little Josephine was very fond of finery and display,' observed Monsieur de Lessay, between two sips of coffee. 'I do not blame her for it; she had good qualities, though rather frivolous in character. She was a Tascher, and she conferred a great honour on Bonaparte by marrying him. To say a Tascher does not, of course, mean a great deal; but to say a Bonaparte simply means nothing at all.'

"'What do you mean by that, Monsieur the Marquis?' demanded Captain Victor.

"'I am not a marquis,' dryly responded Monsieur de Lessay; 'and I mean simply that Bonaparte would have been very well suited had he married one of those cannibal women described by Captain Cook in his voyages — naked, tattooed, with a ring in her nose — devouring with delight putrefied human flesh.'

"I had foreseen it, and in my anguish (O pitiful human heart!) my first idea was about the remarkable exactness of my anticipations. I must say that the captain's reply belonged to the sublime order. He put his arms akimbo, eyed Monsieur de Lessay contemptuously from head to food, and said,

"'Napoleon, Monsieur the Vidame, had another spouse besides Josephine, another spouse besides Marie-Louise. that companion you know nothing of; but I have seen her, close to me. She wears a mantle of azure gemmed with stars; she is crowned with laurels; the Cross-of-Honour flames upon her breast. Her name is GLORY!'

"Monsieur de Lessay set his cup on the mantlepiece and quietly observed,

"'Your Bonaparte was a blackguard!'

"My father rose up calmly, extended his arm, and said very softly to Monsieur de Lessay,

"Whatever the man was who died at St. Helena, I worked for ten years in his government, and my brother-in-law was three times wounded under his eagles. I beg of you, dear sir and friend, never to forget these facts in future.'

"What the sublime and burlesque insolence of the captain could not do, the courteous remonstrance of my father effected immediately, throwing Monsieur de Lessay into a furious passion.

"'I did forget,' he exclaimed, between his set teeth, livid in his rage, and fairly foaming at the mouth; 'the herring-cask always smells of herring and when one has been in the service of rascals — -'

"As he uttered the word, the Captain sprang at his throat; I am sure he would have strangled him upon the spot but for his daughter and me.

"My father, a little paler than his wont, stood there with his arms folded, and watched the scene with a look of inexpressible pity. What followed was still more lamentable — but why dwell further upon the folly of two old men. Finally I succeeded in separating them. Monsieur de Lessay made a sign to his daughter and left the room. As she was following him, I ran out into the stairway after her.

"'Mademoiselle,' I said to her, wildly, taking her hand as I spoke, 'I love you! I love you!'

"For a moment she pressed my hand; her lips opened. What was it that she was going to say to me? But suddenly, lifting her eyes towards her father ascending the stairs, she drew her hand away, and made me a gesture of farewell.

"I never saw her again. Her father went to live in the neighbourhood of the Pantheon, in an apartment which he had rented for the sale of his historical atlas. He died in a few months afterward of an apoplectic stroke. His daughter, I was told, retired to Caen to live with some aged relative. It was there that, later on, she married a bank-clerk, the same Noel Alexandre who became so rich and died so poor.

"As for me, Madame, I have lived alone, at peace with myself; my existence, equally exempt from great pains and great joys, has been tolerably happy. But for many years I could never see an empty chair beside my own of a winter's evening without feeling a sudden painful sinking at my heart. Last year I learned from you, who had known her, the story of her old age and death. I saw her daughter at your house. I have seen her; but I cannot yet say like the aged mad of Scripture, 'And now, O Lord, let thy servant depart in peace!' For if an old fellow like me can be of any use to anybody, I would wish, with your help, to devote my last energies and abilities to the care of this orphan."

I had uttered these last words in Madame de Gabry's own vestibule; and I was about to take leave of my kind guide when she said to me,

"My dear Monsieur, I cannot help you in this matter as much as I would like to do. Jeanne is an orphan and a minor. You cannot do anything for her without the authorisation of her guardian."

"Ah!" I exclaimed, "I had not the least idea in the wold that Jeanne had a guardian!"

Madame de Gabry looked at me with visible surprise. She had not expected to find the old man quite so simple.

She resumed:

"The guardian of Jeanne Alexandre is Maitre Mouche, notary at Levallois-Perret. I am afraid you will not be able to come to any understanding with him; for he is a very serious person."

"Why! good God!" I cried, "with what kind of people can you expect me to have any sort of understanding at my age, except serious persons."

She smiled with a sweet mischievousness — just as my father used to smile — and answered:

"With those who are like you — the innocent folks who wear their hearts on their sleeves. Monsieur Mouche is not exactly that kind. He is cunning and light-fingered. But although I have very little liking for him, we will go together and see him, if you wish, and ask his permission to visit Jeanne, whom he has sent to a boarding-school at Les Ternes, where she is very unhappy."

We agreed at once upon a day; I kissed Madame de Gabry's hands, and we bade each other good-bye.

From May 2 to May 5.

I have seen him in his office, Maitre Mouche, the guardian of Jeanne. Small, thin, and dry; his complexion looks as if it was made out of the dust of his pigeon-holes. He is a spectacled animal; for to imagine him without his spectacles would be impossible. I have heard him speak, this Maitre Mouche; he has a voice like a tin rattle, and he uses choice phrases; but I should have been better pleased if he had not chosen his phrases so carefully. I have observed him, this Maitre Mouche; he is very ceremonious, and watches his visitors slyly out of the corner of his eye.

Maitre Mouche is quite pleased, he informs us; he is delighted to find we have taken such an interest in his ward. But he does not think we are placed in this world just to amuse ourselves. No: he does not believe it; and I am free to acknowledge that anybody in his company is likely to reach the same conclusion, so little is he capable of inspiring joyfulness. He fears that it would be giving his dear ward a false and pernicious idea of life to allow her too much enjoyment. It is for this reason that he requests Madame de Gabry not to invite the young girl to her house except at very long intervals.

We left the dusty notary and his dusty study with a permit in due form (everything which issues from the office of Maitre Mouche is in due form) to visit Mademoiselle Jeanne Alexandre on the first Thursday of each month at Mademoiselle Prefere's private school, Rue Demours, Aux Ternes.

The first Thursday in May I set out to pay a visit to Mademoiselle Prefere, whose establishment I discerned from afar off by a big sign, painted with blue letters. That blue tint was the first indication I received of Mademoiselle Prefere's character, which I was able to see more of later on. A scared-looking servant took my card, and abandoned me without one word of hope at the door of a chilly parlour full of that stale odour peculiar to the dining-rooms of educational establishments. The floor of this parlour had been waxed with such pitiless energy, that I remained

105

for awhile in distress upon the threshold. But happily observing that little strips of woollen carpet had been scattered over the floor in front of each horse-hair chair, I succeeded, by cautiously stepping from one carpet-island to another in reaching the angle of the mantlepiece, where I sat down quite out of breath.

Over the mantelpiece, in a large gilded frame, was a written document, entitled in flamboyant Gothic lettering, Tableau d'Honneur, with a long array of names underneath, among which I did not have the pleasure of finding that of Jeanne Alexandre. After having read over several times the names of those girl-pupils who had thus made themselves honoured in the eyes of Mademoiselle Prefere, I began to feel uneasy at not hearing any one coming. Mademoiselle Prefere would certainly have succeeded in establishing the absolute silence of interstellar spaces throughout her pedagogical domains, had it not been that the sparrows had chosen her yard to assemble in by legions, and chirp at the top of their voices. It was a pleasure to hear them. But there was no way of seeing them — through the ground-glass windows. I had to content myself with the sights of the parlour, decorated from floor to ceiling, on all of its four walls, with drawings executed by the pupils of the institution. There were Vestals, flowers, thatched cottages, column-capitals, and an enormous head of Tatius, King of the Sabines, bearing the signature Estelle Mouton.

I had already passed some time in admiring the energy with which Mademoiselle Mouton had delineated the bushy eyebrows and the fierce gaze of the antique warrior, when a sound, faint like the rustling of a dead leaf moved by the wind, caused me to turn my head. It was not a dead leaf at all — it was Mademoiselle Prefere. With hands jointed before her, she came gliding over the mirror-polish of that wonderful floor as the Saints of the Golden Legend were wont to glide over the crystal surface of the waters. But upon any other occasion, I am sure, Mademoiselle Prefere would not have made me think in the least about those virgins dear to mystical fancy. Her face rather gave me the idea of a russet-apple preserved or a whole winter in an attic by some economical housekeeper. Her shoulders were covered with a fringed pelerine, which had nothing at all remarkable about it, but which she wore as if it were a sacerdotal vestment, or the symbol of some high civic function.

I explained to her the purpose of my visit, and gave her my letter of introduction.

"Ah! — so you are Monsieur Mouche!" she exclaimed. "Is his health VERY good? He is the most upright of men, the most — -"

She did not finish the phrase, but raised her eyes to the ceiling. My own followed the direction of their gaze, and observed a little spiral of paper lace, suspended from the place of the chandelier, which was apparently destined, so far as I could discover, to attract the flies away from the gilded mirror-frames and the Tableau d'Honneur.

"I have met Mademoiselle Jeanne Alexandre," I observed, "at the residence of Madame de Gabry and had reason to appreciate the excellent character and quick intelligence of the young girl. As I used to know her parents very well, the friendship which I felt for them naturally inclines me to take an interest in her."

Mademoiselle Prefere, in lieu of making any reply, sighed profoundly, pressed her mysterious pelerine to her heart, and again contemplated the paper spiral.

At last she observed,

"Since you were once the friend of Monsieur and Madame Alexandre, I hope and trust that, like Monsieur Mouche and myself, you deplore those crazy speculations which led them to ruin, and reduced their daughter to absolute poverty!"

I thought to myself, on hearing these words, how very wrong it is to be unlucky, and how unpardonable such an error on the part of those previously in a position worthy of envy. Their fall at once avenges and flatters us; and we are wholly pitiless.

After having answered, very frankly, that I knew nothing whatever about the history of the bank, I asked the schoolmistress if she was satisfied with Mademoiselle Alexandre.

"That child is indomitable!" cried Mademoiselle Prefere.

And she assumed an attitude of lofty resignation, to symbolise the difficult situation she was placed in by a pupil so hard to train. Then, with more calmness of manner, she added:

"The young person is not unintelligent. But she cannot resign herself to learn things by rule."

What a strange old maid was this Mademoiselle Prefere! She walked without lifting her legs, and spoke without moving her lips! Without, however, considering her peculiarities for more than a reasonable instant, I replied that principles were, no doubt, very excellent things, and that I could trust myself to her judgement in regard to their value; but that, after all, when one had learned something, it very little difference what method had been followed in the learning of it.

Mademoiselle made a slow gesture of dissent. Then with a sigh, she declared,

"Ah, Monsieur! those who do not understand educational methods are apt to have very false ideas on these subjects. I am certain they express their opinions with the best intentions in the world; but they would do better, a great deal better, to leave all such questions to competent people."

I did not attempt to argue further; and simply asked her whether I could see Mademoiselle Alexandre at once.

She looked at her pelerine, as if trying to read in the entanglements of its fringes, as in a conjuring book, what sort of answer she ought to make; then said,

"Mademoiselle Alexandre has a penance to perform, and a class-lesson to give; but I should be very sorry to let you put yourself to the trouble of coming here all to no purpose. I am going to send for her. Only first allow me, Monsieur — as is our custom — to put your name on the visitors' register."

She sat down at the table, opened a large copybook, and, taking out Maitre Mouche's letter again from under her pelerine, where she had placed it, looked at it, and began to write.

"'Bonnard' — with a 'd,' is it not?" she asked. "Excuse me for being so particular; but my opinion is that proper names have an orthography. We have dictation-lessons in proper names, Monsieur, at this school — historical proper names, of course!"

After I had written down my name in a running hand, she inquired whether she should not put down after it my profession, title, quality — such as "retired merchant," "employe," "independent gentleman," or something else. There was a column in her register expressly for that purpose.

"My goodness, Madame!" I said, "if you must absolutely fill that column of yours, put down 'Member of the Institute.'"

It was still Mademoiselle Prefere's pelerine I saw before me; but it was not Mademoiselle Prefere who wore it; it was a totally different person, obliging, gracious, caressing, radiant, happy. Her eyes, smiled; the little wrinkles of her face (there were a vast number of them!) also smiled; her mouth smiled likewise, but only on one side. I discovered afterwards that was her best side. She spoke: her voice had also changed with her manner; it was now sweet as honey.

"You said, Monsieur, that our dear Jeanne was very intelligent. I discovered the same thing myself, and I am proud of being able to agree with you. This young girl has really made me feel a great deal of interest in her. She has what I call a happy disposition.... But excuse me for thus drawing upon your valuable time."

She summoned the servant-girl, who looked much more hurried and scared than before, and who vanished with the order to go and tell Mademoiselle Alexandre that Monsieur Sylvestre Bonnard, Member of the Institute, was waiting to see her in the parlour.

Mademoiselle Prefere had barely time to confide in me that she had the most profound respect for all decisions of the Institute — whatever they might be — when Jeanne appeared, out of breath, red as a poppy, with her eyes very wide open, and her arms dangling helplessly at her sides — charming in her artless awkwardness.

"What a state you are in, my dear child!" murmured Mademoiselle Prefere, with maternal sweetness, as she arranged the girl's collar.

Jeanne certainly did present an odd aspect. Her hair combed back, and imperfectly held by a net from which loose curls were escaping; her slender arms, sheathed down to the elbows in lustring sleeves; her hands, which she did not seem to know what to do with, all red with chillblains; her dress, much too short, revealing that she had on stockings much too large for her, and shoes worn down at the heel; and a skipping-rope tied round her waist in lieu of a belt, — all combined to lend Mademoiselle Jeanne an appearance the reverse of presentable.

"Oh, you crazy girl!" sighed Mademoiselle Prefere, who now seemed no longer like a mother, but rather like an elder sister.

Then she suddenly left the room, gliding like a shadow over the polished floor.

I said to Jeanne,

"Sit down, Jeanne, and talk to me as you would to a friend. Are you not better satisfied here now than you were last year?"

She hesitated; then answered with a good-natured smile of resignation,

"Not much better."

I asked her to tell me about her school life. She began at once to enumerate all her different studies — piano, style, chronology of the Kings of France, sewing, drawing, catechism, deportment... I could never remember them all! She still held in her hands, all unconsciously, the two ends of her skipping-rope, and she raised and lowered them regularly while making her enumeration. Then all at once she became conscious of what she was doing, blushed, stammered, and became so confused that I had to renounce my desire to know the full programme of study adopted in the Prefere Institution.

After having questioned Jeanne on various matters, and obtained only the vaguest of answers, I perceived that her young mind was totally absorbed by the skipping-rope, and I entered bravely into that grave subject.

"So you have been skipping?" I said. "It is a very nice amusement, but one that you must not exert yourself too much at; for any excessive exercise of that kind might seriously injure your health, and I should be very much grieved about it Jeanne — I should be very much grieved, indeed!"

"You are very kind, Monsieur," the young girl said, "to have come to see me and talk to me like this. I did not think about thanking you when I came in, because I was too much surprised. Have you seen Madame de Gabry? Please tell me something about her, Monsieur."

"Madame de Gabry," I answered, "is very well. I can only tell you about her, Jeanne, what an old gardener once said of the lady of the castle, his mistress, when somebody anxiously inquired about her: 'Madame is in her road.' Yes, Madame de Gabry is in her own road; and you know, Jeanne, what a good road it is, and how steadily she can walk upon it. I went out with her the other day, very, very far away from the house; and we talked about you. We talked about you, my child, at your mother's grave."

"I am very glad," said Jeanne.

And then, all at once, she began to cry.

I felt too much reverence for those generous tears to attempt in any way to check the emotion that had evoked them. But in a little while, as the girl wiped her eyes, I asked her,

"Will you not tell me, Jeanne, why you were thinking so much about that skipping-rope a little while ago?"

"Why, indeed I will, Monsieur. It was only because I had no right to come into the parlour with a skipping-rope. You know, of course, that I am past the age for playing at skipping. But when the servant said there was an old gentleman...oh!...I mean...that a gentleman was waiting for me in the parlour, I was making the little girls jump. Then I tied the rope round my waist in a hurry, so that it might not get lost. It was wrong. But I have not been in the habit of having many people come to see me. And Mademoiselle Prefere never lets us off if we commit any breach of deportment: so I know she is going to punish me, and I am very sorry about it."...

"That is too bad, Jeanne!"

She became very grave, and said,

"Yes, Monsieur, it is too bad; because when I am punished myself, I have no more authority over the little girls."

I did not at once fully understand the nature of this unpleasantness; but Jeanne explained to me that, as she was charged by Mademoiselle Prefere with the duties of taking care of the youngest class, of washing and dressing the children, of teaching them how to behave, how to sew, how to say the alphabet, of showing them how to play, and, finally, of putting them to bed at the close of the day, she could not make herself obeyed by those turbulent little folks on the days she was condemned to wear a night-cap in the class-room, or to eat her meals standing up, from a plate turned upside down.

Having secretly admired the punishments devised by the Lady of the Enchanted Pelerine, I responded:

"Then, if I understand you rightly, Jeanne, you are at once a pupil here and a mistress? It is a condition of existence very common in the world. You are punished, and you punish?"

"Oh, Monsieur!" she exclaimed. "No! I never punish!"

"Then, I suspect," said I, "that your indulgence gets you many scoldings from Mademoiselle Prefere?"

She smiled, and blinked.

Then I said to her that the troubles in which we often involve ourselves, by trying to act according to our conscience and to do the best we can, are never of the sort that totally dishearten and weary us, but are, on the contrary, wholesome trials. This sort of philosophy touched her very little. She even appeared totally unmoved by my moral exhortations. But was not this quite natural on her part? — and ought I not to have remembered that it is only those no longer innocent who can find pleasure in the systems of moralists?... I had at least good sense enough to cut short my sermonising.

"Jeanne," I said, "you were asking a moment ago about Madame de Gabry. Let us talk about that Fairy of yours She was very prettily made. Do you do any modelling in wax now?"

"I have not a bit of wax," she exclaimed, wringing her hands — "no wax at all!"

"No wax!" I cried — "in a republic of busy bees?"

She laughed.

"And, then, you see, Monsieur, my FIGURINES, as you call them, are not in Mademoiselle Prefere's programme. But I had begun to make a very small Saint-George for Madame de Gabry — a tiny little Saint-George, with a golden cuirass. Is not that right, Monsieur Bonnard — to give Saint-George a gold cuirass?"

"Quite right, Jeanne; but what became of it?"

"I am going to tell you, I kept it in my pocket because I had no other place to put it, and — and I sat down on it by mistake."

She drew out of her pocket a little wax figure, which had been squeezed out of all resemblance to human form, and of which the dislocated limbs were only attached to the body by their wire framework. At the sight of her hero thus marred, she was seized at once with compassion and gaiety. The latter feeling obtained the mastery, and she burst into a clear laugh, which, however, stopped as suddenly as it had begun.

Mademoiselle Prefere stood at the parlour door, smiling.

"That dear child!" sighed the schoolmistress in her tenderest tone. "I am afraid she will tire you. And, then, your time is so precious!"

I begged Mademoiselle Prefere to dismiss that illusion, and, rising to take my leave, I took from my pocket some chocolate-cakes and sweets which I had brought with me.

"That is so nice!" said Jeanne; "there will be enough to go round the whole school."

The lady of the pelerine intervened.

"Mademoiselle Alexandre," she said, "thank Monsieur for his generosity."

Jeanne looked at her for an instant in a sullen way; then, turning to me, said with remarkable firmness,

"Monsieur, I thank you for your kindness in coming to see me."

"Jeanne," I said, pressing both her hands, "remain always a good, truthful, brave girl. Good-bye."

As she left the room with her packages of chocolate and confectionery, she happened to strike the handles of her skipping-rope against the back of a chair. Mademoiselle Prefere, full of indignation, pressed both hands over her heart, under her pelerine; and I almost expected to see her give up her scholastic ghost.

When we found ourselves alone, she recovered her composure; and I must say, without considering myself thereby flattered, that she smiled upon me with one whole side of her face.

"Mademoiselle," I said, taking advantage of her good humour, "I noticed that Jeanne Alexandre looks a little pale. You know better than I how much consideration and care a young girl requires at her age. It would only be doing you an injustice by implication to recommend her still more earnestly to your vigilance."

These words seemed to ravish her with delight. She lifted her eyes, as in ecstasy, to the paper spirals of the ceiling, and, clasping her hands exclaimed,

"How well these eminent men know the art of considering the most trifling details!"

I called her attention to the fact that the health of a young girl was not a trifling detail, and made my farewell bow. But she stopped me on the threshold to say to me, very confidentially,

"You must excuse me, Monsieur. I am a woman, and I love gloy. I cannot conceal from you the fact that I feel myself greatly honoured by the presence of a Member of the Institute in my humble institution."

I duly excused the weakness of Mademoiselle Prefere; and, thinking only of Jeanne, with the blindness of egotism, kept asking myself all along the road, "What are we going to do with this child?"

June 3.
I had escorted to the Cimetiere de Marnes that day a very aged colleague of mine who, to use the words of Goethe, had consented to die. The great Goethe, whose own vital force was something extraordinary, actually believed that one never dies until one really wants to die — that is to say, when all those energies which resist dissolution, and teh sum of which make up life itself, have been totally destroyed. In other words, he believed that people only die when it is no longer possible for them to live. Good! it is merely a question of properly understanding one another; and when fully comprehended, the magnificent idea of Goethe only brings us quietly back to the song of La Palisse.

Well, my excellent colleague had consented to die — thanks to several successive attacks of extremely persuasive apoplexy — the last of which proved unanswerable. I had been very little acquainted with him during his lifetime; but it seems that I became his friend the moment he was dead, for our colleagues assured me in a most serious manner, with deeply sympathetic countenances, that I should act as one of the pall-bearers, and deliver an address over the tomb.

After having read very badly a short address I had written as well as I could — which is not saying much for it — I started out for a walk in the woods of Ville-d'Avray, and followed, without leaning too much on the Captain's cane, a shaded path on which the sunlight fell, through foliage, in little discs of gold. Never had the scent of grass and fresh leaves, — never had the beauty of the sky over the trees, and the serene might of noble tree contours, so deeply affected my senses and all my being; and the pleasure I felt in that silence, broken only by faintest tinkling sounds, was at once of the senses and of the soul.

I sat down in the shade of the roadside under a clump of young oaks. And there I made a promise to myself not to die, or at least not to consent to die, before I should be again able to sit down under and oak, where — in the great peace of the open country — I could meditate on the nature of the soul and the ultimate destiny of man. A bee, whose brown breast-plate gleamed in the sun like armour of old gold, came to light upon a mallow-flower close by me — darkly rich in colour, and fully opened upon its tufted stalk. It was certainly not the first time I had witnessed so common an incident; but it was the first time that I had watched it with such comprehensive and friendly curiosity. I could discern that there were all sorts of sympathies between the insect and the flower — a thousand singular little relationships which I had never before even suspected.

Satiated with nectar, the insect rose and buzzed away in a straight line, while I lifted myself up as best I could, and readjusted myself upon my legs.

"Adieu!" I said to the flower and to the bee. "Adieu! Heaven grant I may live long enough to discover the secret of your harmonies. I am very tired. But man is so made that he can only find relaxation from one kind of labour by taking up another. The flowers and insects will give me that relaxation, with God's will, after my long researches in philology and diplomatics. How full of meaning is that old myth of Antaeus! I have touched the Earth and I am a new man; and now at seventy years of age, new feelings of curiosity take birth in my mind, even as young shoots sometimes spring up from the hollow trunk of an aged oak!"

June 4.

I like to look out of my window at the Seine and its quays on those soft grey mornings which give such an infinite tenderness of tint to everything. I have seen that azure sky which flings so luminous a calm over the Bay of Naples. But our Parisian sky is more animated, more kindly, more spiritual. It smiles, threatens, caresses — takes an aspect of melancholy or a look of merriment like a human gaze. At this moment it is pouring down a very gentle light on the men and beasts of the city as they accomplish their daily tasks. Over there, on the opposite bank, the stevedores of the Port Saint-Nicholas are unloading a cargo of cow's horns; while two men standing on a gangway are tossing sugar-loaves from one to the other, and thence to somebody in the hold of a steamer. On the north quay, the cab-horses, standing in a line under the shade of the plane-trees each with its head in a nose-bag, are quietly munching their oats, while the rubicund drivers are drinking at the counter of the wine-seller opposite, but all the while keeping a sharp lookout for early customers.

The dealers in second-hand books put their boxes on the parapet. These good retailers of Mind, who are always in the open air, with blouses loose to the breeze, have become so weatherbeaten by the wind, the rain, the frost, the snow, the fog, and the great sun, that they end by looking very much like the old statues of cathedrals. They are all friends of mine, and I scarcely ever pass by their boxes without picking out of one of them some old book which I had always been in need of up to that very moment, without any suspicion of the fact on my part.

Then on my return home I have to endure the outcries of my housekeeper, who accuses me of bursting all my pockets and filling the house with waste paper to attract the rats. Therese is wise about that, and it is because she is wise that I do not listen to her; for in spite of my tranquil mien, I have always preferred the folly of the passions to the wisdom of indifference. But just because my own passions are not of that sort which burst out with violence to devastate and kill, the common mind is not aware of their existence. Nevertheless, I am greatly moved by them at times, and it has more than once been my fate to lose my sleep for the sake of a few pages written by some forgotten monk or printed by some humble apprentice of Peter Schaeffer. And if these fierce enthusiasms are slowly being quenched in me, it is only because I am being slowly quenched myself. Our passions are ourselves. My old books are Me. I am just as old and thumb-worn as they are.

A light breeze sweeps away, along with the dust of the pavements, the winged seeds of the plane trees, and the fragments of hay dropped from the mouths of the horses. The dust is nothing remarkable in itself; but as I watch it flying, I remember a moment in my childhood when I watched just such a swirl of dust; and my old Parisian soul is much affected by that sudden recollection. All that I see from my window — that horizon which extends to the left as far as the hills of Chaillot, and enables me to distinguish the Arc de Triomphe like a die of stone, the Seine, river of glory, and its bridges, the ash-trees of the terrace of the Tuileries, the Louvre of the Renaissance, cut and graven like goldsmithwork; and on my right, towards the Pont-Neuf (pons Lutetiae Novus dictus, as it is named on old engravings), all the old and venerable part of Paris, with its towers and spires: — all that is my life, it is myself; and I should be nothing but for all those things which are thus reflected in me through my thousand varying shades of thought, inspiring me and animating me. That is why I love Paris with an immense love.

And nevertheless I am weary, and I know that there can be no rest for me in the heart of this great city which thinks so much, which has taught me to think, and which for ever urges me to think more. And how avoid being exited among all these books which incessantly tempt my curiosity without ever satisfying it? At one moment it is a date I have to look for; at another it is the name of a place I have to make sure of, or some quaint term of which it is important to determine the exact meaning. Words? — why, yes! words. As a philologist, I am their sovereign; they aer my subjects, and, like a good king, I devote my whole life to them. But shall I not be able to abdicate some day? I have an idea that there is somewhere or other, quite far from here, a certain little cottage where I could enjoy the quiet I so much need, while awaiting that day in which a greater quiet — that which can be never broken — shall come to wrap me all about. I dream of a bench before the threshold, and of fields spreading away out of sight. But I must have a fresh smiling young face beside me, to reflect and concentrate all that freshness of nature. I could then imagine myself a grandfather, and all the long void of my life would be filled....

I am not a violent man, and yet I become easily vexed, and all my works have caused me quite as much pain as pleasure. And I do not know how it is that I still keep thinking about that very conceited and very inconsiderated impertinence which my young friend of the Luxembourg took the liberty to utter about me some three months ago. I do not call him "friend" in irony, for I love studious youth with all it temerities and imaginative eccentricities. Still, my young friend certainly went beyond all bounds. Master Ambroise Pare, who was the first to attempt the ligature of arteries, and who, having commenced his profession at a time when surgery was only performed by quack barbers, nevertheless succeeded in lifting the science to the high place it now occupies, was assailed in his old age by all the young sawbones' apprentices. Being grossly abused during a discussion by some young addlehead who might have been the best son in the world, but who certainly lacked all sense of respect, the old master answered him in his treatise De la Mumie, de la Licorne, des Venins et de la Peste. "I pray him," said the great man — "I pray him, that if he desire to make any contradictions to my reply, he abandon all animosities, and treat the good old man with gentleness." This answer seems admirable from the pen of Ambroise Pare; but even had it been written by a village bonesetter, grown grey in his calling, and mocked by some young stripling, it would still be worthy of all praise.

It might perhaps seem that my memory of the incident had been kept alive only by a base feeling of resentment. I thought so myself at first, and reproached myself for thus dwelling on the saying of a boy who could not yet know the meaning of his own words. But my reflections on this subject subsequently took a better course: that is why I now note them down in my diary. I remembered that one day when I was twenty years old (that was more than half a century ago) I was walking about in that very same garden of the Luxembourg with some comrades. We were talking about our old professors; and one of us happened to name Monsieur Petit-Radel, an estimable and learned man, who was the first to throw some light upon the origins of early Etruscan civilisation, but who had been unfortunate enough to prepare a chronological table of the lovers of Helen. We all laughed a great deal about that chronological table; and I cried out, "Petit-Radel is an ass, not in three letters, but in twelve whole volumes!"

This foolish speech of my adolescence was uttered too lightly to be a weight on my conscience as an old man. May God kindly prove to me some day that I never used an less innocent shaft of speech in the battle of life! But I now ask myself whether I really never wrote, at any time in my life, something quite as unconsciously absurd as the chronological table of the lovers of Helen. The progress of science renders useless the very books which have been the greatest aids to that progress. As those works are no longer useful, modern youth is naturally inclined to believe they never had any value; it despises them, and ridicules them if they happen to contain any superannuated opinion whatever. That is why, in my twentieth year, I amused myself at the expense of Monsieur Petit-Radel and his chronological table; and that was why, the other day, at the Luxembourg, my young and irreverent friend...

"Rentre en toi-meme, Octave, et cesse de te plaindre. Quoi! tu veux qu'on t'epargne et n'as rien epargne!" ["Look into thyself, Octavius, and cease complaining. What! thou wouldst be spared, and thou thyself hast spared none!"]

June 6.

It was the first Thursday in June. I shut up my books and took my leave of the holy abbot Droctoveus, who, being now in the enjoyment of celestial bliss, cannot feel very impatient to behold his name and works glorified on earth through the humble compilation being prepared by my hands. Must I confess it? That mallow-plant I saw visited by a bee the other day has been occupying my thoughts much more than all the ancient abbots who ever bore croisers or wore mitres. There is in one of Sprengel's books which I read in my youth, at that time when I used to read in my youth, at that time when I used to read anything and everything, some ideas about "the loves of flowers" which now return to memory after having been forgotten for half a century, and which to-day interest me so much that I regret not to have devoted the humble capacities of my mind to the study of insects and of plants.

And only awhile ago my housekeeper surprised me at the kitchen window, in the act of examining some wallflowers through a magnifying-glass....

It was while looking for my cravat that I made these reflections. But after searching to no purpose in a great number of drawers, I found myself obliged, after all, to have recourse to my housekeeper. Therese came limping in.

"Monsieur," she said, "you ought to have told me you were going out, and I would have given you your cravat!"

"But Therese," I replied, "would it not be a great deal better to put in some place where I could find it without your help?"

Therese did not deign to answer me.

Therese no longer allows me to arrange anything. I cannot even have a handkerchief without asking her for it; and as she is deaf, crippled, and, what is worse, beginning to lose her memory, I languish in perpetual destitution. But she exercises her domestic authority with such quiet pride that I do not feel the courage to attempt a coup d'etat against her government.

"My cravat! Therese! — do you hear? — my cravat! if you drive me wild like this with your slow ways, it will not be a cravat I shall need, but a rope to hang myself!"

"You must be in a very great hurry, Monsieur," replied Therese. "Your cravat is not lost. Nothing is ever lost in this house, because I have charge of everything. But please allow me the time at least to find it."

"Yet here," I thought to myself — "here is the result of half a century of devotedness and self-sacrifice!... Ah! if by any happy chance this inexorable Therese had once in her whole life, only once, failed in her duty as a servant — if she had ever been at fault for one single instant, she could never have assumed this inflexible authority over me, and I should at least have the courage to resist her. But how can one resist virtue? The people who have no weaknesses are terrible; there is no way of taking advantage of them. Just look at Therese, for example; she has not a single fault for which you can blame her! She has no doubt of herself; nor of God, nor of the world. She is the valiant woman, the wise virgin of Scripture; others may know nothing about her, but I know her worth. In my fancy I always see her carrying a lamp, a humble kitchen lamp, illuminating the beams of some rustic roof — a lamp which will never go out while suspended from that meagre arm of hers, scraggy and strong as a vine-branch.

"Therese, my cravat! Don't you know, wretched woman, that to-day is the first Thursday in June, and that Mademoiselle Jeanne will be waiting for me? The schoolmistress has certainly had the parlour floor vigorously waxed: I am sure one can look at oneself in it now; and it will be quite a consolation for me when I slip and break my old bones upon it — which is sure to happen sooner or later — to see my rueful countenance reflected in it as in a looking-glass. Then taking for my model that amiable and admirable hero whose image is carved upon the handle of Uncle Victor's walking-stick, I will control myself so as not to make too ugly a grimace.... See what a splendid sun! The quays are all gilded by it, and the Seine smiles in countless little flashing wrinkles. The city is gold: a dust-haze, blonde and gold-toned as a woman's hair, floats above its beautiful contours.... Therese, my cravat!... Ah! I can now comprehend the wisdom of that old Chrysal who used to keep his neckbands in a big Plutarch. Hereafter I shall follow his example by laying all my neckties away between the leaves of the Acta Sanctorum."

Therese let me talk on, and keeps looking for the necktie in silence. I hear a gentle ringing at our door-bell.

"Therese," I exclaim; "there is somebody ringing the bell! Give me my cravat, and go to the door; or, rather, go to the door first, and then, with the help of Heaven, you will give me my cravat. But please do not stand there between the clothes-press and the door like an old hack-horse between two saddles.

Therese marched to the door as if advancing upon the enemy. My excellent housekeeper becomes more inhospitable the older she grows. Every stranger is an object of suspicion to her. According to her own assertion, this disposition is the result of a long experience with human nature. I had not the time to consider whether the same experience on the part of another experimenter would produce the same results. Maitre Mouche was waiting to see me in the ante-room.

Maitre Mouche is still more yellow than I had believed him to be. He wears blue glasses, and his eyes keep moving uneasily behind them, like mice running about behind a screen.

Maitre Mouche excuses himself for having intruded upon me at a moment when.... He does not characterise the moment; but I think he means to say a moment in which I happen to be without my cravat. It is not my fault, as you very well know. Maitre Mouche, who does not know, does not appear to be at all shocked, however. He is only afraid that he might have dropped in at the wrong moment. I succeeded in partially reassuring him at once upon that point. He then tells me it is as guardian of Mademoiselle Alexandre that he has come to talk with me. First of all, he desires that I shall not hereafter pay any heed to those restrictions he had at first deemed necessary to put upon the permit given to visit Mademoiselle Jeanne at the boarding-school. Henceforth the establishment of Mademoiselle Prefere will be open to me any day that I might choose to call — between the hours of midday and four o'clock. Knowing the interest I have taken in the young girl, he considers it his duty to give me some information about the person to whom he has confided his ward. Mademoiselle Prefere, whom he has known for many years, is in possession of his utmost confidence. Mademoiselle Prefere is, in his estimation, an enlightened person, of excellent morals, and capable of giving excellent counsel.

"Mademoiselle Prefer," he said to me, "has principles; and principles are rare these days, Monsieur. Everything has been totally changed; and this epoch of ours cannot compare with the preceding ones."

"My stairway is a good example, Monsieur," I replied; "twenty-five years ago it used to allow me to climb it without any trouble, and now it takes my breath away, and wears my legs out before I have climbed half a dozen steps. It has had its character spoiled. Then there are those journals and books I used once to devour without difficulty by moonlight: to-day, even in the brightest sunlight, they mock my curiosity, and exhibit nothing but a blur of white and black when I have not got my spectacles on. Then the gout has got into my limbs. That is another malicious trick of the times!"

"Not only that, Monsieur," gravely replied Maitre Mouche, "but what is really unfortunate in our epoch is that no one is satisfied with his position. From the top of society to the bottom, in every class, there prevails a discontent, a restlessness, a love of comfort...."

"Mon Dieu, Monsieur!" I exclaimed. "You think this love of comfort is a sign of the times? Men have never had at any epoch a love of discomfort. They have always tried to better their condition. This constant effort produces constant changes, and the effort is always going on — that is all there is about it!"

"Ah! Monsieur," replied Maitre Mouche, "it is easy to see that you live in your books — out of the business world altogether. You do not see, as I see them, the conflicts of interest, the struggle for money. It is the same effervescence in all minds, great or small. The wildest speculations are being everywhere indulged in. What I see around me simply terrifies me!"

I wondered within myself whether Maitre Mouche had called upon me only for the purpose of expressing his virtuous misanthropy; but all at once I heard words of a more consoling character issue from his lips. Maitre Mouche began to speak to me of Virginie Prefere as a person worthy of respect, of esteem, and of sympathy, — highly honourable, capable of great devotedness, cultivated, discreet, — able to read aloud remarkably well, extremely modest, and skillful in the art of applying blisters. Then I began to understand that he had only been painting that dismal picture of universal corruption in order the better to bring

124

out, by contrast, the virtues of the schoolmistress. I was further informed that the institution in the Rue Demours was well patronised, prosperous, and enjoyed a high reputation with the public. Maitre Mouche lifted up his hand — with a black woollen glove on it — as if making oath to the truth of these statements. Then he added:

"I am enabled, by the very character of my profession, to know a great deal about people. A notary is, to a certain extent, a father-confessor.

"I deemed it my duty, Monsieur, to give you this agreeable information at the moment when a lucky chance enabled you to meet Mademoiselle Prefere. There is only one thing more which I would like to say. This lady — who is, of course, quite unaware of my action in the matter — spoke to me of you the other day in terms of deepest sympathy. I could only weaken their expression by repeating them to you; and furthermore, I could not repeat them without betraying, to a certain extent, the confidence of Mademoiselle Prefere."

"Do not betray it, Monsieur; do not betray it!" I responded. "To tell you the truth, I had no idea that Mademoiselle Prefere knew anything whatever about me. But since you have the influence of an old friend with her, I will take advantage of your good will, Monsieur, to ask you to exercise that influence in behalf of Mademoiselle Jeanne Alexandre. The child — for she is still a child — is overloaded with work. She is at once a pupil and a mistress — she is overtasked. Besides, she is punished in petty disgusting ways; and hers is one of those generous natures which will be forced into revolt by such continual humiliation."

"Alas!" replied Maitre Mouche, "she must be trained to take her part in the struggle of life. One does not come into this world simply to amuse oneself, and to do just what one pleases."

"One comes into this world," I responded, rather warmly, "to enjoy what is beautiful and what is good, and to do as one pleases, when the things one wants to do are noble, intelligent, and generous. An education which does not cultivate the will, is an education that depraves the mind. It is a teacher's duty to teach the pupil HOW to will."

I perceived that Maitre Mouche began to think me a rather silly man. With a great deal of quiet self-assurance, he proceeded:

"You must remember, Monsieur, that the education of the poor has to be conducted with a great deal of circumspection, and with a view to that future state of dependence they must occupy in society. Perhaps you are not aware that the late Noel Alexandre died a bankrupt, and that his daughter is being educated almost by charity?"

"Oh! Monsieur!" I exclaimed, "do not say it! To say it is to pay oneself back, and then the statement ceases to be true."

"The liabilities of the estate," continued the notary, "exceeded the assets. But I was able to effect a settlement with the creditors in favour of the minor."

He undertook to explain matters in detail. I declined to listen to these explanations, being incapable of understanding business methods in general, and those of Maitre Mouche in particular. The notary then took it upon himself to justify Mademoiselle Prefere's educational system, and observed by way of conclusion,

"It is not by amusing oneself that one can learn."

"It is only by amusing oneself that one can learn," I replied. "The whole art of teaching is only the art of awakening the natural curiosity of young minds for the purpose of satisfying it afterwards; and curiosity itself can be vivid and wholesome only in proportion as the mind is contented and happy. Those acquirements crammed by force into the minds of children simply clog and stifle intelligence. In order that knowledge be properly digested, it must have been swallowed with a good appetite. I know Jeanne! If that child were intrusted to my care, I should make of her — not a learned woman, for I would look to her future happiness only — but a child full of bright intelligence and full of life, in whom everything beautiful in art or nature would awaken some gentle responsive thrill. I would teach her to live in sympathy with all that is beautiful — comely landscapes, the ideal scenes of poetry and history, the emotional charm of noble music. I would make lovable to her everything I would wish her to love. Even her needlework I would make pleasurable to her, by a proper choice of fabrics, the style of embroideries, the designs of lace. I would give her a beautiful dog, and a pony to teach her how to manage animals; I would give her birds to take care of, so that she could learn the value of even a drop of water and a crumb of bread. And in order that she should have a still higher pleasure, I would train her to find delight in exercising charity. And inasmuch as none of us may escape pain, I should teach her that Christian wisdom which elevates us above all suffering, and gives a beauty even to grief itself. That is my idea of the right way to educate a young girl."

"I yield, Monsieur," replied Maitre Mouche, joining his black-gloved hands together.

And he rose.

"Of course you understand," I remarked, as I went to the door with him, "that I do not pretend for a moment to impose my educational system upon Mademoiselle Prefere; it is necessarily a private one, and quite incompatible with the organisation of even the best-managed boarding schools. I only ask you to persuade her to give Jeanne less work and more play, and not to punish her except in case of absolute necessity, and to let her have as much freedom of mind and body as the regulations of the institution permit."

It was with a pale and mysterious smile that Maitre Mouche informed me that my observations would be taken in good part, and should receive all possible consideration.

Therewith he made me a little bow, and took his departure, leaving me with a peculiar feeling of discomfort and uneasiness. I have met a great many strange characters in my time, but never any at all resembling either this notary or this schoolmistress.

July 6.

Maitre Mouche has so much delayed me by his visit that I gave up going to see Jeanne that day. Professional duties kept me very busy for the rest of the week. Although at the age when most men retire altogether from active life, I am still attached by a thousand ties to the society in which I have lived. I have to reside at meetings of academies, scientific congresses, assemblies of various learned bodies. I am overburdened with honorary functions; I have seven of these in one governmental department alone. The bureaux would be very glad to get rid of them. But habit is stronger than both of us together, and I continue to hobble up the stairs of various government buildings. Old clerks point me out to each other as I go by like a ghost wandering through the corridors. When one has become very old one finds it extremely difficult to disappear. Nevertheless, it is time, as the old song says, 'de prendre ma retraite et de songer a faire un fin" — to retire on my pension and prepare myself to die a good death.

An old marchioness, who used to be a friend of Hevetius in her youth, and whom I once met at my father's house when a very old woman, was visited during her last sickness by the priest of her parish, who wanted to prepare her to die.

"Is that really necessary?" she asked. "I see everybody else manage it perfectly well the first time."

My father went to see her very soon afterwards and found her extremely ill.

"Good-evening, my friend!" she said, pressing his hand. "I am going to see whether God improves upon acquaintance."

So were wont to die the belles amies of the philosophers. Such an end is certainly not vulgar nor impertinent, and such levities are not of the sort that emanate from dull minds. Nevertheless, they shock me. Neither my fears nor my hopes could accommodate themselves to such a mode of departure. I would like to make mine with a perfectly collected mind; and that is why I must begin to think, in a year or two, about some way of belonging to myself; otherwise, I should certainly risk.... But, hush! let Him not hear His name and turn to look as He passes by! I can still lift my fagot without His aid.

...I found Jeanne very happy indeed. She told me that, on the Thursday previous, after the visit of her guardian,

Mademoiselle Prefere had set her free from the ordinary regulations and lightened her tasks in several ways. Since that lucky Thursday she could walk in the garden — which only lacked leaves and flowers — as much as she liked; and she had been given facilities to work at her unfortunate little figure of Saint-George.

She said to me, with a smile,

"I know very well that I owe all of this to you."

I tried to talk with her about other matters, but I remarked that she could not attend to what I was saying, in spite of her effort to do so.

"I see you are thinking about something else," I said. "Well, tell me what it is; for, if you do not, we shall not be able to talk to each other at all, which would be very unworthy of both of us."

She answered,

"Oh! I was really listening to you, Monsieur; but it is true that I was thinking about something else. You will excuse me, won't you? I could not help thinking that Mademoiselle Prefere must like you very, very much indeed, to have become so good to me all of a sudden."

Then she looked at me in an odd, smiling, frightened way, which made me laugh.

"Does that surprise you?" I asked.

"Very much," she replied.

"Please tell me why?"

"Because I can see no reason, no reason at all...but there!...no reason at all why you should please Mademoiselle Prefere so much."

"So, then, you think I am very displeasing, Jeanne?"

She bit her lips, as if to punish them for having made a mistake; and then, in a coaxing way, looking at me with great soft eyes, gentle and beautiful as a spaniel's, she said,

"I know I said a foolish think; but, still, I do not see any reason why you should be so pleasing to Mademoiselle Prefere. And, nevertheless, you seem to please her a great deal — a very great deal. She called me one day, and asked me all sorts of questions about you."

"Really?"

"Yes; she wanted to find out all about your house. Just think! she even asked me how old your servant was!"

And Jeanne burst out laughing.

"Well, what do you think about it?" I asked.

She remained a long while with her eyes fixed on the worn-out cloth of her shoes, and seemed to be thinking very deeply. Finally, looking up again, she answered,

"I am distrustful. Isn't it very natural to feel uneasy about what one cannot understand; I know I am foolish; but you won't be offended with me, will you?"

"Why, certainly not, Jeanne. I am not a bit offended with you."

I must acknowledge that I was beginning to share her surprise; and I began to turn over in my old head the singular thought of this young girl — "One is uneasy about what one cannot understand."

But, with a fresh burst of merriment, she cried out,

"She asked me...guess! I will give you a hundred guesses — a thousand guesses. You give it up?... She asked me if you liked good eating."

"And how did you receive this shower of interrogations, Jeanne?"

"I replied, 'I don't know, Mademoiselle.' And Mademoiselle then said to me, 'You are a little fool. The least details of the life of an eminent man ought to be observed. Please to know, Mademoiselle, that Monsieur Sylvestre Bonnard is one of the glories of France!'"

"Stuff!" I exclaimed. "And what did YOU think about it, Mademoiselle?"

"I thought that Mademoiselle Prefere was right. But I don't care at all...(I know it is naughty what I am going to say)...I don't care a bit, not a bit, whether Mademoiselle Prefere is or is not right about anything."

"Well, then, content yourself, Jeanne, Mademoiselle Prefere was not right."

"Yes, yes, she was quite right that time; but I wanted to love everybody who loved you — everybody without exception — and I cannot do it, because it would never be possible for me to love Mademoiselle Prefere."

"Listen, Jeanne," I answered, very seriously, "Mademoiselle Prefere has become good to you; try now to be good to her."

She answered sharply,

"It is very easy for Mademoiselle Prefere to be good to me, and it would be very difficult indeed for me to be good to her."

I then said, in a still more serious tone:

"My child, the authority of a teacher is sacred. You must consider your schoolmistress as occupying the place to you of the mother whom you lost."

I had scarcely uttered this solemn stupidity when I bitterly regretted it. The child turned pale, and the tears sprang to her eyes.

"Oh, Monsieur!" she cried, "how could you say such a thing — YOU? You never knew mamma!"

Ay, just Heaven! I did know her mamma. And how indeed could I have been foolish enough to have said what I did?

She repeated, as if to herself:

"Mamma! my dear mamma! my poor mamma!"

A lucky chance prevented me from playing the fool any further. I do not know how it happened at that moment I looked as if I was going to cry. At my age one does not cry. It must have been a bad cough which brought the tears into my eyes. But, anyhow, appearances were in my favour. Jeanne was deceived by them. Oh! what a pure and radiant smile suddenly shone out under her beautiful wet eyelashes — like sunshine among branches after a summer shower! We took each other by the hand and sat a long while without saying a word — absolutely happy. Those celestial harmonies which I once thought I heard thrilling through my soul while I knelt before that tomb to which a saintly woman had guided me, suddenly awoke again in my heart, slow-

131

swelling through the blissful moments with infinite softness. Doubtless the child whose hand pressed my own also heard them; and then, elevated by their enchantment above the material world, the poor old man and the artless young girl both knew that a tender ghostly Presence was making sweetness all about them.

"My child," I said at last, "I am very old, and many secrets of life, which you will only learn little by little, have been revealed to me. Believe me, the future is shaped out of the past. Whatever you can do to live contentedly here, without impatience and without fretting, will help you live some future day in peace and joy in your own home. Be gentle, and learn how to suffer. When one suffers patiently one suffers less. If you should be badly treated, Madame de Gabry and I would both consider ourselves badly treated in your person."...

"Is your health very good indeed, dear Monsieur?"

It was Mademoiselle Prefere, approaching stealthily behind us, who had asked the question with a peculiar smile. My first idea was to tell her to go to the devil; my second, that her mouth was as little suited for smiling as a frying-pan for musical purposes; my third was to answer her politely and assure her that I hoped she was very well.

She sent the young girl out to take a walk in the garden; then, pressing one hand upon her pelerine and extending the other towards the Tableau d'Honneur, she showed me the name of Jeanne Alexandre written at the head of the list in large text.

"I am very much pleased," I said to her, "to find that you are satisfied with the behaviour of that child. Nothing could delight me more; and I am inclined to attribute this happy result to your affectionate vigilance. I have taken the liberty to send you a few books which I think may serve both to instruct and to amuse young girls. You will be able to judge by glancing over them whether they are adapted to the perusal of Mademoiselle Alexandre and her companions."

The gratitude of the schoolmistress not only overflowed in words, but seemed about to take the form of tearful sensibility. In order to change the subject I observed,

"What a beautiful day this is!"

"Yes," she replied; "and if this weather continues, those dear children will have a nice time for their enjoyment."

"I suppose you are referring to the holidays. But Mademoiselle Alexandre, who has no relatives, cannot go away. What in the world is she going to do all alone in this great big house?"

"Oh, we will do everything we can to amuse her.... I will take her to the museums and — -"

She hesitated, blushed, and continued,

" — and to your house, if you will permit me."

"Why of course!" I exclaimed. "That is a first-rate idea."

We separated very good friends with one another. I with her, because I had been able to obtain what I desired; she with me, for no appreciable motive — which fact, according to Plato, elevated her into the highest rank of the Hierarchy of Souls.

...And nevertheless it is not without a presentiment of evil that I find myself on the point of introducing this person into my house. And I would be very glad indeed to see Jeanne in charge of anybody else rather than of her. Maitre Mouche and Mademoiselle Prefere are characters whom I cannot at all understand. I never can imagine why they say what they do say, nor why they do what they do; they have a mysterious something in common which makes me feel uneasy. As Jeanne said to me a little while ago: "One is uneasy about what one cannot understand."

Alas! at my age one has learned only too well how little sincerity there is in life; one has learned only too well how much one loses by living a long time in this world; and one feels that one can no longer trust any except the young.

August 12.

I waited for them. In fact, I waited for them very impatiently. I exerted all my powers of insinuation and of coaxing to induce Therese to receive them kindly; but my powers in this direction are very limited. They came. Jeanne was neater and

133

prettier than I had ever expected to see her. She has not, it is true, anything approaching the charm of her mother. But to-day, for the first time, I observed that she has a pleasing face; and a pleasing face is of great advantage to a woman in this world. I think that her hat was a little on one side; but she smiled, and the City of Books was all illuminated by that smile.

I watched Therese to see whether the rigid manners of the old housekeeper would soften a little at the sight of the young girl. I saw her turning her lustreless eyes upon Jeanne; I saw her long wrinkled face, her toothless mouth, and that pointed chin of hers — like the chin of some puissant old fairy. And that was all I could see.

Mademoiselle Prefere made her appearance all in blue — advanced, retreated, skipped, tripped, cried out, sighed, cast her eyes down, rolled her eyes up, bewildered herself with excuses — said she dared not, and nevertheless dared — said she would never dare again, and nevertheless dared again — made courtesies innumerable — made, in short, all the fuss she could.

"What a lot of books!" she screamed. "And have you really read them all, Monsieur Bonnard?"

"Alas! I have," I replied, "and that is just the reason that I do not know anything; for there is not a single one of those books which does not contradict some other book; so that by the time one has read them all one does not know what to think about anything. That is just my condition, Madame."

Thereupon she called Jeanne for the purpose of communicating her impressions. But Jeanne was looking out of the window.

"How beautiful it is!" she said to us. "How I love to see the river flowing! It makes you think about all kinds of things."

Mademoiselle Prefere having removed her hat and exhibited a forehead tricked out with blonde curls, my housekeeper sturdily snatched up the hat at once, with the observation that she did not like to see people's clothes scattered over the furniture. Then she approached Jeanne and asked her for her "things," calling her "my little lady!" Where-upon the little lady, giving up her cloak and

134

hat, exposed to view a very graceful neck and a lithe figure, whose outlines were beautifully relieved against the great glow of the open window; and I could have wished that some one else might have seen her at that moment — some one very different from an aged housekeeper, a schoolmistress frizzled like a sheep, and this old humbug of an archivist and paleographer.

"So you are looking at the Seine," I said to her. "See how it sparkles in the sun!"

"Yes," she replied, leaning over the windowbar, "it looks like a flowing of fire. But see how nice and cool it looks on the other side over there under the shadow of the willows! That little spot there pleases me better than all the rest."

"Good!" I answered. "I see that the river has a charm for you. How would you like, with Mademoiselle Prefere's permission, to make a trip to Saint-Cloud? We should certainly be in time to catch the steamboat just below the Pont-Royal."

Jeanne was delighted with my suggestion, and Mademoiselle Prefere willing to make any sacrifice. But my housekeeper was not at all willing to let us go off so unconcernedly. She summoned me into the dining-room, whither I followed her in fear and trembling.

"Monsieur," she said to me as soon as we found ourselves alone, "you never think about anything, and it is always I who have to think about everything. Luckily for you I have a good memory."

I did not think that it was a favourable moment for any attempt to dispel this wild illusion. She continued:

"So you were going off without saying a word to me about what this little lady likes to eat? At her age one does not know anything, one does not care about anything in particular, one eats like a bird. You yourself, Monsieur, are very difficult to please; but at least you know what is good: it is very different with these young people — they do not know anything about cooking. It is often the very best thing which they think the worst, and what is bad seems to them good, because their stomachs are not quite formed yet — so that one never knows just what to do for them.

135

Tell me if the little lady would like a pigeon cooked with green peas, and whether she is fond of vanilla ice-cream."

"My good Therese," I answered, "just do whatever you think best, and whatever that may be I am sure it will be very nice. Those ladies will be quite contented with our humble ordinary fare."

Therese replied, very dryly,

"Monsieur, I am asking you about the little lady: she must not leave this house without having enjoyed herself a little. As for that old frizzle-headed thing, if she doesn't like my dinner she can suck her thumbs. I don't care what she likes!"

My mind being thus set at rest, I returned to the City of Books, where Mademoiselle Prefere was crocheting as calmly as if she were at home. I almost felt inclined myself to think she was. She did not take up much room, it is true, in the angle of the window. But she had chosen her chair and her footstool so well that those articles of furniture seemed to have been made expressly for her.

Jeanne, on the other hand, devoted her attention to the books and pictures — gazing at them in a kindly, expressive, half-sad way, as if she were bidding them an affectionate farewell.

"Here," I said to her, "amuse yourself with this book, which I am sure you cannot help liking, because it is full of beautiful engravings." And I threw open before her Vecellio's collection of costume-designs — not the commonplace edition, by your leave, so meagerly reproduced by modern artists, but in truth a magnificent and venerable copy of that editio princeps which is noble as those noble dames who figure upon its yellowed leaves, made beautiful by time.

While turning over the engravings with artless curiousity, Jeanne said to me,

"We were talking about taking a walk; but this is a great journey you are making me take. And I would like to travel very, very far away!"

"In that case, Mademoiselle," I said to her, "you must arrange yourself as comfortably as possible for travelling. But you are now sitting on one corner of your chair, so that the chair is standing upon only one leg, and that Vecellio must tire your knees. Sit down comfortably; put your chair on its four feet, and put your book on the table."

She obeyed me with a laugh.

I watched her. She cried out suddenly,

"Oh, come look at this beautiful costume!" (It was that of the wife of a Doge of Venice.) "How noble it is! What magnificent ideas it gives one of that life! Oh, I must tell you — I adore luxury!"

"You must not express such thoughts as those, Mademoiselle," said the schoolmistress, lifting up her little shapeless nose from her work.

"Nevertheless, it was a very innocent utterance," I replied. "There are splendid souls in whom the love of splendid things is natural and inborn."

The little shapeless nose went down again.

"Mademoiselle Prefere likes luxury too," said Jeanne; "she cuts out paper trimmings and shades for the lamps. It is economical luxury; but it is luxury all the same."

Having returned to the subject of Venice, we were just about to make the acquaintance of a certain patrician lady attired in an embroidered dalmatic, when I heard the bell ring. I thought it was some peddler with his basket; but the gate of the City of Books opened, and...Well, Master Sylvestre Bonnard, you were wishing awhile ago that the grace of your protegee might be observed by some other eyes than old withered ones behind spectacles. Your wishes have been fulfilled in a most unexpected manner, and a voice cries out to you as to the imprudent Theseus,

"Craignez, Seigneur, craignez que le Ciel rigoureux Ne vous Haisse assez pour exaucer vos voeux! Souvent dans sa colere il recoit nos victimes, Ses presents sont souvent la peine de nos crimes."

["Beware my lord! Beware lest stern Heaven hate you enough to hear your prayers! Often 'tis in wrath that Heaven receives our sacrifices: its gifts are often the punishment of our crimes."]

The gate of the City of Books had opened, and a handsome young man made his appearance, ushered in by Therese. That good old soul only knows how to open the door for people and to shut it behind them; she has no idea whatever of the tact requisite for the waiting-room and for the parlour. It is not in her nature either to make any announcements or to make anybody wait. She either throws people out on the lobby, or simply pitches them at your head.

And here is this handsome young man already inside; and I cannot really take the girl at once and hide her like a secret treasure in the next room. I wait for him to explain himself; he does it without the least embarrassment; but it seems to me that he has already observed the young girl who is still bending over the table looking at Vecellio. As I observe the young man it occurs to me that I have seen him somewhere before, or else I must be very much mistaken. His name is Gelis. That is a name which I have heard somewhere, — I can't remember where. At all events, Monsieur Gelis (since there is a Gelis) is a fine-looking young fellow. He tells me that this is his third class-year at the Ecole des Chartes, and that he has been working for the past fifteen or eighteen months upon his graduation thesis, the subject of which is the Condition of the Benedictine Abbeys in 1700. He has just read my works upon the "Monasticon"; and he is convinced that he cannot terminate this thesis successfully without my advice, to begin with, and in the second place without a certain manuscript which I possess, and which is nothing less than the "Register of the Accounts of the Abbey of Citeaux from 1683 to 1704."

Having thus explained himself, he hands me a letter of introduction bearing the signature of one of the most illustrious of my colleagues.

Good! Now I know who he is! Monsieur Gelis is the very same young man who last year under the chestnut-trees called me an idiot! And while unfolding his letter of introduction I think to myself:

"Aha! my unlucky youth, you are very far from suspecting that I overheard what you said, and that I know what you think of me — or, at least, what you did think of me that day, for these young minds are so fickle? I have got you now, my friend! You have fallen into the lion's den, and so unexpectedly, in good sooth, that the astonished old lion does not know what to do with his prey. But come now, old lion! do not act like an idiot! Is it not possible that you were an idiot? If you are not one now, you certainly were one! You were a fool to have been listening to Monsieur Gelis at the foot of the statue of Marguerite de Valois; you were doubly a fool to have heard what he said; and you were trebly a fool not to have forgotten what it would have been much better never to have heard."

Having thus scolded the old lion, I exhorted him to show clemency. He did not appear to require much coaxing, and gradually became so good-natured that he had some difficulty in restraining himself from bursting out into joyous roarings. From the way in which I had read my colleague's letter one might have supposed me a man who did not know his alphabet. I took a long while to read it; and Monsieur Gelis might have become very tired under different circumstances; but he was watching Jeanne, and endured the trial with exemplary patience. Jeanne occasionally turned her face in our direction. Well you could not expect a person to remain perfectly motionless, could you? Mademoiselle Prefere was arranging her curls, and her bosom occasionally swelled with little sighs. It may be observed that I have myself often been honoured with those little sighs.

"Monsieur," I said, as I folded up the letter, "I shall be very happy to be of any service to you. You are occupied with researches in which I myself have always felt a very lively interest. I have done all that lay in my power. I know, as you do — and still better than you can know — how much there remains to do. The manuscript you asked for is at your disposal; you may take it home with you, but it is not a manuscript of the smallest kind, and I am afraid — -"

"Oh, Monsieur," said Gelis, "big books have never been able to make me afraid of them."

I begged the young man to wait for me, and I went into the next room to get the Register, which I could not find at first, and which I almost despaired of finding, as I discerned, from certain familiar signs, that Therese had been setting the room in order. But the Register was so big and so heavy that, luckily for me, Therese had not been able to put it in order as she had doubtless wished to do. I could scarcely lift it up myself; and I had the pleasure of finding it quite as heavy as I could have hoped.

"Wait, my boy," I said, with a smile which must have been very sarcastic — "wait! I am going to give you something to do which will break your arms first, and afterwards your head. That will be the first vengeance of Sylvestre Bonnard. Later on we shall see what else there is to be done."

When I returned to the City of Books I heard Monsieur Gelis and Mademoiselle Jeanne chatting — chatting together, if you please! as if they were the best friends in the world. Mademoiselle Prefere, being full of decorum, did not say anything; but the other two were chatting like birds. And what about? About the blond tint used by Venetian painters! Yes, about the "Venetian blond." That little serpent of a Gelis was telling Jeanne the secret of the dye with which, according to the best authorities, the women of Titian and of Veronese tinted their hair. And Mademoiselle Jeanne was expressing her opinion very prettily about the honey tint and the golden tint. I understood that that scamp of a Vecellio was responsible — that they had been bending over the book together, and that they had been admiring either that Doge's wife we had been looking at awhile before, or some other patrician woman of Venice.

Never mind! I appeared with my enormous old book, thinking that Gelis was going to make a grimace. It was as much as one could have asked a porter to carry, and my arms were stiff merely with lifting it. But the young man caught it up like a feather, and slipped it under his arm with a smile. Then he thanked me with that sort of brevity which I like, reminded me that he had need of my advice, and, having made an appointment to meet me another day, took his departure after bowing to us with the most perfect self-possession conceivable.

"He seems quite a decent lad," I said.

Jeanne turned over a few more pages of Vecellio, and made no answer.

"Aha!" I thought to myself.... And then we went to Saint-Cloud.

September-December.

The regularity with which visit succeeded visit to the old man's house thereafter made me feel very grateful to Mademoiselle Prefere, who succeeded at last in winning her right to occupy a special corner in the City of Books. She now says "MY chair," "MY footstool," "MY pigeon hole." Her pigeon hole is really a small shelf properly belonging to the poets of La Champagne, whom she expelled therefrom in order to obtain a lodging for her work-bag. She is very amiable, and I must really be a monster not to like her. I can only endure her — in the severest signification of the word. But what would one not endure for Jeanne's sake? Her presence lends to the City of Books a charm which seems to hover about it even after she has gone. She is very ignorant; but she is so finely gifted that whenever I show her anything beautiful I am astounded to find that I had never really seen it before, and that it is she who makes me see it. I have found it impossible so far to make her follow some of my ideas, but I have often found pleasure in following the whimsical and delicate course of her own.

A more practical man than I would attempt to teach her to make herself useful; but is not the capacity of being amiable a useful think in life? Without being pretty, she charms; and the power to charm is perhaps, after all, worth quite as much as the ability to darn stockings. Furthermore, I am not immortal; and I doubt whether she will have become very old when my notary (who is not Maitre Mouche) shall read to her a certain paper which I signed a little while ago.

I do not wish that any one except myself should provide for her, and give her her dowry. I am not, however, very rich, and the paternal inheritance did not gain bulk in my hands. One does not accumulate money by poring over old texts. But my books — at the price which such noble merchandise fetches to-day — are worth something. Why, on that shelf there are some poets of the sixteenth century for which bankers would bid against princes! And I think that those "Heures" of Simon Vostre would not be readily overlooked at the Hotel Sylvestre any more than would those Preces Piae compiled for the use of Queen Claude. I have taken great pains to collect and to preserve all those rare and curious editions which people the City of Books; and for a long time I used to believe that they were as necessary to my life as air and light. I have loved them well, and even now I cannot prevent myself from smiling at them and caressing them. Those morocco bindings are so delightful to the eye! These old vellums are so soft to the touch! There is not a single one among those books which is not worthy, by reason of some special merit, to command the respect of an honourable man. What other owner would ever know how to dip into hem in the proper way? Can I be even sure that another owner would not leave them to decay in neglect, or mutilate them at the prompting of some ignorant whim? Into whose hands will fall that incomparable copy of the "Histoire de l'Abbaye de Saint-Germain-des-Pres," on the margins of which the author himself, in the person of Jacques Bouillard, made such substantial notes in his own handwriting?... Master Bonnard, you are an old fool! Your housekeeper — poor soul! — is nailed down upon her bed with a merciless attack of rheumatism. Jeanne is to come with her chaperon, and, instead of thinking how you are going to receive them, you are thinking about a thousand stupidities. Sylvestre Bonnard, you will never succeed at anything in this world, and it is I myself who tell you so!

And at this very moment I catch sight of them from my window, as they get out of the omnibus. Jeanne leaps down lie a kitten; but Mademoiselle Prefere intrusts herself to the strong arm of the conductor, with the shy grace of a Virginia recovering after the shipwreck, and this time quite resigned to being saved. Jeanne looks up, sees me, laughs, and Mademoiselle Prefere has to prevent her from waving her umbrella at me as a friendly signal. There is a certain stage of cvilisation to which Mademoiselle Jeanne never can be brought. You can teach her all the arts if you like (it is not exactly to Mademoiselle Prefere that I am now speaking); but you will never be able to teach her perfect manners. As a charming child she makes the mistake of being charming only in her own way. Only an old fool like myself could forgive her pranks. As for young fools — and there are several of them still to be found — I do not know what they would think about it; and what they might think is none of my business. Just look at her running along the pavement, wrapped in her cloak, with her hat tilted back on her head, and her feather fluttering in the wind, like a schooner in full rig! And really she has a grace of poise and motion which suggests a fine sailing-vessel — so much so, indeed, that she makes me remember seeing one day, when I was at Havre.... But, Bonnard, my friend, how many times is it necessary to tell you that your housekeeper is in bed, and that you must go and open the door yourself?

Open, Old Man Winter! 'tis Spring who rings the bell.

It is Jeanne herself — Jeanne is all flushed like a rose. Mademoiselle Prefere, indignant and out of breath, has still another whole flight to climb before reaching our lobby.

I explained the condition of my housekeeper, and proposed that we should dine at a restaurant. But Therese — all-powerful still, even upon her sick-bed — decided that we should dine at home, whether we wanted to or no. Respectable people, in her opinion, never dined at restaurants. Moreover, she had made all necessary arrangements — the dinner had been bought; the concierge would cook it.

The audacious Jeanne insisted upon going to see whether the old woman wanted anything. As you might suppose, she was

143

sent back to the parlour with short shrift, but not so harshly as I had feared.

"If I want anybody to do anything for me, which, thank God, I do not," Therese had replied, "I would get somebody less delicate and dainty than you are. What I want is rest. That is a merchandise which is not sold at fairs under the sign of 'Motus with finger on lip.' Go and have your fun, and don't stay here — for old age might be catching."

Jeanne, after telling us what she had said, added that she liked very much to hear old Therese talk. Whereupon Mademoiselle Prefere reproached her for expressing such unladylike tastes.

I tried to excuse her by citing the example of Moliere. Just at that moment it came to pass that, while climbing the ladder to get a book, she upset a whole shelf-row. There was a heavy crash; and Mademoiselle Prefere, being, of course, a very delicate person, almost fainted. Jeanne quickly followed the books to the foot of the ladder. she made one think of a kitten suddenly transformed into a woman, catching mice which had been transformed into old books. While picking them up, she found one which happened to interest her, and she began to read it, squatting down upon her heels. It was the "Prince Grenouille," she told us. Mademoiselle Prefere took occasion to complain that Jeanne had so little taste for poetry. It was impossible to get her to recite Casimir Delavigne's poem on the death of Joan of Arc without mistakes. It was the very most she could do to learn "Le Petit Savoyard." The schoolmistress did not think that any one should read the "Prince Grenouille" before learning by heart the stanzas to Duperrier; and, carried away by her enthusiasm, she began to recite them in a voice sweeter than the bleating of a sheep:

" Ta douleur, Duperrier, sera donc eternelle, Et les tristes discours Que te met en l'esprit l'amitie paternelle L'augmenteront toujours;

. . . .

144

" Je sais de quels appas son enfance etait pleine, Et n'ai pas entrepris, Injurieux ami, de consoler ta peine Avecque son mepris."

Then in ecstacy, she exclaimed,

"How beautiful that is! What harmony! How is it possible for any one not to admire such exquisite, such touching verses! But why did Malherbe call that poor Monsieur Duperrier his injurieux ami at a time when he had been so severely tied by the death of his daughter? Injurieux ami — you must acknowledge that the term is very harsh."

I explained to this poetical person that the phrase "Injurieux ami," which shocked her so much, was in apposition, etc. etc. What I said, however, had so little effect towards clearing her head that she was seized with a severe and prolonged fit of sneezing. Meanwhile it was evident that the history of "Prince Grenouille" had proved extremely funny; for it was all that Jeanne could do, as she crouched down there on the carpet, to keep herself from bursting into a wild fit of laughter. But when she had finished with the prince and princess of the story, and the multitude of their children, she assumed a very suppliant expression, and begged me as a great favour to allow her to put on a white apron and go to the kitchen to help in getting the dinner ready.

"Jeanne," I replied, with the gravity of a master, "I think that if it is a question of breaking plates, knocking off the edges of dishes, denting all the pans, and smashing all the skimmers, the person whom Therese has set to work in the kitchen already will be able to perform her task without assistance; for it seems to me at this very moment I can hear disastrous noises in that kitchen. But anyhow, Jeanne, I will charge you with the duty of preparing the dessert. So go and get your white apron; I will tie it on for you."

Accordingly, I solemnly knotted the linen apron about her waist; and she rushed into the kitchen, where she proceeded at once — as we discovered later on — to prepare various dishes unknown to Vatel, unknown even to that great Careme who began his treatise upon pieces montees with these words: "The Fine Arts are five in number: Painting, Music, Poetry, Sculpture, and Architecture — whereof the principal branch is Confectionery." But I had no reason to be pleased with this little arrangement — for Mademoiselle Prefere, on finding herself alone with me, began to act after a fashion which filled me with frightful anxiety. She gazed upon me with eyes full of tears and flames, and uttered enormous sighs.

"Oh, how I pity you!" she said. "A man like you — a man so superior as you are — having to live alone with a coarse servant (for she is certainly coarse, that is incontestable)! How cruel such a life must be! You have need of repose — you have need of comfort, of care, of every kind of attention; you might fall sick. And yet there is no woman who would not deem it an honour to bear your name, and to share your existence. No, there is none; my own heart tells me so."

And she squeezed both hands over that heart of hers — always so ready to fly away.

I was driven almost to distraction. I tried to make Mademoiselle Prefere comprehend that I had no intention whatever of changing my habits at so advanced an age, and that I found just as much happiness in life as my character and my circumstances rendered possible.

"No, you are not happy!" she cried. "You need to have always beside you a mind capable of comprehending your own. Shake off your lethargy, and cast your eyes about you. Your professional connections are of the most extended character, and you must have charming acquaintances. One cannot be a Member of the Institute without going into society. See, judge, compare. No sensible woman would refuse you her hand. I am a woman, Monsieur; my instinct never deceives me — there is something within me which assures me that you would find happiness in marriage. Women are so devoted, so loving (not all, of course, but some)! And, then, they are so sensitive to glory. Remember that at your age one has need, like Oedipus, of an Egeria! Your cook is no longer able — she is deaf, she is infirm. If anything

146

should happen to you at night! Oh! it makes me shudder even to think of it!"

And she really shuddered — she closed her eyes, clenched her hands, stamped on the floor. Great was my dismay. With awful intensity she resumed,

"Your health — your dear health! The health of a Member of the Institute! How joyfully I would shed the very last drop of my blood to preserve the life of a scholar, of a litterateur, of a man of worth. And any woman who would not do as much, I should despise her! Let me tell you, Monsieur — I used to know the wife of a great mathematician, a man who used to fill whole note-books with calculations — so many note-books that they filled all the cupboards in the house. He had heart-disease, and he was visibly pining away. And I saw that wife of his, sitting there beside him, perfectly calm! I could not endure it. I said to her one day, 'My dear, you have no heart! If I were in your place I should...I should...I do not know what I should do!'"

She paused for want of breath. My situation was terrible. As for telling Mademoiselle Prefere what I really thought about her advice — that was something which I could not even dream of daring to do. For to fall out with her was to lose the chance of seeing Jeanne. So I resolved to take the matter quietly. In any case, she was in my house: that consideration helped me to treat her with something of courtesy.

"I am very old, Mademoiselle," I answered her, "and I am very much afraid that your advice comes to me rather late in life. Still, I will think about it. In the meanwhile let me beg of you to be calm. I think a glass of eau sucree would do you good!"

To my great surprise, these words calmed her at once; and I saw her sit down very quietly in HER corner, close to HER pigeon-hole, upon HER chair, with her feet upon HER footstool.

The dinner was a complete failure. Mademoiselle Prefere, who seemed lost in a brown study, never noticed the fact. As a rule I am very sensitive about such misfortunes; but this one caused Jeanne so much delight that at last I could not help enjoying it myself. Even at my age I had not been able to learn before that a chicken, raw on one side and burned on the other, was a funny thing; but Jeanne's bursts of laughter taught me that it was. That chicken caused us to say a thousand very witty things, which I have forgotten; and I was enchanted that it had not been properly cooked. Jeanne put it back to roast again; then she broiled it; then she stewed it with butter. And every time it came back to the table it was much less appetising and much more mirth-provoking than before. When we did eat it, at last, it had become a thing for which there is no name in any cuisine.

The almond cake was much more extraordinary. It was brought to the table in the pan, because it never could have got out of it. I invited Jeanne to help us all to a piece thinking that I was going to embarrass her; but she broke the pan and gave each of us a fragment. To think that anybody at my age could eat such things was an idea possible only to the very artless mind. Mademoiselle Prefere, suddenly awakened from her dream, indignantly pushed away the sugary splinter of earthenware, and deemed it opportune to inform me that she herself was exceedingly skilful in making confectionery.

"Ah!" exclaimed Jeanne, with an air of surprise not altogether without malice. Then she wrapped all the fragments of the pan in a piece of paper, for the purpose of giving them to her little playmates — especially to the three little Mouton girls, who are naturally inclined to gluttony.

Secretly, however, I was beginning to feel very uneasy. It did not now seem in any way possible to keep much longer upon good terms with Mademoiselle Prefere since her matrimonial fury had this burst forth. And that lady affronted, good-bye to Jeanne! I took advantage of a moment while the sweet soul was busy putting on her cloak, in order to ask Jeanne to tell me exactly what her own age was. She was eighteen years and one month old. I counted on my fingers, and found she would not come of age for another two years and eleven months. And how should we be able to manage during all that time?

At the door Mademoiselle Prefere squeezed my hand with so much meaning that I fairly shook from head to foot.

"Good-bye," I said very gravely to the young girl. "But listen to me a moment: your friend is very old, and might perhaps fail you when you need him most. Promise me never to fail in your duty to yourself, and then I shall have no fear. God keep you, my child!"

After closing the door behind them, I opened the window to get a last look at her as she was going away. But the night was dark, and I could see only two vague shadows flitting across the quay. I heard the vast deep hom of the city rising up about me; and I suddenly felt a great sinking at my heart.

Poor child!

December 15.

The King of Thule kept a goblet of gold which his dying mistress had bequeathed him as a souvenir. When about to die himself, after having drunk from it for the last time, he threw the goblet into the sea. And I keep this diary of memories even as that old prince of the mist-haunted seas kept his carven goblet; and even as he flung away at last his love-pledge, so will I burn this book of souvenirs. Assuredly it is not through any arrogant avarice nor through any egotistical pride, that I shall destroy this record of a humble life — it is only because I fear lest those things which are dear and sacred to me might appear before others, because of my inartistic manner of expression, either commonplace or absurd.

I do not say this in view of what is going to follow. Absurd I certainly must have been when, having been invited to dinner by Mademoiselle Prefere, I took my seat in a bergere (it was really a bergere) at the right hand of that alarming person. The table had been set in a little parlour; and I could observe from the poor way in which it was set out that the schoolmistress was one of those ethereal souls who soar above terrestrial things. Chipped plates, unmatched glasses, knives with loose handles, forks with yellow prongs — there was absolutely nothing wanting to spoil the appetite of an honest man.

I was assured that the dinner had been cooked for me — for me alone — although Maitre Mouche had also been invited. Mademoiselle Prefere must have imagined that I had Sarmatian tastes on the subject of butter; for that which she offered me, served up in little thin pats, was excessively rancid.

The roast very nearly poisoned me. But I had the pleasure of hearing Maitre Mouche and Mademoiselle Prefere discourse upon virtue. I said the pleasure — I ought to have said the shame; for the sentiments to which they gave expression soared far beyond the range of my vulgar nature.

What they said proved to me as clear as day that devotedness was their daily bread, and that self-sacrifice was not less necessary to their existence than air and water. Observing that I was not eating, Mademoiselle Prefere made a thousand efforts to overcome that which she was good enough to term my "discretion." Jeanne was not of the party, because, I was told, her presence at it would have been contrary to the rules, and would have wounded the feelings of the other school-children, among whom it was necessary to maintian a certain equality. I secretly congratulated her upon having escaped from the Merovingian butter; from the huge radishes, empty as funeral-urns; form the leathery roast, and from various other curiosities of diet to which I had exposed myself for the love of her.

The extremely disconsolate-looking servant served up some liquid to which they gave the name of cream — I do not know why — and vanished away like a ghost.

Then Mademoiselle Prefere related to Maitre Mouche, with extraordinary transports of emotion, all that she had said to me in the City of Books, during the time that my housekeeper was sick in bed. Her admiration for a Member of the Institute, her terror lest I should be taken ill while unattended, and the certainty she felt that any intelligent woman would be proud and happy to share my existence — she concealed nothing, but, on the contrary, added many fresh follies to the recital. Maitre Mouche kept nodding his head in approval while cracking nuts. Then, after all this verbiage, he demanded, with an agreeable smile, what my answer had been.

Mademoiselle Prefere, pressing her hand upon her heart and extending the other towards me, cried out,

"He is so affectionate, so superior, so good, and so great! He answered... But I could never, because I am only a humble woman — I could never repeat the words of a Member of the Institute. I can only utter the substance of them. He answered, 'Yes, I understand you — yes.'"

And with these words she reached out and seized one of my hands. Then Maitre Mouche, also overwhelmed with emotion, arose and seized my other hand.

"Monsieur," he said, "permit me to offer my congratulations."

Several times in my life I have known fear; but never before had I experienced any fright of so nauseating a character. A sickening terror came upon me.

I disengaged by two hands, and, rising to my feet, so as to give all possible seriousness to my words, I said,

"Madame, either I explained myself very badly when you were at my house, or I have totally misunderstood you here in your own. In either case, a positive declaration is absolutely necessary. Permit me, Madame, to make it now, very plainly. No — I never did understand you; I am totally ignorant of the nature of this marriage project that you have been planning for me — if you really have been planning one. In any event, I should not think of marrying. It would be unpardonable folly at my age, and even now, at this moment, I cannot conceive how a sensible person like you could ever have advised me to marry. Indeed, I am strongly inclined to believe that I must have been mistaken, and that you never said anything of the kind before. In the latter case, please excuse an old man totally unfamiliar with the usages of society, unaccustomed to the conversation of ladies, and very contrite for his mistake."

Maitre Mouche went back very softly to his place, where, not finding any more nuts to crack, he began to whittle a cork.

Mademoiselle Prefere, after staring at me for a few moments with an expression in her little round dry eyes which I had never seen there before, suddenly resumed her customary sweetness and graciousness. Then she cried out in honeyed tones,

"Oh! these learned men! — these studious men! They are like children. Yes, Monsieur Bonnard, you are a real child!"

Then, turning to the notary, who still sat very quietly in his corner, with his nose over his cork, she exclaimed, in beseeching tones,

"Oh, do not accuse him! Do not accuse him! Do not think any evil of him, I beg of you! Do not think it at all! Must I ask you upon my knees?"

Maitre Mouche continued to examine all the various aspects and surfaces of his cork without making any further manifestation.

I was very indignant; and I know that my cheeks must have been extremely red, if I could judge by the flush of heat which I felt rise to my face. This would enable me to explain the words I heard through all the buzzing in my ears:

"I am frightened about him! our poor friend!... Monsieur Mouche, be kind enough to open a window! It seems to me that a compress of arnica would do him some good."

I rushed out into the street with an unspeakable feeling of shame.

"My poor Jeanne!"

December 20.

I passed eight days without hearing anything further in regard to the Prefere establishment. Then, feeling myself unable to remain any longer without some news of Clementine's daughter, and feeling furthermore that I owed it as a duty to myself not to cease my visits with the school without more serious cause, I took my way to Les Ternes. The parlour seemed to me more cold, more damp, more inhospitable, and more insidious than ever before; and the servant much more silent and much more scared. I asked to see Mademoiselle Jeanne; but, after a very considerable time, it was Mademoiselle Prefere who made her appearance instead — severe and pale, with lips compressed and a hard look in her eyes.

"Monsieur," she said, folding her arms over her pelerine, I regret very much that I cannot allow you to see Mademoiselle Alexandre to-day; but I cannot possibly do it."

"Why not?" I asked in astonishment.

"Monsieur," she replied, "the reasons which compel me to request that your visits shall be less frequent hereafter are of an excessively delicate nature; and I must beg you to spare me the unpleasantness of mentioning them."

"Madame," I replied, "I have been authorized by Jeanne's guardian to see his ward every day. Will you please to inform me of your reasons for opposing the will of Monsieur Mouche?"

"The guardian of Mademoiselle Alexandre," she replied (and she dwelt upon that word "guardian" as upon a solid support), "desires, quite as strongly as I myself do, that your assiduities may come to an end as soon as possible."

"Then, if that be the case," I said, "be kind enough to let me know his reasons and your own."

She looked up at the little spiral of paper on the ceiling, and then replied, with stern composure,

"You insist upon it? Well, although such explanations are very painful for a woman to make, I will yield to your exaction. This house, Monsieur is an honourable house. I have my responsibility. I have to watch like a mother over each one of my pupils. Your assiduities in regard to Mademoiselle Alexandre could not possibly be continued without serious injury to the young girl herself; and it is my duty to insist that they shall cease."

"I do not really understand you," I replied — and I was telling the plain truth. Then she deliberately resumed:

"Your assiduities in this house are being interpreted, by the most respectable and the least suspicious persons, in such a

153

manner that I find myself obliged, both in the interest of my establishment and in the interest of Mademoiselle Alexandre, to see that they end at once."

"Madame," I cried, "I have heard a great many silly things in my life, but never anything so silly as what you have just said!"

She answered me quietly,

"Your words of abuse will not affect me in the slightest. When one has a duty to accomplish, one is strong enough to endure all."

And she pressed her pelerine over her heart once more — not perhaps on this occasion to restrain, but doubtless only to caress that generous heart.

"Madame," I said, shaking my finger at her, "you have wantonly aroused the indignation of an aged man. Be good enough to act in such a fashion that the old man may be able at least to forget your existence, and do not add fresh insults to those which I have already sustained from your lips. I give you fair warning that I shall never cease to look after Mademoiselle Alexandre; and that should you attempt to do her any harm, in any manner whatsoever, you will have serious reason to regret it!"

The more I became excited, the more she became cool; and she answered in a tone of superb indifference:

"Monsieur, I am much too well informed in regard to the nature of the interest which you take in this young girl, not to withdraw her immediately from that very surveillance with which you threaten me. After observing the more than equivocal intimacy in which you are living with your housekeeper, I ought to have taken measures at once to render it impossible for you ever to come into contact with an innocent child. In the future I shall certainly do it. If up to this time I have been too trustful, it is for Mademoiselle Alexandre, and not for you, to reproach me with it. But she is too artless and too pure — thanks to me! — ever to have suspected the nature of that danger into which you were trying to lead her. I scarcely suppose that you will place me under the necessity of enlightening her upon the subject."

"Come, my poor old Bonnard," I said to myself, as I shrugged my shoulders — "so you had to live as long as this in order to learn for the first time exactly what a wicked woman is. And now your knowledge of the subject is complete."

I went out without replying; and I had the pleasure of observing, from the sudden flush which overspread the face of the schoolmistress, that my silence had wounded her far more than my words.

As I passed through the court I looked about me in every direction for Jeanne. She was watching for me, and she ran to me.

"If anybody touches one little hair of your head, Jeanne, write to me! Good-bye!"

"No, not good-bye."

I replied,

"Well, no — not good-bye! Write to me!"

I went straight to Madame de Gabry's residence.

"Madame is at Rome with Monsieur. Did not Monsieur know it?"

"Why, yes," I replied. "Madame wrote to me."...

She had indeed written to me in regard to her leaving home; but my head must have become very much confused, so that I had forgotten all about it. The servant seemed to be of the same opinion, for he looked at me in a way that seemed to signify, "Monsieur Bonnard is doting" — and he leaned down over the balustrade of the stairway to see if I was not going to do something extraordinary before I got to the bottom. But I descended the stairs rationally enough; and then he drew back his head in disappointment.

On returning home I was informed that Monsieur Gelis was waiting for me in the parlour. (This young man has become a constant visitor. His judgement is at fault at times; but his mind is not at all commonplace.) On this occasion, however, his usually welcome visit only embarrassed me. "Alas!" I thought to myself, "I shall be sure to say something very stupid to my young friend to-day, and he also will think that my facilities are becoming impaired. But still I cannot really explain to him that I had first been demanded in wedlock, and subsequently traduced as a man wholly devoid of morals — that even Therese had become an object of suspicion — and that Jeanne remains in the power of the most rascally woman on the face of the earth. I am certainly in an admirable state of mind for conversing about Cistercian abbeys with a young and mischievously minded man. Nevertheless, we shall see — we shall try."...

But Therese stopped me:

"How red you are, Monsieur!" she exclaimed, in a tone of reproach.

"It must be the spring," I answered.

She cried out,

"The spring! — in the month of December?"

That is a fact! this is December. Ah! what is the matter with my head? what a fine help I am going to be to poor Jeanne!

"Therese, take my cane; and put it, if you possibly can, in some place where I shall be able to find it again.

"Good-day, Monsieur Gelis. How are you?"

Undated.

Next morning the old boy wanted to get up; but the old boy could not get up. A merciless invisible hand kept him down upon his bed. Finding himself immovably riveted there, the old boy resigned himself to remain motionless; but his thoughts kept running in all directions.

He must have had a very violent fever; for Mademoiselle Prefere, the Abbots of Saint-Germain-des-Pres, and the servant of Madame de Gabry appeared to him in divers fantastic shapes. The figure of the servant in particular lengthened weirdly over his head, grimacing like some gargoyle of a cathedral. Then it seemed to me that there were a great many people, much too many people, in my bedroom.

This bedroom of mine is furnished after the antiquated fashion. The portrait of my father in full uniform, and the portrait of my mother in her cashmere dress, are suspended on the wall. The wall-paper is covered with green foliage designs. I am aware of all this, and I am even conscious that everything is faded, very much faded. But an old man's room does not require to be pretty; it is enough that it should be clean, and Therese sees to that. At all events my room is sufficiently decorated to please a mind like mine, which has always remained somewhat childish and dreamy. There are things hanging on the wall or scattered over the tables and shelves which usually please my fancy and amuse me. But to-day it would seem as if all those objects had suddenly conceived some kind of ill-will against me. They have all become garish, grimacing, menacing. That statuette, modelled after one of the Theological Virtues of Notre-Dame de Brou, always so ingenuously graceful in its natural condition, is now making contortions and putting out its tongue at me. And that beautiful miniature — in which one of the most skilful pupils of Jehan Fouquet depicted himself, girdled with the cord-girdle of the Sons of St. Francis, offering his book, on bended knee, to the good Duc d'Angouleme — who has taken it out of its frame and put in its place a great ugly cat's head, which stares at me with phosphorescent eyes. And the designs on the wall-paper have also turned into heads — hideous green heads.... But no — I am sure that wall-paper must have foliage-designs upon it at this moment just as it had twenty years ago, and nothing else.... But no, again — I was right before — they are heads, with eyes, noses, mouths — they are heads!... Ah! now I understand! they are both heads and foliage-designs at the same time. I wish I could not see them at all.

And there, on my right, the pretty miniature of the Franciscan has come back again; but it seems to me as if I can only keep it in its frame by a tremendous effort of will, and that the moment I get tired the ugly cat-head will appear in its place. Certainly I am not delirious; I can see Therese very plainly, standing at the foot of my bed; I can hear her speaking to me perfectly well, and I should be able to answer her quite satisfactorily if I were not kept so busy in trying to compel the various objects about me to maintain their natural aspect.

Here is the doctor coming. I never sent for him, but it gives me pleasure to see him. He is an old neighbor of mine; I have never been of much service to him, but I like him very much. Even if I do not say much to him, I have at least full possession of all my faculties, and I even find myself extraordinarily crafty and observant to-day, for I note all his gestures, his every look, the least wrinkling of his face. But the doctor is very cunning, too, and I cannot really tell what he thinks about me. The deep thought of Goethe suddenly comes to my mind and I exclaim,

"Doctor, the old man has consented to allow himself to become sick; but he does not intend, this time at least, to make any further concessions to nature."

Neither the doctor nor Therese laughs at my little joke. I suppose they cannot have understood it.

The doctor goes away; evening comes; and all sorts of strange shadows begin to shape themselves about my bed-curtains, forming and dissolving by turns. And other shadows — ghosts — throng by before me; and through them I can see distinctively the impassive face of my faithful servant. And suddenly a cry, a shrill cry, a great cry of distress, rends my ears. Was it you who called me Jeanne?

The day is over; and the shadows take their places at my bedside to remain with me all through the long night.

Then morning comes — I feel a peace, a vast peace, wrapping me all about.

Art Thou about to take me into Thy rest, my dear Lord God?

February 186-.

The doctor is quite jovial. It seems that I am doing him a great deal of credit by being able to get out of bed. If I must believe him, innumerable disorders must have pounced down upon my poor old body all at the same time.

These disorders, which are the terror of ordinary mankind, have names which are the terror of philologists. They are hybrid names, half Greek, half Latin, with terminations in "itis," indicating the inflammatory condition, and in "algia," indicating pain. The doctor gives me all their names, together with a corresponding number of adjectives ending in "ic," which serve to characterise their detestable qualities. In short, they represent a good half of that most perfect copy of the Dictionary of Medicine contained in the too-authentic box of Pandora.

"Doctor, what an excellent common-sense story the story of Pandora is! — if I were a poet I would put it into French verse. Shake hands, doctor! You have brought me back to life; I forgive you for it. You have given me back to my friends; I thank you for it. You say I am quite strong. That may be, that may be; but I have lasted a very long time. I am a very old article of furniture; I might be very satisfactorily compared to my father's arm-chair. It was an arm-chair which the good man had inherited, and in which he used to lounge from morning until evening. Twenty times a day, when I was quite a baby, I used to climb up and seat myself on one of the arms of that old-fashioned chair. So long as the chair remained intact, nobody paid any particular attention to it. But it began to limp on one foot and then folks began to say that it was a very good chair. Afterwards it became lame in three legs, squeaked with the fourth leg, and lost nearly half of both arms. Then everybody would exclaim, 'What a strong chair!' They wondered how it was that after its arms had been worn off and all its legs knocked out of perpendicular, it could yet preserve the recognisable shape of a chair, remains nearly erect, and still be of some service. The horse-hair came out of its body at last, and it gave up the ghost. And when Cyprien, our servant, sawed up its mutilated members for fire-wood, everybody redoubled their cries of admiration. Oh! what an excellent — what a marvellous chair! It was the chair of Pierre Sylvestre Bonnard, the cloth merchant — of Epimenide Bonnard, his son — of Jean-Baptiste Bonnard, the Pyrrhonian philosopher and Chief of the Third Maritime Division. Oh! what a robust and venerable chair!' In reality it was a dead chair. Well, doctor, I am that chair. You think I am solid because I have been able to resist an attack which would have killed many people, and which only three-fourths killed me. Much obliged! I feel none the less that I am something which has been irremediably damaged."

The doctor tries to prove to me, with the help of enormous Greek and Latin words, that I am really in a very good condition. It would, of course, be useless to attempt any demonstration of this kind in so lucid a language as French. However, I allow him to persuade me at last; and I see him to the door.

"Good! good!" exclaimed Therese; "that is the way to put the doctor out of the house! Just do the same thing once or twice again, and he will not come to see you any more — and so much the better?"

"Well, Therese, now that I have become such a hearty man again, do not refuse to give me my letters. I am sure there must be quite a big bundle of letters, and it would be very wicked to keep me any longer from reading them."

Therese, after some little grumbling, gave me my letters. But what did it matter? — I looked at all the envelopes, and saw that no one of them had been addressed by the little hand which I so much wish I could see here now, turning over the pages of the Vecellio. I pushed the whole bundle of letters away: they had no more interest for me.

April-June

It was a hotly contested engagement.

"Wait, Monsieur, until I have put on my clean things," exclaimed Therese, "and I will go out with you this time also; I will carry your folding-stool as I have been doing these last few days, and we will go and sit down somewhere in the sun."

Therese actually thinks me infirm. I have been sick, it is true, but there is an end to all things! Madame Malady has taken her departure quite awhile ago, and it is now more than three months since her pale and gracious-visaged handmaid, Dame Convalescence, politely bade me farewell. If I were to listen to my housekeeper, I should become a veritable Monsieur Argant, and I should wear a nightcap with ribbons for the rest of my life.... No more of this! — I propose to go out by myself! Therese will not hear of it. She takes my folding-stool, and wants to follow me.

"Therese, to-morrow, if you like, we will take our seats on the sunny side of the wall of La Petite Provence and stay there just as long as you please. But to-day I have some very important affairs to attend to."

"So much the better! But your affairs are not the only affairs in this world."

I beg; I scold; I make my escape.

It is quite a pleasant day. With the aid of a cab and the help of almighty God, I trust to be able to fulfil my purpose.

There is the wall on which is painted in great blue letters the words "Pensionnat de Demoiselles tenu par Mademoiselle Virginie Prefere." There is the iron gate which would give free entrance into the court-yard if it were ever opened. But the lock is rusty, and sheets of zinc put up behind the bars protect the indiscreet observation those dear little souls to whom Mademoiselle Prefere doubtless teaches modesty, sincerity, justice, and disinterestedness. There is a window, with iron bars before it, and panes daubed over with white paint — the window of the domestic offices, like a glazed eye — the only aperture of the building opening upon the exterior world. As for the house-door, through which I entered so often, but which is now closed against me for ever, it is just as I saw it the last time, with its little iron-grated wicket. The single stone step in front of it is deeply worn, and, without having very good eyes behind my spectacles, I can see the little white scratches on the stone which have been made by the nails in the shoes of the girls going in and out. And why cannot I also go in? I have a feeling that Jeanne must be suffering a great deal in this dismal house, and that she calls my name in secret. I cannot go away from the gate! A strange anxiety takes hold of me. I pull the bell. The scared-looking servant comes to the door, even more scared-looking than when I saw her the last time. Strict orders have been given; I am not to be allowed to see Mademoiselle Jeanne. I beg the servant to be so kind as to tell me how the child is. The servant, after looking to her right and then to her left, tells me that Mademoiselle Jeanne is well, and then shuts the door in my face. And I am all alone in the street again.

How many times since then have I wandered in the same way under that wall, and passed before the little door, — full of shame and despair to find myself even weaker than that poor child, who has no other help of friend except myself in the world!

Finally I overcame my repugnance sufficiently to call upon Maitre Mouche. The first thing I remarked was that his office is much more dusty and much more mouldy this year that it was last year. The notary made his appearance after a moment, with his familiar stiff gestures, and his restless eyes quivering behind his eye-glasses. I made my complaints to him. He answered me.... But why should I write down, even in a notebook which I am going to burn, my recollections of a downright scoundrel? He takes sides with Mademoiselle Prefere, whose intelligent mind and irreproachable character he has long appreciated. He does not feel himself in a position to decide the nature of the question at issue; but he must assure me that appearances have been greatly against me. That of course makes no difference to me. He adds — (and this does make some sense to me) — that the small sum which had been placed in his hands to defray the expenses of the education of his ward has been expended, and that, in view of the circumstances, he cannot but gently admire the disinterestedness of Mademoiselle Prefere in consenting to allow Mademoiselle Jeanne to remain with her.

A magnificent light, the light of a perfect day, floods the sordid place with its incorruptible torrent, and illuminates teh person of that man!

And outside it pours down its splendour upon all the wretchedness of a populous quarter.

How sweet it is, — this light with which my eyes have so long been filled, and which ere long I must for ever cease to enjoy! I wander out with my hands behind me, dreaming as I go, following the line of the fortifications; and I find myself after awhile, I know not how, in an out-of-the-way suburb full of miserable little gardens. By the dusty roadside I observe a plant whose flower, at once dark and splendid, seems worthy of association with the noblest and purest mouning for the dead. It is a columbine. Our fathers called it "Our Lady's Glove" — le gant de Notre-Dame. Only such a "Notre-Dame" as might make herself very, very small, for the sake of appearing to little children, could ever slip her dainty fingers into the narrow capsue of that flower.

And there is a big bumble-bee who tries to force himself into the flower, brutally; but his mouth cannot reach the nectar, and the poor glutton strives and strives in vain. He has to give up the attempt, and comes out of the flower all smeared over with pollen. He flies off in his own heavy lumbering way; but there are not many flowers in this portion of the suburbs, which has been defiled by the soot and smoke of factories. So he comes back to the columbine again, and this time he pierces the corolla and sucks the honey through the little hole which he has made; I should never have thought that a bumble-bee had so much sense! Why, that is admirble! The more I observe, them, the more do insects and flowers fill me with astonishment. I am like that good Rollin who went wild with delight over the flowers of his peach-trees. I wish I could have a fine garden, and live at the verge of a wood.

August, September.

It occurred to me one Sunday morning to watch for the moment when Mademoiselle Prefere's pupils were leaving the school in procession to attand Mass at the parish church. I watched them passing two by two, — the little ones first with very serious faces. There were three of them all dressed exactly alike — dumpy, plump, important-looking little creatures, whom I recognized at once as the Mouton girls. Their elder sister is the artist who drew that terrrible head of Tatius, King of the Sabines. Beside the column, the assistant school-teacher, with her prayer-book in her hand, was gesturing and frowning. Then came the next oldest class, and finally the big girls, all whispering to each other, as they went by. But I did not see Jeanne.

I went to police-headquarters and inquired whether they chanced to have, filed away somewhere or other, any information

163

regarding the establishment in the Rue Demours. I succeeded in inducing them to send some female inspectors there. These returned bringing with them the most favourable reports about the establishment. In their opinion the Prefere School was a model school. It is evident that if I were to force an investigation, Mademoiselle Prefere would receive academic honours.

October 3.

This Thursday being a school-holiday I had teh chance of meeting the three little Mouton girls in the vicinity of the Rue Demours. After bowing to their mother, I asked the eldest who appears to be about ten years old, how was her playmate, Mademoiselle Jeanne Alexandre.

The little Mouton girl answered me, all in a breath,

"Jeanne Alexandre is not my playmate. She is only kept in the school for charity — so they make her sweep the class-rooms. It was Mademoiselle who said so. And Jeanne Alexandre is a bad girl; so they lock her up in the dark room — and it serves her right — and I am a good girl — and I am never locked up in the dark room."

The three little girls resumed their walk, and Madame Mouton followed close behind them, looking back over her broad shoulder at me, in a very suspicious manner.

Alas! I find myself reduced to expedients of a questionable character. Madame de Gabry will not come back to Paris for at least three months more, at the very soonest. Without her, I have no tact, I have no common sense — I am nothing but a cumbersome, clumsy, mischief-making machine.

Nevertheless, I cannot possibly permit them to make Jeanne a boarding-school servant!

December 28.

The idea that Jeanne was obliged to sweep the rooms had become absolutely unbearable.

The weather was dark and cold. Night had already begun. I rang the school-door bell with the tranquillity of a resolute man.

164

The moment that the timid servant opened the door, I slipped a gold piece into her hand, and promised her another if she would arrange matters so that I could see Mademoiselle Alexandre. Her answer was,

"In one hour from now, at the grated window."

And she slammed the door in my face so rudely that she knocked my hat into the gutter. I waited for one very long hour in a violent snow-storm; then I approached the window. Nothing! The wind raged, and the snow fell heavily. Workmen passing by with their implements on their shoulders, and their heads bent down to keep the snow from coming in their faces, rudely jostled me. Still nothing. I began to fear I had been observed. I knew that I had done wrong in bribing a servant, but I was not a bit sorry for it. Woe to the man who does not know how to break through social regulations in case of necessity! Another quarter of an hour passed. Nothing. At last the window was partly opened.

"Is that you, Monsieur Bonnard?"

Is that you, Jeanne? — tell me at once what has become of you."

"I am well — very well."

"But what else!"

"They have put me in the kitchen, and I have to sweep the school-rooms."

"In the kitchen! Sweeping — you! Gracious goodness!"

"Yes, because my guardian does not pay for my schooling any longer."

"Gracious goodness! Your guardian seems to me to be a thorough scoundrel."

"Then you know — -"

"What?"

"Oh! don't ask me to tell you that! — but I would rather die than find myself alone with him again."

"And why did you not write to me?"

"I was watched."

At this instant I formed a resolve which nothing in this world could have induced me to change. I did, indeed, have some idea that I might be acting contrary to law; but I did not give myself the least concern about that idea. And, being firmly resolved, I was able to be prudent. I acted with remarkable coolness.

"Jeanne," I asked, "tell me! does that room you are in open into the court-yard?"

"Yes."

"Can you open the street-door from the inside yourself?"

"Yes, — if there is nobody in the porter's lodge."

"Go and see if there is any one there, and be careful that nobody observes you."

Then I waited, keeping a watch on the door and window.

In six or seven seconds Jeanne reappeared behind the bars, and said,

"The servant is in the porter's lodge."

"Very well," I said, "have you a pen and ink?"

"No."

"A pencil?"

"Yes."

"Pass it out here."

I took an old newspaper out of my pocket, and — in a wind which blew almost hard enough to put the street-lamps out, in a downpour of snow which almost blinded me — I managed to wrap up and address that paper to Mademoiselle Prefere.

While I was writing I asked Jeanne,

"When the postman passes he puts the papers and letters in the box, doesn't he? He rings the bell and goes away? Then the servant opens the letter-box and takes whatever she finds there to Mademoiselle Prefere immediately; is not that about the way the thing is managed whenever anything comes by post?"

Jeanne thought it was.

"Then we shall soon see. Jeanne, go and watch again; and, as soon as the servant leaves the lodge, open the door and come out here to me."

Having said this, I put my newspaper in the box, gave the bell a tremendous pull, and then hid myself in the embrasure of a neighbouring door.

I might have been there several minutes, when the little door quivered, then opened, and a young girl's head made its appearance through the opening. I took hold of it; I pulled it towards me.

"Come, Jeanne! come!"

She stared at me uneasily. Certainly she must have been afraid that I had gone mad; but, on the contrary, I was very rational indeed.

"Come, my child! come!"

"Where?"

"To Madame de Gabry's."

Then she took my arm. For some time we ran like a couple of thieves. But running is an exercise ill-suited to one as corpulent as I am, and, finding myself out of breath at last, I stopped and leaned upon something which turned out to be the stove of a dealer in roasted chestnuts, who was doing business at the corner of a wine-seller's shop, where a number of cabmen were drinking. One of them asked us if we did not want a cab. Most assuredly we wanted a cab! The driver, after setting down his glass on the zinc counter, climbed upon his seat and urged his horse forward. We were saved.

"Phew!" I panted, wiping my forehead. For, in spite of the cold, I was perspiring profusely.

What seemed very odd was that Jeanne appeared to be much more conscious than I was of the enormity which we had committed. She looked very serious indeed, and was visibly uneasy.

"In the kitchen!" I cried out, with indignation.

She shook her head, as if to say, "Well, there or anywhere else, what does it matter to me?" And by the light of the street-lamps, I observed with pain that her face was very thin and her features all pinched. I did not find in her any of that vivacity, any of those bright impulses, any of that quickness of expression, which used to please me so much. Her gaze had become timid, her gestures constrained, her whole attitude melancholy. I took her hand — a little cold hand, which had become all hardened and bruised. The poor child must have suffered very much. I questioned her. She told me very quietly that Mademoiselle Prefere had summoned her one day, and called her a little monster and a little viper, for some reason which she had never been able to learn.

She had added, "You shall not see Monsieur Bonnard any more; for he has been giving you bad advice, and he has conducted himself in a most shameful manner towards me." "I then said to her, 'That, Mademoiselle, you will never be able to make me believe.' Then Mademoiselle slapped my face and sent me back to the school-room. The announcement that I should never be allowed to see you again made me feel as if night had come down upon me. Don't you know those evenings when one feels so sad to see the darkness come? — well, just imagine such a moment stretched out into weeks — into whole months! Don't you remember my little Saint-George? Up to that time I had worked at it as well as I could — just simply to work at it — just to amuse myself. But when I lost all hope of ever seeing you again I took my little wax figure, and I began to work at it in quite another way. I did not try to model it with wooden matches any more, as I had been doing, but with hair pins. I even made use of epingles a la neige. But perhaps you do not know what epingles a la neige are? Well, I became more particular about than you can possibly imagine. I put a dragon on Saint-George's helmet; and I passed hours and hours in making a head and eyes and tail for the dragon. Oh the eyes! the eyes, above all! I never stopped working at them till I got them so that they had red pupils and white eye-lids and eye-brows and everything! I know I am very silly; I had an idea that I was going to die as soon as my little Saint-George would be finished. I worked at it during recreation-hours, and Mademoiselle Prefere used to let me alone. One day I learned that you were in the parlour with the schoolmistress; I watched for you; we said 'Au revoir!' that day to each other. I was a little

168

consoled by seeing you. But, some time after that, my guardian came and wanted to make me go to his house, — but please don't ask me why, Monsieur. He answered me, quite gently, that I was a very whimsical little girl. And then he left me alone. But the next day Mademoiselle Prefere came to me with such a wicked look on her face that I was really afraid. She had a letter in her hand. 'Mademoiselle,' she said to me, 'I am informed by your guardian that he has spent all the money which belonged to you. Don't be afraid! I do not intend to abandon you; but, you must acknowledge yourself, it is only right that you should earn your own livelihood.' Then she put me to work house-cleaning; and whenever I made a mistake she would lock me up in the garet for days together. And that is what has happened to me since I saw you last. Even if I had been able to write to you I do not know whether I should have done it, because I did not think you could possibly take me away from the school; and, as Maitre Mouche did not come back to see me, there was no hurry. I thought I could wait for awhile in the garret and the kitchen.

"Jeanne," I cried, "even if we should have to flee to Oceania, the abominable Prefere shall never get hold of you again. I will take a great oath on that! And why should we not go to Oceania? The climate is very healthy; and I read in a newspaper the other day that they have pianos there. But, in the meantime, let us go to the house of Madame de Gabry, who returned to Paris, as luck would have it, some three or four days ago; for you and I are two innocent fools, and we have great need of some one to help us."

Even as I was speaking Jeanne's features suddenly became pale, and seemed to shrink into lifelessness; her eyes became all dim; her lips, half open, contracted with an expression of pain. Then her head sank sideways on her shoulder; — she had fainted.

I lifter her in my arms, and carried her up Madame de Gabry's staircase like a little baby asleep. But I was myself on the point of fainting from emotional excitement and fatigue together, when she came to herself again.

"Ah! it is you." she said: "so much the better!"

Such was our condition when we rang our friend's door-bell.

Same day.

It was eight o'clock. Madame de Gabry, as might be supposed, was very much surprised by our unexpected appearance. But she welcomed the old man and the child with that glad kindness which always expresses itself in her beautiful gestures. It seems to me, — if I might use the language of devotion so familiar to her, — it seems to me as though some heavenly grace streams from her hands when ever she opens them; and even the perfume which impregnates her robes seems to inspire the sweet calm zeal of charity and good works. Surprised she certainly was; but she asked us no question, — and that silence seemed to me admirable.

"Madame," I said to her, "we have both come to place ourselves under your protection. And, first of all, we are going to ask you to give us some super — or to give Jeanne some, at least; for a moment ago, in the carriage, she fainted from weakness. As for myself, I could not eat a bite at this late hour without passing a night of agony in consequence. I hope that Monsieur de Gabry is well."

"Oh, he is here!" she said.

And she called him immediately.

"Come in here, Paul! Come and see Monsieur Bonnard and Mademoiselle Alexandre."

He came. It was a pleasure for me to see his frank broad face, and to press his strong square hand. Then we went, all four of us, into the dining-room; and while some cold meat was being cut for Jeanne — which she never touched notwithstanding — I related our adventure. Paul de Gabry asked me permission to smoke his pipe, after which he listened to me in silence. When I had finished my recital he scratched the short, stiff beard upon his chin, and uttered a tremendous "Sacrebleu!" But, seeing Jeanne stare at each of us in turn, with a frightened look in her face, he added:

"We will talk about this matter to-morrow morning. Come into my study for a moment; I have an old book to show you that I want you to tell me something about."

I followed him into his study, where the steel of guns and hunting knives, suspended against the dark hangings, glimmered in the lamp-light. There, pulling me down beside him upon a leather-covered sofa, he exclaimed,

"What have you done? Great God! Do you know what you have done? Corruption of a minor, abduction, kidnapping! You have got yourself into a nice mess! You have simply rendered yourself liable to a sentence of imprisonment of not less than five nor more than ten years."

"Mercy on us!" I cried; "ten years imprisonment for having saved an innocent child."

"That is the law!" answered Monsieur de Gabry. "You see, my dear Monsieur Bonnard, I happen to know the Code pretty well — not because I ever studied law as a profession, but because, as mayor of Lusance, I was obliged to teach myself something about it in order to be able to give information to my subordinates. Mouche is a rascal; that woman Prefere is a vile hussy; and you are a...Well! I really cannot find a word strong enough to signify what you are!"

After opening his bookcase, where dog-collars, riding-whips, stirrups, spurs, cigar-boxes, and a few books of reference were indiscriminately stowed away, he took out of it a copy of the Code, and began to turn over the leaves.

"'CRIMES AND MISDEMEANOURS'...
'SEQUESTRATION OF PERSONS'

— that is not your case....

'ABDUCTION OF MINORS'

— here we are....'ARTICLE 354': — 'Whosoever shall, either by fraud or violence, have abducted or have caused to be abducted any minor or minors, or shall have enticed them, or turned them away from, or forcibly removed them, or shall have caused them to be enticed, or turned away from or forcibly removed from the places in which they have been placed by those to whose authority or direction they have been submitted or confided, shall be liable to the penalty of imprisonment. See PENAL CODE, 21 and 28.' Here is 21: — 'The term of imprisonment shall not be less than five years.' 28. 'The sentence of imprisonment shall be considered as involving a loss of civil rights.' Now all that is very plain, is it not, Monsieur Bonnard?"

"Perfectly plain."

"Now let us go on: 'ARTICLE 356': — 'In case the abductor be under the age of 21 years at the time of the offense, he shall only be punished with'...But we certainly cannot invoke this artice in your favour. 'ARTICLE 357:': — 'In case the abductor shall have married the girl by him abducted, he can only be prosecuted at the insistence of such persons as, according to the Civil Code, may have the right to demand that the marriage shall be declared null; nor can he be condemned until after the nullity of the marriage shall have been pronounced.' I do not know whether it is a part of your plans to marry Mademoiselle Alexandre! You can see that the code is good-natured about it; it leaves you one door of escape. But no — I ought not to joke with you, because really you have put yourself in a very unfortunate position! And how could a man like you imagine that here in Paris, in the middle of the nineteenth century, a young girl can be abducted with absolute impunity? We are not living in the Middle Ages now; and such things are no longer permitted by law."

"You need not imagine," I replied, "that abduction was lawful under the ancient Code. You will find in Baluze a decree issued by King Cheldebert at Cologne, either in 593 or 594, on the subject: moreoever, everybody knows that the famous 'Ordonance de Blois,' of May 1579, formally enacted that any persons convicted of having suborned any son or daughter under the age of twenty-five years, whether under promise of marriage or otherwise, without the full knowledge, will, or consent of the father, mother, and guardians, should be punished with death; and the ordinance adds: 'Et pareillement seront punis extraordinairement tous ceux qui auront participe audit rapt, et qui auront prete conseil, confort, et aide en aucune maniere que ce soit.' (And in like manner shall be extraordinarily punished all persons whomsoever, who shall have participated in the said abduction, and who shall have given thereunto counsel, succor, or aid in any manner whatsoever.) Those are the exact, or very nearly the exact, terms of the ordinance. As for that article of the Code-Napoleon which you have just told me of, and which excepts from liability to prosecution the abductor who marries the young girl abducted by him, it reminds me that according to the laws of Bretagne, forcible abduction, followed by marriage, was not punished. But this usage, which involved various abuses, was suppressed in 1720 — at least I give you the date within ten years. My memory is not very good now, and the time is long passed when I could repeat by heart without even stopping to take breath, fifteen hundred verses of Girart de Rousillon.

"As far as regards the Capitulary of Charlemagne, which fixes the compensation for abduction, I have not mentioned it because I am sure that you must remember it. So, my dear Monsieur de Gabry, you see abduction was considered as decidedly a punishable offense under the three dynasties of Old France. It is a very great mistake to suppose that the Middle Ages represent a period of social chaos. You must remember, on the contrary — -"

Monsieur de Gabry here interrupted me:

"So," he exclaimed, "you know of the Ordonnacne de Blois, you know Baluze, you know Childebert, you know the Capitularies — and you don't know anything about the Code-Napoleon!"

I replied that, as a matter of fact, I never had read the Code; and he looked very much surprised.

"And now do you understand," he asked, "the extreme gravity of the action you have committed?"

173

I had not indeed been yet able to understand it fully. But little by little, with the aid of Monsieur Paul's very sensible explanations, I reached the conviction at last that I should not be judged in regard to my motives, which were innocent, but only according to my action, which was punishable. Thereupon I began to feel very despondent, and to utter divers lamentations.

"What am I to do?" I cried out, "what am I to do? Am I then irretrievably ruined? — and have I also ruined the poor child whom I wanted to save?"

Monsieur de Gabry silently filled his pipe, and lighted it so slowly that his kind broad face remained for at least three or four minutes glowing red behind the light, like a blacksmith's in the gleam of his forge-fire. Then he said,

"You want to know what to do? Why, don't do anything, my dear Monsieur Bonnard! For God's sake, and for your own sake, don't do anything at all! Your situation is bad enough as it is; don't try to meddle with it now, unless you want to create new difficulties for yourself. But you must promise me to sustain me in any action that I may take. I shall go to see Monsieur Mouche the very first thing to-morrow morning; and if he turns out to be what I think he is — that is to say, a consummate rascal — I shall very soon find means of making him harmless, even if the devil himself should take sides with him. For everything depends on him. As it is too late this evening to take Mademoiselle Jeanne back to her boarding-school, my wife will keep the young lady here to-night. This of course plainly constitues the misdemeanour of complicity; but it saves the girl from anything like an equivocal position. As for you, my dear Monsieur, you just go back to the Quai Malaquais as quickly as you can; and if they come to look for Jeanne there, it will be very easy for you to prove she is not in your house."

While we were thus talking, Madame de Gabry was preparing to make her young lodger comfortable for the night. When she bade me good-bye at the door, she was carrying a pair of clean sheets, scented with lavender, thrown over her arm.

"That," I said, "is a sweet honest smell."

"Well, of course," answered Madame de Gabry, "you must remember we are peasants."

"Ah!" I answered her, "heaven grant that I also may be able one of these days ti becine a peasant! Heaven grant that one of these days I may be able, as you are at Lusance, to inhale the sweet fresh odour of the country, and live in some little house all hidden among trees; and if this wish of mine be too ambitious on the part of an old man whose life is nearly closed, then I will only wish that my winding-sheet may be as sweetly scented with lavender as that linen you have on your arm."

It was agreed that I should come to lunch the following morning. But I was positively forbidden to show myself at the house before midday. Jeanne, as she kissed me good-bye, begged me not to take her back to the school any more. We felt much affected at parting, and very anxious.

I found Therese waiting for me on the landing, in such a condition of worry about me that it had made her furious. She talked of nothing less than keeping me under lock and key in the future.

What a night I passed! I never closed my eyes for one single instant. From time to time I could not help laughing like a boy at the success of my prank; and then again, an inexpressible feeling of horror would come upon me at the thought of being dragged before some magistrate, and having to take my place upon the prisoner's bench, to answer for the crime which I had so naturally committed. I was very much afraid; and nevertheless I felt no remorse or regret whatever. The sun, coming into my room at last, merrily lighted upon the foot of my bed, and then I made this prayer:

"My God, Thou who didst make the sky and the dew, as it is said in 'Tristan,' judge me in Thine equity, not indeed according unto my acts, but according only to my motives, which Thou knowest have been upright and pure; and I will say: Glory to Thee in heaven, and peace on earth to men of good-will. I give into Thy hands the child I stole away. Do that for her which I have not known how to do; guard for her from all her enemies; — and blessed for ever be Thy name!"

December 29.

When I arrived at Madame de Gabry's, I found Jeanne completely transfigured.

Had she also, like myself, at the very first light of dawn, called upon Him who made the sky and the dew? She smiled with such a sweet calm smile!

Madame de Gabry called her away to arrange her hair for the amiable lady had insisted upon combing and plaiting, with her own hands, the hair of the child confided to her care. As I had come a little before the hour agreed upon, I had interrupted this charming toilet. By way of punishment I was told to go and wait in the parlour all by myself. Monsieur de Gabry joined me there in a little while. He had evidently just come in, for I could see on his forehead the mark left my the lining of his hat. His frank face wore an expression of joyful excitement. I thought I had better not ask him any questions; and we all went to lunch. When the servants had finished waiting at table, Monsieur Paul, who had been keeping his good story for the dessert, said to us,

"Well! I went to Levallois."

"Did you see Maitre Mouche?" excitedly inquired Madame de Gabry.

"No," he replied, curiously watching the expression of disappointment upon our faces.

After having amused himself with our anxiety for a reasonable time, the good fellow added:

"Maitre Mouche is no longer at Levallois. Maitre Mouche has gone away from France. The day after to-morrow will make just eight days since he decamped, taking with him all the money of his clients — a tolerably large sum. I found the office closed. A woman who lived close by told me all about it with an abundance of curses and imprecations. The notary did not take the 7:55 train all by himself; he took with him the daughter of the hairdresser of Levallois, a young person quite famous in that part

176

of the country for her beauty and her accomplishments; — they say she could shave better than her father. Well, anyhow Mouche has run away with her; the Commissaire de Police confirmed the fact for me. Now, really, could it have been possible for Maitre Mouche to have left the country at a more opportune moment? If he had only deferred his escapade one week longer, he would have been still the representative of society, and would have had you dragged off to gaol, Monsieur Bonnard, like a criminal. At present we have nothing whatever to fear from him. Here is to the health of Maitre Mouche!" he cried, pouring out a glass of white wine.

I would like to live a long time if it were only to remember that delightful morning. We four were all assembled in the big white dining-room around the waxed oak table. Monsieur Paul's mirth was' of the hearty kind, — even perhaps a little riotous; and the good man quaffed deeply. Madame de Gabry smiled at me, with a smile so sweet, so perfect, and so noble, that I thought such a woman ought to keep smiles like that simply as a reward for good actions, and thus make everybody who knew her do all the good of which they were capable. Then, to reward us for our pains, Jeanne, who had regained something of her former vivacity, asked us in less than a quarter of an hour one dozen questions, to answer which would have required an exhaustive exposition on the nature of man, the nature of the universe, the science of physics and of metaphysics, the Macrocosm and the Microcosm — not to speak of the Ineffable and the Unknowable. Then she drew out of her pocket her little Saint-George, who had suffered most cruelly during our flight. His legs and arms were gone; but he still had his gold helmet with the green dragon on it. Jeanne solemnly pledged herself to make a restoration of him in honour of Madame de Gabry.

Delightful friends! I left them at last overwhelmed with fatigue and joy.

On re-entering my lodgings I had to endure the very sharpest remonstrances from Therese, who said she had given up trying to understand my new way of living. In her opinion Monsieur had really lost his mind.

"Yes, Therese, I am a mad old man and you are a mad old woman. That is certain! May the good God bless us both, Therese, and give us new strength; for we now have new duties to perform. but let me lie down upon the sofa; for I really cannot keep myself on my feet any longer."

January 15, 186-.

"Good-morning, Monsieur," said Jeanne, letting herself in; while Therese remained grumbling in the corridor because she had not been able to get to the door in time.

"Mademoiselle, I beg you will be kind enough to address me very solemnly by my title, and to say to me, 'Good-morning, my guardian.'"

"Then it has all been settled? Oh, how nice!" cried the child, clapping her hands.

"It has all been arranged, Mademoiselle, in the Salle-commune and before the Justice of the Peace; and from to-day you are under my authority.... What are you laughing about, my ward? I see it in your eyes. You have some crazy idea in your head this very moment — some more nonsense, eh?"

"Oh, no! Monsieur.... I mean, my guardian. I was looking at your white hair. It curls out from under the edge of your hat like honeysuckle on a balcony. It is very handsome, and I like it very much!"

"Be good enough to sit down, my ward, and, if you can possibly help it, stop saying ridiculous things, because I have some very serious things to say to you. Listen. I suppose you are not going to insist upon being sent back to the establishment of Mademoiselle Prefere?... No. Well, then, what would you say if I should take you here to live with me, and to finish your education, and keep you here until...what shall I say? — for ever, as the song has it?"

"Oh, Monsieur!" she cried, flushing crimson with pleasure.

I continued,

"Behind there we have a nice little room, which my housekeeper has cleaned up and furnished for you. You are going

178

to take the place of the books which used to be in it; you will succeed them as the day succeeds night. Go with Therese and look at it, and see if you think you will be able to live in it. Madame de Gabry and I have made up our minds that you can sleep there to-night."

She had already started to run; I called her back for a moment.

"Jeanne, listen to me a moment longer! You have always until now made yourself a favourite with my housekeeper, who, like all very old people, is apt to be cross at times. Be gentle and forebearing. Make every allowance for her. I have thought it my duty to make every allowance for her myself, and to put up with all her fits of impatience. Now, let me tell you, Jeanne: — Respect her! And when I say that, I do not forget that she is my servant and yours; neither will she ever allow herself to forget it for a moment. But what I want you to respect in her is her great age and her great heart. She is a humble woman who has lived a very, very long time in the habit of doing good; and she has become hardened and stiffened in that habit. Bear patiently with the harsh ways of that upright soul. If you know how to command, she will know how to obey. Go now, my child; arrange your room in whatever way may seem to you best suited for your studies and for your repose."

Having started Jeanne, with this viaticum, upon her domestic career, I began to read a Review, which, although conducted by very young men, is excellent. The tone of it is somewhat unpolished, but the spirit is zealous. The article I read was certainly far superior, in point of precision and positiveness, to anything of the sort ever written when I was a young man. The author of the article, Monsieur Paul Meyer, points out every error with a remarkably lucid power of incisive criticism.

We used not in my time to criticise with such strict justice. Our indulgence was vast. It went even so far as to confuse the scholar and the ignoramus in the same burst of praise. And nevertheless one must learn how to find fault; and it is even an imperative duty to blame when the blame is deserved.

I remember little Raymond (that was the name we gave him); he did not know anything, and his mind was not a mind capable of absorbing any solid learning; but he was very fond of his mother. We took very good care never to utter a hint of the ignorance of so perfect a son; and, thanks, to our forbearance, little Raymond made his way to the highest positions. He had lost his mother then; but honours of all kinds were showered upon him. He became omnipotent — to the grievous injury of his colleagues and of science.... But here comes my young fiend of the Luxembourg.

"Good-evening, Gelis. You look very happy to-day. What good fortune has come to you, my dear lad?"

His good fortune is that he has been able to sustain his thesis very credibly, and that he has taken high rank in his class. He tells me this with the additional information that my own words, which were incidentally referred to in the course of the examination, had been spoken of by the college professors in terms of the most unqualified praise.

"That is very nice," I replied; "and it makes me very happy, Gelis, to find my old reputation thus associated with your own youthful honours. I was very much interested, you know, in that thesis of yours; — but some domestic arrangements have been keeping me so busy lately that I quite forgot this was the day on which you were to sustain it."

Mademoiselle Jeanne made her appearance very opportunely, as if in order to suggest to him something about the nature of those very domestic arrangements. The giddy girl burst into the City of Books like a fresh breeze, crying at the top of her voice that her room was a perfect little wonder. then she became very red indeed on seeing Monsieur Gelis there. But none of us can escape our destiny.

Monsieur Gelis asked her how she was with the tone of a young fellow who resumes upon a previous acquaintance, and who proposes to put himself forward as an old friend. Oh, never fear! — she had not forgotten him at all; that was very evident from the fact that then and there, right under my nose, they resumed their last year's conversation on the subject of the "Venetian blond"! They continued the discussion after quite an animated fashion. I began to ask myself what right I had to be in the room at all. The only thing I could do in order to make myself heard was to cough. As for getting in a word, they never even gave me a chance. Gelis discoursed enthusiastically, not only about the Venetian colourists, but also upon all other matters relating to nature or to mankind. And Jeanne kept answering him, "Yes, Monsieur, you are right.".... "That is just what I supposed, Monsieur.".... "Monsieur, you express so beautifully just what I feel."... "I am going to think a great deal about what you have just told me, Monsieur."

When I speak, Mademoiselle never answers me in that tone. It is only with the very tip of her tongue that she will even taste any intellectual food which I set before her. Usually she will not touch it at all. But Monsieur Gelis seems to be in her opinion the supreme authority upon all subjects. It was always, "Oh, yes!" — "Oh, of course!" — to all his empty chatter. And, then, the eyes of Jeanne! I had never seen them look so large before; I had never before observed in them such fixity of expression; but her gaze otherwise remained what it always is — artless, frank, and brave. Gelis evidently pleased her; she like Gelis, and her eyes betrayed the fact. They would have published it to the entire universe! All very fine, Master Bonnard! — you have been so deeply interested in observing your ward, that you have been forgetting you are her guardian! You began only this morning to exercise that function; and you can already see that it involves some very delicate and difficult duties. Bonnard, you must really try to devise some means of keeping that young man away from her; you really ought.... Eh! how am I to know what I am to do?...

I have picked up a book at random from the nearest shelf; I open it, and I enter respectfully into the middle of a drama of Sophocles. the older I grow, the more I learn to love the two civilisations of the antique world; and now I always keep the poets of Italy and of Greece on a shelf within easy reach of my arm in the City of Books.

Monsieur and Mademoiselle finally condescend to take some notice of me, now that I seem too busy to take any notice of them. I really think that Mademoiselle Jeanne has even asked me what I am reading. No, indeed, I will not tell her what it is. what I am reading, between ourselves, is the change of that smooth and luminous Chorus which rolls out its magnificent tunefulness through a scene of passionate violence — the Chorus of the Old Men of Thebes — 'Erws avixate...' "Invincible Love, O thou who descendest upon rich houses, — Thou who dost rest upon the delicate cheek of the maiden, — Thou who dost traverse all seas, — surely none among the Immortals can escape Thee, nor indeed any among men who live but for a little space; and he who is possessed by Thee, there is a madness upon him." And when I had re-read that delicious chant, the face of Antigone appeared before me in all its passionless purity. What images! Gods and goddesses who hover in the highest heights of Heaven! The blind old man, the long-wandering beggar-king, led by Antigone, has now been buried with holy rites; and his daughter, fair as the fairest dream ever conceived by human soul, resists the will of the tyrant and gives pious sepulture to her brother. She loves the son of the tyrant, and that son loves her also. And as she goes on her way to execution, the victim of her own sweet piety, the old men sing, "Invincible Love, O Thou who dost descend upon rich houses, — Thou who dost rest upon the delicate cheek of the maiden."...

"Mademoiselle Jeanne, are you really very anxious to know what I am reading? I am reading, Mademoiselle — I am reading that Antigone, having buried the blind old man, wove a fair tapestry embroidered with images in the likeness of laughing faces."

"Ah!" said Gelis, as he burs out laughing "that is not in the text."

"It is a scholium," I said.

"Unpublished," he added, getting up.

I am not an egotist. But I am prudent. I have to bring up this child; she is much too young to be married now. No! I am not an egotist, but I must certainly keep her with me for a few years more — keep her alone with me. She can surely wait until I am dead! Fear not, Antigone, old Oedipus will find holy burial soon enough.

In the meanwhile, Antigone is helping our housekeeper to scrape the carrots. She says she like to do it — that it is in her line, being related to the art of sculpture.

May.

Who would recognise the City of Books now? There are flowers everywhere — even upon all the articles of furniture. Jeanne was right: those roses do look very nice in that blue china vase. She goes to market every day with Therese, under the pretext of helping the old servant to make her purchases, but she never brings anything back with her except flowers. Flowers are really very charming creatures. And one of these days, I must certainly carry out my plan, and devote myself to the study of them, in their own natural domain, in the country — with all the science and earnestness which I possess.

For what have I to do here? Why should I burn my eyes out over these old parchments which cannot now tell me anything worth knowing? I used to study them, these old texts, with the most ardent enjoyment. What was it which I was then so anxious to find in them? The date of a pious foundation — the name of some monkish imagier or copyist — the price of a loaf, of an ox, or of a field — some judicial or administrative enactment — all that, and yet something more, a Something vaguely mysterious and sublime which excited my enthusiasm. But for sixty years I have been searching in vain for that Something. Better men than I — the masters, the truly great, the Fauriels, the Thierrys, who found so many things — died at their task without having been able, any more than I have been, to find that Something which, being incorporeal, has no name, and without which, nevertheless, no great mental work would ever be undertaken in this world. And now that I am only looking for what I should certainly be able to find, I cannot find anything at all; and it is probable that I shall never be able to finish the history of the Abbots of Saint-Germain-des-Pres.

"Guardian, just guess what I have in my handkerchief,"

"Judging from appearances, Jeanne, I should say flowers."

"Oh, no — not flowers. Look!"

I look, and I see a little grey head poking itself out of the handkerchief. It is the head of a little grey cat. The handkerchief opens; the animal leaps down upon the carpet, shakes itself, pricks up first one ear and then the other, and begins to examine with due caution the locality and the inhabitants thereof.

Therese, out of breath, with her basket on her arm, suddenly makes her appearance in time to take an objective part in this examination, which does not appear to result altogether in her favour; for the young cat moves slowly away from her, without, however, venturing near my legs, or approaching Jeanne, who displays extraordinary volubility in the use of caressing appellations. Therese, whose chief fault is her inability to hide her feelings, thereupon vehemently reproaches Mademoiselle for bringing home a cat that she did not know anything about. Jeanne, in order to justify herself, tells the whole story. While she was passing with Therese before a chemist's shop, she saw the assistant kick a little cat into the street. The cat, astonished and frightened, seemed to be asking itself whether to remain in the street where it was being terrified and knocked about by the people passing by, or whether to go back into the chemist's even at the risk of being kicked out a second time. Jeanne thought it was in a very critical position, and understood its hesitation. It looked so stupid; and she knew it looked stupid only because it could not decide what to do. So she took it up in her arms. And as it had not been able to obtain any rest either indoors out out-of-doors, it allowed her to hold it. Then she stroked and petted it to keep it from being afraid, and boldly went to the chemist's assistant and said,

"If you don't like that animal, you mustn't beat it; you must give it to me."

"Take it," said the assistant.

..."Now there!" adds Jeanne, by way of conclusion; and then she changes her voice again to a flute-tone in order to say all kinds of sweet things to the cat.

"He is horribly thin," I observe, looking at the wretched animal; — "moreover, he is horribly ugly." Jeanne thinks he is not ugly at all, but she acknowledges that he looks even more stupid than he looked at first: this time she thinks it not indecision, but surprise, which gives that unfortunate aspect to his countenance. She asks us to imagine ourselves in his place; — then we are obliged to acknowledge that he cannot possibly understand what has happened to him. And then we all burst out laughing in the face of the poor little beast, which maintains the most comical look of gravity. Jeanne wants to take him up; but he hides himself under the table, and cannot even be tempted to come out by the lure of a saucer of milk.

We all turn our backs and promise not to look; when we inspect the saucer again, we find it empty.

"Jeanne," I observe, "your protege has a decidedly tristful aspect of countenance; he is of sly and suspicious disposition; I trust he is not going to commit in the City of Books any such misdemeanours as might render it necessary for us to send him back to his chemist's shop. In the meantime we must give him a name. Suppose we call him 'Don Gris de Gouttiere'; but perhaps that is too long. 'Pill,' 'Drug,' or 'Castor-oil' would be short enough, and would further serve to recall his early condition in life. What do you think about it?

"'Pill' would not sound bad," answers Jeanne, "but it would be very unkind to give him a name which would be always reminding him of the misery from which we saved him. It would be making him pay too dearly for our hospitality. Let us be more generous, and give him a pretty name, in hopes that he is going to deserve it. See how he looks at us! He knows that we are talking about him. And now that he is no longer unhappy, he is beginning to look a great deal less stupid. I am not joking! Unhappiness does make people look stupid, — I am perfectly sure it does."

"Well, Jeanne, if you like, we will call your protege Hannibal. The appropriateness of that name does not seem to strike you at once. But the Angora cat who preceded him here as an intimate of the City of Books, and to whom I was in the habit of telling all my secrets — for he was a very wise and discreet person — used to be called Hamilcar. It is natural that this name should beget the other, and that Hannibal should succeed Hamilcar."

We all agreed upon this point.

"Hannibal!" cried Jeanne, "come here!"

Hannibal, greatly frightened by the strange sonority of his own name, ran to hid himself under a bookcase in an orifice so small that a rat could not have squeezed himself into it.

A nice way of doing credit to so great a name!

I was in a good humour for working that day, and I had just dipped the nib of my pen into the ink-bottle when I heard some one ring. Should any one ever read these pages written by an unimaginative old man, he will be sure to laugh at the way that bell keeps ringing through my narrative, without ever announcing the arrival of a new personage or introducing any unexpected incident. On the stage things are managed on the reverse principle. Monsieur Scribe never has the curtain raised without good reason, and for the greater enjoyment of ladies and young misses. That is art! I would rather hang myself than write a play, — not that I despise life, but because I should never be able to invent anything amusing. Invent! In order to do that one must have received the gift of inspiration. It would be a very unfortunate thing for me to possess such a gift. Suppose I were to invent some monkling in my history of the Abbey of Saint-Germain-des-Pres! What would our young erudites say? What a scandal for the School! As for the Institute, it would say nothing and probably not even think about the matter either. Even if my colleagues still write a little sometimes, they never read. They are of the opinion of Parny, who said,

"Une paisible indifference
Est la plus sage des vertus."

186

["The most wise of the virtues is a calm indifference."]

To be the least wise in order to become the most wise — this is precisely what those Buddhists are aiming at without knowing it. If there is any wiser wisdom than that I will go to Rome to report upon it.... And all this because Monsieur Gelis happened to ring the bell!

This young man has latterly changed his manner completely with Jeanne. He is now quite as serious as he used to be frivolous, and quite as silent as he used to be chatty. And Jeanne follows his example. We have reached the phase of passionate love under constraint. For, old as I am, I cannot be deceived about it: these two children are violently and sincerely in love with each other. Jeanne now avoids him — she hides herself in her room when he comes into the library — but how well she knows how to reach him when she is alone! alone at her piano! Every evening she talks to him through the music she plays with a rich thrill of passional feeling which is the new utterance of her new soul.

Well, why should I not confess it? Why should I not avow my weakness? Surely my egotism would not become any less blameworthy by keeping it hidden from myself? So I will write it. Yes! I was hoping for something else; — yes! I thought I was going to keep her all to myself, as my own child, as my own daughter — not always, of course, not even perhaps for very long, but just for a few short years more. I am so old! Could she not wait? And, who knows? With the help of the gout, I would not have imposed upon her patience too much. That was my wish; that was my hope. I had made my plans — I had not reckoned upon the coming of this wild young man. But the mistake is none the less cruel because my reckoning happened to be wrong. And yet it seems to me that you are condemning yourself very rashly, friend Sylvestre Bonnard: if you did want to keep this young girl a few years longer, it was quite as much in her own interest as in yours. She has a great deal to learn yet, and you are not a master to be despised. When that miserable notary Mouche — who subsequently committed his rascalities at so opportune a moment — paid you the honour of a visit, you explained to him your ideas of education with all the fervour of high enthusiasm. Then you attempted to put that system of yours into practice; — Jeanne is certainly an ungrateful girl, and Gelis a much too seductive young man!

But still, — unless I put him out of the house, which would be a detestably ill-mannered and ill-natured thing to do, — I must continue to receive him. He has been waiting ever so long in my little parlour, in front of those Sevres vases with which King Louis Philippe so graciously presented me. The Moissonneurs and the Pecheurs of Leopold Robert are painted upon those porcelain vases, which Gelis nevertheless dares to call frightfully ugly, with the warm approval of Jeanne, whom he has absolutely bewitched.

"My dear lad, excuse me for having kept you waiting so long. I had a little bit of work to finish."

I am telling the truth. Meditation is work, but of course Gelis does not know what I mean; he thinks I am referring to something archaeological, and, his question in regard to the health of Mademoiselle Jeanne having been answered by a "Very well indeed," uttered in that extremely dry tone which reveals my moral authority as guardian, we begin to converse about historical subjects. We first enter upon generalities. Generalities are sometimes extremely serviceable. I try to inculcate into Monsieur Gelis some respect for that generation of historians to which I belong. I say to him,

"History, which was formerly an art, and which afforded place for the fullest exercise of the imagination, has in our time become a science, the study of which demands absolute exactness of knowledge."

Gelis asks leave to differ from me on this subject. He tells me he does not believe that history is a science, or that it could possibly ever become a science.

"In the first place," he says to me, "what is history? The written representation of past events. But what is an event? Is it merely a commonplace fact? It is any fact? No! You say yourself it is a noteworthy fact. Now, how is the historian to tell whether a fact is noteworthy or not? He judges it arbitrarily, according to his tastes and his caprices and his ideas — in short, as an artist? For facts cannot by reason of their own intrinsic character be divided into historical facts and non-historical facts. But any fact is something exceedingly complex. Will the historian represent facts in all their complexity? No, that is impossible. Then he will represent them stripped of the greater part of the peculiarities which constituted them, and consequently lopped, mutilated, different from what they really were. As for the inter-relation of facts, needless to speak of it! If a so-called historical fact be brought into notice — as is very possible — by one or more facts which are not historical at all, and are for that very reason unknown, how is the historian going to establish the relation of these facts one to another? And in saying this, Monsieur Bonnard, I am supposing that the historian has positive evidence before him, whereas in reality he feels confidence only in such or such a witness for sympathetic reasons. History is not a science; it is an art, and one can succeed in that art only through the exercise of his faculty of imagination."

Monsieur Gelis reminds me very much at this moment of a certain young fool whom I heard talking wildly one day in the garden of the Luxembourg, under the statue of Marguerite of Navarre. But at another turn of the conversation we find ourselves face to face with Walter Scott, whose work my disdainful young friend pleases to term "rococo, troubadourish, and only fit to inspire somebody engaged in making designs for cheap bronze clocks." Those are his very words!

"Why!" I exclaim, zealous to defend the magnificent creator of 'The Bride of Lammermoor' and 'The Fair Maid of Perth,' "the whole past lives in those admirable novels of his; — that is history, that is epic!"

"It is frippery," Gelis answers me.

And, — will you believe it? — this crazy boy actually tells me that no matter how learned one may be, one cannot possibly know just how men used to live five or ten centuries ago, because it is only with the very greatest difficulty that one can picture them to oneself even as they were only ten or fifteen years ago. In his opinion, the historical poem, the historical novel, the historical painting, are all, according to their kind, abominably false as branches of art.

"In all the arts," he adds, "the artist can only reflect his own soul. His work, no matter how it may be dressed up, is of necessity contemporary with himself, being the reflection of his own mind. What do we admire in the 'Divine Comedy' unless it be the great soul of Dante? And the marbles of Michael Angelo, what do they represent to us that is at all extraordinary unless it be Michael Angelo himself? The artist either communicates his own life to his creations, or else merely whittles out puppets and dresses up dolls."

What a torrent of paradoxes and irreverences! But boldness in a young man is not displeasing to me. Gelis gets up from his chair and sits down again. I know perfectly well what is worrying him, and whom he is waiting for. And now he begins to talk to me about his being able to make fifteen hundred francs a year, to which he can add the revenue he derives from a little property that he has inherited — two thousand francs a year more. And I am not in the least deceived as to the purpose of these confidences on his part. I know perfectly well that he is only making his little financial statements in order to persuade me that he is comfortably circumstanced, steady, fond of home, comparatively independent — or, to put the matter in the fewest words possible, able to marry. Quod erat demonstrandum, — as the geometricians say.

He has got up and sat down just twenty times. He now rises for the twenty-first time; and, as he has not been able to see Jeanne, he goes away feeling as unhappy as possible.

The moment he has gone, Jeanne comes into the City of Books, under the pretext of looking for Hannibal. She is also quite unhappy; and her voice becomes singularly plaintive as she calls her pet to give him some milk. Look at that sad little face, Bonnard! Tyrant, gaze upon thy work! Thou hast been able to keep them from seeing each other; but they have now both of them the same expression of countenance, and thou mayest discern from that similarity of expression that in spite of thee they are united in thought. Cassandra, be happy! Bartholo, rejoice! This is what it means to be a guardian! Just see her kneeling down there on the carpet with Hannibal's head between her hands!

Yes, caress the stupid animal! — pity him! — moan over him! — we know very well, you little rogue, the real cause of all these sighs and plaints! Nevertheless, it makes a very pretty picture. I look at it for a long time; then, throwing a glance around my library, I exclaim,

"Jeanne, I am tired of all those books; we must sell them."

September 20.

It is done! — they are betrothed. Gelis, who is an orphan, as Jeanne is, did not make his proposal to me in person. He got one of his professors, an old colleague of mine, highly esteemed for his learning and character, to come to me on his behalf. But what a love messenger! Great Heavens! A bear — neat a bear of the Pyrenees, but a literary bear, and this latter variety of bear is much more ferocious than the former.

"Right or wrong (in my opinion wrong) Gelis says that he does not want any dowry; he takes your ward with nothing but her chemise. Say yes, and the thing is settled! Make haste about it! I want to show you two or three very curious old tokens from Lorraine which I am sure you never saw before."

That is literally what he said to me. I answered him that I would consult Jeanne, and I found no small pleasure in telling him that my ward had a dowry.

Her dowry — there it is in front of me! It is my library. Henri and Jeanne have not even the faintest suspicion about it; and the fact is I am commonly believed to be much richer than I am. I have the face of an old miser. It is certainly a lying face; but its untruthfulness has often won for me a great deal of consideration. There is nobody so much respected in this world as a stingy rich man.

I have consulted Jeanne, — but what was the need of listening for her answer? It is done! They are betrothed.

It would ill become my character as well as my face to watch these young people any longer for the mere purpose of noting down their words and gestures. Noli me tangere: — that is the maxim for all charming love affairs. I know my duty. It is to respect all the little secrets of that innocent soul intrusted to me. Let these children love each other all they can! Never a word of their fervent outpouring of mutual confidences, never a hint of their artless self-betrayals, will be set down in this diary by the old guardian whose authority was so gentle and so brief.

At all events, I am not going to remain with my arms folded; and if they have their business to attend to, I have mine also. I am preparing a catalogue of my books, with a view to having them all sold at auction. It is a task which saddens and amuses me at the same time. I linger over it, perhaps a good deal longer than I ought to do; turning the leaves of all those works which have become so familiar to my thought, to my touch, to my sight — even out of all necessity and reason. But it is a farewell; and it has ever been in the nature of man to prolong a farewell.

This ponderous volume here, which has served me so much for thirty long years, how can I leave it without according it every kindness that a faithful servant deserves? And this one again, which has so often consoled me by its wholesome doctrines, must I not bow down before it for the last time, as to a Master? But each time that I meet with a volume which led me into error, which ever afflicted me with false dates, omissions, lies, and other plagues of the archaeologist, I say to it with bitter joy: "Go! imposter, traitor, false-witness! flee thou far away from me for ever; — vade retro! all absurdly covered with gold as thou art! and I pray it may befall thee — thanks to thy usurped reputation and thy comely morocco attire — to take thy place in the cabinet of some banker-bibliomaniac, whom thou wilt never be able to seduce as thou has seduced me, because he will never read one single line of thee."

I laid aside some books I must always keep — those books which were given to me as souvenirs. As I placed among them the manuscript of the "Golden Legend," I could not but kiss it in memory of Madame Trepof, who remained grateful to me in spite of her high position and all her wealth, and who became my benefactress merely to prove to me that she felt I had once done her a kindness.... Thus I had made a reserve. It was then that, for the first time, I felt myself inclined to commit a deliberate crime. All through that night I was strongly tempted; by morning the temptation had become irresistible. Everybody else in the house was still asleep. I got out of bed and stole softly from my room.

Ye powers of darkness! ye phantoms of the night! if while lingering within my home after the crowing of the cock, you saw me stealing about on tiptoe in the City of Books, you certainly never cried out, as Madame Trepof did at Naples, "That old man has a good-natured round back!" I entered the library; Hannibal, with his tail perpendicularly erected, came to rub himself against my legs and purr. I seized a volume from its shelf, some venerable Gothic text or some noble poet of the Renaissance — the jewel, the treasure which I had been dreaming about all night, I seized it and slipped it away into the very bottom of the closet which I had reserved for those books I intended to retain, and which soon became full almost to bursting. It is horrible to relate: I was stealing from the dowry of Jeanne! And when the crime had been consummated I set myself again sturdily to the task of cataloguing, until Jeanne came to consult me in regard to something about a dress or a trousseau. I could not possibly understand just what she was talking about, through my total ignorance of the current vocabulary of dress-making and linen-drapery. Ah! if a bride of the fourteenth century had come to talk to me about the apparel of her epoch, then, indeed, I should have been able to understand her language! But Jeanne does not belong to my time, and I have to send her to Madame de Gabry, who on this important occasion will take the place of her mother.

...Night has come! Leaning from the window, we gaze at the vast sombre stretch of the city below us, pierced with multitudinous points of light. Jeanne presses her hand to her forehead as she leans upon the window-bar, and seems a little sad. And I say to myself as I watch her: All changes even the most longed for, have their melancholy; for what we leave behind us is a part of ourselves: we must die to one life before we can enter into another!

And as if answering my thought, the young girl murmurs to me,

"My guardian, I am so happy; and still I feel as if I wanted to cry!"

The Last Page

August 21, 1869.

Page eighty-seven.... Only twenty lines more and I shall have finished my book about insects and flowers. Page eighty-seventh and last.... "As we have already seen, the visits of insects are of the utmost importance to plants; since their duty is to carry to the pistils the pollen of the stamens. It seems also that the flower itself is arranged and made attractive for the purpose of inviting this nuptial visit. I think I have been able to show that the nectary of the plant distils a sugary liquid which attracts the insects and obliges it to aid unconsciously in the work of direct or cross fertilisation. The last method of fertilisation is the more common. I have shown that flowers are coloured and perfumed so as to attract insects, and interiorly so constructed as to offer those visitors such a mode of access that they cannot penetrate into the corolla without depositing upon the stigma the pollen with which they have been covered. My most venerated master Sprengel observes in regard to that fine down which lines the corolla of the wood-geranium: 'The wise Author of Nature has never created a single useless hair!' I say in my turn: If that Lily of the Valley whereof the Gospel makes mention is more richly clad than King Solomon in all his glory, its mantle of purple is a wedding-garment, and that rich apparel is necessary to the perpetuation of the species."

"Brolles, August 21, 1869."

Brolles! My house is the last one you pass in the single street of the village, as you go to the woods. It is a gabled house with a slate roof, which takes iridescent tints in the sun like a pigeon's breast. The weather-vane above that roof has won more consideration for me among the country people than all my works upon history and philology. There is not a single child who does not know Monsieur Bonnard's weather-vane. It is rusty, and squeaks very sharply in the wind. Sometimes it refuses to do any work at all — just like Therese, who now allows herself to be assisted by a young peasant girl — though she grumbles a good deal about it. The house is not large, but I am very comfortable in it. My room has two windows, and gets the sun in the morning. The children's room is upstairs. Jeanne and Henri come twice a year to occupy it.

Little Sylvestre's cradle used to be in it. He was a very pretty child, but very pale. When he used to play on the grass, his mother would watch him very anxiously; and every little while she would stop her seweing in order to take him upon her lap. The poor little fellow never wanted to go to sleep. He used to say that when he was asleep he would go away, very far away, to some place where it was all dark, and where he saw things that made him afraid — things he never wanted to see again.

Then his mother would call me, and I would sit down beside his cradle. He would take one of my fingers in his little dry warm hand, and say to me,

"Godfather, you must tell me a story."

Then I would tell him all kinds of stories, which he would listen to very seriously. They all interested him, but there was one especially which filled his little soul with delight. It was "The Blue Bird." Whenever I finished that, he would say to me, "Tell it again! tell it again!" And I would tell it again until his little pale blue-veined head sank back upon the pillow in slumber.

The doctor used to answer all our questions by saying,

"There is nothing extraordinary the matter with him!"

No! There was nothing extraordinary the matter with little Sylvestre. One evening last year his father called me.

"Come," he said, "the little one is still worse."

I approached the cradle over which the mother hung motionless, as if tied down above it by all the powers of her soul.

Little Sylvestre turned his eyes towards me; their pupils had already rolled up beneath his eyelids, and could not descend again.

"Godfather," he said, "you are not to tell me any more stories."

No, I was not to tell him any more stories!

Poor Jeanne! — poor mother!

I am too old now to feel very deeply; but how strangely painful a mystery is the death of a child!

To-day, the father and mother have come to pass six weeks under the old man's roof. I see them now returning from the woods, walking arm-in-arm. Jeanne is closely wrapped in her black shawl, and Henri wears a crape band on his straw hat; but they are both of them radiant with youth, and they smile very sweetly at each other. They smile at the earth which sustains them; they smile at the air which bathes them; they smile at the light which each one sees in the eyes of the other. From my window I wave my handkerchief at them, — and they smile at my old age.

Jeanne comes running lightly up the stairs; she kisses me, and then whispers in my ear something which I divine rather than hear. And I make answer to her: "May God's blessing be with you, Jeanne, and with your husband, and with your children, and with your children's children for ever!"... Et nunc dimittis servum tuum, Domine!

THAIS

Translated By Robert B. Douglas

PART THE FIRST — THE LOTUS

In those days there were many hermits living in the desert. On both banks of the Nile numerous huts, built by these solitary dwellers, of branches held together by clay, were scattered at a little distance from each other, so that the inhabitants could live alone, and yet help one another in case of need. Churches, each surmounted by a cross, stood here and there amongst the huts, and the monks flocked to them at each festival to celebrate the services or to partake of the Communion. There were also, here and there on the banks of the river, monasteries, where the cenobites lived in separate cells, and only met together that they might the better enjoy their solitude.

Both hermits and cenobites led abstemious lives, taking no food till after sunset, and eating nothing but bread with a little salt and hyssop. Some retired into the desert, and led a still more strange life in some cave or tomb.

All lived in temperance and chastity; they wore a hair shirt and a hood, slept on the bare ground after long watching, prayed, sang psalms, and, in short, spent their days in works of penitence. As an atonement for original sin, they refused their body not only all pleasures and satisfactions, but even that care and attention which in this age are deemed indispensable. They believed that the diseases of our members purify our souls, and the flesh could put on no adornment more glorious than wounds and ulcers. Thus, they thought they fulfilled the words of the prophet, "The desert shall rejoice and blossom as the rose."

Amongst the inhabitants of the holy Thebaid, there were some who passed their days in asceticism and contemplation;

others gained their livelihood by plaiting palm fibre, or by working at harvest-time for the neighbouring farmers. The Gentiles wrongly suspected some of them of living by brigandage, and allying themselves to the nomadic Arabs who robbed the caravans. But, as a matter of fact, the monks despised riches, and the odour of their sanctity rose to heaven.

Angels in the likeness of young men, came, staff in hand, as travelers, to visit the hermitages; whilst demons — having assumed the form of Ethiopians or of animals — wandered round the habitations of the hermits in order to lead them into temptation. When the monks went in the morning to fill their pitcher at the spring, they saw the footprints of Satyrs and Aigipans in the sand. The Thebaid was, really and spiritually, a battlefield, where, at all times, and more especially at night, there were terrible conflicts between heaven and hell.

The ascetics, furiously assailed by legions of the damned, defended themselves — with the help of God and the angels — by fasting, prayer, and penance. Sometimes carnal desires pricked them so cruelly that they cried aloud with pain, and their lamentations rose to the starlit heavens mingled with the howls of the hungry hyenas. Then it was that the demons appeared in delightful forms. For though the demons are, in reality, hideous, they sometimes assume an appearance of beauty which prevents their real nature from being recognized. The ascetics of the Thebaid were amazed to see in their cells phantasms of delights unknown even to the voluptuaries of the age. But, as they were under the sign of the Cross, they did not succumb to these temptations, and the unclean spirits, assuming again their true character, fled at daybreak, filled with rage and shame. It was not unusual to meet at dawn one of these beings, flying away and weeping, and replying to those who questioned it, "I weep and groan because one of the Christians who live here has beaten me with rods, and driven me away in ignominy."

The power of the old saints of the desert extended over all sinners and unbelievers. Their goodness was sometimes terrible. They derived from the Apostles authority to punish all offences against the true and only God, and no earthly power could save those they condemned. Strange tales were told in the cities, and even as far as Alexandria, how the earth had opened and swallowed up certain wicked persons whom one of these saints struck with his staff. Therefore they were feared by all evil-doers, and particularly by mimes, mountebanks, married priests, and prostitutes.

Such was the sanctity of these holy men that even wild beasts felt their power. When a hermit was about to die, a lion came and dug a grave with its claws. The saint knew by this that God had called him, and he went and kissed all his brethren on the cheek. Then he lay down joyfully, and slept in the Lord.

Now that Anthony, who was more than a hundred years old, had retired to Mount Colzin with his well-beloved disciples, Macarius and Amathas, there was no monk in the Thebaid more renowned for good works than Paphnutius, the Abbot of Antinoe. Ephrem and Serapion had a greater number of followers, and in the spiritual and temporal management of their monasteries surpassed him. But Paphnutius observed the most rigorous fasts, and often went for three entire days without taking food. He wore a very rough hair shirt, he flogged himself night and morning, and lay for hours with his face to the earth.

His twenty-four disciples had built their huts near his, and imitated his austerities. He loved them all dearly in Jesus Christ, and unceasingly exhorted them to good works. Amongst his spiritual children were men who had been robbers for many years, and had been persuaded by the exhortations of the holy abbot to embrace the monastic life, and who now edified their companions by the purity of their lives. One, who had been cook to the Queen of Abyssinia, and was converted by the Abbot of Antinoe, never ceased to weep. There was also Flavian, the deacon, who knew the Scriptures, and spoke well; but the disciple of Paphnutius who surpassed all the others in holiness was a young peasant named Paul, and surnamed the Fool, because of his extreme simplicity. Men laughed at his childishness, but God favoured him with visions, and by bestowing upon him the gift of prophecy.

Paphnutius passed his life in teaching his disciples, and in ascetic practices. Often did he meditate upon the Holy Scriptures in order to find allegories in them. Therefore he abounded in good works, though still young. The devils, who so rudely assailed the good hermits, did not dare to approach him. At night, seven little jackals sat in the moonlight in front of his cell, silent and motionless, and with their ears pricked up. It was believed that they were seven devils, who, owing to his sanctity, could not cross his threshold.

Paphnutius was born at Alexandria of noble parents, who had instructed him in all profane learning. He had even been allured by the falsehoods of the poets, and in his early youth had been misguided enough to believe that the human race had all been drowned by a deluge in the days of Deucalion, and had argued with his fellow-scholars concerning the nature, the attributes, and even the existence of God. He then led a life of dissipation, after the manner of the Gentiles, and he recalled the memory of those days with shame and horror.

"At that time," he used to say to the brethren, "I seethed in the cauldron of false delights."

He meant by that that he had eaten food properly dressed, and frequented the public baths. In fact, until his twentieth year he had continued to lead the ordinary existence of those times, which now seemed to him rather death than life; but, owing to the lessons of the priest Macrinus, he then became a new man.

The truth penetrated him through and through, and — as he used to say — entered his soul like a sword. He embraced the faith of Calvary, and worshipped Christ crucified. After his baptism he remained yet a year amongst the Gentiles, unable to cast off the bonds of old habits. But one day he entered a church, and heard a deacon read from the Bible, the verse, "If thou wilt be perfect, go and sell that thou hast, and give to the poor." Thereupon he sold all that he had, gave away the money in alms, and embraced the monastic life.

During the ten years that he had lived remote from men, he no longer seethed in the cauldron of false delights, but more profitably macerated his flesh in the balms of penitence.

One day when, according to his pious custom, he was recalling to mind the hours he had lived apart from God, and examining his sins one by one, that he might the better ponder on their enormity, he remembered that he had seen at the theatre at Alexandria a very beautiful actress named Thais. This woman showed herself in the public games, and did not scruple to perform dances, the movements of which, arranged only too cleverly, brought to mind the most horrible passions. Sometimes she imitated the horrible deeds which the Pagan fables ascribe to Venus, Leda, or Pasiphae. Thus she fired all the spectators with lust, and when handsome young men, or rich old ones, came, inspired with love, to hang wreaths of flowers round her door, she welcomed them, and gave herself up to them. So that, whilst she lost her own soul, she also ruined the souls of many others.

She had almost led Paphnutius himself into the sins of the flesh. She had awakened desire in him, and he had once approached the house of Thais. But he stopped on the threshold of the courtesan's house, partly restrained by the natural timidity of extreme youth — he was then but fifteen years old — and partly by the fear of being refused on account of his want of money, for his parents took care that he should commit no great extravagances.

God, in His mercy, had used these two means to prevent him from committing a great sin. But Paphnutius had not been grateful to Him for that, because at that time he was blind to his own interests, and did not know that he was lusting after false delights. Now, kneeling in his cell, before the image of that holy cross on which hung, as in a balance, the ransom of the world, Paphnutius began to think of Thais, because Thais was a sin to him, and he meditated long, according to ascetic rules, on the fearful hideousness of the carnal delights with which this woman had inspired him in the days of his sin and ignorance. After some hours of meditation the image of Thais appeared to him clearly and distinctly. He saw her again, as he had seen her when she tempted him, in all the beauty of the flesh. At first she showed herself like a Leda, softly lying upon a bed of hyacinths, her head bowed, her eyes humid and filled with a strange light, her nostrils quivering, her mouth half open, her breasts like two flowers, and her arms smooth and fresh as two brooks. At this sight Paphnutius struck his breast and said —

"I call Thee to witness, my God, that I have considered how heinous has been my sin."

Gradually the face of the image changed its expression. Little by little the lips of Thais, by lowering at the corners of the mouth, expressed a mysterious suffering. Her large eyes were filled with tears and lights; her breast heaved with sighs, like the sighing of a wind that precedes a tempest. At this sight Paphnutius was troubled to the bottom of his soul. Prostrating himself on the floor, he uttered this prayer —

"Thou who hast put pity in our hearts, like the morning dew upon the fields, O just and merciful God, be Thou blessed! Praise! praise be unto Thee! Put away from Thy servant that false tenderness which tempts to concupiscence, and grant that I may only love Thy creatures in Thee, for they pass away, but Thou endurest for ever. If I care for this woman, it is only because she is Thy handiwork. The angels themselves feel pity for her. Is she not, O Lord, the breath of Thy mouth? Let her not continue to sin with many citizens and strangers. There is great pity for her in my heart. Her wickednesses are abominable, and but to think of them makes my flesh creep. But the more wicked she is, the more do I lament for her. I weep when I think that the devils will torment her to all eternity."

As he was meditating in this way, he saw a little jackal lying at his feet. He felt much surprised, for the door of his cell had been closed since the morning. The animal seemed to read the Abbot's thoughts, and wagged its tail like a dog. Paphnutius made the sign of the cross and the beast vanished. He knew then that, for the first time, the devil had entered his cell, and he uttered a short prayer; then he thought again about Thais.

"With God's help," he said to himself, "I must save her." And he slept.

The next morning, when he had said his prayers, he went to see the sainted Palemon, a holy hermit who lived some distance away. He found him smiling quietly as he dug the ground, as was his custom. Palemon was an old man, and cultivated a little garden; the wild beasts came and licked his hands, and the devils never tormented him.

"May God be praised, brother Paphnutius," he said, as he leaned upon his spade.

"God be praised!" replied Paphnutius. "And peace be unto my brother."

"The like peace be unto thee, brother Paphnutius," said Palemon; and he wiped the sweat from his forehead with his sleeve.

"Brother Palemon, all our discourse ought to be solely the praise of Him who has promised to be wheresoever two or three are gathered together in His Name. That is why I come to you concerning a design I have formed to glorify the Lord."

"May the Lord bless thy design, Paphnutius, as He has blessed my lettuces. Every morning He spreads His grace with the dew on my garden, and His goodness causes me to glorify Him in the cucumbers and melons which He gives me. Let us pray that He may keep us in His peace. For nothing is more to be feared than those unruly passions which trouble our hearts. When these passions disturb us we are like drunken men, and we stagger from right to left unceasingly, and are like to fall miserably. Sometimes these passions plunge us into a turbulent joy, and he who gives way to such, sullies the air with brutish laughter. Such false joy drags the sinner into all sorts of excess. But sometimes also the troubles of the soul and of the senses throw us into an impious sadness which is a thousand times worse than the joy. Brother Paphnutius, I am but a miserable sinner, but I have found, in my long life, that the cenobite has no foe worse than sadness. I mean by that the obstinate melancholy which envelopes the soul as in a mist, and hides from us the light of God. Nothing is more contrary to salvation, and the devil's greatest triumph is to sow black and bitter thoughts in the heart of a good man. If he sent us only pleasurable temptations, he would not be half so much to be feared. Alas! he excels in making us sad. Did he not show to our father Anthony a black child of such surpassing beauty that the very sight of it drew tears? With God's help, our father Anthony avoided the snares of the demon. I knew him when he lived amongst us; he was cheerful with his disciples, and never gave way to melancholy. But did you not come, my brother, to talk to me of a design you had formed in your mind? Let me know what it is — if, at least, this design has for its object the glory of God."

"Brother Palemon, what I propose is really to the glory of God. Strengthen me with your counsel, for you know many things, and sin has never darkened the clearness of your mind."

"Brother Paphnutius, I am not worthy to unloose the latchet of thy sandals, and my sins are as countless as the sands of the desert. But I am old, and I will never refuse the help of my experience."

"I will confide in you, then, brother Palemon, that I am stricken with grief at the thought that there is, in Alexandria, a courtesan named Thais, who lives in sin, and is a subject of reproach unto the people."

"Brother Paphnutius, that is, in truth, an abomination which we do well to deplore. There are many women amongst the Gentiles who lead lives of that kind. Have you thought of any remedy for this great evil?"

"Brother Palemon, I will go to Alexandria and find this woman, and, with God's help, I will convert her; that is my intention; do you approve of it, brother?"

"Brother Paphnutius, I am but a miserable sinner, but our father Anthony used to say, 'In whatsoever place thou art, hasten not to leave it to go elsewhere.'"

"Brother Palemon, do you disapprove of my project?"

"Dear Paphnutius, God forbid that I should suspect my brother of bad intentions. But our father Anthony also said, 'Fishes die on dry land, and so is it with those monks who leave their cells and mingle with the men of this world, amongst whom no good thing is to be found."'

Having thus spoken, the old man pressed his foot on the spade, and began to dig energetically round a fig tree laden with fruit. As he was thus engaged, there was a rustling in the bushes, and an antelope leaped over the hedge which surrounded the garden; it stopped, surprised and frightened, its delicate legs trembling, then ran up to the old man, and laid its pretty head on the breast of its friend.

"God be praised in the gazelle of the desert," said Palemon.

He went to his hut, the light-footed little animal trotting after him, and brought out some black bread, which the antelope ate out of his hand.

Paphnutius remained thoughtful for some time, his eyes fixed upon the stones at his feet. Then he slowly walked back to his cell, pondering on what he had heard. A great struggle was going on in his mind.

"The hermit gives good advice," he said to himself; "the spirit of prudence is in him. And he doubts the wisdom of my intention. Yet it would be cruel to leave Thais any longer in the power of the demon who possesses her. May God advise and conduct me."

As he was walking along, he saw a plover, caught in the net that a hunter had laid on the sand, and he knew that it was a hen bird, for he saw the male fly to the net, and tear the meshes one by one with its beak, until it had made an opening by which its mate could escape. The holy man watched this incident, and as, by virtue of his holiness, he easily comprehended the mystic sense of all occurrences, he knew that the captive bird was no other than Thais, caught in the snares of sin, and that — like the plover that had cut the hempen threads with its beak — he could, by pronouncing the word of power, break the invisible bonds by which Thais was held in sin. Therefore he praised God, and was confirmed in his first resolution. But then seeing the plover caught by the feet, and hampered by the net it had broken, he fell into uncertainty again.

He did not sleep all night, and before dawn he had a vision. Thais appeared to him again. There was no expression of guilty pleasure on her face, nor was she dressed according to custom in transparent drapery. She was enveloped in a shroud, which hid even a part of her face, so that the Abbot could see nothing but the two eyes, from which flowed white and heavy tears.

At this sight he began to weep, and believing that this vision came from God, he no longer hesitated. He rose, seized a knotted stick, the symbol of the Christian faith, and left his cell, carefully closing the door, lest the animals of the desert and the birds of the air should enter, and befoul the copy of the Holy Scriptures which stood at the head of his bed. He called Flavian, the deacon, and gave him authority over the other twenty-three disciples during his absence; and then, clad only in a long cassock, he bent his steps towards the Nile, intending to follow the Libyan bank to the city founded by the Macedonian monarch. He walked from dawn to eve, indifferent to fatigue, hunger, and thirst; the sun was already low on the horizon when he saw the dreadful river, the blood-red waters of which rolled between the rocks of gold and fire.

He kept along the shore, begging his bread at the door of solitary huts for the love of God, and joyfully receiving insults, refusals, or threats. He feared neither robbers nor wild beasts, but he took great care to avoid all the towns and villages he came near. He was afraid lest he should see children playing at knuckle-bones before their father's house, or meet, by the side of the well, women in blue smocks, who might put down their pitcher and smile at him. All things are dangerous for the hermit; it is sometimes a danger for him to read in the Scriptures that the Divine Master journeyed from town to town and supped with His disciples. The virtues that the anchorites embroider so carefully on the tissue of faith, are as fragile as they are beautiful; a breath of ordinary life may tarnish their pleasant colours. For that reason, Paphnutius avoided the towns, fearing lest his heart should soften at the sight of his fellow men.

He journeyed along lonely roads. When evening came, the murmuring of the breeze amidst the tamarisk trees made him shiver, and he pulled his hood over his eyes that he might not see how beautiful all things were. After walking six days, he came to a place called Silsile. There the river runs in a narrow valley, bordered by a double chain of granite mountains. It was there that the Egyptians, in the days when they worshipped demons, carved their idols. Paphnutius saw an enormous sphinx carved in the solid rock. Fearing that it might still possess some diabolical properties, he made the sign of the cross, and pronounced the name of Jesus; he immediately saw a bat fly out of one of the monster's ears, and Paphnutius knew that he had driven out the evil spirits which had been for centuries in the figure. His zeal increased, and picking up a large stone, he threw it in the idol's face. Then the mysterious face of the sphinx expressed such profound sadness that Paphnutius was moved. In fact, the expression of superhuman grief on the stone visage would have touched even the most unfeeling man. Therefore Paphnutius said to the sphinx —

"O monster, be like the satyrs and centaurs our father Anthony saw in the desert, and confess the divinity of Jesus Christ, and I will bless thee in the name of the Father, the Son, and the Holy Ghost."

When he had spoken a rosy light gleamed in the eyes of the sphinx; the heavy eyelids of the monster quivered and the granite lips painfully murmured, as though in echo to the man's voice, the holy name of Jesus Christ; therefore Paphnutius stretched out his right hand, and blessed the sphinx of Silsile.

That being done, he resumed his journey, and the valley having grown wider, he saw the ruins of an immense city. The temples, which still remained standing, were supported by idols which served as columns, and — by the permission of God — these figures with women's heads and cow's horns, threw on Paphnutius a long look which made him turn pale. He walked thus seventeen days, his only food a few raw herbs, and he slept at night in some ruined palace, amongst the wild cats and Pharaoh's rats, with which mingled sometimes, women whose bodies ended in a scaly tail. But Paphnutius knew that these women came from hell, and he drove them away by making the sign of the cross.

On the eighteenth day, he found, far from any village, a wretched hut made of palm leaves, and half buried under the sand which had been driven by the desert wind. He approached it, hoping that the hut was inhabited by some pious anchorite. He saw inside the hovel — for there was no door — a pitcher, a bunch of onions, and a bed of dried leaves.

"This must be the habitation of a hermit," he said to himself. "Hermits are generally to be found near their hut, and I shall not fail to meet this one. I will give him the kiss of peace, even as the holy Anthony did when he came to the hermit Paul, and kissed him three times. We will discourse of things eternal, and perhaps our Lord will send us, by one of His ravens, a crust of bread, which my host will willingly invite me to share with him."

Whilst he was thus speaking to himself, he walked round the hut to see if he could find any one. He had not walked a hundred paces when he saw a man seated, with his legs crossed, by the side of the river. The man was naked; his hair and beard were quite white, and his body redder than brick. Paphnutius felt sure this must be the hermit. He saluted him with the words the monks are accustomed to use when they meet each other.

"Peace be with you, brother! May you some day taste the sweet joys of paradise."

The man did not reply. He remained motionless, and appeared not to have heard. Paphnutius supposed this was due to one of those rhapsodies to which the saints are accustomed. He knelt down, with his hands joined, by the side of the unknown, and remained thus in prayer till sunset. Then, seeing that his companion had not moved, he said to him —

"Father, if you are now out of the ecstasy in which you were lost, give me your blessing in our Lord Jesus Christ."

The other replied without turning his head —

"Stranger, I understand you not, and I know not the Lord Jesus Christ."

"What!" cried Paphnutius. "The prophets have announced Him; legions of martyrs have confessed His name; Caesar himself has worshipped Him, and, but just now, I made the sphinx of Silsile proclaim His glory. Is it possible that you do not know Him?"

"Friend," replied the other, "it is possible. It would even be certain, if anything in this world were certain."

Paphnutius was surprised and saddened by the incredible ignorance of the man.

"If you know not Jesus Christ," he said, "all your works serve no purpose, and you will never rise to life immortal."

The old man replied —

"It is useless to act, or to abstain from acting. It matters not whether we live or die."

"Eh, what?" asked Paphnutius. "Do you not desire to live through all eternity? But, tell me, do you not live in a hut in the desert as the hermits do?"

"It seems so."

"Do I not see you naked, and lacking all things?"

"It seems so."

"Do you not feed on roots, and live in chastity?"

"It seems so."

"Have you not renounced all the vanities of this world?"

"I have truly renounced all those vain things for which men commonly care."

"Then you are like me, poor, chaste, and solitary. And you are not so — as I am — for the love of God, and with a hope of celestial happiness! That I cannot understand. Why are you virtuous if you do not believe in Jesus Christ? Why deprive yourself of the good things of this world if you do not hope to gain eternal riches in heaven?"

"Stranger, I deprive myself of nothing which is good, and I flatter myself that I have found a life which is satisfactory enough, though — to speak more precisely — there is no such thing as a good or evil life. Nothing is itself, either virtuous or shameful, just or unjust, pleasant or painful, good or bad. It is our opinion which gives those qualities to things, as salt gives savour to meats."

"So then, according to you there is no certainty. You deny the truth which the idolaters themselves have sought. You lie in ignorance — like a tired dog sleeping in the mud."

"Stranger, it is equally useless to abuse either dogs or philosophers. We know not what dogs are or what we are. We know nothing."

"Old man, do you belong, then, to the absurd sect of skeptics? Are you one of those miserable fools who alike deny movement and rest, and who know not how to distinguish between the light of the sun and the shadows of night?"

"Friend, I am truly a skeptic, and of a sect which appears praiseworthy to me, though it seems ridiculous to you. For the same things often assume different appearances. The pyramids of Memphis seem at sunrise to be cones of pink light. At sunset they look like black triangles against the illuminated sky. But who shall solve the problem of their true nature? You reproach me with denying appearances, when, in fact, appearances are the only realities I recognize. The sun seems to me illuminous, but its nature is unknown to me. I feel that fire burns — but I know not how or why. My friend, you understand me badly. Besides, it is indifferent to me whether I am understood one way or the other."

"Once more. Why do you live on dates and onions in the desert? Why do you endure great hardships? I endure hardships equally great, and, like you, I live in abstinence and solitude. But then it is to please God, and to earn eternal happiness. And that is a reasonable object, for it is wise to suffer now for a future gain. It is senseless, on the contrary, to expose yourself voluntarily to useless fatigue and vain sufferings. If I did not believe — pardon my blasphemy, O uncreated Light! — if I did not believe in the truth of that which God has taught us by the voice of the prophets, by the example of His Son, by the acts of the Apostles, by the authority of councils, and by the testimony of the martyrs,

— if I did not know that the sufferings of the body are necessary for the salvation of the soul — if I were, like thee, lost in ignorance of sacred mysteries — I would return at once amongst the men of this day, I would strive to acquire riches, that I might live in ease, like those who are happy in this world, and I would say to the votaries of pleasure, 'Come, my daughters, come, my servants, come and pour out for me your wines, your philtres, your perfumes.' But you, foolish old man! you deprive yourself of all these advantages; you lose without hope of any gain; you give without hope of any return, and you imitate foolishly the noble deeds of us anchorites, as an impudent monkey thinks, by smearing a wall, to copy the picture of a clever artist. What, then, are your reasons, O most besotted of men?"

Paphnutius spoke with violence and indignation, but the old man remained unmoved.

"Friend," he replied, gently, "what matter the reasons of a dog sleeping in the dirt or a mischievous ape?"

Paphnutius' only aim was the glory of God. His anger vanished, and he apologized with noble humility.

"Pardon me, old man, my brother," he said, "if zeal for the truth has carried me beyond proper bounds. God is my witness, that it is thy errors and not thyself that I hate. I suffer to see thee in darkness, for I love thee in Jesus Christ, and care for thy salvation fills my heart. Speak! give me your reasons. I long to know them that I may refute them."

The old man replied quietly —

"It is the same to me whether I speak or remain silent. I will give my reasons without asking yours in return, for I have no interest in you at all. I care neither for your happiness nor your misfortune, and it matters not to me whether you think one way or another. Why should I love you, or hate you? Aversion and sympathy are equally unworthy of the wise man. But since you question me, know then that I am named Timocles, and that I was born at Cos, of parents made rich by commerce. My father was a ship-owner. In intelligence he much resembled Alexander, who is surnamed the Great. But he was not so gross. In short, he was a man of no great parts. I had two brothers, who, like him, were ship-owners. As for me, I followed wisdom. My eldest brother was compelled by my father to marry a Carian woman, named Timaessa, who displeased him so greatly that he could not live with her without falling into a deep melancholy. However, Timaessa inspired our younger brother with a criminal passion, and this passion soon turned to a furious madness. The Carian woman hated them both equally; but she loved a flute-player, and received him at night in her chamber. One morning he left there the wreath which he usually wore at feasts. My two brothers, having found this wreath, swore to kill the flute-player, and the next day they caused him to perish under the lash, in spite of his tears and prayers. My sister-in-law felt such grief that she lost her reason, and these three poor wretches became beasts rather than human beings, and wandered insane along the shores of Cos, howling like wolves and foaming at the mouth, and hooted at by the children, who threw shells and stones at them. They died, and my father buried them with his own hands. A little later his stomach refused all nourishment, and he died of hunger, though he was rich enough to have bought all the meats and fruits in the markets of Asia. He was deeply grieved at having to leave me his fortune. I used it in travels. I visited Italy, Greece, and Africa without meeting a single person who was either wise or happy. I studied philosophy at Athens and Alexandria, and was deafened by noisy arguments. At last I wandered as far as India, and I saw on the banks of the Ganges a naked man, who had sat there motionless with his legs crossed for more than thirty years. Climbing plants twined round his dried up body, and the birds built their nests in his hair. Yet he lived. At the sight of him I called to mind Timaessa, the flute-player, my two brothers, and my father, and I realized that this Indian was a wise man. 'Men,' I said to myself, 'suffer because they are deprived of that which they believe to be good; or because, possessing it they fear to lose it; or because they endure that which they believe to be an evil. Put an end to all beliefs of this kind, and the evils would disappear.' That is why I resolved henceforth to deem nothing an advantage, to tear myself entirely from the good things of this world, and to live silent and motionless, like the Indian."

Paphnutius had listened attentively to the old man's story.

"Timocles of Cos," he replied, "I own that your discourse is not wholly devoid of sense. It is, in truth, wise to despise the riches of this world. But it would be absurd to despise also your eternal welfare, and render yourself liable to be visited by the wrath of God. I grieve at your ignorance, Timocles, and I will instruct you in the truth, in order that knowing that there really exists a God in three hypostases, you may obey this God as a child obeys its father."

Timocles interrupted him.

"Refrain, stranger, from showing me your doctrines, and do not imagine that you will persuade me to share your opinions. All discussions are useless. My opinion is to have no opinion. My life is devoid of trouble because I have no preferences. Go thy ways, and strive not to withdraw me from the beneficent apathy in which I am plunged, as though in a delicious bath, after the hardships of my past days."

Paphnutius was profoundly instructed in all things relating to the faith. By his knowledge of the human heart, he was aware that the grace of God had not fallen on old Timocles, and the day of salvation for this soul so obstinately resolved to ruin itself had not yet come. He did not reply, lest the power given for edification should turn to destruction. For it sometimes happens, in disputing with infidels, that the means used for their conversion may steep them still farther in sin. Therefore they who possess the truth should take care how they spread it.

"Farewell, then, unhappy Timocles," he said; and heaving a deep sigh, he resumed his pious pilgrimage through the night.

In the morning, he saw the ibises motionless on one leg at the edge of the water, which reflected their pale pink necks. The willows stretched their soft grey foliage to the bank, cranes flew in a triangle in the clear sky, and the cry of unseen herons was heard from the sedges. Far as the eye could reach, the river rolled its broad green waters o'er which white sails, like the wings of birds, glided, and here and there on the shores, a white house shone out. A light mist floated along the banks, and from out the shadow of the islands, which were laden with palms, flowers, and fruits, came noisy flocks of ducks, geese, flamingoes, and teal. To the left, the grassy valley extended to the desert its fields and orchards in joyful abundance; the sun shone on the yellow wheat, and the earth exhaled forth its fecundity in odorous wafts. At this sight, Paphnutius fell on his knees, and cried —

"Blessed be the Lord, who has given a happy issue to my journey. O God, who spreadest Thy dew upon the fig trees of the Arsiniote, pour Thy grace upon Thais, whom Thou hast formed with Thy love, as Thou hast the flowers and trees of the field. May she, by Thy loving care, flourish like a sweet-scented rose in the heavenly Jerusalem."

And every time that he saw a tree covered with blossom, or a bird of brilliant plumage, he thought of Thais. Keeping along the left arm of the river and through a fertile and populous district, he reached, in a few days, the city of Alexandria, which the Greeks have surnamed the Beautiful and the Golden. The sun had risen an hour, when he beheld, from the top of a hill, the vast city, the roofs of which glittered in the rosy light. He stopped, and folded his arms on his breast.

"There, then," he said, "is the delightful spot where I was born in sin; the bright air where I breathed poisonous perfumes; the sea of pleasure where I heard the songs of the sirens. There is my cradle, after the flesh; my native land — in the parlance of the men of these days! A rich cradle, an illustrious country, in the judgment of men! It is natural that thy children should reverence thee like a mother, Alexandria, and I was begotten in thy magnificently adorned breast. But the ascetic despises nature, the mystic scorns appearances, the Christian regards his native land as a place of exile, the monk is not of this earth. I have turned away my heart from loving thee, Alexandria. I hate thee! I hate thee for thy riches, thy science, thy pleasures, and thy beauty. Be accursed, temple of demons! Lewd couch of the Gentiles, tainted pulpit of Arian heresy, be thou accursed! And thou, winged son of heaven who led the holy hermit Anthony, our father, when he came from the depths of the desert, and entered into the citadel of idolatry to strengthen the faith of believers and the confidence of martyrs, beautiful angel of the Lord, invisible child, first breath of God, fly thou before me, and cleanse, by the beating of thy wings, the corrupted air I am about to breathe amongst the princes of darkness of this world!"

Having thus spoken, he resumed his journey. He entered the city by the Gate of the Sun. This gate was a handsome structure of stone. In the shadow of its arch, crowded some poor wretches, who offered lemons and figs for sale, or with many groans and lamentations, begged for an obolus.

An old woman in rags, who was kneeling there, seized the monk's cassock, kissed it, and said —

"Man of the Lord, bless me, that God may bless me. I have suffered many things in this world that I may have joys in the world to come. You come from God, O holy man, and that is why the dust of your feet is more precious than gold."

"The Lord be praised!" said Paphnutius, and with his half-closed hand he made the sign of redemption on the old woman's head.

But hardly had he gone twenty paces down the street, than a band of children began to jeer at him, and throw stones, crying —

"Oh, the wicked monk! He is blacker than an ape, and more bearded than a goat! He is a skulker! Why not hang him in an orchard, like a wooden Priapus, to frighten the birds? But no; he would draw down the hail on the apple-blossom. He brings bad luck. To the ravens with the monk! to the ravens!" and stones mingled with the cries.

"My God, bless these poor children!" murmured Paphnutius.

And he pursued his way, thinking.

"I was worshipped by the old woman, and hated and despised by these children. Thus the same object is appreciated differently by men who are uncertain in their judgment and liable

215

to error. It must be owned that, for a Gentile, old Timocles was not devoid of sense. Though blind, he knew he was deprived of light. His reasoning was much better than that of these idolaters, who cry from the depths of their thick darkness, 'I see the day!' Everything in this world is mirage and moving sand. God alone is steadfast."

He passed through the city with rapid steps. After ten years of absence he would still recognize every stone, and every stone was to him a stone of reproach that recalled a sin. For that reason he struck his naked feet roughly against the kerb-stones of the wide street, and rejoiced to see the bloody marks of his wounded feet. Leaving on his left the magnificent portico of the Temple of Serapis, he entered a road lined with splendid mansions, which seemed to be drowsy with perfumes. Pines, maples, and larches raised their heads above the red cornices and golden acroteria. Through the half-open doors could be seen bronze statues in marble vestibules, and fountains playing amidst foliage. No noise troubled the stillness of these quiet retreats. Only the distant strains of a flute could be heard. The monk stopped before a house, rather small, but of noble proportions, and supported by columns as graceful as young girls. It was ornamented with bronze busts of the most celebrated Greek philosophers.

He recognized Plato, Socrates, Aristotle, Epicurus, and Zeno, and having knocked with the hammer against the door, he waited, wrapped in meditation.

"It is vanity to glorify in metal these false sages; their lies are confounded, their souls are lost in hell, and even the famous Plato himself, who filled the earth with his eloquence, now disputes with the devils."

A slave opened the door, and seeing a man with bare feet standing on the mosaic threshold, said to him roughly —

"Go and beg elsewhere, stupid monk, or I will drive you away with a stick."

"Brother," replied the Abbott of Antinoe, "all that I ask is that you conduct me to your master, Nicias."

The slave replied, more angrily than before —

"My master does not see dogs like you."

"My son," said Paphnutius, "will you please do what I ask, and tell your master that I desire to see him.

"Get out, vile beggar!" cried the porter furiously; and he raised his stick and struck the holy man, who, with his arms crossed upon his breast, received unmovedly the blow, which fell full in his face, and then repeated gently —

"Do as I ask you, my son, I beg."

The porter tremblingly murmured —

"Who is this man who is not afraid of suffering?"

And he ran and told his master.

Nicias had just left the bath. Two pretty slave girls were scraping him with strigils. He was a pleasant-looking man, with a kind smile. There was an expression of gentle satire in his face. On seeing the monk, he rose and advanced with open arms.

"It is you!" he cried, "Paphnutius, my fellow-scholar, my friend my brother! Oh, I knew you again, though, to say the truth, you look more like a wild animal than a man. Embrace me. Do you remember the time when we studied grammar, rhetoric, and philosophy together? You were, even then, of a morose and wild character, but I liked you because of your complete sincerity. We used to say that you looked at the universe with the eyes of a wild horse, and it was not surprising you were dull and moody. You needed a pinch of Attic salt, but your liberality knew no bounds. You cared nothing for either your money or your life. And you had the eccentricity of genius, and a strange character which interested me deeply. You are welcome, my dear Paphnutius, after ten years of absence. You have quitted the desert; you have renounced all Christian superstitions, and now return to your old life. I will mark this day with a white stone."

"Crobyle and Myrtale," he added, turning towards the girls, "perfume the feet, hands, and beard of my dear guest."

They smiled, and had already brought the basin, the phials, and the metal mirror. But Paphnutius stopped them with an imperious gesture, and lowered his eyes that he might not look upon them, for they were naked. Nicias brought cushions for

217

him, and offered him various meats and drinks, which Paphnutius scornfully refused.

"Nicias," he said, "I have not renounced what you falsely call the Christian superstition, which is the truth of truths. 'In the beginning was the Word, and the Word was with God, and the Word was God. All things were made by Him, and without Him was not anything made that was made. In Him was the life, and the life was the light of men.'"

"My dear Paphnutius," replied Nicias, who had now put on a perfumed tunic, "do you expect to astonish me by reciting a lot of words jumbled together without skill, which are no more than a vain murmur? Have you forgotten that I am a bit of a philosopher myself? And do you think to satisfy me with some rags, torn by ignorant men from the purple garment of AEmilius, when AEmilius, Porphyry, and Plato, in all their glory, did not satisfy me! The systems devised by the sages are but tales imagined to amuse the eternal childishness of men. We divert ourselves with them, as we do with the stories of *The Ass*, *The Tub*, and *The Ephesian Matron*, or any other Milesian fable."

And, taking his guest by the arm, he led him into a room where thousands of papyri were rolled up and lay in baskets.

"This is my library," he said. "It contains a small part of the various systems which the philosophers have constructed to explain the world. The Serapeium itself, with all its riches, does not contain them all. Alas! they are but the dreams of sick men."

He compelled his guest to sit down in an ivory chair, and sat down himself. Paphnutius scowled gloomily at all the books in the library, and said —

"They ought all to be burned."

"Oh, my dear guest, that would be a pity!" replied Nicias. "For the dreams of sick men are sometimes amusing. Besides, if we should destroy all the dreams and visions of men, the earth would lose its form and colours, and we should all sleep in a dull stupidity."

Paphnutius continued in the same strain as before —

"It is certain that the doctrines of the pagans are but vain lies. But God, who is the truth, revealed Himself to men by miracles, and He was made flesh, and lived among us."

Nicias replied —

"You speak well, my dear Paphnutius, when you say that he was made flesh. A God who thinks, acts, speaks, who wanders through nature, like Ulysses of old on the glaucous sea, is altogether a man. How do you expect that we should believe in this new Jupiter, when the urchins of Athens, in the time of Pericles, no longer believed in the old one?

"But let us leave all that. You did not come here; I suppose, to argue about the three hypostases. What can I do for you, my dear fellow-scholar?"

"A good deed," replied the Abbot of Antinoe. "Lend me a perfumed tunic, like the one you have just put on. Be kind enough to add to the tunic, gilt sandals, and a vial of oil to anoint my beard and hair. It is needful also, that you should give me a purse with a thousand drachmae in it. That, O Nicias, is what I came to ask of you, for the love of God, and in remembrance of our old friendship."

Nicias made Crobyle and Myrtale bring his richest tunic; it was embroidered, after the Asiatic fashion, with flowers and animals. The two girls held it open, and skillfully showed its bright colours, waiting till Paphnutius should have taken off the cassock which covered him down to his feet. But the monk having declared that they should rather tear off his flesh than this garment, they put on the tunic over it. As the two girls were pretty, they were not afraid of men, although they were slaves. They laughed at the strange appearance of the monk thus clad. Crobyle called him her dear satrap, as she presented him with the mirror, and Myrtale pulled his beard. But Paphnutius prayed to the Lord, and did not look at them. Having tied on the gilt sandals, and fastened the purse to his belt, he said to Nicias, who was looking at him with an amused expression —

"O Nicias, let not these things be an offence in your eyes. For know that I shall make pious use of this tunic, this purse, and these sandals."

"My dear friend," replied Nicias, "I suspect no evil, for I believe that men are equally incapable of doing evil or doing good. Good and evil exist only in the opinion. The wise man has only custom and usage to guide him in his acts. I conform with all the prejudices which prevail at Alexandria. That is why I pass for an honest man. Go, friend, and enjoy yourself."

But Paphnutius thought that it was needful to inform his host of his intention.

"Do you know Thais," he said, "who acts in the games at the theatre?"

"She is beautiful," replied Nicias, "and there was a time when she was dear to me. For her sake, I sold a mill and two fields of corn, and I composed in her honour three books full of detestably bad verses. Surely beauty is the most powerful force in the world, and were we so made that we could possess it always, we should care as little as may be for the demiurgos, the logos, the aeons, and all the other reveries of the philosophers. But I am surprised, my good Paphnutius, that you should have come from the depths of the Thebaid to talk about Thais."

Having said this, he sighed gently. And Paphnutius gazed at him with horror, not conceiving it possible that a man should so calmly avow such a sin. He expected to see the earth open, and Nicias swallowed up in flames. But the earth remained solid, and the Alexandrian silent, his forehead resting on his hand, and he smiling sadly at the memories of his past youth. The monk rose, and continued in solemn tones —

"Know then, O Nicias, that, with the aid of God, I will snatch this woman Thais from the unclean affections of the world, and give her as a spouse to Jesus Christ. If the Holy Spirit does not forsake me, Thais will leave this city and enter a nunnery."

"Beware of offending Venus," replied Nicias. "She is a powerful goddess, she will be angry with you if you take away her chief minister."

"God will protect me," said Paphnutius. "May He also illumine thy heart, O Nicias, and draw thee out of the abyss in which thou art plunged."

And he stalked out of the room. But Nicias followed him, and overtook him on the threshold, and placing his hand on his shoulder whispered into his ear the same words —

"Beware of offending Venus; her vengeance is terrible."

Paphnutius, disdainful of these trivial words, left without turning his head. He felt only contempt for Nicias; but what he could not bear was the idea that his former friend had received the caresses of Thais. It seemed to him that to sin with that woman was more detestable than to sin with any other. To him this appeared the height of iniquity, and he henceforth looked upon Nicias as an object of execration. He had always hated impurity, but never before had this vice appeared so heinous to him; never before had it so seemed to merit the anger of Jesus Christ and the sorrow of the angels.

He felt only a more ardent desire to save Thais from the Gentiles, and that he must hasten to see the actress in order to save her. Nevertheless, before he could enter her house, he must wait till the heat of the day was over, and now the morning had hardly finished. Paphnutius wandered through the most frequented streets. He had resolved to take no food that day, in order to be the less unworthy of the favours he had asked of the Lord. To the great grief of his soul, he dared not enter any of the churches in the city, because he knew they were profaned by the Arians, who had overturned the Lord's table. For, in fact, these heretics, supported by the Emperor of the East, had driven the patriarch Athanasius from his episcopate, and sown trouble and confusion among the Christians of Alexandria.

He therefore wandered about aimlessly, sometimes with his eyes fixed on the ground in humility, and sometimes raised to heaven in ecstasy. After some time, he found himself on the quay.

Before him lay the harbour, in which were sheltered innumerable ships and galleys, and beyond them, smiling in blue and silver, lay the perfidious sea. A galley, which bore a Nereid at its prow, had just weighed anchor. The rowers sang as the oars struck the water; and already the white daughter of the waters, covered with humid pearls, showed no more than a flying profile to the monk. Steered by her pilot, she cleared the passage leading from the basin of the Eunostos, and gained the high seas, leaving a glittering trail behind her.

"I also," thought Paphnutius, "once desired to embark singing on the ocean of the world. But I soon saw my folly, and the Nereid did not carry me away."

Lost in his thoughts, he sat down upon a coil of rope, and went to sleep. During his sleep, he had a vision. He seemed to hear the sound of a clanging trumpet, and the sky became blood red, and he knew that the day of judgment had come. Whilst he was fervently praying to God, he saw an enormous monster coming towards him, bearing on its forehead a cross of light, and he recognized the sphinx of Silsile. The monster seized him between its teeth, without hurting him, and carried him in its mouth, as a cat carries a kitten. Paphnutius was thus conveyed across many countries, crossing rivers and traversing mountains, and came at last to a desert place, covered with scowling rocks and hot cinders. The ground was rent in many places, and through these openings came a hot air. The monster gently put Paphnutius down on the ground, and said —

"Look!"

And Paphnutius, leaning over the edge of the abyss, saw a river of fire which flowed in the interior of the earth, between two cliffs of black rocks. There, in a livid light, the demons tormented the souls of the damned. The souls preserved the appearance of the bodies which had held them, and even wore some rags of clothing. These souls seemed peaceful in the midst of their torments. One of them, tall and white, his eyes closed, a white fillet across his forehead, and a sceptre in his hand, sang; his voice filled the desert shores with harmony; he sang of gods and heroes.

Little green devils pierced his lips and throat with red-hot irons. And the shade of Homer still sang. Near by, old Anaxagoras, bald and hoary, traced figures in the dust with a compass. A demon poured boiling oil into his ear, yet failed, however, to disturb the sage's meditations. And the monk saw many other persons, who, on the dark shore by the side of the burning river, read, or quietly meditated, or conversed with other spirits while walking, — like the sages and pupils under the shadow of the sycamore trees of Academe. Old Timocles alone had withdrawn from the others, and shook his head like a man who denies. One of the demons of the abyss shook a torch before his eyes, but Timocles would see neither the demon nor the torch.

Mute with surprise at this spectacle, Paphnutius turned to the monster. It had disappeared, and, in place of the sphinx, the monk saw a veiled woman, who said —

"Look and understand. Such is the obstinacy of these infidels, that, even in hell, they remain victims of the illusions which deluded them when on earth. Death has not undeceived them; for it is very plain that it does not suffice merely to die in order to see God. Those who are ignorant of the truth whilst living, will be ignorant of it always. The demons which are busy torturing these souls, what are they but agents of divine justice? That is why these souls neither see them nor feel them. They were ignorant of the truth, and therefore unaware of their own condemnation, and God Himself cannot compel them to suffer.

"God can do all things," said the Abbot of Antinoe.

"He cannot do that which is absurd," replied the veiled woman. "To punish them, they must first be enlightened, and if they possessed the truth, they would be like unto the elect."

Vexed and horrified, Paphnutius again bent over the edge of the abyss. He saw the shade of Nicias smiling, with a wreath of flowers on his head, sitting under a burnt myrtle tree. By his side was Aspasia of Miletus, gracefully draped in a woolen cloak, and they seemed to talk together of love and philosophy; the expression of her face was sweet and noble. The rain of fire which fell on them was as a refreshing dew, and their feet pressed the burning soil as though it had been tender grass. At this sight Paphnutius was filled with fury.

"Strike him, O God! strike him!" he cried. "It is Nicias! Let him weep! let him groan! let him grind his teeth! He sinned with Thais!"

And Paphnutius woke in the arms of a sailor, as strong as Hercules, who cried —

"Quietly! quietly! my friend! By Proteus, the old shepherd of the seals, you slumber uneasily. If I had not caught hold of you, you would have tumbled into the Eunostos. It is as true as that my mother sold salt fish, that I saved your life."

"I thank God," replied Paphnutius.

And, rising to his feet, he walked straight before him, meditating on the vision which had come to him whilst he was asleep.

"This vision," he said to himself, "is plainly an evil one; it is an insult to divine goodness to imagine hell is unreal. The dream certainly came from the devil."

He reasoned thus because he knew how to distinguish between the dreams sent by God and those produced by evil angels. Such discernment is useful to the hermit, who lives surrounded by apparitions, and who, in avoiding men, is sure to meet with spirits. The deserts are full of phantoms. When the pilgrims drew near the ruined castle, to which the holy hermit, Anthony, had retired, they heard a noise like that which goes up from the public square of a large city at a great festival. The noise was made by the devils, who were tempting the holy man.

Paphnutius remembered this memorable example. He also called to mind St. John the Egyptian, who for sixty years was tempted by the devil. But John saw through all the tricks of the demon. One day, however, the devil, having assumed the appearance of a man, entered the grotto of the venerable John, and said to him, "John, you must continue to fast until to-morrow evening." And John, believing that it was an angel who spoke, obeyed the voice of the demon, and fasted the next day until the vesper hour. That was the only victory that the Prince of

Darkness ever gained over St. John the Egyptian, and that was but a trifling one. It was therefore not astonishing that Paphnutius knew at once that the vision which had visited him in his sleep was an evil one.

Whilst he was gently remonstrating with God for having given him into the power of the demons, he felt himself pushed and dragged amidst a crowd of people who were all hurrying in the same direction. As he was unaccustomed to walk in the streets of a city, he was shoved and knocked from one passer to another like an inert mass; and being embarrassed by the folds of his tunic, he was more than once on the point of falling. Desirous of knowing where all these people could be going, he asked one of them the cause of this hurry.

"Do you not know, stranger," replied he, "that the games are about to begin, and that Thais will appear on the stage? All the citizens are going to the theatre, and I also am going. Would you like to accompany me?"

It occurred to him at once that it would further his design to see Thais in the games, and Paphnutius followed the stranger. In front of them stood the theatre, its portico ornamented with shining masks, and its huge circular wall covered with innumerable statues. Following the crowd, they entered a narrow passage, at the end of which lay the amphitheatre, glittering with light. They took their places on one of the seats, which descended in steps to the stage, which was empty but magnificently decorated. There was no curtain to hide the view, and on the stage was a mound, such as used to be erected in old times to the shades of heroes. This mound stood in the midst of a camp. Lances were stacked in front of the tents, and golden shields hung from masts, amidst boughs of laurel and wreaths of oak. On the stage all was silence, but a murmur like the humming of bees in a hive rose from the vast hemicycle filled with spectators. All their faces, reddened by the reflection from the purple awning which waved above them, turned with attentive curiosity towards the large, silent stage, with its tomb and tents. The women laughed and ate lemons, and the regular theatre-goers called gaily to one another from their seats.

Paphnutius prayed inwardly, and refrained from uttering any vain words, but his neighbour began to complain of the decline of the drama.

"Formerly," he said, "clever actors used to declaim, under a mask, the verses of Euripides and Menander. Now they no longer recite dramas, they act in dumb show; and of the divine spectacles with which Bacchus was honoured in Athens, we have kept nothing but what a barbarian — a Scythian even — could understand — attitude and gesture. The tragic mask, the mouth of which was provided with metal tongues that increased the sound of the voice; the cothurnus, which raised the actors to the height of gods; the tragic majesty and the splendid verses that used to be sung, have all gone. Pantomimists, and dancing girls with bare faces, have replaced Paulus and Roscius. What would the Athenians of the days of Pericles have said if they had seen a woman on the stage? It is indecent for a woman to appear in public. We must be very degenerate to permit it. It is as certain as that my name is Dorion, that woman is the natural enemy of man, and a disgrace to human kind."

"You speak wisely," replied Paphnutius; "woman is our worst enemy. She gives us pleasure, and is to be feared on that account."

"By the immovable gods," cried Dorion, "it is not pleasure that woman gives to man, but sadness, trouble, and black cares. Love is the cause of our most biting evils. Listen, stranger. When I was a young man I visited Troezene, in Argolis, and I saw there a myrtle of a most prodigious size, the leaves of which were covered with innumerable pinholes. And this is what the Troezenians say about that myrtle. Queen Phaedra, when she was in love with Hippolytos, used to recline idly all day long under this same tree. To beguile the tedium of her weary life she used to draw out the golden pin which held her fair locks, and pierce with it the leaves of the sweet-scented bush. All the leaves were riddled with holes. After she had ruined the poor young man whom she pursued with her incestuous love, Phaedra, as you know, perished miserably. She locked herself up in her bridal chamber, and hanged herself by her golden girdle from an ivory peg. The gods willed that the myrtle, the witness of her bitter misery, should continue to bear, in its fresh leaves, the marks of the pin-holes. I picked one of these leaves, and placed it at the head of my bed, that by the sight of it I might take warning against the folly of love, and conform to the doctrine of the divine Epicurus, my master, who taught that all lust is to be feared. But, properly speaking, love is a disease of the liver, and one is never sure of not catching the malady."

Paphnutius asked —

"Dorion, what are your pleasures?"

Dorion replied sadly —

"I have only one pleasure, and, it must be confessed, that it is not a very exciting one; it is meditation. When a man has a bad digestion, he must not look for any others."

Taking advantage of these words, Paphnutius proceeded to initiate the Epicurean into those spiritual joys which the contemplation of God procures. He began —

"Hear the truth, Dorion, and receive the light."

But he saw then that all heads were turned towards him, and everybody was making signs for him to be quiet. Dead silence prevailed in the theatre, broken at last by the strains of heroic music.

The play began. The soldiers left their tents, and were preparing to depart, when a prodigy occurred — a cloud covered the summit of the funeral pile. Then the cloud rolled away, and the ghost of Achilles appeared, clad in golden armour. Extending his arms towards the warriors, he seemed to say to them, "What! do you depart, children of Danaos? do you return to the land I shall never behold again, and leave my tomb without any offerings?" Already the principal Greek chieftains pressed to the foot of the pile. Acamas, the son of Theseus, old Nestor, Agamemnon, bearing a sceptre and with a fillet on his brow, gazed at the prodigy. Pyrrhus, the young son of Achilles, was prostrate in the dust. Ulysses, recognizable by the cap which covered his curly hair, showed by his gestures that he acquiesced in the demand of the hero's shade. He argued with Agamemnon, and their words might be easily guessed —

"Achilles," said the King of Ithaca, "is worthy to be honoured by us, for he died gloriously for Hellas. He demands that the daughter of Priam, the virgin Polyxena, should be immolated on his tomb. Greeks! appease the manes of the hero, and let the son of Peleus rejoice in Hades."

But the king of kings replied —

"Spare the Trojan virgins we have torn from the altars. Sufficient misfortunes have already fallen on the illustrious race of Priam."

He spoke thus because he shared the couch of the sister of Polyxena, and the wise Ulysses reproached him for preferring the couch of Cassandra to the lance of Achilles.

The Greeks showed they shared the opinion of Ulysses, by loudly clashing their weapons. The death of Polyxena was resolved on, and the appeased shade of Achilles vanished. The music — sometimes wild and sometimes plaintive — followed the thoughts of the personages in the drama. The spectators burst into applause.

Paphnutius, who applied divine truth to everything murmured —

"This fable shows how cruel the worshippers of false gods were."

"All religions breed crimes," replied the Epicurean. "Happily, a Greek, who was divinely wise, has freed men from foolish terrors of the unknown — "

Just at that moment, Hecuba, her white hair disheveled, her robe tattered, came out of the tent in which she was kept captive. A long sigh went up from the audience, when her woeful figure appeared. Hecuba had been warned by a prophetic dream, and lamented her daughter's fate and her own. Ulysses approached her, and asked her to give up Polyxena. The old mother tore her hair, dug her nails into her cheeks, and kissed the hands of the cruel chieftain, who, with unpitying calmness, seemed to say —

"Be wise, Hecuba, and yield to necessity. There are amongst us many old mothers who weep for their children, now sleeping under the pines of Ida."

And Hecuba, formerly queen of the most flourishing city in Asia, and now a slave, bowed her unhappy head in the dust.

Then the curtain in front of one of the tents was raised, and the virgin Polyxena appeared. A tremor passed through all the spectators. They had recognized Thais. Paphnutius saw again the woman he had come to seek. With her white arm she held above her head the heavy curtain. Motionless as a splendid statue, she stood, with a look of pride and resignation in her violet eyes, and her resplendent beauty made a shudder of commiseration pass through all who beheld her.

A murmur of applause uprose, and Paphnutius, his soul agitated, and pressing both hands to his heart, sighed —

"Why, O my God, hast thou given this power to one of Thy creatures?"

Dorion was not so disturbed. He said —

"Certainly the atoms, which have momentarily met together to form this woman, present a combination which is agreeable to the eye. But that is but a freak of nature, and the atoms know not what they do. They will some day separate with the same indifference as they came together. Where are now the atoms which formed Lais or Cleopatra? I must confess that women are sometimes beautiful. But they are liable to grievous afflictions, and disgusting inconveniences. That is patent to all thinking men, though the vulgar pay no attention to it. And women inspire love, though it is absurd and ridiculous to love them."

Such were the thoughts of the philosopher and the ascetic as they gazed on Thais. They neither of them noticed Hecuba, who turned to her daughter, and seemed to say by her gestures —

"Try to soften the cruel Ulysses. Employ your tears, your beauty, and your youth."

Thais — or rather Polyxena herself — let fall the curtain of the tent. She made a step forward, and all hearts were conquered. And when, with firm but light steps, she advanced towards Ulysses, her rhythmic movements, which were accompanied by the sound of flutes, created in all present such happy visions, that it seemed as though she were the divine centre of all the harmonies of the world. All eyes were bent on her; the other actors were obscured by her effulgence, and were not noticed. The play continued, however.

The prudent son of Laertes turned away his head, and hid his hand under his mantle, in order to avoid the looks and kisses of the suppliant. The virgin made a sign to him to fear nothing. Her tranquil gaze said —

"I follow you, Ulysses, and bow to necessity — because I wish to die. Daughter of Priam, and sister of Hector, my couch, which was once worthy of Kings, shall never receive a foreign master. Freely do I quit the light of day."

Hecuba, lying motionless in the dust, suddenly rose and enfolded her daughter in a last despairing embrace. Polyxena gently, but resolutely, removed the old arms which held her. She seemed to say —

"Do not expose yourself, mother, to the fury of your master. Do not wait until he drags you ignominiously on the ground in tearing me from your arms. Better, O well-beloved mother, to give me your wrinkled hand, and bend your hollow cheeks to my lips."

The face of Thais looked beautiful in its grief. The crowd felt grateful to her for showing them the forms and passions of life endowed with superhuman grace, and Paphnutius pardoned her present splendour on account of her coming humility, and glorified himself in advance for the saint he was about to give to heaven.

The drama neared its end. Hecuba fell as though dead, and Polyxena, led by Ulysses, advanced towards the tomb, which was surrounded by the chief warriors. A dirge was sung as she mounted the funeral pile, on the summit of which the son of Achilles poured out libations from a gold cup to the manes of the hero. When the sacrificing priests stretched out their arms to seize her, she made a sign that she wished to die free and unbound, as befitted the daughter of so many kings. Then, tearing aside her robe, she bared her bosom to the blow. Pyrrhus, turning away his head, plunged his sword into her heart, and by a skilful trick, the blood gushed forth over the dazzling white breast of the virgin, who, with head thrown back, and her eyes swimming in the horrors of death, fell with grace and modesty.

Whilst the warriors enshrouded the victim with a veil, and covered her with lilies and anemones, terrified screams and groans rent the air, and Paphnutius, rising from his seat, prophesied in a loud voice.

"Gentiles? vile worshippers of demons! And you Arians more infamous than the idolaters! — learn! That which you have just seen is an image and a symbol. There is a mystic meaning in this fable, and very soon the woman you see there will be offered, a willing and happy sacrifice, to the risen God."

But already the crowd was surging in dark waves towards the exits. The Abbot of Antinoe, escaping from the astonished Dorion, gained the door, still prophesying.

An hour later he knocked at the door of the house of Thais.

The actress then lived in the rich Racotis quarter, near the tomb of Alexander, in a house surrounded by shady gardens, in which a brook, bordered with poplars, flowed amidst artificial rocks. An old black slave woman, loaded with rings, opened the door, and asked what he wanted.

"I wish to see Thais," he replied. "God is my witness that I came here for no other purpose."

As he wore a rich tunic, and spoke in an imperious manner, the slave allowed him to enter.

"You will find Thais," she said, "in the Grotto of Nymphs."

PART THE SECOND — THE PAPYRUS

Thais was born of free, but poor, parents, who were idolaters. When she was a very little girl, her father kept, at Alexandria, near the Gate of the Moon, an inn, which was frequented by sailors. She still retained some vivid, but disconnected, memories of her early youth. She remembered her father, seated at the corner of the hearth with his legs crossed — tall, formidable, and quiet, like one of those old Pharaohs who are celebrated in the ballads sung by blind men at the street corners. She remembered also her thin, wretched mother, wandering like a hungry cat about the house, which she filled with the tones of her sharp voice, and the glitter of her phosphorescent eyes. They said in the neighbourhood that she was a witch, and changed into an owl at night, and flew to see her lovers. It was a lie. Thais knew well, having often watched her, that her mother practiced no magic arts, but that she was eaten up with avarice, and counted all night the gains of the day. The idle father and the greedy mother let the child live as best it could, like one of the fowls in the poultry-yard. She became very clever in extracting, one by one, the oboli from the belt of some drunken sailor, and in amusing the drinkers with artless songs and obscene words, the meaning of which she did not know. She passed from knee to knee, in a room reeking with the odours of fermented drinks and resiny wine-skins; then, her cheeks sticky with beer and pricked by rough beards, she escaped, clutching the oboli in her little hand, and ran to buy honey-cakes from an old woman who crouched behind her baskets under the Gate of the Moon. Every day the same scenes were repeated, the sailors relating their perilous adventures, then playing at dice or knuckle-bones, and blaspheming the gods, amid their shouting for the best beer of Cilicia.

Every night the child was awakened by the quarrels of the drunkards. Oyster-shells would fly across the tables, cutting the heads of those they hit, and the uproar was terrible. Sometimes she saw, by the light of the smoky lamps, the knives glitter, and the blood flow.

It humiliated her to think that the only person who showed her any human kindness in her young days was the mild and gentle Ahmes. Ahmes, the house-slave, a Nubian blacker than the pot he gravely skimmed, was as good as a long night's sleep. Often he would take Thais on his knee, and tell her old tales about underground treasure-houses constructed for avaricious kings, who put to death the masons and architects. There were also tales about clever thieves who married kings' daughters, and courtesans who built pyramids. Little Thais loved Ahmes like a father, like a mother, like a nurse, and like a dog. She followed the slave into the cellar when he went to fill the amphorae, and into the poultry-yard amongst the scraggy and ragged fowls, all beak, claws, and feathers, who flew swifter than eagles before the knife of the black cook. Often at night, on the straw, instead of sleeping, he built for Thais little water-mills, and ships no bigger than his hand, with all their rigging.

He had been badly treated by his masters; one of his ears was torn, and his body covered with scars. Yet his features always wore an air of joyous peace. And no one ever asked him whence he drew the consolation in his soul, and the peace in his heart. He was as simple as a child. As he performed his heavy tasks, he sang, in a harsh voice, hymns which made the child tremble and dream. He murmured, in a gravely joyous tone —

"Tell us, Mary, what thou hast seen where thou hast been?
I saw the shroud and the linen cloths, and the angels
seated on the tomb.
And I saw the glory of the Risen One."
She asked him —
"Father, why do you sing about angels seated on a tomb?"
And he replied —
"Little light of my eyes, I sing of the angels because Jesus, our Lord, is risen to heaven."

Ahmes was a Christian. He had been baptized, and was known as Theodore at the meetings of the faithful, to which he went secretly during the hours allowed him for sleep.

At that time the Church was suffering the severest trials. By order of the Emperor, the churches had been thrown down, the holy books burned, the sacred vessels and candlesticks melted. The Christians had been deprived of all their honours, and expected nothing but death. Terror reigned over all the community at Alexandria, and the prisons were crammed with victims. It was whispered with horror amongst the faithful, that in Syria, in Arabia, in Mesopotamia, in Cappadocia, in all the empire, bishops and virgins had been flogged, tortured, crucified or thrown to wild beasts. Then Anthony, already celebrated for his visions and his solitary life, a prophet, and the head of all the Egyptian believers, descended like an eagle from his desert rock on the city of Alexandria, and, flying from church to church, fired the whole community with his holy ardour. Invisible to the pagans, he was present at the same time at all the meetings of Christians, endowing all with the spirit of strength and prudence by which he was animated. Slaves, in particular, were persecuted with singular severity. Many of them, seized with fright, denied the faith. Others, and by far the greater number, fled to the desert, hoping to live there, either as hermits or robbers. Ahmes, however, frequented the meetings as usual, visited the prisoners, buried the martyrs, and joyfully professed the religion of Christ. The great Anthony, who saw his unshaken zeal, before he returned into the desert, pressed the black slave in his arms, and gave him the kiss of peace.

When Thais was seven years old, Ahmes began to talk to her of God.

"The good Lord God," he said, "lived in heaven like a Pharaoh, under the tents of His harem, and under the trees of His gardens. He was the Ancient of Ancients, and older than the world; and He had but one Son, the Prince Jesus, whom He loved with all His heart, and who surpassed in beauty the virgins and the angels. And the good Lord God said to Prince Jesus —

"'Leave My harem and My palace, and My date trees and My running waters. Descend to earth for the welfare of men. There Thou shalt be like a little child, and Thou shalt live poor amongst the poor. Suffering shall be Thy daily bread, and Thou shalt weep so profusely that Thy tears shall form rivers, in which the tired slave shall bathe with delight. Go, My Son!'

"Prince Jesus obeyed the good Lord, and He came down to earth, to a place named Bethlehem of Judaea. And He walked in fields, amidst the flowering anemones, saying to His companion —

"'Blessed are they who hunger, for I will lead them to My Father's table! Blessed are they who thirst, for they shall drink of the fountains of heaven! Blessed are they who weep, for I will dry their tears with veils finer than those of the almehs!'

"That is why the poor loved Him, and believed in Him. But the rich hated Him; fearing that He should raise the poor above them. At that time, Cleopatra and Caesar were powerful on the earth. They both hated Jesus, and they ordered the judges and priests to put Him to death. To obey the Queen of Egypt, the princes of Syria erected a cross on a high mountain, and they caused Jesus to die on this cross. But women washed His corpse, and buried it; and Prince Jesus, having broken the door of His tomb, rose again to the good Lord, His Father.

"And, from that time, all those who believed in Him go to heaven.

"The Lord God opens His arms, and says to them —

"'Ye are welcome, because ye love the Prince, My Son. Wash, and then eat.'

"They bathe to the sound of beautiful music, and, all the time they are eating, they see almehs dancing, and they listen to tales that never end. They are dearer to the good Lord God than the light of His eyes, because they are His guests, and they shall have for their portion the carpets of His house, and the pomegranates of His gardens."

Ahmes often spoke in this strain, and thus taught the truth to Thais. She wondered, and said —

"I should like to eat the pomegranates of the good Lord."

Ahmes replied —

"Only those who are baptized may taste the fruits of heaven."

And Thais asked to be baptized. Seeing by this that she believed in Jesus, the slave resolved to instruct her more fully, so that, being baptized, she might enter the Church; and he loved her as his spiritual daughter.

The child, unloved and uncared for by its selfish parents, had no bed in the house. She slept in a corner of the stable amongst the domestic animals, and there Ahmes came to her every night secretly.

He gently approached the mat on which she lay, and sat down on his heels, his legs bent and his body straight — a position hereditary to his race. His face and his body, which was clothed in black, were invisible in the darkness; but his big white eyes shone out, and there came from them a light like a ray of dawn through the chinks of a door. He spoke in a husky, monotonous tone, with a slight nasal twang that gave it the soft melody of music heard at night in the streets. Sometimes the breathing of an ass, or the soft lowing of an ox, accompanied, like a chorus of invisible spirits, the voice of the slave as he recited the gospels. His words flowed gently in the darkness, which they filled with zeal, mercy, and hope; and the neophyte, her hand in that of Ahmes, lulled by the monotonous sounds, and the vague visions in her mind, slept calm and smiling, amid the harmonies of the dark night and the holy mysteries, gazed down on by a star, which twinkled between the joists of the stable-roof.

The initiation lasted a whole year, till the time when the Christians joyfully celebrate the festival of Easter. One night in the holy week, Thais, who was already asleep on her mat, felt herself lifted by the slave, whose eyes gleamed with a strange light. He was clad, not as usual in a pair of torn drawers, but in a long white cloak, beneath which he pressed the child, whispering to her —

"Come, my soul! Come, light of my eyes! Come, little sweetheart! Come and be clad in the baptismal robes!"

He carried the child pressed to his breast. Frightened and yet curious, Thais, her head out of the cloak, threw her arms round her friend's neck, and he ran with her through the darkness. They went down narrow, black alleys; they passed through the Jews' quarter; they skirted a cemetery, where the osprey uttered its dismal cry; they traversed an open space, passing under crosses on which hung the bodies of victims, and on the arms of the crosses the ravens clacked their beaks. Thais hid her head in the slave's breast. She did not dare to peep out all the rest of the way. Soon it seemed to her that she was going down under ground. When she reopened her eyes she found herself in a narrow cave, lighted by resin torches, on the walls of which were painted standing figures, which seemed to move and live in the flickering glare of the torches. They were men clad in long tunics and carrying branches of palm, and around them were lambs, doves, and tendrils of vine.

Amongst these figures, Thais recognized Jesus of Nazareth, by the anemones flowering at his feet. In the centre of the cave, near a large stone font filled with water, stood an old man clad in a scarlet dalmatic embroidered with gold, and on his head a low mitre. His thin face ended in a long beard. He looked gentle and humble, in spite of his rich costume. This was Bishop Vivantius, an exiled dignitary of the Church of Cyrene, who now gained his livelihood by weaving common stuffs of goats' hair. Two poor children stood by his side. Close by, an old Negress unfolded a little white robe. Ahmes set the child down on the ground, and kneeling before the Bishop, said —

"Father, this is the little soul, the child of my soul. I have brought her that you may, according to your promise, and if it please your holiness, bestow on her the baptism of life."

At these words the Bishop opened his arms, and showed his mutilated hands. His nails had been torn out because he had maintained the faith in the days of persecution. Thais was frightened, and threw herself into the arms of Ahmes. But the kind words of the priest reassured her.

"Fear nothing, dearly beloved little one. Thou hast here a spiritual father, Ahmes, who is called Theodore amongst the faithful, and a kind mother in grace, who has prepared for thee, with her own hands, a white robe."

And turning towards the Negress —

"She is called Nitida," he added, "and is a slave in this world, but in heaven she will be a spouse of Jesus."

Then he said to the child neophyte —

"Thais, dost thou believe in God, the Father Almighty; and in His only Son, who died for our salvation; and in all that the apostles taught?"

"Yes," replied together the negro and Negress, who held her by each hand.

By the Bishop's orders, Nitida knelt down and undressed Thais. The child was quite naked; round her neck was an amulet. The Pontiff plunged her three times into the baptismal font. The acolytes brought the oil, with which Vivantius anointed the catechumen, and the salt, a morsel of which he placed on her tongue. Then, having dried that body which was destined, after many trials, to life immortal, the slave Nitida put on Thais the white robe she had woven.

The Bishop gave to each and all the kiss of peace, and, the ceremony being terminated, took off his sacerdotal insignia.

When they had left the crypt, Ahmes said —

"We ought to rejoice that we have this day brought a soul to the good Lord God; let us go to the house of your Holiness and spend the rest of the night in rejoicing."

"Thou hast well said, Theodore," replied the Bishop, and he led the little band to his house, which was quite near. It consisted of a single room, furnished with a couple of looms, a heavy table, and a worn-out carpet. As soon as they had entered,

"Nitida," cried the Nubian, "bring hither the stove and the jar of oil, and we will have a good supper."

Saying thus, he drew from under his cloak some little fish which he had kept concealed, and lighted a fire and fried them. The Bishop, the girl, the two boys, and the two slaves sat in a ring on the carpet, ate the fried fish, and blessed the Lord. Vivantius spoke of the torture he had undergone, and prophesied the speedy triumph of the Church. His language was grotesque, and full of word-play and rhetorical tropes. He compared the life of the just to a tissue of purple, and to explain the mystery of baptism, he said —

"The Divine Spirit floated on the waters, and that is why Christians receive the baptism of water. But demons also inhabit the brooks; springs consecrated to nymphs are especially dangerous, and there are certain waters which cause various maladies, both of the soul and of the body."

Sometimes he spoke enigmatically, and the child listened to him with profound awe and wonder. At the end of the repast he offered his guests a little wine, and this unloosed their tongues, and they began to sing lamentations and hymns. Ahmes and Nitida then rose, and danced a Nubian dance which they had learned as children, and which, no doubt, had been danced by their tribe since the early ages of the world. It was a love dance; waving their arms, and moving their bodies in rhythmic measure, they feigned, in turn, to fly from and to pursue each other. Their big eyes rolled, and they showed their gleaming teeth in broad grins.

In this strange manner did Thais receive the holy rite of baptism.

She loved amusements, and, as she grew, vague desires were created in her mind. All day long she danced and sang with the children in the streets, and when at night she returned to her father's house, she was still singing —

"Crooked twist, why do you stay in the house? I comb the wool, and the Miletan threads. Crooked twist, what did your son die of? He fell from the white horses into the sea."

She now began to prefer the company of boys and girls to that of the gentle and quiet Ahmes. She did not notice that her friend was not so often with her. The persecution having relented, the Christians were able to assemble more regularly, and the Nubian frequented these meetings assiduously. His zeal increased, and he sometimes uttered mysterious threats. He said that the rich would not keep their wealth. He went to the public places to which the poorer Christians used to resort, and assembling together all the poor wretches who were lying in the shade of the old walls, he announced to them that all slaves would soon be free, and that the day of justice was at hand.

"In the kingdom of God," he said, "the slaves will drink new wine and eat delicious fruits; whilst the rich, crouching at their feet like dogs, will devour the crumbs from their table."

These sayings were noised abroad through all that quarter of the city, and the masters feared that Ahmes might incite the slaves to revolt. The innkeeper hated him intensely, though he carefully concealed his rancour.

One day, a silver salt-cellar, reserved for the table of the gods, disappeared from the inn. Ahmes was accused of having stolen it — out of hate to his master and to the gods of the empire. There was no proof of the accusation, and the slave vehemently denied the charge. Nevertheless, he was dragged before the tribunal, and as he had the reputation of being a bad servant, the judge condemned him to death.

"As you did not know how to make a good use of your hands," he said, "they will be nailed to the cross."

Ahmes heard the verdict quietly, bowed to the judge most respectfully, and was taken to the public prison. During the three days that remained to him, he did not cease to preach the gospel to the prisoners, and it was related afterwards that the criminals, and the jailer himself, touched by his words, believed in Jesus crucified.

He was taken to the very place which one night, less than two years before, he had crossed so joyfully, carrying in his cloak little Thaïs, the daughter of his soul, his darling flower. When his hands were nailed to the cross, he uttered no complaint, but many times he sighed and murmured, "I thirst."

His agony lasted three days and three nights. It seemed hardly possible that human flesh could have endured such prolonged torture. Many times it was thought he was dead; the flies clustered on his eyelids, but suddenly he would reopen his bloodshot eyes. On the morning of the fourth day, he sang, in a voice clearer and purer than that of a child —

"Tell us, Mary, what thou hast seen where thou hast been?"

Then he smiled and said —

"They come, the angels of the good Lord. They bring me wine and fruit. How refreshing is the fanning of their wings!"

And he expired.

His features preserved in death an expression of ecstatic happiness. Even the soldiers who guarded the cross were struck with wonder. Vivantius, accompanied by some of the Christian brethren, claimed the body, and buried it with the remains of the other martyrs in the crypt of St. John the Baptist, and the Church venerated the memory of Saint Theodore the Nubian.

Three years later, Constantine, the conqueror of Maxentius, issued an edict which granted toleration to the Christians, and the believers were not henceforth persecuted, except by heretics.

Thais had completed her eleventh year when her friend was tortured to death, and she felt deeply saddened and shocked. Her soul was not sufficiently pure to allow her to understand that the slave Ahmes was blessed both in his life and his death. The idea sprang up in her little mind that no one can be good in this world except at the cost of the most terrible sufferings. And she was afraid to be good, for her delicate flesh could not bear pain.

At an early age, she had given herself to the lads about the port, and she followed the old men who wandered about the quarter in the evening, and with what she received from them she bought cakes and trinkets.

As she did not take home any of the money she gained, her mother continually ill-treated her. To get out of reach of her mother's arm, she often ran, bare-footed, to the city walls, and hid with the lizards. There she thought with envy of the ladies she had seen pass her, richly dressed, and in a litter surrounded by slaves.

One day, when she had been beaten more brutally than usual, she was crouching down beside the gate, motionless and sulky, when an old woman stopped in front of her, looked at her for some moments in silence, and then cried —

"Oh, the pretty flower! the beautiful child! Happy is the father who begot thee, and the mother who brought thee into the world!"

Thais remained silent, with her eyes fixed on the ground. Her eyelids were red, and it was evident she had been weeping.

"My white violet," continued the old woman, "is not your mother happy to have nourished a little goddess like you, and does not your father, when he sees you, rejoice from the bottom of his heart?"

To which the child replied, as though talking to herself —

"My father is a wine-skin swollen with wine, and my mother a greedy horse-leech."

The old woman glanced to right and left, to see if she were observed. Then, in a fawning voice —

"Sweet flowering hyacinth, beautiful drinker of light, come with me, and you shall have nothing to do but dance and smile. I will feed you on honey cakes, and my son — my own son — will love you as his eyes. My son is handsome and young; he has but little beard on his chin; his skin is soft, and he is, as they say, a little Acharnian pig."

Thais replied —

"I am quite willing to go with you."

And she rose and followed the old woman out of the city.

The old woman, who was named Moeroe, went from city to city with a troupe of girls and boys, whom she taught to dance, and then hired out to rich people to appear at feasts.

Guessing that Thais would soon develop into a most beautiful woman, she taught her — with the help of a whip — music and prosody, and she flogged with leather thongs those beautiful legs, when they did not move in time to the strains of the cithara. Her son — a decrepit abortion, of no age and no sex — ill-treated the child, on whom he vented the hate he had for all womankind. Like the dancing-girls whose grace he affected, he knew, and taught Thais, the art of pantomime, and how to mimic, by expression, gesture, and attitude, all human passions, and more especially the passions of love. He was a clever master, though he disliked his work; but he was jealous of his pupil, and as soon as he discovered that she was born to give men pleasure, he scratched her cheeks, pinched her arms, or pricked her legs, as a spiteful girl would have done. Thanks, however, to his lessons, she quickly became an excellent musician, pantomimist, and dancer. The brutality of her master did not at all surprise her; it seemed natural to her to be badly treated. She even felt some respect for the old woman, who knew music and drank Greek wine. Moeroe, when she came to Antioch, praised her pupil to the rich merchants of the city who gave banquets, both as a dancer and a flute-player. Thais danced and pleased. She accompanied the rich bankers, when they left the table, into the shady groves on the banks of the Orontes. She gave herself to all, for she knew nothing of the price of love. But one night that she had danced before the most fashionable young men of the city, the son of the pro-consul came to her, radiant with youth and pleasure, and said, in a voice that seemed redolent of kisses —

"Why am I not, Thais, the wreath which crowns your hair, the tunic which enfolds your beautiful form, the sandal on your pretty foot? I wish you to tread me under foot as a sandal; I wish my caresses to be your tunic and your wreath. Come, sweet girl! come to my house, and let us forget the world."

She looked at him whilst he was speaking, and saw that he was handsome. Suddenly she felt a cold sweat on her face. She turned green as grass; she reeled; a cloud descended before her eyes. He again implored her to come with him, but she refused. His ardent looks, his burning words were vain, and when he took her in his arms to try and drag her away, she pushed him off rudely. Then he implored her, and shed tears. But a new, unknown, and invincible passion dominated her heart, and she still resisted.

"What madness!" said the guests. "Lollius is noble, handsome, and rich, and a dancing-girl treats him with scorn!"

243

Lollius returned home alone that night, quite love-sick. He came in the morning, pale and red-eyed, and hung flowers at the dancing-girl's door.

But Thais was frightened and troubled; she avoided Lollius, and yet he was continually in her mind. She suffered, and she did not know the cause of her complaint. She wondered why she had thus changed, and why she was melancholy. She recoiled from all her lovers; they were hateful to her. She loathed the light of day, and lay on her bed all day, sobbing, and with her head buried in the pillows. Lollius contrived to gain admittance, and came many times, but neither his pleadings nor his execrations had any effect on the obdurate girl. In his presence, she was as timid as a virgin, and would say nothing but —

"I will not! I will not!"

But at the end of a fortnight she gave in, for she knew that she loved him; she went to his house and lived with him. They were supremely happy. They passed their days shut up together, gazing into each other's eyes, and babbling a childish jargon. In the evening, they walked on the lonely banks of the Orontes, and lost themselves in the laurel woods. Sometimes they rose at dawn, to go and gather hyacinths on the slopes of Sulpicus. They drank from the same cup, and he would take a grape from between her lips with his mouth.

Moeroe came to Lollius, and cried and shrieked that Thais should be restored to her.

"She is my daughter," she said, "my daughter, who has been torn from me. My perfumed flower — my own bowels — !"

Lollius gave her a large sum of money, and sent her away. But, as she came back to demand some more gold staters, the young man had her put in prison, and the magistrates having discovered that she was guilty of many crimes, she was condemned to death, and thrown to the wild beasts.

Thais loved Lollius with all the passion of her mind, and the bewilderment of innocence. She told him, and told him truly from the bottom of her heart —

"I have never loved any one but you."

244

Lollius replied —

"You are not like any other woman."

The spell lasted six months, but it broke at last. Thais suddenly felt that her heart was empty and lonely. Lollius no longer seemed the same to her. She thought —

"What can have thus changed me in an instant? How is it that he is now like any other man, and no longer like himself?"

She left him, not without a secret desire to find Lollius again in another, as she no longer found him in himself. She thought it would be less dull to live with someone she had never loved, than with one she had ceased to love. She appeared, in the company of rich debauchees, at those sacred feasts at which naked virgins danced in the temples, and troops of courtesans swam across the Orontes. She took part in all the pleasures of the fashionable and depraved city; and she assiduously frequented the theatres, at which clever mimes from all countries performed amidst the applause of a crowd greedy for excitement.

She carefully observed the mimes, dancers, comedians, and especially the women, who in tragedies represented goddesses in love with young men, or mortals loved by the gods. Having discovered the secrets by which they pleased the audience, she thought to herself that she was more beautiful and could act better. She went to the manager, and asked to be admitted into the troupe. Thanks to her beauty, and to the lessons she had received from old Moeroe, she was received, and appeared on the stage in the part of Dirce.

She met with but indifferent success, for she was inexperienced, and the admiration of the spectators had not been aroused by hearing her praises sung. But after she had played small parts for a few months, the power of her beauty burst forth with such effect that all the city was moved. All Antioch crowded to the theatre. The imperial magistrates and the chief citizens were compelled, by the force of public opinion, to show themselves there. The porters, sweepers, and dock labourers went without bread and garlic, that they might pay for their places. Poets composed epigrams in her honour. Bearded philosophers inveighed against her in the baths and gymnasia; when her litter passed, Christian priests turned away their heads. The threshold of her door was wreathed with flowers, and sprinkled with blood. She received so much money from her lovers that it was no longer counted, but measured by the medimnus, and all the treasure hoarded by miserly old men was poured out at her feet. But she was placid and unmoved. She rejoiced, with quiet pride, in the admiration of the public and the favour of the gods, and was so much loved that she loved herself.

After she had several years enjoyed the admiration and affection of the Antiochians, she was taken with a desire to revisit Alexandria, and show her glory in that city in which, as a child, she had wandered in want and shame, hungry and lean as a grasshopper in the middle of a dusty road. The golden city joyfully welcomed her, and loaded her with fresh riches; when she appeared in the games it was a triumph. Countless admirers and lovers came to her. She received them with indifference, for she at last despaired of meeting another Lollius.

Amongst many others, she met the philosopher Nicias, who desired to possess her, although he professed to have no desires. In spite of his riches, he was intelligent and modest. But his delicate wit and beautiful sentiments failed to charm her. She did not love him and sometimes his refined irony even irritated her. His perpetual doubts hurt her, for he believed in nothing, and she believed in everything. She believed in divine providence, in the omnipotence of evil spirits, in spells, exorcisms, and eternal justice; she believed in Jesus Christ, and in the goddess of good of the Syrians; she believed also that bitches barked when black Hecate passed through the streets, and that a woman could inspire love by pouring a philtre into a cup wrapped in the bleeding skin of a sheep. She thirsted for the unknown; she called on nameless gods, and lived in perpetual expectation. The future frightened her, and yet she wished to know it. She surrounded herself with priests of Isis, Chaldean magi, pharmacopolists, and professors of the black arts, who invariably deceived her, though she never tired of being deceived. She feared death, and she saw it everywhere. When she yielded to pleasure, it seemed to her that an icy finger would suddenly touch her on the bare shoulder, and she turned pale, and cried with terror, in the arms which embraced her.

Nicias said to her —

"What does it matter, O my Thais, whether we descend to eternal night with white locks and hollow cheeks, or, whether this very day, now laughing to the vast sky, shall be our last? Let us enjoy life; we shall have greatly lived if we have greatly loved. There is no knowledge except that of the senses; to love is to understand. That which we do not know does not exist. What good is it to worry ourselves about nothing?"

She replied angrily —

"I despise men like you, who hope for nothing and fear nothing. I wish to know! I wish to know!"

In order to understand the secret of life, she set to work to read the books of the philosophers, but she did not understand them. The further the years of her childhood receded from her, the more anxious she was to recall them. She loved to traverse at night, in disguise, the alleys, squares, and places where she had grown up so miserably. She was sorry she had lost her parents, and especially that she had not been able to love them. When she met any Christian priest, she thought of her baptism, and felt troubled. One night, when enveloped in a long cloak, and her fair hair hidden under a black hood, she was wandering, according to custom, about the suburbs of the city, she found herself — without knowing how she came there — before the poor little church of St. John the Baptist. They were singing inside the church, and a bright light glimmered through the chinks of the door. There was nothing strange in that, as, for the past twenty years, the Christians, protected by the conqueror of Maxentius, had publicly solemnized their festivals. But these hymns seemed more like an ardent appeal to the soul. As if she had been invited to the mysteries, she pushed the door open with her arm, and entered the building. She found a numerous assembly of women, children, and old men, on their knees before a tomb, which stood against the wall. The tomb was nothing but a stone coffer, roughly sculptured with vine tendrils and bunches of grapes; yet it had received great honours, and was covered with green palms and wreaths of red roses. All round, innumerable lights gleamed out of the heavy shadow, in which the smoke of Arabian gums seemed like the folds of angels' robes, and the paintings on the walls visions of Paradise. Priests, clad in white, were prostrate at the foot of the sarcophagus. The hymns they sang with the people expressed the delight of suffering, and mingled, in a triumphal mourning, so much joy with so much grief, that Thais, in listening to them, felt the pleasures of life and the terrors of death flowing, at the same time, through her re-awakened senses.

When they had finished singing, the believers rose, and walked in single file to the tomb, the side of which they kissed. They were common men, accustomed to work with their hands. They advanced with a heavy step, the eyes fixed, the jaw dropped, but they had an air of sincerity. They knelt down, each in turn, before the sarcophagus, and put their lips to it. The women lifted their little children in their arms, and gently placed their cheek to the stone.

Thais, surprised and troubled, asked a deacon why they did so.

"Do you not know, woman," replied the deacon, "that we celebrate to-day the blessed memory of St. Theodore the Nubian, who suffered for the faith in the days of the Emperor Diocletian? He lived virtuously and died a martyr, and that is why, robed in white, we bear red roses to his glorious tomb."

On hearing these words, Thais fell on her knees, and burst into tears. Half-forgotten recollections of Ahmes returned to her mind. On the memory of this obscure, gentle, and unfortunate man, the blaze of candles, the perfume of roses, the clouds of incense, the music of hymns, the piety of souls, threw all the charms of glory. Thais thought in the dazzling glare —

"He was good, and now he has become great and glorious. Why is it that he is elevated above other men? What is this unknown thing which is more than riches or pleasure?"

She rose slowly, and turned towards the tomb of the saint who had loved her, those violet eyes, now filled with tears which glittered in the candle-light; then, with bowed head, humble, slow, and the last, with those lips on which so many desires hung, she kissed the stone of the slave's tomb.

When she returned to her house, she found Nicias, who, with his hair perfumed, and his tunic thrown open, was reading a treatise on morals whilst waiting for her. He advanced with open arms.

"Naughty Thais," he said, in a laughing voice, "whilst I was waiting for you to come, do you know what I saw in this manuscript, written by the gravest of Stoics? Precepts of virtue and noble maxims: No! On the staid papyrus, I saw dance thousands and thousands of little Thaises. Each was no bigger than my finger, and yet their grace was infinite, and all were the only Thais. There were some who flaunted in mantles of purple and gold; others, like a white cloud, floated in the air in transparent drapery. Others again, motionless and divinely nude, the better to inspire pleasure, expressed no thought. Lastly, there were two, hand in hand; two so alike that it was impossible to distinguish one from the other. Both smiled. The first said, 'I am love.' The other, 'I am death.'"

Thus speaking, he pressed Thais in his arms, and not noticing the sullen look in her downcast eyes, he went on adding thought to thought, heedless of the fact that they were all lost upon her.

"Yes, when I had before my eyes the line in which it was written, 'Nothing should deter you from improving your mind,' I read, 'The kisses of Thais are warmer than fire, and sweeter than honey.' That is how a philosopher reads the books of other philosophers — and that is your fault, you naughty child. It is true that, as long as we are what we are, we shall never find anything but our own thoughts in the thoughts of others, and that all of us are somewhat inclined to read books as I have read this one."

She did not hear him; her soul was still before the Nubian's tomb. As he heard her sigh, he kissed her on the neck, and said —

"Do not be sad, my child. We are never happy in this world, except when we forget the world.

"Come, let us cheat life — it is sure to take its revenge. Come, let us love!"

But she pushed him away.

"*We* love!" she cried bitterly. "*You* never loved any one. And *I* do not love *you!* No! I do not love you! I hate you! Go! I hate you! I curse and despise all who are happy, and all who are rich! Go! Go! Goodness is only found amongst the unfortunate. When I was a child I knew a black slave who died on the cross. He was good; he was filled with love, and he knew the secret of life. You are not worthy to wash his feet. Go! I never wish to see you again!"

She threw herself on her face on the carpet, and passed the night sobbing and weeping, and forming resolutions to live, in future, like Saint Theodore, in poverty and humbleness.

The next day, she devoted herself again to those pleasures to which she was addicted. As she knew that her beauty, though still intact, would not last very long, she hastened to derive all the enjoyment and all the fame she could from it. At the theatre, where she acted and studied more than ever, she gave life to the imagination of sculptors, painters, and poets. Recognizing that there was in the attitudes, movements, and walk of the actress, an idea of the divine harmony which rules the spheres, wise men and philosophers considered that such perfect grace was a virtue in itself, and said, "Thais also is a geometrician!" The ignorant, the poor, the humble, and the timid before whom she consented to appear, regarded her as a blessing from heaven. Yet she was sad amidst all the praise she received, and dreaded death more than ever. Nothing was able to set her mind at rest, not even her house and gardens, which were celebrated, and a proverb throughout the city.

The gardens were planted with trees, brought at great expense from India and Persia. They were watered by a running brook, and colonnades in ruins, and imitation rocks, arranged by a skilful artist, were reflected in a lake, which also mirrored the statues that stood round it. In the middle of the garden was the Grotto of Nymphs, which owed its name to three life-size figures of women, which stood on the threshold. They were represented as divesting themselves of their garments, and about to bathe. They anxiously turned their heads, fearing to be seen, and looked as though they were alive. The only light which entered the building came, tempered and iridescent, through thin sheets of water. All the walls were hung — as in the sacred grottoes — with wreaths, garlands, and votive pictures, in which the beauty of Thais was celebrated. There were also tragic and comic masks, bright with colours; and paintings representing theatrical scenes or grotesque figures, or fabulous animals. On a stele in the centre stood a little ivory Eros of wonderful antique workmanship. It was a gift from Nicias. In one of the bays was a figure of a goat in black marble, with shining agate eyes. Six alabaster kids crowded round its teats; but, raising its cloven hoofs and its ugly head, it seemed impatient to climb the rocks. The floor was covered with Byzantine carpets, pillows embroidered by the yellow men of Cathay, and the skins of Libyan lions. Perfumed smoke arose from golden censers. Flowering plants grew in large onyx vases. And at the far end, in the purple shadow, gleamed the gold nails on the shell of a huge Indian tortoise turned upside down, which served as the bed of the actress. It was here that every day, to the murmur of the water, and amid perfumes and flowers, Thais reclined softly, and conversed with her friends, while awaiting the hour of supper, or meditated in solitude on theatrical art, or on the flight of years.

On the afternoon after the games, Thais was reposing in the Grotto of Nymphs. She had noticed in her mirror the first signs of the decay of her beauty, and she was frightened to think that white hair and wrinkles would at last come. She vainly tried to comfort herself with the assurance that she could recover her fresh complexion by burning certain herbs and pronouncing a few magic words. A pitiless voice cried, "You will grow old Thais;

you will grow old." And a cold sweat of terror bedewed her forehead. Then, on looking at herself again in the mirror with infinite tenderness, she found that she was still beautiful and worthy to be loved. She smiled to herself, and murmured, "There is not a woman in Alexandria who can rival me in suppleness or grace or movement, or in splendour of arms, and the arms, my mirror, are the real chains of love!"

While she was thus thinking she saw an unknown man — thin, with burning eyes and unkempt beard, and clad in a richly embroidered robe — standing before her. She let fall her mirror, and uttered a cry of fright.

Paphnutius stood motionless, and seeing how beautiful she was, he murmured this prayer from the bottom of his heart —

"Grant, my God, that the face of this woman may not be a temptation, but may prove salutary to Thy servant."

Then, forcing himself to speak, he said —

"Thais, I live in a far country, and the fame of thy beauty has led me to thee. It is said that thou art the most clever of actresses and the most irresistible of women. That which is related of thy riches and thy love affairs seems fabulous, and calls to mind the old story of Rhodope, whose marvelous history is known by heart to all the boatmen on the Nile. Therefore I was seized with a desire to know thee, and I see that the truth surpasses the rumour. Thou art a thousand times more clever and more beautiful than is reported. And now that I see thee, I say to myself, 'It is impossible to approach her without staggering like a drunken man.'"

The words were feigned; but the monk, animated by pious zeal, uttered them with real warmth. Thais gazed, without displeasure, at this strange being who had frightened her. The rough, wild aspect, and the fiery glances of his eyes, astonished her. She was curious to learn the state of life of a man so different from all others she had met. She replied, with gentle raillery —

"You seem prompt to admire, stranger. Beware that my looks do not consume you to the bones! Beware of loving me!"

He said —

"I love thee, O Thais! I love thee more than my life, and more than myself. For thee I have quitted the desert; for thee my lips — vowed to silence — have pronounced profane words; for thee I have seen what I ought not to have seen, and heard what it was forbidden to me to hear; for thee my soul is troubled, my heart is open, and the thoughts gush out like the running springs at which the pigeons drink; for thee I have walked day and night across sandy deserts teeming with reptiles and vampires; for thee I have placed my bare foot on vipers and scorpions! Yes, I love thee! I love thee, but not like those men who, burning with the lusts of the flesh, come to thee like devouring wolves or furious bulls. Thou art dear to them as is the gazelle to the lion. Their ravening lusts will consume thee to the soul, O woman! I love thee in spirit and in truth; I love thee in God, and for ever and ever; that which is in my breast is named true zeal and divine charity. I promise thee better things than drunkenness crowned with flowers or the dreams of a brief night. I promise thee holy feasts and celestial suppers. The happiness that I bring thee will never end; it is unheard-of, it is ineffable, and such that if the happy of this world could only see a shadow of it they would die of wonder."

Thais laughed mischievously.

"Friend," she said, "show me this wonderful love. Make haste! Long speeches would be an insult to my beauty; let us not lose a moment. I am impatient to taste the felicity you announce; but, to say the truth, I fear that I shall always remain ignorant of it, and that all you have promised me will vanish in words. It is easier to promise a great happiness than to give it. Everyone has a talent of some sort. I fancy that yours is to make long speeches. You speak of an unknown love. It is so long since kisses were first exchanged that it would be very extraordinary if there still remained secrets in love. On this subject lovers know more than philosophers."

"Do not jest, Thais. I bring thee the unknown love."

"Friend, you come too late. I know every kind of love."

"The love that I bring thee abounds with glory, whilst the loves that thou knowest breed only shame."

Thais looked at him with an angry eye, a frown gathered on her beautiful face.

"You are very bold, stranger, to offend your hostess. Look at me, and say if I resemble a creature crushed down with shame. No, I am not ashamed, and all others who live like me are not ashamed either, although they are not so beautiful or so rich as I am. I have sown pleasure in my footsteps, and I am celebrated for that all over the world. I am more powerful than the masters of the world. I have seen them at my feet. Look at me, look at these little feet; thousands of men would pay with their blood for the happiness of kissing them. I am not very big, and I do not occupy much space on the earth. To those who look at me from the top of the Serapeium, when I pass in the street, I look like a grain of rice; but that grain of rice has caused among men, griefs, despairs, hates, and crimes enough to have filled Tartarus. Are you not mad to talk to me of shame when all around proclaims my glory?"

"That which is glory in the eyes of men, is infamy before God. O woman, we have been nourished in countries so different, that it is not surprising we have neither the same language nor the same thoughts! Yet Heaven is my witness that I wish to agree with thee, and that it is my intention not to leave thee until we share the same sentiments. Who will inspire me with burning words that will melt thee like wax in my breath, O woman, that the fingers of my desires may mould thee as they wish? What virtue will deliver thee to me, O dearest of souls, that the spirit which animates me, creating thee a second time, may imprint on thee a fresh beauty, and that thou mayest cry, weeping for joy, 'It is only now that I am born'? Who will cause to gush in my heart a fount of Siloam, in which thou mayest bathe and recover thy first purity? Who will change me into a Jordan, the waves of which sprinkled on thee, will give thee life eternal?"

Thais was no longer angry.

"This man," she thought, "talks of life eternal and all that he says seems written on a talisman. No doubt he is a mage, and

254

knows secret charms against old age and death," and she resolved to offer herself to him. Therefore, pretending to be afraid of him, she retired a few steps to the end of the grotto, and sitting down on the edge of the bed, artfully pulled her tunic across her breast; then, motionless and mute and her eyes cast down, she waited. Her long eyelashes made a soft shadow on her cheeks. Her entire attitude expressed modesty; her naked feet swung gently, and she looked like a child sitting thinking on the bank of a brook. But Paphnutius looked at her, and did not move. His trembling knees hardly supported him, his tongue dried in his mouth, a terrible buzzing rang in his ears. But all at once his sight failed, and he could see nothing before him but a thick cloud. He thought that the hand of Jesus had been laid on his eyes, to hide this woman from them. Reassured by such succour, strengthened and fortified, he said with a gravity worthy of an old hermit of the desert —

"If thou givest thyself to me, thinkest thou it is hidden from God?"

She shook her head.

"God? Who forces Him to keep His eye always upon the Grotto of Nymphs? Let Him go away if we offend Him! But why should we offend Him? Since He has created us, He can be neither angry nor surprised to see us as He made us, and acting according to the nature He has given us. A good deal too much is said on His behalf, and He is often credited with ideas He never had. You yourself, stranger, do you know His true character? Who are you that you should speak to me in His name?"

At this question the monk, opening his borrowed robe, showed the cassock, and said —

"I am Paphnutius, Abbot of Antinoe, and I come from the holy desert. The hand that drew Abraham from Chaldaea and Lot from Sodom has separated me from the present age. I no longer existed for the men of this century. But thy image appeared to me in my sandy Jerusalem, and I knew that thou wert full of corruption, and death was in thee. And now I am before thee, woman, as before a grave, and I cry unto thee, 'Thais, arise!'"

At the words, Paphnutius, monk, and abbot, she had turned pale with fright. And now, with disheveled hair and joined hands, weeping and groaning, she dragged herself to the feet of the saint.

"Do not hurt me! Why have you come? What do you want of me? Do not hurt me! I know that the saints of the desert hate women who, like me, are made to please. I am afraid that you hate me, and want to hurt me. Go! I do not doubt your power. But know, Paphnutius, that you should neither despise me nor hate me. I have never, like many of the men I know, laughed at your voluntary poverty. In your turn, do not make a crime of my riches. I am beautiful, and clever in acting. I no more chose my condition than my nature. I was made for that which I do. I was born to charm men. And you yourself, did you not say just now that you loved me? Do not use your science against me. Do not pronounce magic words which would destroy my beauty, or change me into a statue of salt. Do not terrify me! I am already too frightened. Do not kill me! I am so afraid of death."

He made a sign to her to rise, and said —

"Child, have no fear. I will utter no word of shame or scorn. I come on behalf of Him who sat on the edge of the well, and drank of the pitcher which the woman of Samaria offered to Him; and who, also, when He supped at the house of Simon, received the perfumes of Mary. I am not without sin that I should throw the first stone. I have often badly employed the abundant grace which God has bestowed upon me. It was not anger, but pity, which took me by the hand to conduct me here. I can, without deceit, address thee in words of love, for it is the zeal in my heart which has brought me to thee. I burn with the fire of charity, and if thy eyes, accustomed only to the gross sights of the flesh, could see things in their mystic aspect, I should appear unto thee as a branch broken off the burning bush which the Lord showed on the mountain to Moses of old, that he might understand true love — that which envelops us, and which, so far from leaving behind it mere coals and ashes, purifies and perfumes for ever that which it penetrates."

"I believe you, monk, and no longer fear either deceit or ill-will from you. I have often heard talk of the hermits of the Thebaid. Marvelous things have been told concerning Anthony and Paul. Your name is not unknown to me, and I have heard say that, though you are still young, you equal in virtue the oldest anchorites. As soon as I saw you, and without knowing who you were, I felt that you were no ordinary man. Tell me! can you do for me that which neither the priests of Isis, nor of Hermes, nor of the celestial Juno, nor the Chaldean soothsayers, nor the Babylonian magi have been able to effect? Monk, if you love me, can you prevent me from dying?"

"Woman, whosoever wishes to live shall live. Flee from the abominable delights in which thou diest for ever. Snatch from the devils, who will burn it most horribly, that body which God kneaded with His spittle and animated with his own breath. Thou art consumed with weariness; come, and refresh thyself at the blessed springs of solitude; come and drink of those fountains which are hidden in the desert, and which gush forth to heaven. Careworn soul, come, and possess that which thou desirest! Heart greedy for joy, come and taste true joys — poverty, retirement, self-forgetfulness, seclusion in the bosom of God. Enemy of Christ now, and to-morrow His well-beloved, come to Him! Come, thou whom I have sought, and thou wilt say, 'I have found love!'"

Thais seemed lost in meditation on things afar.

"Monk," she asked, "if I adjure all pleasures and do penance, is it true that I shall be born again in heaven, my body intact in all its beauty?"

"Thais, I bring thee eternal life. Believe me, for that which I announce to thee is the truth."

"Who will assure me that it is the truth?"

"David and the prophets, the Scriptures, and the wonders that thou shalt behold."

"Monk, I should like to believe you, for I must confess that I have not found happiness in this world. My lot in life is better than that of a queen, and yet I have many bitternesses and misfortunes, and I am infinitely weary of my existence. All women envy me, and yet sometimes I have envied the lot of a toothless old woman who, when I was a child, sold honey-cakes under one of the city gates. Often has the idea flashed across my mind that only the poor are good, happy, and blessed, and that there must be great gladness in living humble and obscure. Monk, you have agitated a storm in my soul, and brought to the surface that which lay at the bottom. Who am I to believe, alas! and what is to become of me — and what is life?"

Whilst she thus spoke, Paphnutius was transfigured; celestial joy beamed in his face.

"Listen!" he said. "I was not alone when I entered this house. Another accompanied me, another who stands by my side. Him thou canst not see, because thy eyes are yet unworthy to behold Him; but soon thou shalt see Him in all His glorious splendour, and thou wilt say, 'He alone is to be adored.' But now, if He had not placed His gentle hands before my eyes, O Thais, I should perhaps have fallen into sin with thee, for of myself I am but weak and sinful. But He saved us both. He is as good as He is powerful, and His name is the Saviour. He was promised to the world, by David and the prophets, worshipped in His cradle by the shepherds and the magi, crucified by the Pharisees, buried by the holy women, revealed to the world by the apostles, testified to by the martyrs. And now, having learned that thou fearest death, O woman, He has come to thy house to prevent thee from dying. Art Thou not here present with me, Jesus, at this moment, as Thou didst appear to the men of Galilee, in those wonderful days when the stars, which came down with thee from heaven, were so near the earth that the holy innocents could take them in their hands, when they played in their mothers' arms on the terraces of Bethlehem? Is it not true, Jesus, that Thou art here present, and that Thou showest me in reality Thy precious body? Is not Thy face here, and that tear which flows down Thy cheek a real tear? Yes, the angel of eternal justice shall receive it, and it shall be the ransom of the soul of Thais. Art Thou not here, Jesus? Jesus, Thy loving lips open. Thou canst speak; speak, I hear Thee! And thee,

258

Thais, happy Thais! listen to what the Saviour Himself says to thee; it is He who speaks, not I. He says, 'I have sought thee long, O My lost sheep! I have found thee at last! Fly from Me no more. Let Me take thee by the hands, poor little one, and I will bear thee on My shoulders to the heavenly fold. Come, My Thais! come, My chosen one! come, and weep with Me!'"

And Paphnutius fell on his knees, his eyes filled with ecstasy. And then Thais saw in his face the likeness of the living Christ.

"O vanished days of my childhood!" she sobbed. "O sweet father Ahmes! good Saint Theodore, why did I not die in thy white mantle whilst thou didst bear me, in the first dawn of day, yet fresh from the waters of baptism!"

Paphnutius advanced towards her, crying —

"Thou art baptized! O divine wisdom! O Providence! O great God! I know now the power which drew me to thee. I know what rendered thee so dear and so beautiful in my eyes. It was the virtue of the baptismal water, which made me leave the shadow of God, where I lived, to seek thee in the poisoned air where men dwell. A drop — a drop, no doubt, of the water which washed thy body — has been sprinkled in my face. Come, O my sister, and receive from thy brother the kiss of peace."

And the monk touched with his lips the forehead of the courtesan.

Then he was silent, letting God speak, and nothing was heard in the Grotto of Nymphs but the sobs of Thais, mingled with the rippling of the running water.

She wept without trying to stop her tears, when two black slaves appeared, loaded with stuffs, perfumes, and garlands.

"It was hardly the right time to weep," she said, trying to smile. "Tears redden the eyes and spoil the complexion, and I must sup tonight with some friends, and want to be beautiful, for there will be women there quick to spy out marks of care on my face. These slaves come to dress me. Withdraw, my father, and allow them to do their work. They are clever and experienced, and I pay them well for their services. You see that one who wears thick rings of gold, and shows such white teeth. I took her from the wife of the pro-consul."

Paphnutius had at first a thought of dissuading Thais, as earnestly as he could, from going to this supper. But he determined to act prudently, and asked what persons she would meet there.

She replied that there would be the host, old Cotta, the Prefect of the Fleet, Nicias, and several other philosophers who loved an argument, the poet Callicrates, the high priest of Serapis, some young men whose chief amusement was training horses, and lastly some women, of whom there was little to be said except that they were young. Then, by a supernatural inspiration —

"Go amongst them, Thais," said the monk. "Go! But I will not leave thee. I will go with thee to this banquet, and will remain by thy side without saying a word."

She burst out laughing. And whilst her two black slaves were busy dressing her, she cried —

"What will they say when they see that I have a monk of the Thebaid for my lover?"

THE BANQUET

When, followed by Paphnutius, Thais entered the banqueting-room, the guests were already, for the most part, assembled, and reclining on their couches before the horseshoe table, which was covered with glittering vessels. In the centre of the table stood a silver basin, surmounted by four figures of satyrs, who poured out from wine-skins on the boiled fish a kind of pickle in which they floated. When Thais appeared, acclamations arose from all sides.

Greetings to the sister of the Graces!

To the silent Melpomene, who can express all things with her looks!

Salutation to the well-beloved of gods and men!

To the much desired!

To her who gives suffering and its cure!

To the pearl of Racotis!

To the rose of Alexandria!

She waited impatiently till this torrent of praise had passed, and then said to Cotta, the host —

"Lucius, I have brought you a monk of the desert, Paphnutius, the Abbot of Antinoe. He is a great saint, whose words burn like fire."

Lucius Aurelius Cotta, the Prefect of the Fleet, rose, and replied —

"You are welcome, Paphnutius, you who profess the Christian faith. I myself have some respect of a religion that has now become imperial. The divine Constantine has placed your co-religionists in the front rank of the friends of the empire. Latin wisdom ought, in fact, to admit your Christ into our pantheon. It was a maxim of our forefathers that there was something divine in every god. But no more of that. Let us drink and enjoy ourselves while there is yet time."

Old Cotta spoke tranquilly. He had just studied a new model for a galley, and had finished the sixth book of his history of the Carthaginians. He felt sure he had not lost his day, and was satisfied with himself and the gods.

"Paphnutius," he added, "you see here several men who are worthy to be loved — Hermodorus, the High Priest of Serapis; the philosophers Dorion, Nicias, and Zenothemis; the poet Callicrates; young Chereas and young Aristobulus, both sons of dear old comrades; and near them Philina and Drosea, who deserve to be praised for their beauty."

Nicias embraced Paphnutius, and whispered in his ear —

"I warned you, brother, that Venus was powerful. It is her gentle force that has brought you here in spite of yourself. Listen: you are a man full of piety, but if you do not confess that she is the mother of the gods, your ruin is certain. Do you know that the old mathematician, Melanthes, used to say, 'I cannot demonstrate the properties of a triangle without the aid of Venus'?"

Dorion, who had for some seconds been looking at the new-comer, suddenly clapped his hands and uttered a cry of surprise.

"It is he, friends! His look, his beard, his tunic — it is he himself! I met him at the theatre whilst our Thais was acting. He was furiously excited, and spoke with violence, as I can testify. He is an honest man, but he will abuse us all; his eloquence is terrible. If Marcus is the Plato of the Christians, Paphnutius is the Demosthenes. Epicurus, in his little garden, never heard the like."

Philina and Drosea, however, devoured Thais with their eyes. She wore on her fair hair a wreath of pale violets, each flower of which recalled, in a paler hue, the colour of her eyes, so that the flowers looked like softened glances, and the eyes like sparkling flowers. It was the peculiar gift of this woman; on her everything lived, and was soul and harmony. Her robe, which was of mauve spangled with silver, trailed in long folds with a grace that was almost melancholy and was not relieved by either bracelets or necklaces. The chief charm of her appearance was her beautiful bare arms. The two friends were obliged to admire, in spite of themselves the robe and head-dress of Thais, though they said nothing to her on the subject.

"How beautiful you are!" said Philina. "You could not have been more so when you came to Alexandria. Yet my mother, who remembers seeing you then, says there were few women who were worthy to be compared with you."

"Who is the new lover you have brought?" asked Drosea. "He has a strange, wild appearance. If there are shepherds of elephants, assuredly he must resemble one. Where did you find such a wild-looking friend, Thais? Was it amongst the troglodytes who live under the earth, and are grimy with the smoke of Hades?"

But Philina put her finger on Drosea's lips.

"Hush! the mysteries of love must remain secret, and it is forbidden to know them. For my own part, certainly, I would rather be kissed by the mouth of smoking Etna than by the lips of that man. But our dear Thais, who is beautiful and adorable as the goddesses, should, like the goddesses, grant all requests, and not, like us, only those of nice young men."

"Take care, both of you!" replied Thais. "He is a mage and an enchanter. He hears words that are whispered, and even thoughts. He will tear out your heart while you are asleep, and put a sponge in its place, and the next day, when you drink water, you will be choked to death."

She watched them grow pale, then she turned away from them, and sat on a couch by the side of Paphnutius. The voice of Cotta, kind but imperious, was suddenly heard above the murmur of conversation.

"Friends, let each take his place! Slaves, pour out the honeyed wine!"

Then, the host raising his cup —

"Let us first drink to the divine Constantine and the genius of the empire. The country should be put first of all, even above the gods, for it contains them all."

All the guests raised their full cups to their lips. Paphnutius alone did not drink, because Constantine had persecuted the Nicaean faith, and because the country of the Christian is not of this world.

Dorion, having drunk, murmured —

"What is one's country? A flowing river. The shores change, and the waves are incessantly renewed."

"I know, Dorion," replied the Prefect of the Fleet, "that you care little for the civic virtues, and you think that the sage ought to hold himself aloof from all affairs. I think, on the contrary, that an honest man should desire nothing better than to fill a responsible post in the State. The State is a noble thing."

Hermodorus, the High Priest of Serapis, spoke next —

"Dorion has asked, 'What is one's country?' I will reply that the altars of the gods and the tombs of ancestors make one's country. A man is a fellow-citizen by association of memories and hopes."

Young Aristobulus interrupted Hermodorus.

"By Castor! I saw a splendid horse to-day. It belonged to Demophoon. It has a fine head, small jaw, and strong forelegs. It carries its neck high and proud, like a cock."

But young Chereas shook his head.

"It is not such a good horse as you say, Aristobulus. Its hoofs are thin, and the pasterns are too low; the animal will soon go lame."

They were continuing their dispute, when Drosea uttered a piercing shriek.

"Oh! I nearly swallowed a fish-bone, as long and much sharper than a style. Luckily, I was able to get it out of my throat in time! The gods love me!"

"Did you say, Drosea, that the gods loved you?" asked Nicias, smiling. "Then they must share the same infirmities as men. Love presupposes unhappiness on the part of whoever suffers from it, and is a proof of weakness. The affection they feel for Drosea is a great proof of the imperfection of the gods."

At these words Drosea flew into a great rage.

"Nicias, your remarks are foolish and not to the point. But that is your character — you never understand what is said, and reply in words devoid of sense."

Nicias smiled again.

"Talk away, talk away, Drosea. Whatever you say, we are glad every time you open your mouth. Your teeth are so pretty!"

At that moment, a grave-looking old man, negligently dressed, walking slowly, with his head high, entered the room, and gazed at the guests quietly. Cotta made a sign to him to take a place by his side, on the same couch.

"Eucrites," he said, "you are welcome. Have you composed a new treatise on philosophy this month? That would make, if I calculate correctly, the ninety-second that has proceeded from the Nile reed you direct with an Attic hand."

Eucrites replied, stroking his silver beard —

"The nightingale was created to sing, and I was created to praise the immortal gods."

DORION. Let us respectfully salute, in Eucrites, the last of the stoics. Grave and white, he stands in the midst of us like the image of an ancestor. He is solitary amidst a crowd of men, and the words he utters are not heard.

EUCRITES. You deceive yourself, Dorion. The philosophy of virtue is not dead. I have numerous disciples in Alexandria, Rome, and Constantinople. Many of the slaves, and some of the nephews of Caesar, now know how to govern themselves, to live independently, and being unconcerned with all affairs, they enjoy boundless happiness. Many of them have revived, in their own person, Epictetus and Marcus Aurelius. But if it were true that virtue were for ever extinguished upon the earth, in what way would the loss of it affect my happiness, since it did not depend on me whether it existed or perished? Only fools, Dorion, place their happiness out of their own power. I desire nothing that the gods do not wish, and I desire all that they do wish. By that means I render myself like unto them, and share their infallible content. If virtue perishes, I consent that it should perish, and that consent fills me with joy, as the supreme effort of my reason or my courage. In all things my wisdom will copy the divine wisdom, and the copy will be more valuable than the model; it will have cost greater care and more work.

NICIAS. I understand. You put yourself on the same level as divine providence. But if virtue consists only in effort, Eucrites, and in that intense application by which the disciples of Zeno pretend to render themselves equal to the gods, the frog, which swelled itself out to try and become as big as the ox, accomplished a masterpiece of stoicism.

EUCRITES. You jest, Nicias, and, as usual, you excel in ridicule. But if the ox of which you speak is really a god, like Apis, or like that subterranean ox whose high priest I see here, and if the frog, being wisely inspired, succeed in equaling it, would it not be, in fact, more virtuous than the ox, and could you refrain from admiring such a courageous little animal!

Four servants placed on the table a wild pig, still covered with its bristles. Little pigs, made of pastry, surrounded the animal, as though they would suckle, to show that it was a sow.

Zenothemis, turning towards the monk, said —

"Friends, a guest has come hither to join us. The illustrious Paphnutius, who leads such an extraordinary life of solitude, is our unexpected guest."

COTTA. You may even add, Zenothemis, that the place of honour is due to him, because he came without being invited.

ZENOTHEMIS. Therefore, we ought, my dear Lucius, to make him the more welcome, and strive to do that which would be most agreeable to him. Now it is certain that such a man cares less for the perfumes of meat than for the perfumes of fine thoughts. We shall, doubtless, please him by discussing the doctrine he professes, which is that of Jesus crucified. For my own part, I shall the more willingly discuss this doctrine, because it keenly interests me, on account of the number and the diversity of the allegories it contains. If one may guess at the spirit by the letter, it is filled with truths, and I consider that the Christian books abound in divine revelations. But I should not, Paphnutius, grant equal merit to the Jewish books. They were inspired not, as it was said, by the Spirit of God, but by an evil genius. Iaveh, who dictated them, was one of those spirits who people the lower air, and cause the greater part of the evils, from which we suffer; but he surpassed all the others in ignorance and ferocity. On the contrary, the serpent with golden wings, which twined its azure coils round the tree of knowledge, was made up of light and love. A combat between these two powers — the one of light and the other of darkness — was, therefore, inevitable. It occurred soon after the creation of the world. God had hardly begun to rest after His labors; Adam and Eve, the first man and the first woman, lived happy and naked in the Garden of Eden, when Iaveh conceived — to their misfortune — the design of governing them and all the generations which Eve already bore in her splendid loins. As he possessed neither the compass nor the lyre, and was equally ignorant of the science which commands and the art which persuades, he frightened these two poor children by hideous apparitions, capricious threats, and thunder-bolts. Adam and Eve, feeling his shadow upon them, pressed closer to one another, and their love waxed stronger in fear. The serpent took pity on them, and determined to instruct them, in order that, possessing knowledge, they might no longer be misled by lies. Such an undertaking required extreme prudence, and the frailty of the first human couple rendered it almost hopeless. The well-intentioned demon essayed it, however. Without the knowledge of Iaveh — who pretended to see everything, but, in reality, was not very sharp-sighted — he approached these two beings, and charmed their eyes by the splendour of his coat and the brilliancy of his wings. Then he interested their minds by forming before them, with his body, definite figures, such as the circle, the ellipse, and the spiral, the wonderful properties of which have since been recognized by the Greeks. Adam meditated on these figures more than Eve did. But when the serpent began to speak, and taught the most sublime truths — those which cannot be demonstrated — he found that Adam being made of red earth, was of too dull a nature to understand these subtle distinctions, but that Eve, on the contrary, being more tender and more sensitive, was easily impressed. Therefore he conversed with her alone, in the absence of her husband, in order to initiate her first —

DORION. Permit me, Zenothemis, to interrupt you. I speedily recognized in the myth you have explained to us an episode in the war of Pallas Athene against the giants. Iaveh much resembles Typhoon, and Pallas is represented by the Athenians with a serpent at her side. But what you have said causes me considerable doubt as to the intelligence or good faith of the serpent of whom you have spoken. If he had really possessed knowledge, would he have entrusted it to a woman's little head, which was incapable of containing it? I should rather consider that he was like Iaveh, ignorant and a liar, and that he chose Eve because she was easily seduced, and he imagined that Adam would have more intelligence and perception.

ZENOTHEMIS. Learn, Dorion, that it is not by perception and intelligence, but by sensibility, that the highest and purest truths are reached. That is why women, who, generally, are less reflective but more sensitive than men, rise more easily to the knowledge of things divine. In them is the gift of prophecy, and it is not without reason that Apollo Citharedes, and Jesus of Nazareth, are sometimes represented clad, like women, in flowing robes. The initiator was therefore wise — whatever you may say to the contrary, Dorion — in bestowing light, not on the duller Adam, but on Eve, who was whiter than milk or the stars. She freely listened to him, and allowed herself to be led to the tree of knowledge, the branches of which rose to heaven, and which was bathed with the divine spirit as with a dew. This tree was covered with leaves which spoke all the languages of future races of men, and their united voices formed a perfect harmony. Its abundant fruit gave to the initiated who tasted it the knowledge of metals, stones, and plants, and also of physical and moral laws; but this fruit was like fire, and those who feared suffering and death did not dare to put it to their lips. Now, as she had listened attentively to the lessons of the serpent, Eve despised these empty terrors, and wished to taste the fruit which gave the knowledge of God. But, as she loved Adam, and did not wish him to be inferior to her, she took him by the hand and led him to the wonderful tree. Then she picked one of the burning apples, bit it, and proffered it to her companion. Unfortunately, Iaveh, who was by chance walking in the garden, surprised them, and seeing that they had become wise, he fell into a most ungovernable rage. It is in his jealous fits that he is most to be feared. Assembling all his forces, he created such a turmoil in the lower air that these two weak beings were terrified. The fruit fell from the man's hand, and the woman, clinging to the neck of her luckless husband, said, "I too will be ignorant and suffer with him." The triumphant Iaveh kept Adam and Eve and all their seed in a condition of hebetude and terror. His art, which consisted only in being able to make huge meteors, triumphed over the science of the serpent, who was a musician and geometrician. He made men unjust, ignorant, and cruel, and caused evil to reign in the earth. He persecuted Cain and his sons because they were skilful workmen; he exterminated the Philistines because they composed Orphic poems, and fables like those of AEsop. He was the implacable enemy of science and beauty, and for long ages the human race expiated, in blood and tears, the defeat of the winged serpent. Fortunately, there arose among the Greeks learned men, such as Pythagoras, and Plato, who recovered by the force of genius, the figures and the ideas which the enemy of Iaveh had vainly tried to teach the first woman. The soul of the serpent was in them; and that is why the serpent, as Dorion has said, is honoured by the Athenians. Finally, in these latter days, there appeared, under human form, three celestial spirits — Jesus of Galilee, Basilides, and Valentinus — to whom it was given to pluck the finest fruits of that tree of knowledge, whose roots pass through all the earth, and whose top reaches to the highest heaven. I have said all this in vindication of the Christians, to whom the errors of the Jews are too often imputed.

DORION. If I understood you aright, Zenothemis, you said that three wonderful men — Jesus, Basilides, and Valentinus — had discovered secrets which had remained hidden from Pythagoras and Plato, and all the philosophers of Greece, and even from the divine Epicurus, who, however, has freed men from the dread of empty terrors. You would greatly oblige me by telling me by what means these three mortals acquired knowledge which had eluded the most contemplative sages.

ZENOTHEMIS. Must I repeat to you, Dorion, that science and cogitation are but the first steps to knowledge, and that ecstasy alone leads to eternal truth?

HERMODORUS. It is true, Zenothemis, that the soul is nourished on ecstasy, as the cicada is nourished on dew. But we may even say more: the mind alone is capable of perfect rapture. For man is of a threefold nature, composed of material body, of a soul which is more subtle, but also material, and of an incorruptible mind. When, emerging from the body as from a palace suddenly given over to silence and solitude and flying through the gardens of the soul, the mind diffuses itself in God, it tastes the delights of an anticipated death, or rather of a future life, for to die is to live; and in that condition, partaking of divine purity, it possesses both infinite joy and complete knowledge. It enters into the unity which is All. It is perfected.

NICIAS. That is very fine; but, to say the truth, Hermodorus, I do not see much difference between All and Nothing. Words even seem to fail to make the distinction. Infinity is terribly like nothingness — they are both inconceivable to the mind. In my opinion perfection costs too dear; we pay for it with all our being, and to possess it must cease to exist. That is a calamity from which God Himself is not free, for the philosophers are doing their best to perfect Him. After all, if we do not know what it is *not* to be, we are equally ignorant what it is to *be*. We know nothing. It is said that it is impossible for men to agree on this question. I believe — in spite of our noisy disputes — that it is, on the contrary, impossible for men not to become some day all at unity buried under the mass of contradictions, a Pelion on Ossa, which they themselves have raised.

COTTA. I am very fond of philosophy, and study it in my leisure time. But I never understand it well, except in Cicero's books. Slaves, pour out the honeyed wine!

CALLICRATES. It is a singular thing, but when I am hungry I think of the time when the tragic poets sat at the boards of good tyrants, and my mouth waters. But when I have tasted the excellent wine that you give us so abundantly, generous Lucius, I dream of nothing but civil wars and heroic combats. I blush to live in such inglorious times; I invoke the goddess of Liberty; and I pour out my blood — in imagination — with the last Romans on the field of Philippi.

COTTA. In the days of the decline of the Republic my ancestors died with Brutus — for liberty. But there is reason to suspect that what the Roman people called liberty was only in reality the right to govern themselves. I do not deny that liberty is the greatest boon a nation can have. But the longer I live the more

I am persuaded that only a strong government can bestow it on the citizens. For forty years I have filled high positions in the State, and my long experience has shown me that when the ruling power is weak the people are oppressed. Those, therefore, who — like the great majority of rhetoricians — try to weaken the government, commit an abominable crime. An autocrat, who governs by his single will, may sometimes cause most deplorable results; but if he governs by popular consent there is no remedy possible. Before the majesty of the Roman arms had bestowed peace upon all the world, the only nations which were happy were those which were ruled over by intelligent despots.

HERMODORUS. For my part, Lucius, I believe that there is no such thing as a good form of government, and that we shall never discover one, because the Greeks, who had so many excellent ideas, were never able to find one. In that respect, therefore, all hope of ultimate success is taken from us. Unmistakable signs show that the world is about to fall into ignorance and barbarism. It has been our lot, Lucius, to witness terrible events. Of all the mental satisfactions which intelligence, learning, and virtue can give, all that remains is the cruel pleasure of watching ourselves die.

COTTA. It is true that the rapacity of the people, and the boldness of the barbarians, are threatening evils. But with a good fleet, a good army, and plenty of money —

HERMODORUS. What is the use of deceiving ourselves? The dying empire will become an easy prey to the barbarians. Cities which were built by Hellenic genius, or Latin patience, will soon be sacked by drunken savages. Neither art nor philosophy will exist any longer on the earth. The statues of the gods will be overturned in the temples, and in men's hearts as well. Darkness will overcome all minds, and the world will die. Can we believe that the Sarmatians will ever devote themselves to intelligent work, that the Germani will cultivate music and philosophy, and that the Quadi and the Marcomani will adore the immortal gods? No! we are sliding toward the abyss. Our old Egypt, which was the cradle of the world, will be its burial vault; Serapis, the god of

Death, will receive the last adoration of mortals, and I shall have been the last priest of the last god.

At this moment a strange figure raised the tapestry, and the guests saw before them a little hunchback, whose bald skull rose in a point. He was clad, in the Asiatic fashion, in a blue tunic, and wore round his legs, like the barbarians, red breeches, spangled with gold stars. On seeing him, Paphnutius recognized Marcus the Arian, and fearing lest a thunderbolt should fall from heaven, he covered his head with his arms, and grew pale with fright. At this banquet of the demons, neither the blasphemies of the pagans, nor the horrible errors of the philosophers, had had any effect on him, but the mere presence of the heretic quenched his courage. He would have fled, but his eyes met those of Thais, and he felt at once strengthened. He read in her soul that she, who was predestined to become a saint, already protected him. He seized the skirt of her long, flowing robe, and inwardly prayed to the Saviour Jesus.

A murmur of acclamation welcomed the arrival of the personage who had been called the Christian Plato. Hermodorus was the first to speak.

"Most illustrious Marcus, we rejoice to see you amongst us, and it may be said that you come at the right moment. We know nothing of the Christian doctrine, beyond what is publicly taught. Now, it is certain that a philosopher, like you, cannot think as the vulgar think, and we are curious to know your opinion of the principal mysteries of the religion you profess. Our dear friend, Zenothemis, who, as you know, is always hunting for symbolic meanings, just now questioned the illustrious Paphnutius concerning the Jewish books. But Paphnutius made no reply, and we should not be surprised at that, as our guest has made a vow of silence, and God has sealed his tongue in the desert. But you Marcus, who have spoken at the Christian synods, and even at the councils of the divine Constantine, can if you wish, satisfy our curiosity by revealing to us the philosophic truths which are wrapped up in the Christian fables. Is not the first of these truths the existence of an only God — in whom, for my part, I fervently believe?"

MARCUS. Yes, venerable brethren, I believe in an only God, not begotten — the only Eternal, the origin of all things.

NICIAS. We know, Marcus, that your God created the world. That must certainly have been a great crisis in His existence. He had already existed an eternity before He could make up His mind to it. But I must, in justice, confess that His situation was a most difficult one. He must continue inactive if He would remain perfect, and must act if He would prove to Himself His own existence. You assure me that He decided to act. I am willing to believe you, although it was an unpardonable imprudence on the part of a perfect God. But tell us, Marcus, how He set about making the world.

MARCUS. Those who, without being Christians, possess, like Hermodorus and Zenothemis, the principles of knowledge, are aware that God did not create the world personally without an intermediary. He gave birth to an only Son, by whom all things were made.

HERMODORUS. That is quite true, Marcus; and this Son is worshipped under the various names of Hermes, Mithra, Adonis, Apollo, and Jesus.

MARCUS. I should not be a Christian if I gave Him any other names than those of Jesus Christ, and Saviour. He is the true Son of God. But He is not eternal, since He had a beginning; as to thinking that He existed before He was begotten, we must leave that absurdity to the Nicaean mules, and the obstinate ass who too long governed the Church of Alexandria under the accursed name of Athanasius.

At these words Paphnutius, white with horror and his face bedewed with the sweat of agony made the sign of the cross, but maintained a sublime silence.

Marcus continued —

"It is clear that the foolish Nicene Creed is a treason against the majesty of the only God, by compelling Him to share His indivisible attributes with His own emanation — the Mediator by whom all things were made. Cease jesting at the true God of the Christians, Nicias, and learn that, like the lilies of the field, He toils not, neither does He spin. It was not He who was the worker, it was His only Son, Jesus, who, having created the world, came afterwards to repair His handiwork. For the creation could not be perfect, and evil was necessarily mingled with good."

NICIAS. What is "good," and what is "evil"?

There was a moment's silence, during which Hermodorus, his arm extended on the cloth, pointed to a little ass in Corinthian metal which bore two baskets — the one containing white olives, the other black olives.

"You see these olives," he said. "The contrast between the colours is pleasant to the eye, and we are content that these should be light and those should be dark. But, if they were endowed with thought and knowledge, the white would say, It is good for an olive to be white, it is bad for it to be black; and the black olives would hate the white olives. We judge better, for we are as much above them as the gods are above us. For man, who only sees a part of things, evil is an evil; for God, who understands all things, evil is a good. Doubtless ugliness is ugly, and not beautiful; but if all were beautiful, the whole would not be beautiful. It is, then, well that there should be evil, as the second Plato, far greater than the first, has demonstrated."

EUCRITES. Let us talk more morally. Evil is an evil — not for the world, of which it cannot destroy the indestructible harmony but for the sinner who does it, and cannot help doing it.

COTTA. By Jupiter? that is a good argument.

EUCRITES. The world is a tragedy by an excellent poet. God, who composed it, has intended each of us to play a part in it. If he wills that you shall be a beggar, a prince, or a cripple, make the best of the part assigned you.

NICIAS. Assuredly it would be well that the cripple should limp like Hephaistos: it would be well that the madman should indulge in all the fury of Ajax, that the incestuous woman should repeat the crimes of Phaedra, that the traitor should betray, that the rascal should lie, and the murderer kill, and when the piece was played, all the actor — kings, just men, bloody tyrants, pious virgins, immodest wives, noble-minded citizens, and cowardly assassins — should receive from the poet an equal share in the felicitations.

EUCRITES. You distort my thought, Nicias, and change a beautiful young girl into a hideous Gorgon. I am sorry for you, if you are so ignorant of the nature of the gods, of justice, and of the eternal laws.

ZENOTHEMIS. For my part, friends, I believe in the reality of good and evil. But I am convinced that there is not a single human action — were it even the kiss of Judas — which does not bear within itself the germ of redemption. Evil contributes to the ultimate salvation of men, and, in that respect issues from Good, and shares the merits belonging to Good. This has been admirably expressed by the Christians, in the myth concerning the man with red hair, who, in order to betray his master, gave him the kiss of peace, and by such act assured the salvation of men. Therefore, nothing is, in my opinion, more unjust and absurd than the hate with which certain disciples of Paul, the tentmaker, pursue the most unfortunate of the apostles of Jesus without realizing that the kiss of Iscariot — prophesied by Jesus Himself — was necessary, according to their own doctrine, for the redemption of men, and that if Judas had not received the thirty pieces, the divine wisdom would have been impugned, Providence frustrated, its designs upset, and the world given over to evil, ignorance, and death.

MARCUS. Divine wisdom foresaw that Judas, though he was not obliged to give the traitor's kiss, would give it, notwithstanding. It thus employed the sin of Iscariot as a stone in the marvelous edifice of the redemption.

ZENOTHEMIS. I spoke just now, Marcus, as though I believed that the redemption of men had been accomplished by Jesus crucified, because I know that such is the belief of the Christians, and I borrowed their opinion that I might the better show the mistake of those who believe in the eternal damnation of Judas. But, in reality, Jesus was, in my eyes, but the precursor of Basilides and Valentinus. As to the mystery of the redemption, I will tell you, my dear friends — if you are at all curious to hear it — how it was really accomplished on earth.

The guests made a sign of assent. Like the Athenian virgins with the baskets sacred to Ceres, twelve young girls, bearing on their heads baskets filled with pomegranates and apples, entered the room with a light step, in time to the music of an invisible flute. They placed the baskets on the table, the flute ceased, and Zenothemis spoke as follows —

"When Eunoia, 'the thought of God,' had created the world, she confided the government of the earth to the angels. But they did not preserve the dispassion befitting masters. Seeing that the daughters of men were fair, they surprised them in the evening by the wellside, and united themselves to them. From these unions sprang a turbulent race, who covered the earth with injustice and cruelty, and the dust of the roads drank up the blood of the innocent. The sight of this caused Eunoia infinite grief.

"'See what I have done!' she sighed, leaning towards the world. 'My poor children are plunged in misery, and by my fault. Their suffering is my crime, and I will expiate it. God Himself, who only thinks through me, would be powerless to restore them to their pristine purity. That which is done is done, and the creation will remain for ever imperfect. But, at least, I will not forsake my creatures. If I cannot make them happy, like me, I can make myself unhappy, like them. Since I committed the mistake of giving them bodies which dishonour them, I will myself assume a body like unto theirs, and will go and live amongst them.'

"Having thus spoken, Eunoia descended to the earth, and was incarnate in the breast of a woman of Argos. She was born small and feeble, and received the name of Helen. She submitted to all the labours of this life, but soon grew in grace and beauty, and became the most desired of women, as she had determined, in order that her mortal body might be tried by the most supreme defilements. An inert prey to lascivious and violent men, she

276

suffered rape and adultery, in expiation of all the adulteries, all the violences, all the iniquities, and caused, by her beauty, the ruin of nations, that God might pardon the sins of the universe. And never was the celestial thought, never was Eunoia, so adorable as in those days when, as a woman, she prostituted herself to heroes and shepherds. The poets surmised her divinity when they painted her so peaceful, superb, and fatal, and when they addressed that invocation to her, 'A soul as serene as a calm upon the waters.'

"Thus was Eunoia led by pity into evil and suffering. She died, and the Argives still show her tomb — for it was necessary that she should know death after lust, and taste the bitter fruit she had sown. But, emerging from the decomposed flesh of Helen, she became incarnate again as a woman, and again suffered every form of insult and outrage. Thus, passing from body to body, throughout all the evil ages, she takes upon her the sins of the world. Her sacrifice will not be in vain. Joined to us by the bonds of the flesh, loving us, and weeping with us, she will effect her redemption and ours, and will carry us, clinging to her white breast, into the peace of the regained paradise."

HERMODORUS. This myth was not unknown to me. I remembered having heard that, in one of her metamorphoses, the divine Helen lived with the magician, Simon, in the reign of the Emperor Tiberius. I thought, however, that her perdition was involuntary, and that she was dragged down by the angels in their fall.

ZENOTHEMIS. It is true, Hermodorus, that men who were not properly initiated in the mysteries have imagined that the sad Eunoia was not a party to her own downfall. But if it were as they assert Eunoia would not be the expiating courtesan, the victim covered with stains of all sorts, the bread steeped in the wine of our shame, the pleasant offering, the meritorious sacrifice, the holocaust, the smoke of which rises to God. If they were not voluntary, there would be no merit in her sins.

CALLICRATES. Does anyone know, Zenothemis in what country, under what name, in what adorable form, this ever-renascent Helen is living now?

ZENOTHEMIS. A man would have to be very wise indeed to discover such a secret. And wisdom, Callicrates, is not given to poets, who live in the rude world of forms and amuse themselves, like children, with sounds and empty shows.

CALLICRATES. Beware of offending the gods, impious Zenothemis; the poets are dear to them. The first laws were dictated in verse by the immortals themselves, and the oracles of the gods are poems. Hymns have a pleasant sound to celestial ears. Who does not know that the poets are prophets, and that nothing is hidden from them? Being a poet myself, and crowned with Apollo's laurel, I will make known to all the last incarnation of Eunoia. The eternal Helen is close to us; she is looking at us, and we are looking at her. You see that woman reclining on the cushions of her couch — so beautiful and so contemplative — whose eyes shed tears, and whose lips abound with kisses! It is she! Lovely as in the time of Priam and the halcyon days of Asia, Eunoia is now called Thais.

PHILINA. What do you say, Callicrates? Our dear Thais knew Paris, Menelaus, and the Achaians who fought before Ilion! Was the Trojan horse big, Thais?

ARISTOBULUS. Who speaks of a horse?

"I have drunk like a Thracian!" cried Chereas and he rolled under the table.

Callicrates, raising his cup, cried —

"If we drink like desperate men, we die unavenged!"

Old Cotta was asleep, and his bald head nodded slowly above his broad shoulders.

For some time past Dorion had seemed to be greatly excited under his philosophic cloak. He reeled up to the couch of Thais.

"Thais, I love you, although it is unseemly in me to love a woman."

THAIS. Why did you not love me before?

DORION. Because I had not supped.

278

THAIS. But I, my poor friend, have drunk nothing but water; therefore you must excuse me if I do not love you.

Dorion did not wait to hear more, but made towards Drosea, who had made a sign to him in order to get him away from her friend. Zenothemis took the place he had left, and gave Thais a kiss on the mouth.

THAIS. I thought you more virtuous.

ZENOTHEMIS. I am perfect, and the perfect are subject to no laws.

THAIS. But are you not afraid of sullying your soul in a woman's arms?

ZENOTHEMIS. The body may yield to lust without the soul being concerned.

THAIS. Go away! I wish to be loved with body and soul. All these philosophers are old goats.

The lamps died out one by one. The pale rays of dawn, which entered between the openings of the hangings, shone on the livid faces and swollen eyes of the guests. Aristobulus was sleeping soundly by the side of Chereas, and, in his dreams, devoting all his grooms to the ravens. Zenothemis pressed in his arms the yielding Philina; Dorion poured on the naked bosom of Drosea drops of wine, which rolled like rubies on the white breast, which was shaking with laughter, and the philosopher tried to catch these drops with his lips, as they rolled on the slippery flesh. Eucrites rose, and placing his arm on the shoulder of Nicias, led him to the end of the hall.

"Friend," he said, smiling, "if you can still think at all — of what are you thinking?"

"I think that the love of women is like a garden of Adonis."

"What do you mean by that?"

"Do you not know, Eucrites, that women make little gardens on the terraces, in which they plant boughs in clay pots in honour of the lover of Venus? These boughs flourish a little time, and then fade."

"What does that signify, Nicias? That it is foolish to attach importance to that which fades?"

"If beauty is but a shadow, desire is but a lightning flash. What madness it is, then, to desire beauty! Is it not rational, on the contrary, that that which passes should go with that which does not endure, and that the lightning should devour the gliding shadow?"

"Nicias, you seem to me like a child playing at knuckle-bones. Take my advice — be free! By liberty only can you become a man."

"How can a man be free, Eucrites, when he has a body?"

"You shall see presently, my son. Presently you will say, 'Eucrites was free.'"

The old man spoke, leaning against a porphyry pillar, his face lighted by the first rays of dawn. Hermodorus and Marcus had approached, and stood before him by the side of Nicias; and all four, regardless of the laughter and cries of the drinkers, conversed on things divine. Eucrites expresses himself so wisely and eloquently, that Marcus said —

"You are worthy to know the true God."

Eucrites replied —

"The true God is in the heart of the wise man."

Then they spoke of death.

"I wish," said Eucrites, "that it may find me occupied in correcting my faults, and attentive to all my duties. In the face of death I will raise my pure hands to heaven, and I will say to the gods, 'Your images, gods, that you have placed in the temple of my soul, I have not profaned; I have hung there my thoughts, as well as garlands, fillets, and wreaths. I have lived according to your providence. I have lived enough.'"

Thus speaking, he raised his arms to heaven, and he remained thoughtful a moment. Then he continued, with extreme joy —

"Separate thyself from life, Eucrites, like the ripe olive which falls; returning thanks to the tree which bore thee, and blessing the earth, thy nurse."

At these words, drawing from the folds of his robe a naked dagger, he plunged it into his breast.

Those who listened to him sprang forward to seize his hand, but the steel point had already penetrated the heart of the sage. Eucrites had already entered into his rest. Hermodorus and Nicias bore the pale and bleeding body to one of the couches, amidst the shrill shrieks of the women, the grunts of the guests disturbed in their sleep, and the heavy breathing of the couples hidden in the shadow of the tapestry. Cotta, an old soldier, who slept lightly, woke, approached the corpse, examined the wound, and cried —

"Call Aristaeus, my physician!"

Nicias shook his head.

"Eucrites is no more," he said. "He wished to die as others wish to love. He has, like all of us, obeyed his inexpressible desire. And, lo, now he is like unto the gods, who desire nothing."

Cotta struck his forehead.

"Die! To want to die when he might still serve the State! What nonsense!"

Paphnutius and Thais remained motionless and mute, side by side, their souls overflowing with disgust, horror, and hope.

Suddenly the monk seized the hand of the actress, and stepping over the drunkards, who had fallen close to the lascivious couples, and treading in the wine and blood spilt upon the floor, he led her out of the house.

The sun had risen over the city. Long colonnades stretched on both sides of the deserted street, and at the end shone the dome of Alexander's tomb. Here and there on the pavement lay broken wreaths and extinguished torches. Fresh wafts of the sea could be felt in the air. Paphnutius, with a look of disgust, tore off his rich robe and trampled the fragments under his feet.

"Thou hast heard them, my Thais!" he cried. "They have spat forth every sort of folly and abomination. They dragged the Divine Creator of all things down the gemonies of the devils of hell, impudently denied the existence of Good and Evil, blasphemed Jesus, and exalted Judas. And the most infamous of all, the jackal of darkness, the stinking beast, the Arian full of corruption and death, opened his mouth like a yawning sepulchre.

My Thais, thou hast seen these filthy snails crawling towards thee and defiling thee with their sticky sweat; thou hast seen others, like brutes, sleeping under the heels of their slaves; thou hast seen them coupling like beasts on the carpet they had fouled with their vomit; thou hast seen a foolish old man shed a blood yet viler than the wine which flowed at his debauch, and at the end of the orgy throw himself in the face of the unforeseen Christ. Praise be to God! Thou hast seen error and recognized how hideous it was. Thais, Thais, Thais, recall to mind the follies of these philosophers, and say if thou wilt go mad with them! Remember the looks, the gestures, the laughs of their fitting companions, those two lascivious and malicious strumpets, and say if thou wilt remain like unto them."

Thais, her heart stirred with horror and disgust at all she had seen and heard that night, and feeling the indifference and brutality, the malicious jealousy of women, the heavy weight of useless hours, sighed.

"I am weary to death, O my father! Where shall I find rest? I feel that my face is burning, my head empty, and my arms are so tired that I should not have the strength to seize happiness were it within reach of my hand."

Paphnutius gazed at her with loving pity.

"Courage, O my sister! The hour of rest rises for thee, white and pure as the vapours thou seest rise from the gardens and waters."

They were near the house of Thais, and could see, above the wall, the tops of the sycamore and fir trees, which surrounded the Grotto of Nymphs, tremble in the morning breeze. In front of them was a public square, deserted, and surrounded with steles and votive statues, and having at each end a semicircular marble seat, supported by figures of monsters. Thais fell on one of these seats. Then, looking anxiously at the monk, she asked —

"What must I do?"

"Thou must," replied the monk, "follow Him who has come to seek thee. He will separate thee from this present life, as the vintager gathers the cluster that would have rotted on the tree,

and bears it to the wine-press to change it into perfumed wine.
Listen! there is, a dozen hours from Alexandria, towards the west,
not far from the sea, a nunnery, the rules of which, a masterpiece
of wisdom, deserve to be put in lyric verse and sung to the sound
of the theorbo and tambourines. It may truly be said that the
women who are there, submissive to these rules, have their feet
upon earth and their faces in heaven. They desire to be poor, that
Jesus may love them, modest, that He may gaze upon them;
chaste that He may wed them. He visits them every day in the
guise of a gardener, His feet bare, His beautiful hands open —
even as He showed Himself to Mary at the entrance of the tomb.
I will conduct thee this very day to this nunnery, my Thais, and
soon, commingling with these holy women, thou wilt share in
their heavenly conversation. They await thee as a sister. On the
threshold of the convent, their mother, the pious Albina, will give
thee the kiss of peace and will say, 'My daughter, thou art
welcome!'"

The courtesan uttered a cry of amazement.

"Albina! a daughter of the Caesars! The great niece of the
Emperor Carus!"

"She herself! Albina, who, born in the purple, has donned
the serge, and a daughter of the masters of this world, has risen to
the rank of servant of Jesus Christ. She will be thy mother."

Thais rose and said —

"Take me to the house of Albina."

And Paphnutius, completing his victory —

"Surely I will conduct thee thither, and there I will place
thee in a cell, where thou shalt weep for thy sins. For it is not
fitting that thou shouldst mingle with the daughters of Albina
until thou art cleansed from thy sins. I will seal the door, and
there, a happy prisoner, thou wilt wait in tears till Jesus Himself
come, as a sign of pardon, to break the seal that I have placed.
And doubt not that He will come, Thais, and how the flesh of
thy soul will tremble when thou shalt feel the fingers of Light
placed upon thy eyes to dry thy tears!"

Thais said a second time —

"Take me, my father, to the house of Albina."

His heart filled with joy, Paphnutius gazed around him, and tasted, almost without fear, the pleasure of contemplating the works of creation; his eyes drank in with joy God's light, and unknown breezes fanned his cheeks. Suddenly, seeing at one of the corners of the public square the little door which led to Thais' house, and remembering that the trees, whose foliage he had been admiring, shaded the courtesan's garden, he thought of all the impurities which there sullied the air, to-day so light and pure, and his soul was so grieved that bitter tears sprang to his eyes.

"Thais," he said, "we must fly without looking back. But we must not leave behind us the instruments, the witnesses, the accomplices of thy past crimes; those heavy hangings, those beds, carpets, perfume censers and lamps, which would proclaim thy infamy! Dost thou wish that, animated by the demons, and carried by the evil spirit that is in them, those accursed belongings should pursue thee even to the desert? It is but too true that there are tables which bring ruin, seats which serve as the instruments of devils, which act, speak, strike the ground, and pass through the air. Let all perish which has seen thy shame! Hasten, Thais, and, whilst the city is yet asleep, order thy slaves to make, in the centre of this place, a pile, upon which we will burn all the abominable riches thy dwelling contains."

Thais consented.

"Do as you will, my father," she said. "I know that spirits often dwell in inanimate objects. At night some articles of furniture talk, either by giving knocks at regular intervals or by emitting little flashes of light as signals. And even more. Have you remarked, my father, at the entrance to the Grotto of Nymphs, on the right, a statue of a naked woman about to bathe? One day I saw, with my own eyes, that statue turn its head like a living person, and then return to its ordinary attitude. I was terrified. Nicias, to whom I related this prodigy, laughed at me; yet there must be some magic in that statue, for it inspired with violent desires a certain Dalmatian, who was insensible to my beauty. It is certain that I have lived amongst enchanted things, and that I was exposed to the greatest perils, for men have been strangled by the embraces of a bronze statue. Yet it would be a pity to destroy valuable works made with rare skill, and to burn my carpets and tapestry would be a great loss. The beautiful colours of some of them are truly wonderful, and they cost much money to those who gave them to me. I also possess cups, statues, and pictures of great price. I do not think they ought to perish. But you know what is necessary. Do as you will, my father."

Thus saying, she followed the monk to the little door at which so many garlands and wreaths had been hung, and, when it was opened, she told the porter to call together all the slaves in the house. Four Indians, who were employed in the kitchen, were the first to appear. They were all four yellow men, and each had but one eye. It had cost Thais much trouble, and given her amusement, to get together these four slaves of the same race, and all afflicted with the same infirmity. When they attended at table they excited the curiosity of the guests, and Thais made them relate the story of their lives. These four waited in silence. Their assistants followed them. Then came the stablemen, the huntsmen, the litter-bearers, and the running footmen with muscles like iron, two gardeners hirsute as Priapus, six ferocious looking negroes, three Greek slaves — one a grammarian, another a poet, and the third a singer. They all stood, ranged in order, on the public square, and were presently joined by the Negresses — curious, suspicious, rolling big round eyes, and each with a huge mouth slit to her earrings. Lastly, adjusting their veils and languidly dragging their feet, which were shackled with light gold chains, appeared six sulky-looking, beautiful white slave-girls. When they were all assembled, Thais, pointing to Paphnutius, said —

"Do whatever this man commands you; for the spirit of God is in him, and if you disobey him you will fall dead."

For she had heard, and really believed, that the earth would open and swallow up in flames and smoke any impious wretch whom a saint of the desert struck with his staff.

Paphnutius sent away the women and the Greek men-slaves, and said to the others —

"Bring wood to the middle of this place, make a huge fire, and throw into it pell-mell all that there is in the house and grotto."

They were astonished, and stood motionless, looking at their mistress. And they still stood inactive and silent, and pressed against each other, elbow to elbow, suspecting that the order was a joke.

"Obey!" said the monk.

Several of them were Christians. They understood the command, and went to the house to fetch wood and torches. The others were not indisposed to imitate them, for, being poor, they hated riches and had a natural instinct for destruction. Whilst they were building the pile, Paphnutius said to Thais —

"I thought at one time of fetching the treasurer of one of the churches of Alexandria (if there still remain one worthy of the name of church, and that is not defiled by the Arian beasts) and giving him thy goods, woman, that he might distribute them to widows, and change the proceeds of crime into the treasure of justice. But such a thought did not come from God, and I cast it from me, for assuredly it would be a great offence to the well-beloved of Jesus Christ to offer them the spoils of thy lust. Thais, all that thou hast touched must be devoured by the fire, even to its very soul. Thanks be to Heaven, these tunics and veils, which have seen kisses more innumerable than the waves of the sea, will only feel now the lips and tongues of the flames. Hasten, slaves! More wood! More links and torches! And thou, woman, return to thy house, strip thyself of thy shameful robes, and ask of the most humble of thy slaves, as an undeserving favour, the tunic that she puts on when she scrubs the floors."

Thais obeyed. Whilst the Indians knelt down and blew the embers, the negroes threw on the pile coffers of ivory, ebony, or cedar, which broke open and let out wreaths, garlands, and necklaces. The smoke rose in a dark column, as in the holocausts of the old religion. Then the fire, which had been smouldering, burst out suddenly with a roar as of some monstrous animal, and the almost invisible flames began to devour their valuable prey. The slaves worked more eagerly; they joyfully dragged out rich carpets, veils embroidered with silver, and flowered tapestry. They staggered under the weight of tables, couches, thick cushions, and beds with gold nails. Three strong Ethiopians came hugging the coloured statues of the nymphs, one of which had been loved as though it were a mortal; and they looked like huge apes carrying off women. And when the beautiful naked forms fell from the arms of these monsters, and were broken on the stones, a deep groan was heard.

At that moment Thais appeared, her hair unloosed and streaming over her shoulders, barefooted, and clad in a clumsy coarse garment which seemed redolent with divine voluptuousness merely from having touched her body. Behind her came a gardener, carrying, half hidden in his long beard, an ivory Eros.

She made a sign to the man to stop, and approaching Paphnutius, showed him the little god.

"My father," she asked, "should this also be thrown into the flames? It is of marvelous antique work, and is worth a hundred times its weight in gold. Its loss would be irreparable, for there is not a sculptor in the world capable of making such a beautiful Eros. Remember also, my father, that this child is Love, and he should not be harshly treated. Believe me, Love is a virtue, and if I have sinned, it is not through him, my father, but against him. Never shall I regret aught that he has caused me to do, and I deplore only those things I have done contrary to his commands. He does not allow women to give themselves to those who do not come in his name. For that reason he ought to be honoured. Look, Paphnutius, how pretty this little Eros is! With what grace he hides himself in the gardener's beard! One day Nicias, who loved me then, brought it to me and said, 'It will remind you of me.' But the roguish boy did not remind me of Nicias, but of a young man I knew at Antioch. Enough riches have been destroyed upon this pile, my father! Preserve this Eros, and place it in some monastery. Those who see it will turn their hearts towards God, for love leads naturally to heavenly thoughts."

The gardener, already believing that the little Eros was saved, smiled on it as though it had been a child, when Paphnutius, snatching the god from the arms which held it, threw it into the flames, crying —

"It is enough that Nicias has touched it to make it replete with every sort of poison!"

Then, seizing by armfuls the sparkling robes, the purple mantles, the golden sandals, the combs, strigils, mirrors, lamps, theorbos, and lyres, he threw them into this furnace, more costly than the funeral pile of Sardanapalus, whilst, drunken with the rage of destruction, the slaves danced round, uttering wild yells amid a shower of sparks and ashes.

One by one, the neighbours, awakened by the noise, opened the windows, and rubbing their eyes, looked out to see whence the smoke came. Then they came down, half dressed, and drew near the fire.

"What does it mean?" they wondered.

Amongst them were merchants from whom Thais had often bought perfumes and stuffs, and they looked on anxiously with long, yellow faces, unable to comprehend what was going on. Some young debauchees, who, returning from a supper, passed by there, preceded by their slaves, stopped, their heads crowned with flowers, their tunics floating, and uttered loud cries. Attracted by curiosity, the crowd increased unceasingly, and soon it was known that Thais had been persuaded by the Abbot of Antinoe to burn her riches and retire to a nunnery.

The shopkeepers thought to themselves —

"Thais is going to leave the city; we shall sell no more to her; it is dreadful to think of. What will become of us without her? This monk has driven her mad. He is ruining us. Why let him do it? What is the use of the laws? Are there no magistrates in Alexandria? Thais does not think about us and our wives and our poor children. It is a public scandal. She ought to be compelled to stay in the city."

288

The young men, on their part, also thought —

"If Thais is going to renounce acting and love, our chief amusements will be taken from us. She was the glory, delight, and honour of the stage. She was the joy even of those who had never possessed her. The women we loved, we loved in her. There were no kisses given in which she was altogether absent, for she was the joy of all voluptuaries, and the mere thought that she breathed amongst us excited us to pleasure."

Thus thought the young men, and one of them, named Cerons, who had held her in his arms, cried out upon the abduction, and blasphemed against Christ. In every group the conduct of Thais was severely criticized.

"It is a shameful flight!"

"A cowardly desertion!"

"She is taking the bread out of our mouths."

"She is robbing our children."

"She ought at least to pay for the wreaths I have sold to her."

"And the sixty robes she has ordered of me."

"She owes money to everybody."

"Who will represent Iphigenia, Electra, and Polyxena when she is gone? The handsome Polybia herself will not make such a success as she has done."

"Life will be dull when her door is closed."

"She was the bright star, the soft moon of the Alexandrian sky."

All the most notorious mendicants of the city — cripples, blind men, and paralytics — had by this time assembled in the place; and crawling through the remnants of the riches, they groaned —

"How shall we live when Thais is no longer here to feed us? Every day the fragments from her table fed two hundred poor wretches, and her lovers, when they quitted her, threw us as they passed handfuls of silver pieces."

Some thieves, too, also mingled with the crowd, and created a deafening clamour, and pushed their neighbours, to increase disorder, and take advantage of the tumult to filch some valuable object.

Old Taddeus, who sold Miletan wool and Tarentan linen, and to whom Thais owed a large sum of money, alone remained calm and silent in the midst of the uproar. He listened and watched, and gently stroking his goat-beard, seemed thoughtful. At last he approached young Cerons, and pulling him by the sleeve, whispered —

"You are the favoured lover of Thais, handsome youth; show yourself, and do not allow this monk to carry her off."

"By Pollux and his sister, he shall not!" cried Cerons. "I will speak to Thais, and without flattering myself, I think she will listen to me rather than to that sooty-faced Lapithan. Place! Place, dogs!"

And striking with his fist the men, upsetting the old women and treading on the young children, he reached Thais, and taking her aside —

"Dearest girl," he said, "look at me, remember, and tell me truly if you renounce love."

But Paphnutius threw himself between Thais and Cerons.

"Impious wretch!" he cried, "beware and touch her not; she is sacred — she belongs to God."

"Get away, baboon!" replied the young man furiously. "Let me speak to my sweetheart, or if not I will drag your obscene carcass by the beard to the fire, and roast you like a sausage."

And he put his hand on Thais. But, pushed away by the monk with unexpected force, he staggered back four paces and fell at the foot of the pile amongst the scattered ashes.

Old Taddeus, meanwhile, had been going from one to the other, pulling the ears of the slaves and kissing the hands of the masters, inciting each and all against Paphnutius, and had already formed a little band resolutely determined to oppose the monk who would steal Thais from them.

Cerons rose, his face black, his hair singed, and choking with smoke and rage. He blasphemed against the gods, and threw himself amongst the assailants, behind whom the beggars crawled, shaking their crutches. Paphnutius was soon enclosed in a circle of menacing fists, raised sticks, and cries of death.

"To the ravens with the monk! to the ravens!"

"No; throw him in the fire! Burn him alive!"

Seizing his fair prey, he pressed her to his heart.

"Impious men," he cried in a voice of thunder, "strive not to tear the dove from the eagle of the Lord. But rather copy this woman, and like she turn your filth into gold. Imitate her example, and renounce the false wealth which you think you hold and which holds you. Hasten! the day is at hand, and divine patience begins to grow weary. Repent, confess your sins, weep and pray. Walk in the footsteps of Thaïs. Hate your offenses, which are as great as hers. Which of you, poor or rich, merchants, soldiers, slaves or eminent citizens, would dare to say, before God, that he was better than a prostitute? You are all nothing but living filth, and it is by a miracle of divine goodness that you do not suddenly turn into streams of mire."

Whilst he spoke flames shot from his eyes; an it seemed as though live coals came from his lips and those who surrounded him were obliged to hear him in spite of themselves.

But old Taddeus did not remain idle. He picked up stones and oyster shells, which he hid in the skirt of his tunic, and not daring to throw them himself slipped them into the hands of the beggars. Soon the stones began to fly, and a well-directed shell cut Paphnutius' face. The blood, which flowed down the dark face of the martyr, dropped in a new baptism on the head of the penitent, and Thaïs, half stifled in the monk's embrace and her delicate skin scratched by the coarse cassock, felt a thrill of horror and fright.

At that moment a man elegantly dressed, and with a wreath of wild celery on his head, opened a road for himself through the furious crowd, and cried —

"Stop! Stop! This monk is my brother!"

It was Nicias, who, having closed the eyes of the philosopher Eucrites, was passing through the square to return to his house, and saw, without very much surprise (for nothing

291

astonished him), the smoking pile, Thais clad an a serge cassock, and Paphnutius being stoned.

He repeated —

"Stop, I tell you; spare my old fellow-scholar; respect the beloved head of Paphnutius!"

But, being only used to subtle disquisitions with philosophers, he did not possess that imperious energy which commands vulgar minds. He was not listened to. A shower of stones and shells fell on the monk, who, protecting Thais with his body, praised the Lord whose goodness turned his wounds into caresses. Despairing of making himself heard, and feeling but too sure that he could not save his friend either by force or persuasion, Nicias resigned himself to the will of the gods — in whom he had little confidence — when the idea occurred to him to use a stratagem which his contempt for men had suddenly suggested to him. He took from his girdle his purse, which was full of gold and silver, for he was a pleasure-loving and charitable man, and running up to the men who were throwing the stones, he chinked the money in their ears. At first they paid no attention to him, their fury being too great; but little by little their looks turned towards the chinking gold, and soon their arms dropped and no longer menaced their victim. Seeing that he had attracted their eyes and minds, Nicias opened his purse and threw some pieces of gold and silver amongst the crowd. The more greedy of them stooped to pick it up. The philosopher, pleased at his first success, adroitly threw deniers and drachmas here and there. At the sound of the pieces of money rattling on the pavement, the persecutors of Paphnutius threw themselves on the ground. Beggars, slaves, and trades people scrambled after the money, whilst, grouped round Cerons, the patricians watched the struggle and laughed heartily. Cerons himself quite forgot his wrath. His friends encouraged the rivals, chose competitors, and made bets, and urged on the miserable wretches as they would have done fighting dogs. A cripple without legs having succeeded in seizing a drachma, the applause was frenetic. The young men themselves began to throw money, and nothing was to be seen in the square but a multitude of backs, rising and falling like waves of the sea, under a shower of coins. Paphnutius was forgotten.

Nicias ran up to him, covered him with his cloak, and dragged him and Thais into by-streets where they were safe from pursuit. They ran for some time in silence, and when they thought they were out of reach of their enemies, they ceased running, and Nicias said, in a tone of raillery in which a little sadness was mingled —

"It is finished then! Pluto ravishes Proserpine, and Thais will follow my fierce-looking friend whithersoever he will lead her."

"It is true, Nicias," replied Thais, "that I am tired of living with men like you, smiling, perfumed, kindly egoists. I am weary of all I know, and I am, therefore, going to seek the unknown. I have experienced joy that was not joy, and here is a man who teaches me that sorrow is true joy. I believe him, for he knows the truth."

"And I, sweetheart," replied Nicias, smiling, "I know the truths. He knows but one, I know them all. I am superior to him in that respect, but to tell the truth, it doesn't make me any the prouder nor any the happier."

Then, seeing that the monk was glaring fiercely at him —

"My dear Paphnutius, do not imagine that I think you extremely absurd, or even altogether unreasonable. And if I were to compare your life with mine, I could not say which is preferable in itself. I shall presently go and take the bath which Crobyle and Myrtale have prepared for me; I shall eat the wing of a Phasian pheasant; then I shall read — for the hundredth time — some fable by Apuleius or some treatise by Porphyry. You will return to your cell, where, leaning like a tame camel, you will ruminate on — I know not what — formulas of incarnations you have long chewed and rechewed, and in the evening you will swallow some radishes without any oil. Well, my dear friend, in accomplishing these acts, so different apparently, we are both obeying the same sentiment, the only motive for all human actions; we are both seeking our own pleasure, and striving to

293

attain the same end — happiness, the impossible happiness. It would be folly on my part to say you were wrong, dear friend, even though I think myself in the right.

"And you, my Thais, go and enjoy yourself, and be more happy still, if it be possible, in abstinence and austerity than you have been in riches and pleasure. On the whole, I should say you were to be envied. For if in our whole lives, Paphnutius and I have pursued but one kind of pleasurable satisfaction, you in your life, dear Thais, have tasted diverse joys such as it is rarely given to the same person to know. I should really like to be for one hour, a saint like our dear friend Paphnutius. But that is not possible. Farewell, then, Thais! Go where the secret forces of nature and your destiny conduct you! Go, and take with you, whithersoever you go, the good wishes of Nicias! I know that is mere foolishness, but can I give you anything more than barren regrets and vain wishes in payment for the delicious illusions which once enveloped me when I was in your arms, and of which only the shadow now remains to me? Farewell, my benefactress! Farewell, goodness that is ignorant of its own existence, mysterious virtue, joy of men! Farewell to the most adorable of the images that nature has ever thrown — for some unknown reasons — on the face of this deceptive world!"

Whilst he spoke, deep wrath had been brewing in the monk's heart, and it now broke forth in imprecations.

"Avaunt, cursed wretch! I scorn thee and hate thee. Go, child of hell, a thousand times worse than those poor lost ones who just now threw stones and insults at me! They knew not what they did, and the grace of God, which I implored for them, may some day descend into their hearts. But thou, detestable Nicias, thou art but a perfidious venom and a bitter poison. Thy mouth breathes despair and death. One of thy smiles contains more blasphemy than issues in a century from the smoking lips of Satan. Avaunt, backslider!"

Nicias looked at him.

"Farewell, my brother," he said, "and may you preserve until your life's end your store of faith, hate, and love. Farewell, Thais!

294

It is in vain that you will forget me, because I shall ever remember you."

On quitting them he walked thoughtfully through the winding streets in the vicinity of the great cemetery of Alexandria, which are peopled by the makers of funeral urns. Their shops were full of clay figures painted in bright colours and representing gods and goddesses, mimes, women, winged sprites, &c., such as were usually buried with the dead. He fancied that perhaps some of the little images which he saw there might be the companions of his eternal sleep; and it seemed to him that a little Eros, with its tunic tucked up, laughed at him mockingly. He looked forward to his death, and the idea was painful to him. To cure his sadness he tried to philosophize, and reasoned thus —

"Assuredly," he said to himself, "time has no reality. It is a simple illusion of our minds. Then, if it does not exist, how can it bring death to me? Does that mean that I shall live for ever? No, but I conclude therefrom that my death is, always has been, as it always will be. I do not feel it yet, but it is in me, and I ought not to fear it, for it would be folly to dread the coming of that which has arrived. It exists, like the last page of a book I read and have not finished."

This argument occupied him all the rest of the way, but without making him more cheerful; and his mind was filled with dismal thoughts when he arrived at the door of his house and heard the merry laughter of Crobyle and Myrtale, who were playing at tennis whilst they were waiting for him.

Paphnutius and Thais left the city by the Gate of the Moon, and followed the coast.

"Woman," said the monk, "all that great blue sea could not wash away thy pollutions."

He spoke with scorn and anger.

"More filthy than a bitch or a sow, thou hast prostituted to pagans and infidels a body which the Eternal had intended for a tabernacle, and thy impurities are such that, now that thou knowest the truth, thou canst not unite thy lips or join thy hands without a horror of thyself rising in thy heart."

She followed him meekly, over stony roads, under a burning sun. Her knees ached from fatigue, and her throat was parched with thirst. But, far from feeling any of the pity which softens the hearts of the profane, Paphnutius rejoiced at these propitiatory sufferings of the flesh which had so sinned. So infuriated was he with holy zeal that he would have liked to cut with rods the body that had preserved its beauty as a shining witness to its infamy. His meditations augmented his pious fury, and remembering that Thais had received Nicias in her bed, that idea seemed so horrible to him that his blood all flowed back to his heart, and his breast felt ready to burst. His curses were stifled in his throat, and he could only grind his teeth. He sprang forward and stood before her, pale, terrible, and filled with the Spirit of God — looked into her very soul, and then spat in her face.

She calmly wiped her face and continued to walk on. He followed, glaring at her in pious anger, as if she had been hell itself. He was thinking how he could avenge Christ in order that Christ should not avenge Himself, when he saw a drop of blood that had dripped from the foot of Thais on the sand. Then a hitherto unknown influence entered his opened heart, sobs rose to his lips, he wept, he ran and knelt before her, called her his sister, and kissed her bleeding feet. He murmured a hundred times, "My sister, my sister, my mother, O most holy!"

He prayed —

"Angels of heaven, receive carefully this drop of blood, and bear it before the throne of the Lord. And may a miraculous anemone blossom on the sand sprinkled with the blood of Thais, that those who see the flower may recover purity of heart and feeling. O holy, holy, most holy Thais!"

As he prayed and prophesied thus, a lad passed on an ass. Paphnutius ordered him to descend, seated Thais on the ass, and led it by the bridle. Towards evening they came to a canal shaded by fine trees; he tied the ass to the trunk of a date palm, and sitting on a mossy stone he shared with Thais a loaf, which they ate with salt and hyssop. They drank fresh water in their hands, and talked of things eternal. She said —

"I have never drunk water so pure nor breathed an air so light, and I feel that God floats in the breezes that pass."

"Look! it is the evening, O my sister. The blue shadows of night cover the hills. But soon thou wilt see shining in the dawn the tabernacles of Light; soon thou wilt behold shine forth the roses of the eternal morning."

They journeyed all night, and, while the crescent moon gleamed on the silver crests of the waves, they sang psalms and hymns. When the sun rose, the Libyan desert stretched before them like a huge lion-skin. At the edge of the desert, and close to a few palm-trees, some white huts shimmered in the morning light.

"Are those the tabernacles of Light, father?" asked Thaïs.

"Even so, my daughter and my sister. Yonder is the House of Salvation, where I will confine you with my own hands."

Soon they saw a number of women busy around the buildings, like bees round their hives. There were some who baked bread, or prepared vegetables; many were spinning wool, and the light of heaven shone upon them like a smile of God. Others meditated in the shade of the tamarisk trees; their white hands hung by their sides, for, being filled with love, they had chosen the part of Magdalen, and performed no work but prayer, contemplation, and ecstasy. They were, therefore, called the Marys, and were clad in white. Those who worked with their hands were called the Marthas, and wore blue robes. All wore the hood, but the younger ones allowed a few curls to show on their foreheads — unintentionally, it is to be presumed, since it was forbidden by the rules. A very old lady, tall and white, walked from cell to cell, leaning on a staff of hard wood. Paphnutius approached her respectfully, kissed the hem of her veil, and said
—

"The peace of the Lord be with thee, venerable Albina. I have brought to the hive, of which thou art queen, a bee I found lost on a flowerless road. I took it in the palm of my hand, and revived it with my breath. I give it to thee."

And he pointed to the actress, who knelt down before the daughter of the Caesars.

Albina cast a piercing glance on Thais, ordered her to rise, kissed her on the forehead, and then, turning to the monk —

"We will place her," she said, "amongst the Marys."

Paphnutius then related how Thais had been brought to the House of Salvation, and asked that she should be at once confined in a cell. The abbess consented, and led the penitent to a hut, which had remained empty since the death of the virgin Laeta, who had sanctified it. In this narrow chamber there was but a bed, a table, and a pitcher, and Thais when she crossed the threshold, felt filled with ineffable joy.

"I wish to close the door myself," said Paphnutius, "and put thereon a seal, which Jesus will come and break with His own hands."

He went to the side of the spring, and took a handful of wet clay, mixed with it a little spittle and a hair from his head, and plastered it across the chink of the door. Then, approaching the window, near which Thais stood peaceful and happy, he fell on his knees and praised the Lord three times.

"How beautiful are the feet of her who walketh in the paths of righteousness! How beautiful are her feet, and how resplendent her face!"

He rose, lowered his hood over his eyes, and walked away slowly.

Albina called one of her virgins.

"My daughter," she said, "take to Thais those things which are needful for her — bread, water, and a flute with three holes."

PART THE THIRD — THE EUPHORBIA

Paphnutius had returned to the holy desert. He took, near Athribis, the boat which went up the Nile to carry food to the monastery of Abbot Serapion. When he disembarked, his disciples advanced to meet him with great demonstrations of joy. Some raised their arms to heaven; others, prostrate on the ground, kissed the Abbot's sandals. For they knew already what the saint had accomplished in Alexandria. The monks generally received, by rapid and unknown means, information concerning the safety or glory of the Church. News spread through the desert with the rapidity of the simoom.

When Paphnutius strode across the sand, his disciples followed him, praising the Lord. Flavian, who was the oldest member of the brotherhood, was suddenly seized with a pious frenzy and began to sing an inspired hymn —

"O blessed day! Now is our father restored to us. He has returned laden with fresh merits, of which we reap the benefit. For the virtues of the father are the wealth of the children, and the sanctity of the Abbot illuminates every cell. Paphnutius, our father, has given a new spouse to Jesus Christ. By his wondrous art, he has changed a black sheep into a white sheep. And now, behold, he has returned to us, laden with fresh merits. Like unto the bee of the Arsinoetid, heavy with the nectar of flowers. Even as the ram of Nubia, which could hardly bear the weight of its abundant wool. Let us celebrate this day by mingling oil with our food."

When they came to the door of the Abbot's cell, they fell on their knees, and said —

"Let our father bless us, and give each of us a measure of oil to celebrate his return."

Paul the Fool, who alone had remained standing, asked, "Who is this man?" and did not recognize Paphnutius. But no one paid any attention to what he said, as he was known to be devoid of intelligence, though filled with piety.

The Abbot of Antinoe, locked in his cell, thought —

"I have at last regained the haven of my repose and happiness. I have returned to my fortress of contentment. But how is it that this roof of rushes, so dear to me, does not receive me as a friend, and the walls say not to me, 'Thou art welcome.' Nothing has changed, since my departure, in this abode I have chosen. There is my table and my bed. There is the mummy's head which has so often inspired me with salutary thoughts; and there is the book in which I have so often sought conceptions of God. And yet nothing that I left is here. The things appear grievously despoiled of their customary charm, and it seems to me as though I saw them to-day for the first time. When I look at that table and couch, that in former days I made with my own hands, that black, dried head, these rolls of papyrus filled with the sayings of God, I seem to see the belongings of a dead man. After having known them all so well, I know them no longer. Alas! since nothing around me has really changed, it is I who am no longer what I was. I am another. I am the dead man! What has happened, my God? What has been taken from me? What is left unto me? And who am I?"

And it especially perplexed him to find, in spite of himself, that his cell was small, whereas, when viewed by the eye of faith, he ought to consider it immense, because the infinitude of God began there.

He began to pray, with his face against the ground, and felt a little happier. He had hardly been an hour in prayer, when a vision of Thais passed before his eyes. He returned thanks to God

—

"Jesus! it is Thou who hast sent her. I acknowledge in that Thy wonderful goodness; Thou wouldst please me, reassure me and comfort me by the sight of her whom I have given to Thee. Thou; presentest her to my eyes with her smile now disarmed; her grace, now become innocent; her beauty from which I have extracted the sting. To please me, my God, thou showest her to me as I have prepared and purified her for Thy designs, as one friend pleasantly reminds another of the rich gift he has received from him. Therefore I see this woman with delight, being assured that the vision comes from Thee. Thou dost not forget that I have given her to Thee, Jesus. Keep her, since she pleases Thee, and suffer not her beauty to give joy to any but Thyself."

He could not sleep all night, and he saw Thais more distinctly than he had seen her in the Grotto of Nymphs. He commended himself, saying —

"What I have done, I have done to the glory of God."

Yet, to his great surprise, his heart was not at ease. He sighed.

"Why art thou sad, O my soul, and why dost thou trouble me?"

And his mind was still perturbed. Thirty days he remained in that condition of sadness which precedes the sore trials of a solitary monk. The image of Thais never left him day or night. He did not try to banish it, because he still thought it came from God, and was the image of a saint. But one morning she visited him in a dream, her hair crowned with violets, and her very gentleness seemed so formidable, that he uttered a cry of fright, and woke in an icy sweat. His eyes were still heavy with sleep, when he felt a moist warm breath on his face. A little jackal, its two paws placed on the side of the bed, was panting its stinking breath in his face, and grinning at him.

Paphnutius was greatly astonished, and it seemed to him as though a tower had given way under his feet. And, in fact, he had fallen, for his self-confidence had gone. For some time he was incapable of thought and when he did recover himself, his meditations only increased his perplexity.

"It is one of two things," he said to himself; "either this vision, like the preceding ones, came from God, and was a good vision, and it is my natural perversity which has misrepresented it, as wine turns sour in a dirty cup. I have, by my unworthiness, changed instruction into reproach, of which this diabolical jackal immediately took advantage. Or else this vision came, not from God, but, on the contrary, from the devil, and was evil. In that case I should doubt whether the former ones had, as I thought, a celestial origin. I am therefore incapable of that discernment which is necessary for the ascetic. In either case it is plain that God is no longer with me, — of which I feel the effects, though I cannot explain the cause."

He reasoned in this way, and anxiously asked —

"Just God, what trials dost Thou appoint for Thy servants if the apparitions of Thy saints are a danger for them? Give me to discern, by an intelligible sign, that which comes from Thee, and that which comes from the other."

And as God, whose designs are inscrutable, did not see fit to enlighten his servant, Paphnutius, lost in doubt, resolved not to think of Thais any more. But his resolutions were vain. Though absent, she was ever with him. She gazed at him whilst he read, or meditated, or prayed, or met his eyes wherever he looked. Her imaginary approach was heralded by a slight sound, such as is made by a woman's dress when she walks, and the visions had more verisimilitude than reality itself, which moves and is confused, whereas the phantoms which are caused by solitude are fixed and unchangeable. She came under various appearances — sometimes pensive, her head crowned with her last perishable wreath, clad as at the banquet at Alexandria, in a mauve robe spangled with silver flowers; sometimes voluptuously in a cloud of light veils, and bathed in the warm shadows of the Grotto of Nymphs; sometimes in a serge cassock, pious and radiant with celestial joy; sometimes tragic, her eyes swimming in the terrors of death, and showing her bare breast bedewed with the blood from her pierced heart. What disturbed him the most in these visions was that the wreaths, tunics, and veils, that he had burned with his own hands, should thus return; it became evident to him that these things had an imperishable soul, and he cried —

"Lo, all the countless souls of the sins of Thais come upon me!"

When he turned away his head, he felt that Thais was behind him, and that made him feel still more uneasy. His torture was cruel. But as his soul and body remained pure in the midst of all his temptations, he trusted in God, and gently complained to Him.

302

"My God, if I went so far to seek her amongst the Gentiles, it was for Thy sake, and not for mine. It would not be just that I should suffer for what I have done in Thy behalf. Protect me, sweet Jesus! My Saviour, save me! Suffer not the phantom to accomplish that which the body could not. As I have triumphed over the flesh, suffer not the shadow to overthrow me. I know that I am now exposed to greater dangers than I ever ran. I feel and know that the dream has more power than the reality. And how could it be otherwise, since it is itself but a higher reality? It is the soul of things. Plato, though he was but an idolater, has testified to the real existence of ideas. At that banquet of demons to which Thou accompaniedst me, Lord, I heard men — sullied with crimes truly, but certainly not devoid of intelligence — agree to acknowledge that we see real objects in solitude, meditation, and ecstasy; and Thy Scriptures, my God, many times affirm the virtue of dreams, and the power of visions formed either by Thee, great God, or by Thy adversary."

There was a new man in him and now he reasoned with God, but God did not choose to enlighten him. His nights were one long dream, and his days did not differ from his nights. One morning he awoke uttering sighs, such as issue, by moonlight, from the tombs of the victims of crimes. Thais had come, showing her bleeding feet, and whilst he wept, she had slipped into his couch. There was no longer any doubt; the image of Thais was an impure image.

His heart filled with disgust, he leaped out of his profaned couch, and hid his face in his hands that he might not see the daylight. The hours passed, but they did not remove his shame. All was quiet in the cell. For the first time for many long days, Paphnutius was alone. The phantom had at last left him, and even its absence seemed dreadful. Nothing, nothing to distract his mind from the recollection of the dream. Full of horror, he thought —

"Why did I not drive her away? Why did I not tear myself from her cold arms and burning knees?"

He no longer dared to pronounce the name of God near that horrible couch, and he feared that his cell being profaned, the demons might freely enter at any hour. His fears did not deceive him. The seven little jackals, which had never crossed the threshold, entered in a file, and went and hid under the bed. At the vesper hour, there came an eighth, the stench of which was horrible. The next day, a ninth joined the others, and soon there were thirty, then sixty, then eighty. They became smaller as they multiplied, and being no bigger than rats, they covered the floor, the couch, and the stool. One of them jumped on the little table by the side of the bed, and standing with its four feet together on the death's head, looked at the monk with burning eyes. And every day fresh jackals came.

To expiate the abominable sin of his dream, and flee from impure thoughts, Paphnutius determined to leave his cell, which had now become polluted, go far into the desert, and practice unheard-of austerities, strange labours, and fresh works of grace. But before putting his design into action, he went to see old Palemon and ask his advice.

He found him in his garden watering his lettuces. It was the evening. The blue Nile flowed at the foot of violet hills. The good old man was walking slowly, in order not to frighten a pigeon that had perched on his shoulder.

"The Lord be with thee, brother Paphnutius," he said. "Admire his goodness; He sends me the animals that He has created that I may converse with them of His works, and praise Him in the birds of the air. Look at this pigeon; note the changing hues of its neck, and say, is it not a beautiful work of God? But have you not come to talk with me, brother, on some pious subject? If so, I will put down my watering-pot, and listen to you."

Paphnutius told the old man about his journey, his return, the visions of his days and the dreams of his nights, — without omitting the sinful one — and the pack of jackals.

"Do you not think, father," he added, "that I ought to bury myself in the desert, and perform some extraordinary austerities that would even astonish the devil?"

"I am but a poor sinner," replied Palemon, "and I know little about men, having passed all my life in this garden, with gazelles, little hares and pigeons. But it seems to me, brother, that your distemper comes from your having passed too suddenly from the noisy world to the calm of solitude. Such sudden transitions can but do harm to the health of the soul. You are, brother, like a man who exposes himself, almost at the same time, to great heat and great cold. A cough shakes him, and fever torments him. In your place, brother Paphnutius, instead of retiring at once into some awful desert, I should take such amusements as are fitting to a monk and a holy abbot. I should visit the monasteries in the neighbourhood. Some of them are wonderful, it is said. That of Abbot Serapion contains, I have been told, a thousand four hundred and thirty-two cells, and the monks are divided into as many legions as there are letters in the Greek alphabet. I am even informed that a certain analogy is observed between the character of the monks and the shape of the letter by which they are designated, and that, for example, those who are placed under Z have a tortuous character, whilst those under I have an upright mind. If I were you, brother, I should go and assure myself of this with my own eyes, and I should know no rest until I had seen such a wonderful thing. I should not fail to study the regulations of the various communities which are scattered along the banks of the Nile, so as to be able to compare one with another. Such study is befitting a religious man like yourself. You have heard say, no doubt, that Abbot Ephrem has drawn up for his monastery pious regulations of great beauty. With his permission, you might make a copy of them, as you are a skilful penman. I could not do so, for my hands, accustomed to wield the spade, are too awkward to direct the thin reed of the scribe over the papyrus. But you have the knowledge of letters, brother, and should thank God for it, for beautiful writing cannot be too much admired. The work of the copyist and the reader is a

305

great safeguard against evil thoughts. Brother Paphnutius, why do you not write out the teachings of our fathers, Paul and Anthony? Little by little you would recover, in these pious works, peace of soul and mind; solitude would again become pleasant to your heart, and soon you would be in a condition to recommence those ascetic works which your journey has interrupted. But you must not expect much benefit from excessive penitence. When he was amongst us, our Father Anthony used to say, 'Excessive fasting produces weakness, and weakness begets idleness. There are some monks who ruin their body by fasts improperly prolonged. Of them it may be said that they plunge a dagger into their own breast, and deliver themselves up unresistingly into the power of the devil.' So said the holy man, Anthony. I am but a foolish old man, but, by the grace of God, I have remembered what our father told us."

Paphnutius thanked Palemon and promised to think over his advice. When he had passed the fence of reeds which enclosed the little garden, he turned round and saw the good old gardener engaged in watering his salads, whilst the pigeon walked about on his bent back, and at that sight Paphnutius felt ready to weep.

On returning to his cell, he found there a strange turmoil, as though it were filled with grains of sand blown about by a strong wind, and on looking closer, he saw these moving bodies were myriads of little jackals. That night he saw in a dream, a high stone column surmounted by a human face, and he heard a voice which said —

"Ascend this pillar!"

On awaking, he felt confident that this dream had been sent from heaven. He called his disciples, and addressed them in these words —

"My beloved sons, I must leave you, and go where God sends me. During my absence obey Flavian as you would me, and take care of our brother Paul. Bless you. Farewell."

As he strode away, they remained prostrate on the ground, and when they raised their heads, they saw his tall dark figure on the sandy horizon.

He walked day and night until he reached the ruins of the temple, formerly built by the idolaters, in which he had slept amongst the scorpions and sirens on his former strange journey. The walls, covered with magic signs, were still standing. Thirty immense columns, which terminated in human heads or lotus flowers, still supported a heavy stone entablature. But, at one end of the temple, a pillar had shaken off its old burden, and stood isolated. It had for its capital the head of a woman which smiled, with long eyes and rounded cheeks, and on her forehead cow's horns.

Paphnutius, on seeing it, recognized the column which had been shown him in his dream, and he calculated that it was thirty-two cubits high. He went to the neighbouring village, and ordered a ladder of that height to be made; and when the ladder was placed against the pillar, he ascended, knelt down on the top, and said to the Lord —

"Here, then, O God, is the abode Thou hast chosen for me. May I remain here, in Thy Grace, until the hour of my death."

He had brought no provisions with him, trusting in divine providence, and expecting that charitable peasants would give him all that he needed. And, in fact, the next day, about the ninth hour, women came with their children, bringing bread, dates, and fresh water, which the boys carried to the top of the column.

The top of the pillar was not large enough to allow the monk to lie at full length, so that he slept with his legs crossed and his head on his breast, and sleep was a more cruel torture to him than his wakeful hours. At dawn the ospreys brushed him with their wings, and he awoke filled with pain and terror.

It happened that the carpenter who had made the ladder feared God. Disturbed at the thought that the saint was exposed to the sun and rain, and fearing that he might fall in his sleep, this pious man constructed a roof and a railing on the top of the column.

Soon the report of this extraordinary existence spread from village to village, and the labourers of the valley came on Sundays, with their wives and children, to look at the stylite. The disciples of Paphnutius, having learned with surprise the place of this wonderful retreat, came to him, and obtained from him permission to build their huts at the foot of the column. Every morning they came and stood in a circle round the master, and received from him the words of instruction.

"My sons," he said to them, "continue like those little children whom Jesus loved. That is the way of salvation. The sin of the flesh is the source and origin of all sins; they spring from it as from a parent. Pride, avarice, idleness, anger, and envy are its dearly beloved progeny. I have seen this in Alexandria; I have seen rich men carried away by the vice of lust, which, like a river with a turbid flood, swept them into the gulf of bitterness."

The abbots Ephrem and Serapion, being informed of his strange proceeding, wished to behold him with their own eyes. Seeing from afar, on the river, the triangular sail which was bringing them to him, Paphnutius could not prevent himself from thinking that God had made him an example to all solitary monks. The two abbots, when they saw him, did not conceal their surprise; and, having consulted together, they agreed in condemning such an extraordinary penance, and exhorted Paphnutius to come down.

"Such a mode of life is contrary to all usage," they said; "it is peculiar, and against all rules."

But Paphnutius replied —

"What is the monastic life if not peculiar? And ought not the deeds of a monk to be as eccentric as he is himself? It was a sign from God that caused me to ascend here; it is a sign from God that will make me descend."

Every day religious men came to join the disciples of Paphnutius, and they built for themselves shelters round the aerial hermitage. Several of them, to imitate the saint, mounted the ruins of the temple; but, being reproved by their brethren, and conquered by fatigue, they soon gave up these attempts.

Pilgrims flocked from all parts. There were some who had come long distances, and were hungry and thirsty. The idea occurred to a poor widow of selling fresh water and melons.

Against the foot of the column, behind her bottles of red clay, her cups and her fruit under an awning of blue-and-white striped canvas, she cried, "Who wants to drink?" Following the example of this widow, a baker brought some bricks and made an oven close by, in the hope of selling loaves and cakes to visitors. As the crowd of visitors increased unceasingly, and the inhabitants of the large cities of Egypt began to come, some man, greedy of gain, built a caravanserai to lodge the guests and their servants, camels, and mules. Soon there was, in front of the column, a market to which the fishermen of the Nile brought their fish, and the gardeners their vegetables. A barber, who shaved people in the open air, amused the crowd with his jokes. The old temple, so long given over to silence and solitude was filled with countless sights and sounds of life. The innkeepers turned the subterranean vaults into cellars and nailed on the old pillars signs surmounted by the figure of the holy Paphnutius, and bearing this inscription in Greek and Egyptian — *"Pomegranate wine, fig wine, and genuine Cilician beer sold here."* On the walls, sculptured with pure and graceful carvings, the shop-keepers hung ropes of onions, and smoked fish, dead hares, and the carcasses of sheep. In the evening, the old occupants of the ruins, the rats, scuttled in a long row to the river, whilst the ibises, suspiciously craning their necks, perched on the high cornices, to which rose the smoke of the kitchens, the shouts of the drinkers, and the cries of the tapsters. All around, builders laid out streets, and masons constructed convents, chapels, and churches. By the end of six months a city was established with a guardhouse, a tribunal, a prison, and a school, kept by an old blind scribe.

The pilgrims were innumerable. Bishops and other Church dignitaries, came, full of admiration. The Patriarch of Antioch, who chanced to be in Egypt at that time, came with all his clergy. He highly approved of the extraordinary conduct of the stylite, and the heads of the Libyan Church followed, in the absence of Athanasius, the opinion of the Patriarch. Having learned which, Abbots Ephrem and Serapion came to the feet of Paphnutius to apologies for their former mistrust. Paphnutius replied —

"Know, my brothers, that the penance I endure is barely equal to the temptations which are sent me, the number and force of which astound me. A man, viewed externally, is but small, and, from the height of the pillar to which God has called me, I see human beings moving about like ants. But, considered internally, man is immense; he is as large as the world, for he contains it. All that is spread before me — these monasteries, these inns, the boats on the river, the villages, and what I see in the distance of fields, canals, sand, and mountains — is nothing in respect to what is in me. I carry in my heart countless cities and illimitable deserts. And evil — evil and death — spread over this immensity, cover them all, as night covers the earth. I am, in myself alone, a universe of evil thoughts."

He spoke thus because the desire for woman was in him.

The seventh month, there came from Alexandria, Bubastis and Sais, women who had long been barren, hoping to obtain children by the intercession of the holy man and the virtues of his pillar. They rubbed their sterile bodies against the stone. There followed a procession, as far as the eye could reach, of chariots, palanquins, and litters, which stopped and pushed and jostled below the man of God. From them came sick people terrible to see. Mothers brought to Paphnutius young boys whose limbs were twisted, their eyes starting, their mouth foaming, their voices hoarse. He laid his hands upon them. Blind men approached, groping with their hands, and raising towards him a face pierced with two bleeding holes. Paralytics displayed before him the heavy immobility, the deadly emaciation, and the hideous contractions of their limbs; lame men showed him their club feet; women with cancer, holding their bosoms with both hands, uncovered before him their breasts devoured by the invisible vulture. Dropsical women, swollen like wine skins were placed on the ground before him. He blessed them. Nubians, afflicted with elephantiasis, advanced with heavy steps and looked at him with streaming eyes and expressionless countenances. He made the sign of the cross over them. A young girl of Aphroditopolis was brought to him on a litter; after having vomited blood, she had

310

slept for three days. She looked like a waxen image, and her parents, who thought she was dead, had placed a palm leaf on her breast. Paphnutius having prayed to God, the young girl raised her head and opened her eyes.

As the people reported everywhere the miracles which the saint had performed, unfortunate persons afflicted with that disease which the Greeks call "the divine malady," came from all parts of Egypt in incalculable legions. As soon as they saw the pillar, they were seized with convulsions, rolled on the ground, writhed, and twisted themselves into a ball. And — though it is hardly to be believed — the persons present were in their turn seized with a violent delirium, and imitated the contortions of the epileptics. Monks and pilgrims, men and women, wallowed and struggled pell-mell, their limbs twisted, foaming at the mouth, eating handfuls of earth and prophesying. And Paphnutius at the top of his pillar felt a thrill of horror pass through him, and cried to God —

"I am the scapegoat, and I take upon me all the impurities of these people, and that is why, Lord, my body is filled with evil spirits."

Every time that a sick person went away healed, the people applauded, carried him in triumph, and ceased not to repeat —

"We behold another well of Siloam!"

Hundreds of crutches already hung round the wonderful column; grateful women suspended wreaths and votive images there. Some of the Greeks inscribed distiches, and as every pilgrim carved his name, the stone was soon covered as high as a man could reach with an infinity of Latin, Greek, Coptic, Punic, Hebrew, Syrian, and magic characters.

When the feast of Easter came there was such an affluence of people to this city of miracles that old men thought that the days of the ancient mysteries had returned. All sorts of people, in all sorts of costumes, were to be seen there; the striped robes of the Egyptians, the burnoose of the Arabs, the white drawers of the Nubians, the short cloak of the Greeks, the long toga of the Romans, the scarlet breeches of the barbarians, the gold-spangled robes of the courtesans. A veiled woman would pass on an ass, preceded by black eunuchs, who cleared a passage for her by the free use of their sticks. Acrobats, having spread a carpet on the ground, juggled and performed skilful tricks before a circle of silent spectators. Snake-charmers unrolled their living girdles. A glittering, dusty, noisy, chattering crowd! The curses of the camel-drivers beating the animals; the cries of the hawkers who sold amulets against leprosy and the evil eye; the psalmody of the monks reciting verses of the Bible; the shrieking of the women who were prophesying; the shouting of the beggars singing old songs of the harem; the bleating of sheep; the braying of asses; the sailors calling tardy passengers; all these confused noises caused a deafening uproar, over which dominated the strident voices of the little naked negro boys, running about everywhere selling fresh dates.

And all these human beings stifled under the white sky, in a heavy atmosphere laden with the perfumes of women, the odour of negroes, the fumes of cooking and the smoke of gums, which the devotees bought of the shepherds to burn before the saint.

When night came, fires, torches, and lanterns were lighted everywhere, and nothing was to be seen but red shadows and black shapes. Standing amidst a circle of squatting listeners, an old man, his face lighted by a smoky lamp, related how, formerly, Bitiou had enchanted his heart, torn it from his breast, placed it in an acacia, and then transformed himself into a tree. He made gestures, which his shadow repeated with absurd exaggerations, and the audience uttered cries of admiration. In the taverns, the drinkers, lying on couches, called for beer and wine. Dancing girls, with painted eyes and bare stomachs, performed before them religious or lascivious scenes. In retired corners, young men played dice or other games, and old men followed prostitutes. Above all these rose the solitary, unchanging column; the head with the cow's horns gazed into the shadow, and above it Paphnutius watched between heaven and earth. All at once the moon rose over the Nile, like the bare shoulder of a goddess. The hills gleamed with blue light, and Paphnutius thought he saw the

312

body of Thais shinning in the glimmer of the waters amidst the sapphire night.

The days passed, and the saint still lived on his pillar. When the rainy season came, the waters of heaven, filtering through the cracks in the roof, wetted his body; his stiff limbs were incapable of movement. Scorched by the sun, and reddened by the dew, his skin broke; large ulcers devoured his arms and legs. But the desire of Thais still consumed him inwardly, and he cried —

"It is not enough, great God! More temptations! More unclean thoughts! More horrible desires! Lord, lay upon me all the lusts of men, that I may expiate them all! Though it is false that the Greek bitch took upon herself all the sins of the world, as I heard an impostor once declare, yet there is a hidden meaning in the fable, the truth of which I now recognize. For it is true that the sins of the people enter the soul of the saints, and are lost there as in a well. Thus it is that the souls of the just are polluted with more filth than is ever found in the soul of the sinner. And, for that reason, I praise Thee, O my God, for having made me the cesspool of the world."

One day, a rumour ran through the holy city, and even reached the ears of the hermit: a very great personage, a man occupying a high position, the Prefect of the Alexandrian fleet, Lucius Aurelius Cotta, was about to visit the city — was, indeed, now on his way.

The news was true. Old Cotta, who was inspecting the canals and the navigation of the Nile, had many times expressed a desire to see the stylite and the new city, to which the name of Stylopolis had been given. The Stylopolitans saw the river covered with sails one morning. Cotta appeared on board a golden galley hung with purple, and followed by all his fleet. He landed, and advanced, accompanied by a secretary carrying his tablets, and Aristaeus, his physician, with whom he liked to converse.

A numerous suite walked behind him, and the shore was covered with *laticlaves* and military uniforms. He stopped, some paces from the column, and began to examine the stylite, wiping

313

his face meanwhile with the skirt of his toga. Being of a naturally curious disposition, he had observed many things in the course of his long voyages. He liked to remember them, and intended to write, after he had finished his Punic history, a book on the remarkable things he had witnessed. He seemed much interested by the spectacle before him.

"This is very curious!" he said, puffing and blowing. "And — which is a circumstance worthy of being recorded — this man was my guest. Yes, this monk supped with me last year, after which he carried off an actress."

Turning to his secretary —

"Note that, my son, on my tablets; also the dimensions of the column, not omitting the shape of the top of it."

Then, wiping his face again —

"Persons deserving of belief have assured me that this monk has not left his column for a single moment since he mounted it a year ago. Is that possible, Aristaeus?"

"That which is possible to a lunatic or a sick man," replied Aristaeus, "would be impossible to a man sound in body and mind. Do you know, Lucius, that sometimes diseases of the mind or body give to those afflicted by them a strength which healthy men do not possess? For, as a matter of fact, there is no such thing as good health or bad health. There are only different conditions of the organs. Having studied what are called maladies, I have come to consider them as necessary forms of life. I take pleasure in studying them in order to be able to conquer them. Some of them are worthy of admiration, and conceal, under apparent disorder, profound harmonies; for instance, a quartan fever is certainly a very pretty thing! Sometimes certain affections of the body cause a rapid augmentation of the faculties of the mind. You know Creon? When he was a child, he stuttered and was stupid. But, having cracked his skull by tumbling off a ladder, he became an able lawyer, as you are aware. This monk must be affected in some hidden organ. Moreover, this kind of existence is not so extraordinary as it appears to you, Lucius. I may remind you that the gymnosophists of India can remain motionless, not merely for a year, but during twenty, thirty, or forty years."

"By Jupiter!" cried Cotta, "that is a strange madness. For man was born to move and act, and idleness is an unpardonable crime, because it is an injury to the State. I do not know of any religion in which such an objectionable practice is permitted, though it possibly may be in some of the Asiatic creeds. When I was Governor of Syria, I found *phalli* erected in the porches at the city of Hera. A man ascended, twice a year, and remained there for a week. The people believed that this man talked with the gods, and interceded with them for the prosperity of Syria. The custom appeared senseless to me; nevertheless I did nothing to put it down. For I consider that a functionary ought not to interfere with the manners and customs of the people, but on the contrary, to see that they are preserved. It is not the business of the government to force a religion on a people, but to maintain that which exists, which, whether good or bad, has been regulated by the spirit of the time, the place, and the race. If it endeavours to put down a religion, it proclaims itself revolutionary in its spirit, and tyrannical in its acts, and is justly detested. Besides, how are you to raise yourself above the superstitions of the vulgar, except by understanding them and tolerating them? Aristaeus, I am of opinion that I should leave this nephelo-coccygian in the air, exposed only to the indignities the birds shower on him. I should not gain anything by having him pulled down, but I should by taking note of his thoughts and beliefs."

He puffed, coughed, and placed his hand on the secretary's shoulder.

"My child, note down that, amongst certain sects of Christians, it is considered praiseworthy to carry off courtesans and live upon columns. You may add that these customs are evidence of the worship of genetic divinities. But on this point we ought to question him himself."

Then, raising his head, and shading his eyes with his hand, to keep off the sun, he shouted —

"Hallo, Paphnutius! If you remember that you were once my guest, answer me. What are you doing up there? Why did you go up, and why do you stay there? Has this column any phallic signification in your mind?"

Paphnutius, considering Cotta as nothing but an idolater, did not deign to reply. But his disciple, Flavian, approached, and said —

"Illustrious Sir, this holy man takes the sins of the world upon him, and cures diseases."

"By Jupiter! Do you hear, Aristaeus?" cried Cotta. "This nephelo-coccygian practices medicine, like you. What do you think of so high a rival?"

Aristaeus shook his head.

"It is very possible that he may cure certain diseases better than I can; such, for instance, as epilepsy, vulgarly called the divine malady, although all maladies are equally divine, for they all come from the gods. But the cause of this disease lies, partly, in the imagination, and you must confess, Lucius, that this monk, perched up on the head of a goddess, strikes the minds of the sick people more forcibly than I, bending over my mortars and phials in my laboratory, could ever do. There are forces, Lucius, infinitely more powerful than reason and science."

"What are they?" asked Cotta.

"Ignorance and folly," replied Aristaeus.

"I have rarely seen a more curious sight," continued Cotta, "and I hope that some day an able writer will relate the foundation of Stylopolis. But even the most extraordinary spectacles should not keep, longer than is befitting, a serious and busy man from his work. Let us go and inspect the canals. Farewell, good Paphnutius! or rather, till our next meeting! If ever you should come down to earth again, and revisit Alexandria, do not fail to come and sup with me."

These words, heard by all present, passed from mouth to mouth, and being repeated by the believers, added greatly to the reputation of Paphnutius. Pious minds amplified and transformed them, and it was stated that Paphnutius, from the top of his pillar, had converted the Prefect of the Fleet to the faith of the apostles and the Nicaean fathers. The believers found a figurative meaning in the last words uttered by Aurelius Cotta; to them, the supper to which this important personage had invited the ascetic, was a holy communion, a spiritual repast, a celestial banquet. The story of this meeting was embroidered with wonderful details, which those who invented were the first to believe. It was said that when Cotta, after a long argument, had embraced the truth, an angel had come from heaven to wipe the sweat from his brow. The physician and secretary of the Prefect of the Fleet had also, it was asserted, been converted at the same time. And, the miracle being public and notorious, the deacons of the principal churches of Libya recorded it amongst the authentic facts. After that, it could be said, without any exaggeration, that the whole world was seized with a desire to see Paphnutius, and that, in the West as well as the East, all Christians turned their astonished eyes towards him. The most celebrated cities of Italy sent deputations to him, and the Roman Caesar, the divine Constantine who favoured the Christian religion, wrote him a letter which the legates brought to him with great ceremony. But one night, whilst the budding city at his feet slept in the dew, he heard a voice, which said —

"Paphnutius, thou art become celebrated by thy works and powerful by thy word. God has raised thee up for His glory. He has chosen thee to work miracles, heal the sick, convert the Pagans, enlighten sinners, confound the Arians, and establish peace in the Church."

Paphnutius replied —

"God's will be done!"

The voice continued —

"Arise, Paphnutius, and go seek in his palace the impious Constans, who, far from imitating the wisdom of his brother, Constantine, inclines to the errors of Arius and Marcus. Go! The bronze gates shall fly open before thee, and thy sandals shall resound on the golden floor of the basilica before the throne of the Caesars, and thy awe-inspiring voice shall change the heart of the son of Constantinus. Thou shalt reign over a peaceful and powerful Church. And, even as the soul directs the body, so shall the Church govern the empire. Thou shalt be placed above senators, comites, and patricians. Thou shalt repress the greed of the people, and check the boldness of the barbarians. Old Cotta, knowing that thou art the head of the government, will seek the honour of washing thy feet. At thy death thy *cilicium* shall be taken to the patriarch of Alexandria, and the great Athanasius, white with glory, shall kiss it as the relic of a saint. Go!"

Paphnutius replied —

"Let the will of God be accomplished!"

And making an effort to stand up, he prepared to descend. But the voice, divining his intention, said —

"Above all, descend not by the ladder. That would be to act like an ordinary man, and to be unconscious of the gifts that are in thee. A great saint, like thee, ought to fly through the air. Leap! the angels are there to support thee. Leap, then!"

Paphnutius replied —

"The will of God be done, on earth as it is in heaven."

Extending his long arms like the ragged wings of a huge sick bird, he was about to throw himself down, when, suddenly, a hideous mocking laugh rang in his ears. Terrified, he asked —

"Who laughs thus?"

"Ah? ah!" screamed the voice, "we are yet but at the beginning of our friendship; thou wilt some day be better acquainted with me. My friend, it was I who caused thee to ascend here, and I ought to be satisfied at the docility with which thou hast accomplished my wishes. Paphnutius, I am pleased with thee."

Paphnutius murmured, in a voice stifled by fear —

"Avaunt, avaunt! I know thee now; thou art he who carried Jesus to a pinnacle of the temple, and showed him all the kingdoms of this world."

He fell, affrighted, on the stone.

"Why did I not know this sooner?" he thought. "More wretched than the blind, deaf, and paralyzed who trust in me, I have lost all knowledge of things supernatural, and am more depraved than the maniacs who eat earth and approach dead bodies. I can no longer distinguish between the clamours of hell and the voices of heaven. I have lost even the intuition of the new-born child, who cries when its nurse's breast is taken from it, of the dog that scents out its master's footsteps, of the plant that turns towards the sun. I am the laughing-stock of the devils. So, then, it is Satan who led me here. When he elevated me on this pedestal, lust and pride mounted with me. It is not the magnitude of my temptations which terrifies me. Anthony, on his mountain, suffers the same. I wish that all their swords may pierce my flesh, before the eyes of the angels. I have even learned to like my sufferings. But God does not speak to me, and His silence astonishes me. He has left me — and I had but Him to look to. He leaves me alone in the horror of His absence. He flies from me. I will follow after Him. This stone burns my feet. Let me leave quickly, and come up with God."

With that he seized the ladder which stood against the column, put his feet on it, and having descended a rung, found himself face to face with the monster's head; she smiled strangely. He was certain then that what he had taken for the site of his rest and glory, was but the diabolical instrument of his trouble and damnation. He hastily descended and touched the soil. His feet had forgotten their use, and he reeled. But, feeling on him the shadow of the cursed column, he forced himself to run. All slept. He traversed, without being seen, the great square surrounded by wine-shops, inns, and caravanserais, and threw himself into a by-street which led towards the Libyan Hills. A dog pursued him, barking, and stopped only at the edge of the desert. Paphnutius went through a country where there was no road but the trail of wild beasts. Leaving behind him the huts abandoned by the coiners, he continued all night and all day his solitary flight.

At last, almost ready to expire with hunger, thirst, and fatigue, and not knowing if God was still far from him, he came to a silent city which extended from right to left, and stretched away till it was lost in the blue horizon. The buildings, which were widely separated and like each other, resembled pyramids cut off at half their height. They were tombs. The doors were broken, and in the shadow of the chambers could be seen the gleaming eyes of hyenas and wolves who brought forth their young there, whilst the dead bodies lay on the threshold, despoiled by robbers, and gnawed by the wild beasts. Having passed through this funeral city, Paphnutius fell exhausted before a tomb which stood near a spring surrounded by palm trees. This tomb was much ornamented, and, as there was no door to it, he saw inside it a painted chamber, in which serpents bred.

"Here," he sighed, "is the abode I have chosen; the tabernacle of my repentance and penitence."

He dragged himself to it, drove out the reptiles with his feet, and remained prostrate on the stone floor for eighteen hours, at the end of which time he went to the spring, and drank out of his hand. Then he plucked some dates and some stalks of lotus, the seeds of which he ate. Thinking this kind of life was good, he made it the rule of his existence. From morning to night he never lifted his forehead from the stone.

One day, whilst he was thus prostrated, he heard a voice which said —

"Look at these images, that thou mayest learn."

Then, raising his head, he saw, on the walls of the chamber, paintings which represented lively and domestic scenes. They were of very old work, and marvelously lifelike. There were cooks who blew the fire, with their cheeks all puffed out; others plucked geese, or cooked quarters of sheep in stew-pans. A little farther, a hunter carried on his shoulders a gazelle pierced with arrows. In one place, peasants were sowing, reaping, or gathering. In another, women danced to the sounds of viols, flutes, and harp. A young girl played the theorbo. The lotus flower shone in her hair, which was neatly braided. Her transparent dress let the pure forms of her body be seen. Her bosom and mouth were perfect. The face was turned in profile, and the beautiful eye looked straight before her. The whole figure was exquisite. Paphnutius having examined it, lowered his eyes, and replied to the voice —

"Why dost thou command me to look at these images? No doubt they represent the terrestrial life of the idolater whose body rests here, under my feet, at the bottom of a well, in a coffin of black basalt. They recall the life of a dead man, and are, despite their bright colours, the shadows of a shadow. The life of a dead man! O vanity!"

"He is dead, but he lived," replied the voice; "and thou wilt die, and wilt not have lived."

From that day, Paphnutius had not a moment's rest. The voice spoke to him incessantly. The girl with the theorbo looked fixedly at him from underneath the long lashes of her eye. At last she also spoke —

"Look. I am mysterious and beautiful. Love me. Exhaust in my arms the love which torments you. What use is it to fear me? You cannot escape me; I am the beauty of woman. Whither do you think to fly from me, senseless fool? You will find my likeness in the radiance of flowers, and in the grace of the palm trees, in the flight of pigeons, in the bounds of the gazelle, in the rippling of brooks, in the soft light of the moon, and if you close your eyes, you will find me within yourself. It is a thousand years since the man who sleeps here, swathed in linen, in a bed of black stone, pressed me to his heart. It is a thousand years since he received the last kiss from my mouth, and his sleep is yet redolent with it. You know me well, Paphnutius. How is it you have not recognized me? I am one of the innumerable incarnations of Thais. You are a learned monk, and well skilled in the knowledge of things. You have traveled, and it is by travel a man learns the most. Often a day passed abroad will show more novelties than ten years passed at home. You have heard that Thais lived formerly in Argos, under the name of Helen. She had another existence in Thebes Hecatompyle. And I was Thais of Thebes. How is it you have not guessed it? I took, when I was alive, a large share in the sins of this world, and now reduced here to the condition of a shadow, I am still quite capable of taking your sins upon me, beloved monk. Whence comes your surprise? It was certain that, wherever you went, you would find Thais again."

He struck his forehead against the pavement, and uttered a cry of terror. And every night the player of the theorbo left the wall, approached him, and spoke in a clear voice mingled with soft breathing. And as the holy man resisted the temptations she gave him, she said to him —

"Love me; yield, friend. As long as you resist me I shall torment you. You do not know what the patience of a dead woman is. I shall wait, if necessary, till you are dead. Being a sorceress, I shall put into your lifeless body a spirit who will reanimate it, and who will not refuse me what I have asked in vain of you. And think, Paphnutius, what a strange situation when your blessed soul sees, from the height of heaven, its own body given up to sin. God, who has promised to return you this body after the day of judgment and the end of time, will Himself be much puzzled. How can He place in celestial glory a human form inhabited by a devil, and guarded by a sorceress? You have not thought of that difficulty. Nor God either, perhaps. Between ourselves, He is not very knowing. Any ordinary magician can easily deceive Him, and if He had not His thunder, and the cataracts of heaven, the village urchins would pull His beard. He has certainly not as much sense as the old serpent, His adversary. He, indeed, is a wonderful artist. If I am so beautiful, it is because he adorned me with all my attractions. It was he who taught me how to braid my hair, and to make for myself rosy fingers with agate nails. You have misunderstood him. When you came to live in this tomb, you drove out with your feet the serpents which were here, without troubling yourself to know whether they were of his family, and you crushed their eggs. I am afraid, my poor friend, you will have a troublesome business on your hands. You were warned, however, that he was a musician and a lover. What have you done? You have quarreled with science and beauty. You are altogether miserable, and Iaveh does not come to your help. It is not probable that he will come. Being as great as all things, he cannot move for want of space, and if, by an impossibility, he made the least movement, all creation would be pushed out of place. My handsome hermit, give me a kiss."

Paphnutius was aware that great prodigies are performed by magic arts. He thought — not without much uneasiness —

"Perhaps the dead man buried at my feet knows the words written in that mysterious book which exists hidden, not far from here, at the bottom of a royal tomb. By virtue of these words, the dead, taking the form which they had upon earth, see the light of the sun and the smiles of women."

His chief fear was that the girl with the theorbo and the dead man might come together, as they did in their lifetime, and that he should see them unite. Sometimes he thought he heard the sound of kissing.

He was troubled in his mind, and now, in the absence of God he feared to think as much as to feel. One evening, when he was kneeling prostrate according to his custom, an unknown voice said to him —

"Paphnutius, there are on earth more people than you imagine, and if I were to show you what I have seen, you would die of astonishment. There are men with a single eye in the middle of their forehead. There are men who have but one leg, and advance by jumps. There are men who change their sex, and the females become males. There are men-trees, who shoot out roots in the ground. And there are men with no head, with two eyes, a nose, and a mouth in their breast. Can you honestly believe that Jesus Christ died for the salvation of these men?"

Another time he had a vision. He saw, in a strong light, a broad road, rivulets, and gardens. On the road, Aristobulus and Chereas passed at a gallop on their Syrian horses, and the joyous ardour of the race reddened the cheeks of the two young men. Beneath a portico, Callicrates recited his verses; satisfied pride trembled in his voice and shone in his eyes. In the garden, Zenothemis picked apples of gold, and caressed a serpent with azure wings. Clad in white, and wearing a shining mitre, Hermodorus meditated beneath a sacred persea, which bore, instead of flowers, small heads of pure profile, wearing, like the Egyptian goddesses, vultures, hawks, or the shining disk of the moon; whilst in the background, by the side of a fountain, Nicias

323

studied, on an armillary sphere, the harmonious movements of the stars.

Then a veiled woman approached the monk, holding in her hand a branch of myrtle. She said to him —

"Look! Some seek eternal beauty, and place their ephemeral life in the infinite. Others live without much thought. But by that alone they submit to fair Nature, and they are happy and beautiful in the joy of living only, and give glory to the supreme artist of all things; for man is a noble hymn to God. All think that happiness is innocent, and that pleasure is permitted to man. Paphnutius, if they are right, what a dupe you have been!"

And the vision vanished.

Thus was Paphnutius tempted unceasingly in body and mind. Satan never gave him a minute's repose. The solitude of the tomb was more peopled than the streets of a great city. The devils shouted with laughter, and millions of imps, evil genii, and phantoms imitated all the ordinary transactions of life. In the evening, when he went to the spring, satyrs and nymphs capered round him, and tried to drag him into their lascivious dances. The demons no longer feared him. They loaded him with insults, obscene jests, and blows. One day a devil, no longer than his arm, stole the cord he wore round his waist.

He said to himself —

"Thought, whither hast thou led me?"

And he resolved to work with his hands, in order to give his mind that rest of which it had need. Near the spring, some banana trees, with large leaves, grew under the shade of the palms. He cut the stalks, and carried them to the tomb. He crushed them with a stone, and reduced them to fibres, as he had seen rope makers do. For he intended to make a cord, to replace that which the devil had stolen. The demons were somewhat displeased at this; they ceased their clamour, and the girl with the theorbo no longer continued her magic arts, but remained quietly on the wall. The courage and faith of Paphnutius increased whilst he pounded the banana stems.

"With Heaven's help," he said to himself, "I shall subdue the flesh. As to my soul, its confidence is still unshaken. In vain do the devils, and that accursed woman, try to instill into my mind doubts as to the nature of God. I will reply to them, by the mouth of the Apostle John, 'In the beginning was the Word, and the Word was God.' That I firmly believe, and that which I believe is absurd, I believe still more firmly. In fact it should be absurd. If it were not so, I should not believe; I should know. And it is not that which we know which gives eternal life; it is faith only that saves."

He exposed the separated fibres to the sun and the dew, and every morning he took care to turn them, to prevent them rotting; and he rejoiced to find that he had become as simple as a child. When he had twisted his cord, he cut reeds to make mats and baskets. The sepulchral chamber resembled a basket-maker's workshop, and Paphnutius could pass without difficulty from work to prayer. Yet still God was not merciful to him, for one night he was awakened by a voice which froze him with horror, for he guessed that it was the voice of the dead man.

The voice called quickly, in a light whisper —

"Helen! Helen! come and bathe with me! come quickly!"

A woman, whose mouth was close to the monk's ear, replied —

"Friend, I cannot rise; a man is lying on me."

Paphnutius suddenly perceived that his cheek rested on a woman's breast. He recognized the player of the theorbo, who, partly relieved of his weight, raised her breast. He clung tightly to the sweet, warm, perfumed body, and consumed with the desire of damnation, he cried —

"Stay, stay, my heavenly one!"

But she was already standing on the threshold. She laughed, and her smile gleamed in the silver rays of the moon.

"Why should I stay?" she said. "The shadow of a shadow is enough for a lover endowed with such a lively imagination. Besides, you have sinned. What more was needed?"

Paphnutius wept in the night, and when the dawn came, he murmured a prayer that was a meek complaint —

"Jesus, my Jesus, why hast Thou forsaken me! Thou seest the danger in which I am. Come, and help me, sweet Saviour. Since Thy Father no longer loves me, and does not hear me, remember that I have but Thee. From Him nothing is to be hoped; I cannot comprehend Him, and He cannot pity me. But Thou was born of a woman, and that is why I trust in Thee. Remember that Thou wast a man. I pray to Thee, not because Thou art God of God, Light of light, very God of very God, but because Thou hast lived poor and humble on this earth where now I suffer, because Satan has tempted Thy flesh, because the sweat of agony has bedewed Thy face. It is to Thy humanity that I pray, Jesus, my brother Jesus!"

When he had thus prayed, wringing his hands, a terrible peal of laughter shook the walls of the tomb, and the voice which rang in his ears on the top of the column, said jeeringly —

"That is a prayer worthy of the breviary of Marcus, the heretic. Paphnutius is an Arian! Paphnutius is an Arian!"

As though thunderstruck, the monk fell senseless.

*****

When he reopened his eyes, he saw around him monks wearing black hoods, who poured water on his temples, and recited exorcisms. Many others were standing outside, carrying palm leaves.

"As we passed through the desert," said one of them, "we heard cries issuing from this tomb, and, having entered, we found you lying unconscious on the floor. Doubtless the devils had thrown you down, and had fled at our approach."

Paphnutius, raising his head, asked in a feeble voice —

"Who are you, my brothers? And why do you carry palms in your hands? Is it for my burial?"

One of them replied —

"Brother, do you not know that our father, Anthony, now a hundred and five years old, having been warned of his approaching end, has come down from Mount Colzin, to which

326

he had retired, to bless his numerous spiritual children? We are going with palm leaves to greet our holy father. But how is it, brother, that you are ignorant of such a great event? Can it be possible that no angel came to this tomb to inform you?"

"Alas!" replied Paphnutius, "I am not worthy of such a favour, and the only denizens of this abode are demons and vampires. Pray for me. I am Paphnutius, Abbot of Antinoe, the most wretched of the servants of God."

At the name of Paphnutius, all waved their palm leaves and murmured his praises. The monk who had previously spoken, cried in surprise —

"Can it be that thou art that holy Paphnutius, celebrated for so many works that it was supposed he would some day equal the great Anthony himself? Most venerable, it was thou who convertedst to God the courtesan, Thais, and who, raised upon a high column, was carried away by the seraphs. Those who watched by night, at the foot of the pillar, saw thy blessed assumption. The wings of the angels encircled thee in a white cloud, and with thy right hand extended thou didst bless the dwellings of man. The next day, when the people saw thou wert no longer there, a long groan rose to the summit of the discrowned pillar. But Flavian, thy disciple, reported the miracle, and took thy place as the head. But a foolish man, of the name of Paul, tried to contradict the general opinion. He asserted that he had seen thee, in a dream, carried away by the devils; the people wanted to stone him, and it was a miracle that he escaped death. I am Zozimus, abbot of these solitary monks whom thou seest prostrate at thy feet. Like them, I kneel before thee, that thou mayest bless the father with the children. Then thou shalt relate to us the marvels which God has deigned to accomplish by thy means."

"Far from having favoured me as thou believest," replied Paphnutius, "the Lord has tried me with terrible temptations. I was not carried away by angels. But a shadowy wall is raised in front of my eyes, and moves before me. I have lived in a dream. Without God all is a dream. When I made my journey to

Alexandria, I heard, in a short space of time, many discourses, and I learned that the army of errors was innumerable. It pursues me, and I am compassed about with swords."

Zozimus replied —

"Venerable father, we must remember that the saints, and especially the solitary saints, undergo terrible trials. If thou wast not carried to heaven by the seraphs, it is certain that the Lord granted that favour to thy image, for Flavian, the monks, and the people were witnesses of thy assumption."

Paphnutius resolved to go and receive the blessing of Anthony.

"Brother Zozimus," he said, "give me one of these palm leaves, and let us go and meet our father."

"Let us go," replied Zozimus; "military order is most befitting for monks, who are God's soldiers. Thou and I, being abbots, will march in front, and the others shall follow us, singing psalms."

They set out on their march, and Paphnutius said —

"God is unity, for He is the truth, which is one. The world is many, because it is error. We should turn away from all the sights of nature, even those which appear the most innocent. Their diversity renders them pleasant, which is a sign that they are evil. For that reason, I cannot see a tuft of papyrus by the side of still waters without my soul being imbued with melancholy. All things that the senses perceive are detestable. The least grain of sand brings danger. Everything tempts us. Woman is but a combination of all the temptations scattered in the thin air, on the flowering earth, in the clear waters. Happy is he whose soul is a sealed vase! Happy is he who knows how to be deaf, dumb, and blind, and who knows nothing of the world, in order that he may know God!"

Zozimus, having meditated upon these words, replied as follows —

"Venerable father, it is fitting that I should avow my sins to thee, since thou hast shown me thy soul. Thus we shall confess to each other, according to the apostolic custom. Before I was a monk, I led an abominable life. At Madaura, a city celebrated for its courtesans, I sought out all kinds of worldly love. Every night I supped in company with young debauchees and female flute players, and I took home with me the one who pleased me the best. A saint like thee could never imagine to what a pitch the fury of my desires carried me. Suffice it to say that it spared neither matrons nor nuns, and spread adultery and sacrilege everywhere. I excited my senses with wine, and was justly known as the heaviest drinker in Madaura. Yet I was a Christian, and, in all my follies, kept my faith in Jesus crucified. Having devoured my substance in riotous living, I was beginning to feel the first attacks of poverty, when I saw one of my companions in pleasure suddenly struck with a terrible disease. His knees could not sustain him; his twitching hands refused to obey him; his glazed eyes closed. Only horrible groans came from his breast. His mind, heavier than his body, slumbered. To punish him for having lived like a beast, God had changed him into a beast. The loss of my property had already inspired me with salutary reflections, but the example of my friend was of yet greater efficacy; it made such an impression on my heart that I quitted the world and retired into the desert. There I have enjoyed for twenty years a peace that nothing has troubled. I work with my monks as weaver, architect, carpenter, and even as scribe, though, to say the truth, I have little taste for writing, having always preferred action to thought. My days are full of joy, and my nights without dreams, and I believe that the grace of the Lord is in me, because, even in the midst of the most frightful sins, I have never lost hope."

On hearing these words, Paphnutius lifted his eyes to heaven and murmured —

"Lord, Thou lookest with kindness upon this man polluted by adultery, sacrilege, and so many crimes, and Thou turnest away from me, who have always kept Thy commandments! How inscrutable is Thy justice, O my God! and how impenetrable are Thy ways!"

Zozimus extended his arms.

"Look, venerable father! On both sides of the horizon are long, black files that look like emigrant ants. They are our brothers, who, like us, are going to meet Anthony."

When they came to the place of meeting, they saw a magnificent spectacle. The army of monks extended, in three ranks, in an immense semicircle. In the first rank stood the old hermits of the desert, cross in hand, and with long beards that almost touched the ground. The monks, governed by the abbots Ephrem and Serapion, and also all the cenobites of the Nile, formed the second line. Behind them appeared the ascetics, who had come from their distant rocks. Some wore, on their blackened and dried-up bodies, shapeless rags; others had for their only clothes, bundles of reeds held together by withies. Many of them were naked, but God had covered them with a fell of hair as thick as a sheep's fleece. All held branches of palm; they looked like an emerald rainbow, or they might have been also compared to the host of the elect — the living walls of the city of God.

Such perfect order reigned in the assembly, that Paphnutius found, without difficulty, the monks he governed. He placed himself near them, after having taken care to hide his face under his hood, that he might remain unknown, and not disturb them in their pious expectation. Suddenly, an immense shout arose —

"The saint!" they all cried. "The saint! Behold the great saint, against whom hell has not prevailed, the well-beloved of God! Our father, Anthony!"

Then a great silence followed, and every forehead was lowered to the sand.

From the summit of a dune, in the vast void space, Anthony advanced, supported by his beloved disciples, Macarius and Amathas. He walked slowly, but his figure was still upright, and showed the remains of a superhuman strength. His white beard spread over his broad chest, his polished skull reflected the rays of sunlight like the forehead of Moses. The keen gaze of the eagle was in his eyes; the smile of a child shone on his round cheek. To bless his people, he raised his arms, tired by a century of

330

marvellous works, and his voice burst forth for the last time, with the words of love.

"How goodly are thy tents, O Jacob, and thy tabernacles, O Israel!"

Immediately, from one end to the other of the living wall, like a peal of harmonious thunder, the psalm, "Blessed is the man that feareth the Lord," broke forth.

Accompanied by Macarius and Amathas, Anthony passed along the ranks of the old hermits, anchorites, and cenobites. This seer, who had beheld heaven and hell; this hermit, who from a cave in the rock, governed the Christian Church; this saint, who had sustained the faith of the martyrs; this scholar, whose eloquence had paralyzed the heretics, spoke tenderly to each of his sons, and bade them a kindly farewell, on the eve of the blessed death, which God, who loved him, had at last promised him.

He said to the abbots Ephrem and Serapion —

"You command large armies, and you are both great generals. Therefore, you shall put on in heaven an armour of gold, and the Archangel Michael shall give you the title of kiliarchs of his hosts."

Perceiving the old man Philemon, he embraced him, and said —

"Behold, the kindest and best of all my children. His soul exhales a perfume as sweet as the flower of the beans he sows every year."

To Abbot Zozimus he addressed these words —

"Thou hast never mistrusted divine goodness, and therefore the peace of the Lord is in thee. The lily of thy virtues has flowered upon the dunghill of thy corruption."

To all he spoke words of unerring wisdom.

To the old hermits he said —

"The apostle saw, round the throne of God, eighty old men seated, clad in white robes, and wearing crowns on their heads."

To the young men —

"Be joyful; leave sadness to the happy ones of this world."

331

Thus he passed along the front of his filial army, exhorting and comforting. Paphnutius, seeing him approach, fell on his knees, his heart torn by fear and hope.

"My father! my father!" he cried in his agony. "My father! come to my help, for I perish. I have given to God the soul of Thaïs; I have lived upon the top of a column, and in the chamber of a tomb. My forehead, unceasingly in the dust, has become horny as a camel's knee. And yet God has gone from me. Bless me, my father, and I shall be saved; shake the hyssop, and I shall be washed, and I shall shine as the snow."

Anthony did not reply. He turned to the monks of Antinoe those eyes whose looks no man could sustain. He gazed for a long time at Paul, called the Fool; then he made a sign to him to approach. And, as all were astonished that the saint should address himself to a man who was not in his senses, Anthony said —

"God has granted to him more grace than to any of you. Lift thy eyes, my son Paul, and tell me what thou seest in heaven."

Paul the Fool raised his eyes; his face shone, and his tongue was unloosed.

"I see in heaven," he said, "a bed adorned with hangings of purple and gold. Around it three virgins keep constant watch that no soul may approach it, except the chosen one for whom the bed is prepared."

Believing that this bed was the symbol of his glorification, Paphnutius had already begun to return thanks to God. But Anthony made a sign to him to be silent, and to listen to the Fool, who murmured in his ecstasy —

"The three virgins speak to me; they say unto me: 'A saint is about to quit the earth; Thaïs of Alexandria is dying. And we have prepared the bed of her glory, for we are her virtues — Faith, Fear, and Love.'"

Anthony asked —

"Sweet child, what else seest thou?"

Paul gazed vacantly from the zenith to the nadir, and from west to east, when suddenly his eyes fell on the Abbot of Antinoe.

His face grew pale with a holy terror, and his eyeballs reflected invisible flames.

"I see," he murmured, "three demons, who, full of joy, prepare to seize that man. One of them is like unto a tower, one to a woman, and one to a mage. All three bear their name, marked with red-hot iron; the first on the forehead, the second on the belly, the third on the breast, and those names are — Pride, Lust, and Doubt. I have finished."

Having spoken thus, Paul, with haggard eyes and hanging jaw, returned to his old simple ways.

And, as the monks of Antinoe looked anxiously at Anthony, the saint pronounced these words —

"God has made known His just judgment. Let us bow to Him and hold our peace."

He passed. He bestowed blessings as he went. The sun, now descended to the horizon, enveloped him in its glory, and his shadow, immeasurably elongated by a miracle from heaven, unrolled itself behind him like an endless carpet, as a sign of the long remembrance this great saint would leave amongst men.

Upright, but thunderstruck, Paphnutius saw and heard nothing more. One word alone rang in his ears, "Thais is dying!" The thought had never occurred to him. Twenty years had he contemplated a mummy's head, and yet the idea that death would close the eyes of Thais astonished him hopelessly.

"Thais is dying!" An incomprehensible saying! "Thais is dying!" In those three words what a new and terrible sense! "Thais is dying!" Then why the sun, the flowers, the brooks, and all creation? "Thais is dying!" What good was all the universe? Suddenly he sprang forward. "To see her again, to see her once more!" He began to run. He knew not where he was, or whither he went, but instinct conducted him with unerring certainty; he went straight to the Nile. A swarm of sails covered the upper waters of the river. He sprang on board a barque manned by Nubians, and lying in the forepart of the boat, his eyes devouring space, he cried, in grief and rage —

"Fool, fool, that I was, not to have possessed Thais whilst there was yet time! Fool to have believed that there was anything else in the world but her! Oh, madness! I dreamed of God, of the salvation of my soul, of life eternal — as if all that counted for anything when I had seen Thais! Why did I not feel that blessed eternity was in a single kiss of that woman, and that without her life was senseless, and no more than an evil dream? Oh, stupid fool! thou hast seen her, and thou hast desired the good things of the other world! Oh, coward! thou hast seen her, and thou hast feared God! God! heaven! what are they? And what have they to offer thee which are worth the least title of that which she would have given thee? Oh, miserable, senseless fool, who sought divine goodness elsewhere than on the lips of Thais! What hand was upon thy eyes? Cursed be he who blinded thee then! Thou couldst have bought, at the price of thy damnation, one moment of her love, and thou hast not done it! She opened to thee her arms — flesh mingled with the perfume of flowers — and thou wast not engulfed in the unspeakable enchantments of her unveiled breast. Thou hast listened to the jealous voice which said to thee, 'Refrain!' Dupe, dupe, miserable dupe! Oh, regrets! Oh, remorse! Oh, despair! Not to have the joy to carry to hell the memory of that never-to-be-forgotten hour, and to cry to God, 'Burn my flesh, dry up all the blood in my veins, break all my bones, thou canst not take from me the remembrance which sweetens and refreshes me for ever and ever!' . . . Thais is dying! Preposterous God, if thou knewest how I laugh at Thy hell! Thais is dying, and she will never be mine — never! never!"

And as the boat came down the river with the current, he remained whole days lying on his face, and repeating —

"Never! never! never!"

Then, at the idea that she had given herself to others, and not to him; that she had poured forth an ocean of love, and he had not wetted his lips therein, he stood up, savagely wild, and howled with grief. He tore his breast with his nails, and bit the flesh of his arms. He thought —

"If I could but kill all those she has loved!"

334

The idea of these murders filled him with delicious fury. He dreamed of killing Nicias slowly and leisurely, looking him full in the eyes whilst he murdered him. Then suddenly his fury melted away. He wept, he sobbed. He became feeble and meek. An unknown tenderness softened his soul. He longed to throw his arms round the neck of the companion of his childhood and say to him, "Nicias, I love thee, because thou hast loved her. Talk to me about her. Tell me what she said to thee." And still, without ceasing, the iron of that phrase entered into his soul — "Thais is dying!"

"Light of day, silvery shadows of night stars, heavens, trees with trembling crests, savage beasts, domestic animals, all the anxious souls of men, do you not hear? 'Thais is dying!' Disappear, ye lights, breezes, and perfumes! Hide yourselves, ye shapes and thoughts of the universe! 'Thais is dying!' She was the beauty of the world, and all that drew near to her grew fairer in the reflection of her grace. The old man and the sages who sat near her, at the banquet at Alexandria, how pleasant they were, and how fascinating was their conversation! A host of brilliant thoughts sprang to their lips, and all their ideas were steeped in pleasure. And it was because the breath of Thais was on them that all they said was love, beauty, truth. A delightful impiety lent its grace to their discourse. They thoroughly expressed all human splendour. Alas! all that is but a dream. Thais is dying! Oh, how easy it will be to me to die of her death! But canst thou only die, withered embryo, fetus steeped in gall and scalding tears? Miserable abortion, dost thou think thou canst taste death, thou who hast never known life? If only God exists, that he may damn me. I hope for it — I wish it. God, I hate Thee — dost Thou hear? Overwhelm me with Thy damnation. To compel Thee to, I spit in Thy face. I must find an eternal hell, to exhaust the eternity of rage which consumes me."

✺✺✺✺✺

The next day, at dawn, Albina received the Abbot of Antinoe at the nunnery.

"Thou art welcome to our tabernacles of peace, venerable father, for no doubt, thou comest to bless the saint thou hast given us. Thou knowest that God, in his mercy, has called her to Him; how couldst thou fail to know tidings that the angels have carried from desert to desert? It is true that Thais is about to meet her blessed death. Her labours are accomplished, and I ought to inform thee, in a few words, as to her conduct whilst she was still amongst us. After thy departure, when she was confined in a cell sealed with thy seal, I sent her, with her food, a flute, similar to those which girls of her profession play at banquets. I did that to prevent her from falling into a melancholy mood, and that she should not show less skill and talent before God than she had shown before men. In this I showed prudence and foresight, for all day long Thais praised the Lord upon the flute, and the virgins, who were attracted by the sound of this invisible flute, said, 'We hear the nightingale of the heavenly groves, the dying swan of Jesus crucified.' Thus did Thais perform her penance, when, after sixty days, the door which thou hadst sealed opened of itself, and the clay seal was broken without being touched by any human hand. By that sign I knew that the trial thou hadst imposed upon her was at an end, and that God had pardoned the sins of the flute-player. From that time she has shared the ordinary life of my nuns, working and praying with them. She was an example to them by the modesty of her acts and words, and seemed like a statue of purity amongst them. Sometimes she was sad; but those clouds soon passed. When I saw that she was really drawn towards God by faith, hope, and love, I did not hesitate to employ her talent, and even her beauty, for the improvement of her sisters. I asked her to represent before us the actions of the famous women and wise virgins of the Scriptures. She acted Esther, Deborah, Judith, Mary, the sister of Lazarus, and Mary, the mother of Jesus. I know, venerable father, that thy austere mind is alarmed at the idea of these performances. But thou thyself wouldest have been touched if thou hadst seen her in these pious scenes, shedding real tears, and raising to heaven arms graceful as palm leaves. I have long governed a community of women, and I make it a rule never to oppose their nature. All seeds give not the same flowers. Not all souls are sanctified in the same way. It must also not be forgotten that Thais gave herself to God whilst she was still beautiful, and such a sacrifice is, if not unexampled, at least very rare. This beauty — her natural vesture — has not left her during the three months' fever of which she is dying. As, during her illness, she has incessantly asked to see the sky, I have her carried every morning into the courtyard, near the well, under the old fig tree, in the shade of which the abbesses of this convent are accustomed to hold their meetings. Thou wilt find her there, venerable father; but hasten, for God calls her, and this night a shroud will cover that face which God made both to shame and to edify this world."

Paphnutius followed her into a courtyard flooded with the morning light. On the edge of the brick roofs, the pigeons formed a string of pearls. On a bed, in the shade of the fig tree, Thais lay quite white, her arms crossed. By her side stood veiled women, reciting the prayers for the dying.

"Have mercy, upon me, O God, according to Thy loving kindness: according unto the multitude of Thy tender mercies blot out my transgressions."

He called her —

"Thais!"

She raised her eyelids, and turned the whites of her eyes in the direction of the voice.

Albina made a sign to the veiled women to retire a few paces.

"Thais!" repeated the monk.

She raised her head; a light breath came from her pale lips.

"Is it thou, my father? . . . Dost thou remember the water of the spring, and the dates that we picked? . . . That day, my father, love was born in my heart — the love of life eternal."

She was silent, and her head fell back.

Death was upon her, and the sweat of the last agony bedewed her forehead. A pigeon broke the still silence with its plaintive cooing. Then the sobs of the monk mingled with the psalms of the virgins.

"Wash me thoroughly from mine iniquity, and cleanse me from my sin. For I acknowledge my transgressions: and my sin is ever before me."

Suddenly Thais sat up in the bed. Her violet eyes opened wide, and with a rapt gaze, her arms stretched towards the distant hills, she said in a clear, fresh voice —

"Behold them — the roses of the eternal dawn!"

Her eyes shone; a slight flush suffused her face. She had revived, more sweet and more beautiful than ever. Paphnutius knelt down, and threw his long black arms around her.

"Do not die!" he cried, in a strange voice, which he himself did not recognize. "I love thee! Do not die! Listen, my Thais. I have deceived thee? I was but a wretched fool. God, heaven — all that is nothing. There is nothing true but this worldly life, and the love of human beings. I love thee! Do not die! That would be impossible — thou art too precious! Come, come with me! Let us fly? I will carry thee far away in my arms. Come, let us love! Hear me, O my beloved, and say, 'I will live; I wish to live.' Thais, Thais, arise!"

She did not hear him. Her eyes gazed into infinity.

She murmured —

"Heaven opens. I see the angels, the prophets, and the saints. . . . The good Theodore is amongst them, his hands filled with flowers; he smiles on me and calls me. . . . Two angels come to me. They draw near. . . . How beautiful they are! I see God!"

She uttered a joyful sigh, and her head fell back motionless on the pillow. Thais was dead.

Paphnutius held her in a last despairing embrace; his eyes devoured her with desire, rage, and love.

Albina cried to him —

"Avaunt, accursed wretch!"

And she gently placed her fingers on the eyelids of the dead girl. Paphnutius staggered back, his eyes burning with flames and feeling the earth open beneath his feet.

The virgins chanted the song of Zacharias:

"Blessed be the Lord God of Israel."

Suddenly their voices stayed in their throat. They had seen the monk's face, and they fled in affright, crying —

"A vampire! A vampire!"

He had become so repulsive, that passing his hand over his face, he felt his own hideousness.

THE RED LILY
BOOK I
CHAPTER I
"I NEED LOVE"

She gave a glance at the armchairs placed before the chimney, at the tea-table, which shone in the shade, and at the tall, pale stems of flowers ascending above Chinese vases. She thrust her hand among the flowery branches of the guelder roses to make their silvery balls quiver. Then she looked at herself in a mirror with serious attention. She held herself sidewise, her neck turned over her shoulder, to follow with her eyes the spring of her fine form in its sheath-like black satin gown, around which floated a light tunic studded with pearls wherein sombre lights scintillated. She went nearer, curious to know her face of that day. The mirror returned her look with tranquility, as if this amiable woman whom she examined, and who was not unpleasing to her, lived without either acute joy or profound sadness.

On the walls of the large drawing-room, empty and silent, the figures of the tapestries, vague as shadows, showed pallid among their antique games and dying graces. Like them, the terra-cotta statuettes on slender columns, the groups of old Saxony, and the paintings of Sevres, spoke of past glories. On a pedestal ornamented with precious bronzes, the marble bust of some princess royal disguised as Diana appeared about to fly out of her turbulent drapery, while on the ceiling a figure of Night, powdered like a marquise and surrounded by cupids, sowed flowers. Everything was asleep, and only the crackling of the logs and the light rattle of Therese's pearls could be heard.

Turning from the mirror, she lifted the corner of a curtain and saw through the window, beyond the dark trees of the quay, the Seine spreading its yellow reflections. Weariness of the sky and of the water was reflected in her fine gray eyes. The boat passed, the 'Hirondelle', emerging from an arch of the Alma Bridge, and carrying humble travelers toward Grenelle and Billancourt. She followed it with her eyes, then let the curtain fall, and, seating herself under the flowers, took a book from the table.

On the straw-colored linen cover shone the title in gold: 'Yseult la Blonde', by Vivian Bell. It was a collection of French verses composed by an Englishwoman, and printed in London. She read indifferently, waiting for visitors, and thinking less of the poetry than of the poetess, Miss Bell, who was perhaps her most agreeable friend, and whom she almost never saw; who, at every one of their meetings, which were so rare, kissed her, calling her "darling," and babbled; who, plain yet seductive, almost ridiculous, yet wholly exquisite, lived at Fiesole like a philosopher, while England celebrated her as her most beloved poet. Like Vernon Lee and like Mary Robinson, she had fallen in love with the life and art of Tuscany; and, without even finishing her Tristan, the first part of which had inspired in Burne-Jones dreamy aquarelles, she wrote Provencal verses and French poems expressing Italian ideas. She had sent her 'Yseult la Blonde' to "Darling," with a letter inviting her to spend a month with her at Fiesole. She had written: "Come; you will see the most beautiful things in the world, and you will embellish them."

And "darling" was saying to herself that she would not go, that she must remain in Paris. But the idea of seeing Miss Bell in Italy was not indifferent to her. And turning the leaves of the book, she stopped by chance at this line:

Love and gentle heart are one.

And she asked herself, with gentle irony, whether Miss Bell had ever been in love, and what manner of man could be the ideal of Miss Bell. The poetess had at Fiesole an escort, Prince Albertinelli. He was very handsome, but rather coarse and vulgar; too much so to please an aesthete who blended with the desire for love the mysticism of an Annunciation.

"Good-evening, Therese. I am positively worn out."

The Princess Seniavine had entered, supple in her furs, which almost seemed to form a part of her dark beauty. She seated herself brusquely, and, in a voice at once harsh yet caressing, said:

"This morning I walked through the park with General Lariviere. I met him in an alley and made him go with me to the bridge, where he wished to buy from the guardian a learned magpie which performs the manual of arms with a gun. Oh! I am so tired!"

"But why did you drag the General to the bridge?"

"Because he had gout in his toe."

Therese shrugged her shoulders, smiling:

"You squander your wickedness. You spoil things."

"And you wish me, dear, to save my kindness and my wickedness for a serious investment?"

Therese made her drink some Tokay.

Preceded by the sound of his powerful breathing, General Lariviere approached with heavy state and sat between the two women, looking stubborn and self-satisfied, laughing in every wrinkle of his face.

"How is Monsieur Martin-Belleme? Always busy?"

Therese thought he was at the Chamber, and even that he was making a speech there.

Princess Seniavine, who was eating caviar sandwiches, asked Madame Martin why she had not gone to Madame Meillan's the day before. They had played a comedy there.

"A Scandinavian play? Was it a success?"

"Yes — I don't know. I was in the little green room, under the portrait of the Duc d'Orleans. Monsieur Le Menil came to me and did me one of those good turns that one never forgets. He saved me from Monsieur Garain."

The General, who knew the Annual Register, and stored away all useful information, pricked up his ears.

"Garain," he asked, "the minister who was in the Cabinet when the princes were exiled?"

"Himself. I was excessively agreeable to him. He talked to me of the yearnings of his heart and he looked at me with alarming tenderness. And from time to time he gazed, with sighs, at the portrait of the Duc d'Orleans. I said to him: 'Monsieur Garain, you are making a mistake. It is my sister-in-law who is an Orleanist. I am not.' At this moment Monsieur Le Menil came to escort me to the buffet. He paid great compliments — to my

343

horses! He said, also, there was nothing so beautiful as the forest in winter. He talked about wolves. That refreshed me."

The General, who did not like young men, said he had met Le Menil the day before in the forest, galloping, with vast space between himself and his saddle.

He declared that old cavaliers alone retained the traditions of good horsemanship; that people in society now rode like jockeys.

"It is the same with fencing," he added. "Formerly — "

Princess Seniavine interrupted him:

"General, look and see how charming Madame Martin is. She is always charming, but at this moment she is prettier than ever. It is because she is bored. Nothing becomes her better than to be bored. Since we have been here, we have bored her terribly. Look at her: her forehead clouded, her glance vague, her mouth dolorous. Behold a victim!"

She arose, kissed Therese tumultuously, and fled, leaving the General astonished.

Madame Martin-Belleme prayed him not to listen to what the Princess had said.

He collected himself and asked:

"And how are your poets, Madame?"

It was difficult for him to forgive Madame Martin her preference for people who lived by writing and were not of his circle.

"Yes, your poets. What has become of that Monsieur Choulette, who visits you wrapped in a red muffler?"

"My poets? They forget me, they abandon me. One should not rely on anybody. Men and women — nothing is sure. Life is a continual betrayal. Only that poor Miss Bell does not forget me. She has written to me from Florence and sent her book."

"Miss Bell? Isn't she that young person who looks, with her yellow waving hair, like a little lapdog?"

He reflected, and expressed the opinion that she must be at least thirty.

An old lady, wearing with modest dignity her crown of white hair, and a little vivacious man with shrewd eyes, came in suddenly — Madame Marmet and M. Paul Vence. Then, carrying himself very stiffly, with a square monocle in his eye, appeared M. Daniel Salomon, the arbiter of elegance. The General hurried out.

They talked of the novel of the week. Madame Marmet had dined often with the author, a young and very amiable man. Paul Vence thought the book tiresome.

"Oh," sighed Madame Martin, "all books are tiresome. But men are more tiresome than books, and they are more exacting."

Madame Marmet said that her husband, who had much literary taste, had retained, until the end of his days, a horror of naturalism. She was the widow of a member of the 'Academie des Inscriptions', and plumed herself upon her illustrious widowhood. She was sweet and modest in her black gown and her beautiful white hair.

Madame Martin said to M. Daniel Salomon that she wished to consult him particularly on the picture of a group of beautiful children.

"You will tell me if it pleases you. You may also give me your opinion, Monsieur Vence, unless you disdain such trifles."

M. Daniel Salomon looked at Paul Vence through his monocle with disdain. Paul Vence surveyed the drawing-room.

"You have beautiful things, Madame. That would be nothing. But you have only beautiful things, and all serve to set off your own beauty."

She did not conceal her pleasure at hearing him speak in that way. She regarded Paul Vence as the only really intelligent man she knew. She had appreciated him before his books had made him celebrated. His ill-health, his dark humor, his assiduous labor, separated him from society. The little bilious man was not very pleasing; yet he attracted her. She held in high esteem his profound irony, his great pride, his talent ripened in solitude, and she admired him, with reason, as an excellent writer, the author of powerful essays on art and on life.

Little by little the room filled with a brilliant crowd. Within the large circle of armchairs were Madame de Wesson, about whom people told frightful stories, and who kept, after twenty years of half-smothered scandal, the eyes of a child and cheeks of virginal smoothness; old Madame de Morlaine, who shouted her witty phrases in piercing cries; Madame Raymond, the wife of the Academician; Madame Garain, the wife of the exminister; three other ladies; and, standing easily against the mantelpiece, M. Berthier d'Eyzelles, editor of the 'Journal des Debats', a deputy who caressed his white beard while Madame de Morlaine shouted at him:

"Your article on bimetallism is a pearl, a jewel! Especially the end of it."

Standing in the rear of the room, young clubmen, very grave, lisped among themselves:

"What did he do to get the button from the Prince?"

"He, nothing. His wife, everything."

They had their own cynical philosophy. One of them had no faith in promises of men.

"They are types that do not suit me. They wear their hearts on their hands and on their mouths. You present yourself for admission to a club. They say, 'I promise to give you a white ball. It will be an alabaster ball — a snowball! They vote. It's a black ball. Life seems a vile affair when I think of it."

"Then don't think of it."

Daniel Salomon, who had joined them, whispered in their ears spicy stories in a lowered voice. And at every strange revelation concerning Madame Raymond, or Madame Berthier, or Princess Seniavine, he added, negligently:

"Everybody knows it."

Then, little by little, the crowd of visitors dispersed. Only Madame Marmet and Paul Vence remained.

The latter went toward Madame Martin, and asked:

"When do you wish me to introduce Dechartre to you?"

It was the second time he had asked this of her. She did not like to see new faces. She replied, unconcernedly:

"Your sculptor? When you wish. I saw at the Champ de Mars medallions made by him which are very good. But he does not work much. He is an amateur, is he not?"

"He is a delicate artist. He does not need to work in order to live. He caresses his figures with loving slowness. But do not be deceived about him, Madame. He knows and he feels. He would be a master if he did not live alone. I have known him since his childhood. People think that he is solitary and morose. He is passionate and timid. What he lacks, what he will lack always to reach the highest point of his art, is simplicity of mind. He is restless, and he spoils his most beautiful impressions. In my opinion he was created less for sculpture than for poetry or philosophy. He knows a great deal, and you will be astonished at the wealth of his mind."

Madame Marmet approved.

She pleased society by appearing to find pleasure in it. She listened a great deal and talked little. Very affable, she gave value to her affability by not squandering it. Either because she liked Madame Martin, or because she knew how to give discreet marks of preference in every house she went, she warmed herself contentedly, like a relative, in a corner of the Louis XVI chimney, which suited her beauty. She lacked only her dog.

"How is Toby?" asked Madame Martin. "Monsieur Vence, do you know Toby? He has long silky hair and a lovely little black nose."

Madame Marmet was relishing the praise of Toby, when an old man, pink and blond, with curly hair, short-sighted, almost blind under his golden spectacles, rather short, striking against the furniture, bowing to empty armchairs, blundering into the mirrors, pushed his crooked nose before Madame Marmet, who looked at him indignantly.

It was M. Schmoll, member of the Academie des Inscriptions. He smiled and turned a madrigal for the Countess Martin with that hereditary harsh, coarse voice with which the Jews, his fathers, pressed their creditors, the peasants of Alsace, of Poland, and of the Crimea. He dragged his phrases heavily. This great philologist knew all languages except French. And Madame Martin enjoyed his affable phrases, heavy and rusty like the iron-work of brica-brac shops, among which fell dried leaves of anthology. M. Schmoll liked poets and women, and had wit.

Madame Marmet feigned not to know him, and went out without returning his bow.

When he had exhausted his pretty madrigals, M. Schmoll became sombre and pitiful. He complained piteously. He was not decorated enough, not provided with sinecures enough, nor well fed enough by the State — he, Madame Schmoll, and their five daughters. His lamentations had some grandeur. Something of the soul of Ezekiel and of Jeremiah was in them.

Unfortunately, turning his golden-spectacled eyes toward the table, he discovered Vivian Bell's book.

"Oh, 'Yseult La Blonde'," he exclaimed, bitterly. "You are reading that book, Madame? Well, learn that Mademoiselle Vivian Bell has stolen an inscription from me, and that she has altered it, moreover, by putting it into verse. You will find it on page 109 of her book: 'A shade may weep over a shade.' You hear, Madame? 'A shade may weep over a shade.' Well, those words are translated literally from a funeral inscription which I was the first to publish and to illustrate. Last year, one day, when I was dining at your house, being placed by the side of Mademoiselle Bell, I quoted this phrase to her, and it pleased her a great deal. At her request, the next day I translated into French the entire inscription and sent it to her. And now I find it changed in this volume of verses under this title: 'On the Sacred Way' — the sacred way, that is I."

And he repeated, in his bad humor:

"I, Madame, am the sacred way."

He was annoyed that the poet had not spoken to him about this inscription. He would have liked to see his name at the top of the poem, in the verses, in the rhymes. He wished to see his name everywhere, and always looked for it in the journals with which his pockets were stuffed. But he had no rancor. He was not really angry with Miss Bell. He admitted gracefully that she was a distinguished person, and a poet that did great honor to England.

When he had gone, the Countess Martin asked ingenuously of Paul Vence if he knew why that good Madame Marmet had looked at M. Schmoll with such marked though silent anger. He was surprised that she did not know.

"I never know anything," she said.

"But the quarrel between Schmoll and Marmet is famous. It ceased only at the death of Marmet.

"The day that poor Marmet was buried, snow was falling. We were wet and frozen to the bones. At the grave, in the wind, in the mud, Schmoll read under his umbrella a speech full of jovial cruelty and triumphant pity, which he took afterward to the newspapers in a mourning carriage. An indiscreet friend let Madame Marmet hear of it, and she fainted. Is it possible, Madame, that you have not heard of this learned and ferocious quarrel?

"The Etruscan language was the cause of it. Marmet made it his unique study. He was surnamed Marmet the Etruscan. Neither he nor any one else knew a word of that language, the last vestige of which is lost. Schmoll said continually to Marmet: 'You do not know Etruscan, my dear colleague; that is the reason why you are an honorable savant and a fair-minded man.' Piqued by his ironic praise, Marmet thought of learning a little Etruscan. He read to his colleague a memoir on the part played by flexions in the idiom of the ancient Tuscans."

Madame Martin asked what a flexion was.

"Oh, Madame, if I explain anything to you, it will mix up everything. Be content with knowing that in that memoir poor Marmet quoted Latin texts and quoted them wrong. Schmoll is a Latinist of great learning, and, after Mommsen, the chief epigraphist of the world.

"He reproached his young colleague — Marmet was not fifty years old — with reading Etruscan too well and Latin not well enough. From that time Marmet had no rest. At every meeting he was mocked unmercifully; and, finally, in spite of his softness, he got angry. Schmoll is without rancor. It is a virtue of his race. He does not bear ill-will to those whom he persecutes. One day, as he went up the stairway of the Institute with Renan and Oppert, he met Marmet, and extended his hand to him. Marmet refused to take it, and said 'I do not know you.' — 'Do you take me for a Latin inscription?' Schmoll replied. Marmet died and was buried because of that satire. Now you know the reason why his widow sees his enemy with horror."

"And I have made them dine together, side by side."

"Madame, it was not immoral, but it was cruel."

"My dear sir, I shall shock you, perhaps; but if I had to choose, I should like better to do an immoral thing than a cruel one."

A young man, tall, thin, dark, with a long moustache, entered, and bowed with brusque suppleness.

"Monsieur Vence, I think that you know Monsieur Le Menil."

They had met before at Madame Martin's, and saw each other often at the Fencing Club. The day before they had met at Madame Meillan's.

"Madame Meillan's — there's a house where one is bored," said Paul Vence.

"Yet Academicians go there," said M. Robert Le Menil. "I do not exaggerate their value, but they are the elite."

Madame Martin smiled.

"We know, Monsieur Le Menil, that at Madame Meillan's you are preoccupied by the women more than by the Academicians. You escorted Princess Seniavine to the buffet and talked to her about wolves."

"What wolves?"

"Wolves, and forests blackened by winter. We thought that with so pretty a woman your conversation was rather savage!"

Paul Vence rose.

"So you permit, Madame, that I should bring my friend Dechartre? He has a great desire to know you, and I hope he will not displease you. There is life in his mind. He is full of ideas."

"Oh, I do not ask for so much," Madame Martin said. "People that are natural and show themselves as they are rarely bore me, and sometimes they amuse me."

When Paul Vence had gone, Le Menil listened until the noise of footsteps had vanished; then, coming nearer:

"To-morrow, at three o'clock? Do you still love me?"

He asked her to reply while they were alone. She answered that it was late, that she expected no more visitors, and that no one except her husband would come.

He entreated. Then she said:

"I shall be free to-morrow all day. Wait for me at three o'clock."

He thanked her with a look. Then, placing himself on at the other side of the chimney, he asked who was that Dechartre whom she wished introduced to her.

"I do not wish him to be introduced to me. He is to be introduced to me. He is a sculptor."

He deplored the fact that she needed to see new faces, adding:

"A sculptor? They are usually brutal."

"Oh, but this one does so little sculpture! But if it annoys you that I should meet him, I will not do so."

"I should be sorry if society took any part of the time you might give to me."

"My friend, you can not complain of that. I did not even go to Madame Meillan's yesterday."

"You are right to show yourself there as little as possible. It is not a house for you."

He explained. All the women that went there had had some spicy adventure which was known and talked about. Besides, Madame Meillan favored intrigue. He gave examples. Madame Martin, however, her hands extended on the arms of the chair in charming restfulness, her head inclined, looked at the dying embers in the grate. Her thoughtful mood had flown. Nothing of it remained on her face, a little saddened, nor in her languid body, more desirable than ever in the quiescence of her mind. She kept

351

for a while a profound immobility, which added to her personal attraction the charm of things that art had created.

He asked her of what she was thinking. Escaping the magic of the blaze in the ashes, she said:

"We will go to-morrow, if you wish, to far distant places, to the odd districts where the poor people live. I like the old streets where misery dwells."

He promised to satisfy her taste, although he let her know that he thought it absurd. The walks that she led him sometimes bored him, and he thought them dangerous. People might see them.

"And since we have been successful until now in not causing gossip — "

She shook her head.

"Do you think that people have not talked about us? Whether they know or do not know, they talk. Not everything is known, but everything is said."

She relapsed into her dream. He thought her discontented, cross, for some reason which she would not tell. He bent upon her beautiful, grave eyes which reflected the light of the grate. But she reassured him.

"I do not know whether any one talks about me. And what do I care? Nothing matters."

He left her. He was going to dine at the club, where a friend was waiting for him. She followed him with her eyes, with peaceful sympathy. Then she began again to read in the ashes.

She saw in them the days of her childhood; the castle wherein she had passed the sweet, sad summers; the dark and humid park; the pond where slept the green water; the marble nymphs under the chestnut-trees, and the bench on which she had wept and desired death. To-day she still ignored the cause of her youthful despair, when the ardent awakening of her imagination threw her into a troubled maze of desires and of fears. When she was a child, life frightened her. And now she knew that life is not worth so much anxiety nor so much hope; that it is a very ordinary thing. She should have known this. She thought:

"I saw mamma; she was good, very simple, and not very happy. I dreamed of a destiny different from hers. Why? I felt around me the insipid taste of life, and seemed to inhale the future like a salt and pungent aroma. Why? What did I want, and what did I expect? Was I not warned enough of the sadness of everything?"

She had been born rich, in the brilliancy of a fortune too new. She was a daughter of that Montessuy, who, at first a clerk in a Parisian bank, founded and governed two great establishments, brought to sustain them the resources of a brilliant mind, invincible force of character, a rare alliance of cleverness and honesty, and treated with the Government as if he were a foreign power. She had grown up in the historical castle of Joinville, bought, restored, and magnificently furnished by her father. Montessuy made life give all it could yield. An instinctive and powerful atheist, he wanted all the goods of this world and all the desirable things that earth produces. He accumulated pictures by old masters, and precious sculptures. At fifty he had known all the most beautiful women of the stage, and many in society. He enjoyed everything worldly with the brutality of his temperament and the shrewdness of his mind.

Poor Madame Montessuy, economical and careful, languished at Joinville, delicate and poor, under the frowns of twelve gigantic caryatides which held a ceiling on which Lebrun had painted the Titans struck by Jupiter. There, in the iron cot, placed at the foot of the large bed, she died one night of sadness and exhaustion, never having loved anything on earth except her husband and her little drawing-room in the Rue Maubeuge.

She never had had any intimacy with her daughter, whom she felt instinctively too different from herself, too free, too bold at heart; and she divined in Therese, although she was sweet and good, the strong Montessuy blood, the ardor which had made her suffer so much, and which she forgave in her husband, but not in her daughter.

But Montessuy recognized his daughter and loved her. Like most hearty, full-blooded men, he had hours of charming gayety.

Although he lived out of his house a great deal, he breakfasted with her almost every day, and sometimes took her out walking. He understood gowns and furbelows. He instructed and formed Therese. He amused her. Near her, his instinct for conquest inspired him still. He desired to win always, and he won his daughter. He separated her from her mother. Therese admired him, she adored him.

In her dream she saw him as the unique joy of her childhood. She was persuaded that no man in the world was as amiable as her father.

At her entrance in life, she despaired at once of finding elsewhere so rich a nature, such a plenitude of active and thinking forces. This discouragement had followed her in the choice of a husband, and perhaps later in a secret and freer choice.

She had not really selected her husband. She did not know: she had permitted herself to be married by her father, who, then a widower, embarrassed by the care of a girl, had wished to do things quickly and well. He considered the exterior advantages, estimated the eighty years of imperial nobility which Count Martin brought. The idea never came to him that she might wish to find love in marriage.

He flattered himself that she would find in it the satisfaction of the luxurious desires which he attributed to her, the joy of making a display of grandeur, the vulgar pride, the material domination, which were for him all the value of life, as he had no ideas on the subject of the happiness of a true woman, although he was sure that his daughter would remain virtuous.

While thinking of his absurd yet natural faith in her, which accorded so badly with his own experiences and ideas regarding women, she smiled with melancholy irony. And she admired her father the more.

After all, she was not so badly married. Her husband was as good as any other man. He had become quite bearable. Of all that she read in the ashes, in the veiled softness of the lamps, of all her reminiscences, that of their married life was the most vague. She found a few isolated traits of it, some absurd images, a fleeting and fastidious impression. The time had not seemed long and had left nothing behind. Six years had passed, and she did not even remember how she had regained her liberty, so prompt and easy had been her conquest of that husband, cold, sickly, selfish, and polite; of that man dried up and yellowed by business and politics, laborious, ambitious, and commonplace. He liked women only through vanity, and he never had loved his wife. The separation had been frank and complete. And since then, strangers to each other, they felt a tacit, mutual gratitude for their freedom. She would have had some affection for him if she had not found him hypocritical and too subtle in the art of obtaining her signature when he needed money for enterprises that were more for ostentation than real benefit. The man with whom she dined and talked every day had no significance for her.

With her cheek in her hand, before the grate, as if she questioned a sibyl, she saw again the face of the Marquis de Re. She saw it so precisely that it surprised her. The Marquis de Re had been presented to her by her father, who admired him, and he appeared to her grand and dazzling for his thirty years of intimate triumphs and mundane glories. His adventures followed him like a procession. He had captivated three generations of women, and had left in the heart of all those whom he had loved an imperishable memory. His virile grace, his quiet elegance, and his habit of pleasing had prolonged his youth far beyond the ordinary term of years. He noticed particularly the young Countess Martin. The homage of this expert flattered her. She thought of him now with pleasure. He had a marvellous art of conversation. He amused her. She let him see it, and at once he promised to himself, in his heroic frivolity, to finish worthily his happy life by the subjugation of this young woman whom he appreciated above every one else, and who evidently admired him. He displayed, to capture her, the most learned stratagems. But she escaped him very easily.

She yielded, two years later, to Robert Le Menil, who had desired her ardently, with all the warmth of his youth, with all the simplicity of his mind. She said to herself: "I gave myself to him because he loved me." It was the truth. The truth was, also, that a dumb yet powerful instinct had impelled her, and that she had obeyed the hidden impulse of her being. But even this was not her real self; what awakened her nature at last was the fact that she believed in the sincerity of his sentiment. She had yielded as soon as she had felt that she was loved. She had given herself, quickly, simply. He thought that she had yielded easily. He was mistaken. She had felt the discouragement which the irreparable gives, and that sort of shame which comes of having suddenly something to conceal. Everything that had been whispered before her about other women resounded in her burning ears. But, proud and delicate, she took care to hide the value of the gift she was making. He never suspected her moral uneasiness, which lasted only a few days, and was replaced by perfect tranquility. After three years she defended her conduct as innocent and natural.

Having done harm to no one, she had no regrets. She was content. She was in love, she was loved. Doubtless she had not felt the intoxication she had expected, but does one ever feel it? She was the friend of the good and honest fellow, much liked by women who passed for disdainful and hard to please, and he had a true affection for her. The pleasure she gave him and the joy of being beautiful for him attached her to this friend. He made life for her not continually delightful, but easy to bear, and at times agreeable.

That which she had not divined in her solitude, notwithstanding vague yearnings and apparently causeless sadness, he had revealed to her. She knew herself when she knew him. It was a happy astonishment. Their sympathies were not in their minds. Her inclination toward him was simple and frank, and at this moment she found pleasure in the idea of meeting him the next day in the little apartment where they had met for three years. With a shake of the head and a shrug of her shoulders, coarser than one would have expected from this exquisite woman, sitting alone by the dying fire, she said to herself: "There! I need love!"

CHAPTER II
"ONE CAN SEE THAT YOU ARE YOUNG!"

It was no longer daylight when they came out of the little apartment in the Rue Spontini. Robert Le Menil made a sign to a coachman, and entered the carriage with Therese. Close together, they rolled among the vague shadows, cut by sudden lights, through the ghostly city, having in their minds only sweet and vanishing impressions while everything around them seemed confused and fleeting.

The carriage approached the Pont-Neuf. They stepped out. A dry cold made vivid the sombre January weather. Under her veil Therese joyfully inhaled the wind which swept on the hardened soil a dust white as salt. She was glad to wander freely among unknown things. She liked to see the stony landscape which the clearness of the air made distinct; to walk quickly and firmly on the quay where the trees displayed the black tracery of their branches on the horizon reddened by the smoke of the city; to look at the Seine. In the sky the first stars appeared.

"One would think that the wind would put them out," she said.

He observed, too, that they scintillated a great deal. He did not think it was a sign of rain, as the peasants believe. He had observed, on the contrary, that nine times in ten the scintillation of stars was an augury of fine weather.

Near the little bridge they found old iron-shops lighted by smoky lamps. She ran into them. She turned a corner and went into a shop in which queer stuffs were hanging. Behind the dirty panes a lighted candle showed pots, porcelain vases, a clarinet, and a bride's wreath.

He did not understand what pleasure she found in her search.

"These shops are full of vermin. What can you find interesting in them?"

"Everything. I think of the poor bride whose wreath is under that globe. The dinner occurred at Maillot. There was a

357

policeman in the procession. There is one in almost all the bridal processions one sees in the park on Saturdays. Don't they move you, my friend, all these poor, ridiculous, miserable beings who contribute to the grandeur of the past?"

Among cups decorated with flowers she discovered a little knife, the ivory handle of which represented a tall, thin woman with her hair arranged a la Maintenon. She bought it for a few sous. It pleased her, because she already had a fork like it. Le Menil confessed that he had no taste for such things, but said that his aunt knew a great deal about them. At Caen all the merchants knew her. She had restored and furnished her house in proper style. This house was noted as early as 1690. In one of its halls were white cases full of books. His aunt had wished to put them in order. She had found frivolous books in them, ornamented with engravings so unconventional that she had burned them.

"Is she silly, your aunt?" asked Therese.

For a long time his anecdotes about his aunt had made her impatient. Her friend had in the country a mother, sisters, aunts, and numerous relatives whom she did not know and who irritated her. He talked of them with admiration. It annoyed her that he often visited them. When he came back, she imagined that he carried with him the odor of things that had been packed up for years. He was astonished, naively, and he suffered from her antipathy to them.

He said nothing. The sight of a public-house, the panes of which were flaming, recalled to him the poet Choulette, who passed for a drunkard. He asked her if she still saw that Choulette, who called on her wearing a mackintosh and a red muffler.

It annoyed her that he spoke like General Lariviere. She did not say that she had not seen Choulette since autumn, and that he neglected her with the capriciousness of a man not in society.

"He has wit," she said, "fantasy, and an original temperament. He pleases me."

And as he reproached her for having an odd taste, she replied:

"I haven't a taste, I have tastes. You do not disapprove of them all, I suppose."

He replied that he did not criticize her. He was only afraid that she might do herself harm by receiving a Bohemian who was not welcome in respectable houses.

She exclaimed:

"Not welcome in respectable houses — Choulette? Don't you know that he goes every year for a month to the Marquise de Rieu? Yes, to the Marquise de Rieu, the Catholic, the royalist. But since Choulette interests you, listen to his latest adventure. Paul Vence related it to me. I understand it better in this street, where there are shirts and flowerpots at the windows.

"This winter, one night when it was raining, Choulette went into a public-house in a street the name of which I have forgotten, but which must resemble this one, and met there an unfortunate girl whom the waiters would not have noticed, and whom he liked for her humility. Her name was Maria. The name was not hers. She found it nailed on her door at the top of the stairway where she went to lodge. Choulette was touched by this perfection of poverty and infamy. He called her his sister, and kissed her hands. Since then he has not quitted her a moment. He takes her to the coffee-houses of the Latin Quarter where the rich students read their reviews. He says sweet things to her. He weeps, she weeps. They drink; and when they are drunk, they fight. He loves her. He calls her his chaste one, his cross and his salvation. She was barefooted; he gave her yarn and knitting-needles that she might make stockings. And he made shoes for this unfortunate girl himself, with enormous nails. He teaches her verses that are easy to understand. He is afraid of altering her moral beauty by taking her out of the shame where she lives in perfect simplicity and admirable destitution."

Le Menil shrugged his shoulders.

"But that Choulette is crazy, and Paul Vence has no right to tell you such stories. I am not austere, assuredly; but there are immoralities that disgust me." They were walking at random. She fell into a dream.

"Yes, morality, I know — duty! But duty — it takes the devil to discover it. I can assure you that I do not know where duty is. It's like a young lady's turtle at Joinville. We spent all the evening looking for it under the furniture, and when we had found it, we went to bed."

He thought there was some truth in what she said. He would think about it when alone.

"I regret sometimes that I did not remain in the army. I know what you are going to say — one becomes a brute in that profession. Doubtless, but one knows exactly what one has to do, and that is a great deal in life. I think that my uncle's life is very beautiful and very agreeable. But now that everybody is in the army, there are neither officers nor soldiers. It all looks like a railway station on Sunday. My uncle knew personally all the officers and all the soldiers of his brigade. Nowadays, how can you expect an officer to know his men?"

She had ceased to listen. She was looking at a woman selling fried potatoes. She realized that she was hungry and wished to eat fried potatoes.

He remonstrated:

"Nobody knows how they are cooked."

But he had to buy two sous' worth of fried potatoes, and to see that the woman put salt on them.

While Therese was eating them, he led her into deserted streets far from the gaslights. Soon they found themselves in front of the cathedral. The moon silvered the roofs.

"Notre Dame," she said. "See, it is as heavy as an elephant yet as delicate as an insect. The moon climbs over it and looks at it with a monkey's maliciousness. She does not look like the country moon at Joinville. At Joinville I have a path — a flat path — with the moon at the end of it. She is not there every night; but she returns faithfully, full, red, familiar. She is a country neighbor. I go seriously to meet her. But this moon of Paris I should not like to know. She is not respectable company. Oh, the things that she has seen during the time she has been roaming around the roofs!"

He smiled a tender smile.

"Oh, your little path where you walked alone and that you liked because the sky was at the end of it! I see it as if I were there."

It was at the Joinville castle that he had seen her for the first time, and had at once loved her. It was there, one night, that he had told her of his love, to which she had listened, dumb, with a pained expression on her mouth and a vague look in her eyes.

The reminiscence of this little path where she walked alone moved him, troubled him, made him live again the enchanted hours of his first desires and hopes. He tried to find her hand in her muff and pressed her slim wrist under the fur.

A little girl carrying violets saw that they were lovers, and offered flowers to them. He bought a two-sous' bouquet and offered it to Therese.

She was walking toward the cathedral. She was thinking: "It is like an enormous beast — a beast of the Apocalypse."

At the other end of the bridge a flower-woman, wrinkled, bearded, gray with years and dust, followed them with her basket full of mimosas and roses. Therese, who held her violets and was trying to slip them into her waist, said, joyfully:

"Thank you, I have some."

"One can see that you are young," the old woman shouted with a wicked air, as she went away.

Therese understood at once, and a smile came to her lips and eyes. They were passing near the porch, before the stone figures that wear sceptres and crowns.

"Let us go in," she said.

He did not wish to go in. He declared that the door was closed. She pushed it, and slipped into the immense nave, where the inanimate trees of the columns ascended in darkness. In the rear, candles were moving in front of spectre-like priests, under the last reverberations of the organs. She trembled in the silence, and said:

"The sadness of churches at night moves me; I feel in them the grandeur of nothingness."

361

He replied:

"We must believe in something. If there were no God, if our souls were not immortal, it would be too sad."

She remained for a while immovable under the curtains of shadow hanging from the arches. Then she said:

"My poor friend, we do not know what to do with this life, which is so short, and yet you desire another life which shall never finish."

In the carriage that took them back he said gaily that he had passed a fine afternoon. He kissed her, satisfied with her and with himself. But his good-humor was not communicated to her. The last moments they passed together were spoiled for her always by the presentiment that he would not say at parting the thing that he should say. Ordinarily, he quitted her brusquely, as if what had happened were not to last. At every one of their partings she had a confused feeling that they were parting forever. She suffered from this in advance and became irritable.

Under the trees he took her hand and kissed her.

"Is it not rare, Therese, to love as we love each other?"

"Rare? I don't know; but I think that you love me."

"And you?"

"I, too, love you."

"And you will love me always?"

"What does one ever know?"

And seeing the face of her lover darken:

"Would you be more content with a woman who would swear to love only you for all time?"

He remained anxious, with a wretched air. She was kind and she reassured him:

"You know very well, my friend, that I am not fickle."

Almost at the end of the lane they said good-by. He kept the carriage to return to the Rue Royale. He was to dine at the club and go to the theatre, and had no time to lose.

Therese returned home on foot. Opposite the Trocadero she remembered what the old flower-woman had said: "One can see that you are young." The words came back to her with a significance not immoral but sad. "One can see that you are young!" Yes, she was young, she was loved, and she was bored to death.

CHAPTER III
A DISCUSSION ON THE LITTLE CORPORAL

In the centre of the table flowers were disposed in a basket of gilded bronze, decorated with eagles, stars, and bees, and handles formed like horns of plenty. On its sides winged Victorys supported the branches of candelabra. This centrepiece of the Empire style had been given by Napoleon, in 1812, to Count Martin de l'Aisne, grandfather of the present Count Martin-Belleme. Martin de l'Aisne, a deputy to the Legislative Corps in 1809, was appointed the following year member of the Committee on Finance, the assiduous and secret works of which suited his laborious temperament. Although a Liberal, he pleased the Emperor by his application and his exact honesty. For two years he was under a rain of favors. In 1813 he formed part of the moderate majority which approved the report in which Laine censured power and misfortune, by giving to the Empire tardy advice. January 1, 1814, he went with his colleagues to the Tuileries. The Emperor received them in a terrifying manner. He charged on their ranks. Violent and sombre, in the horror of his present strength and of his coming fall, he stunned them with his anger and his contempt.

He came and went through their lines, and suddenly took Count Martin by the shoulders, shook him and dragged him, exclaiming: "A throne is four pieces of wood covered with velvet? No! A throne is a man, and that man is I. You have tried to throw mud at me. Is this the time to remonstrate with me when there are two hundred thousand Cossacks at the frontiers? Your Laine is a wicked man. One should wash one's dirty linen at home." And while in his anger he twisted in his hand the embroidered collar of the deputy, he said: "The people know me. They do not know you. I am the elect of the nation. You are the obscure delegates of a department." He predicted to them the fate of the Girondins. The noise of his spurs accompanied the sound of his voice. Count Martin remained trembling the rest of his life, and tremblingly recalled the Bourbons after the defeat of the

Emperor. The two restorations were in vain; the July government and the Second Empire covered his oppressed breast with crosses and cordons. Raised to the highest functions, loaded with honors by three kings and one emperor, he felt forever on his shoulder the hand of the Corsican. He died a senator of Napoleon III, and left a son agitated by the same fear.

This son had married Mademoiselle Belleme, daughter of the first president of the court of Bourges, and with her the political glories of a family which gave three ministers to the moderate monarch. The Bellemes, advocates in the time of Louis XV, elevated the Jacobin origins of the Martins. The second Count Martin was a member of all the Assemblies until his death in 1881. His son took without trouble his seat in the Chamber of Deputies. Having married Mademoiselle Therese Montessuy, whose dowry supported his political fortune, he appeared discreetly among the four or five bourgeois, titled and wealthy, who rallied to democracy, and were received without much bad grace by the republicans, whom aristocracy flattered.

In the dining-room, Count Martin-Belleme was doing the honors of his table with the good grace, the sad politeness, recently prescribed at the Elysee to represent isolated France at a great northern court. From time to time he addressed vapid phrases to Madame Garain at his right; to the Princess Seniavine at his left, who, loaded with diamonds, felt bored. Opposite him, on the other side of the table, Countess Martin, having by her side General Lariviere and M. Schmoll, member of the Academie des Inscriptions, caressed with her fan her smooth white shoulders. At the two semicircles, whereby the dinner-table was prolonged, were M. Montessuy, robust, with blue eyes and ruddy complexion; a young cousin, Madame Belleme de Saint-Nom, embarrassed by her long, thin arms; the painter Duviquet; M. Daniel Salomon; then Paul Vence and Garain the deputy; Belleme de Saint-Nom; an unknown senator; and Dechartre, who was dining at the house for the first time. The conversation, at first trivial and insignificant, was prolonged into a confused murmur, above which rose Garain's voice:

"Every false idea is dangerous. People think that dreamers do no harm. They are mistaken: dreamers do a great heal of harm. Even apparently inoffensive utopian ideas really exercise a noxious influence. They tend to inspire disgust at reality."

"It is, perhaps, because reality is not beautiful," said Paul Vence.

M. Garain said that he had always been in favor of all possible improvements. He had asked for the suppression of permanent armies in the time of the Empire, for the separation of church and state, and had remained always faithful to democracy. His device, he said, was "Order and Progress." He thought he had discovered that device.

Montessuy said:

"Well, Monsieur Garain, be sincere. Confess that there are no reforms to be made, and that it is as much as one can do to change the color of postage-stamps. Good or bad, things are as they should be. Yes, things are as they should be; but they change incessantly. Since 1870 the industrial and financial situation of the country has gone through four or five revolutions which political economists had not foreseen and which they do not yet understand. In society, as in nature, transformations are accomplished from within."

As to matters of government his ideas were terse and decided. He was strongly attached to the present, heedless of the future, and the socialists troubled him little. Without caring whether the sun and capital should be extinguished some day, he enjoyed them. According to him, one should let himself be carried. None but fools resisted the current or tried to go in front of it.

But Count Martin, naturally sad, had, dark presentiments. In veiled words he announced catastrophes. His timorous phrases came through the flowers, and irritated M. Schmoll, who began to grumble and to prophesy. He explained that Christian nations were incapable, alone and by themselves, of throwing off barbarism, and that without the Jews and the Arabs Europe

366

would be to-day, as in the time of the Crusades, sunk in ignorance, misery, and cruelty.

"The Middle Ages," he said, "are closed only in the historical manuals that are given to pupils to spoil their minds. In reality, barbarians are always barbarians. Israel's mission is to instruct nations. It was Israel which, in the Middle Ages, brought to Europe the wisdom of ages. Socialism frightens you. It is a Christian evil, like priesthood. And anarchy? Do you not recognize in it the plague of the Albigeois and of the Vaudois? The Jews, who instructed and polished Europe, are the only ones who can save it to-day from the evangelical evil by which it is devoured. But they have not fulfilled their duty. They have made Christians of themselves among the Christians. And God punishes them. He permits them to be exiled and to be despoiled. Anti-Semitism is making fearful progress everywhere. From Russia my co-religionists are expelled like savage beasts. In France, civil and military employments are closing against Jews. They have no longer access to aristocratic circles. My nephew, young Isaac Coblentz, has had to renounce a diplomatic career, after passing brilliantly his admission examination. The wives of several of my colleagues, when Madame Schmoll calls on them, display with intention, under her eyes, anti-Semitic newspapers. And would you believe that the Minister of Public Instruction has refused to give me the cross of the Legion of Honor for which I have applied? There's ingratitude! Anti-Semitism is death — it is death, do you hear? to European civilization."

The little man had a natural manner which surpassed all the art in the world. Grotesque and terrible, he threw the table into consternation by his sincerity. Madame Martin, whom he amused, complimented him on this:

"At least," she said, "you defend your co-religionists. You are not, Monsieur Schmoll, like a beautiful Jewish lady of my acquaintance who, having read in a journal that she received the elite of Jewish society, went everywhere shouting that she had been insulted."

"I am sure, Madame, that you do not know how beautiful and superior to all other moralities is Jewish morality. Do you know the parable of the three rings?"

This question was lost in the murmur of the dialogues wherein were mingled foreign politics, exhibitions of paintings, fashionable scandals, and Academy speeches. They talked of the new novel and of the coming play. This was a comedy. Napoleon was an incidental character in it.

The conversation settled upon Napoleon I, often placed on the stage and newly studied in books — an object of curiosity, a personage in the fashion, no longer a popular hero, a demi-god, wearing boots for his country, as in the days when Norvins and Beranger, Charlet and Raffet were composing his legend; but a curious personage, an amusing type in his living infinity, a figure whose style is pleasant to artists, whose movements attract thoughtless idlers.

Garain, who had founded his political fortune on hatred of the Empire, judged sincerely that this return of national taste was only an absurd infatuation. He saw no danger in it and felt no fear about it. In him fear was sudden and ferocious. For the moment he was very quiet; he talked neither of prohibiting performances nor of seizing books, of imprisoning authors, or of suppressing anything. Calm and severe, he saw in Napoleon only Taine's 'condottiere' who kicked Volney in the stomach. Everybody wished to define the true Napoleon. Count Martin, in the face of the imperial centrepiece and of the winged Victorys, talked suitably of Napoleon as an organizer and administrator, and placed him in a high position as president of the state council, where his words threw light upon obscure questions. Garain affirmed that in his sessions, only too famous, Napoleon, under pretext of taking snuff, asked the councillors to pass to him their gold boxes ornamented with miniatures and decked with diamonds, which they never saw again. The anecdote was told to him by the son of Mounier himself.

Montessuy esteemed in Napoleon the genius of order. "He liked," he said, "work well done. That is a taste most persons have lost."

The painter Duviquet, whose ideas were those of an artist, was embarrassed. He did not find on the funeral mask brought from St. Helena the characteristics of that face, beautiful and powerful, which medals and busts have consecrated. One must be convinced of this now that the bronze of that mask was hanging in all the old shops, among eagles and sphinxes made of gilded wood. And, according to him, since the true face of Napoleon was not that of the ideal Napoleon, his real soul may not have been as idealists fancied it. Perhaps it was the soul of a good bourgeois. Somebody had said this, and he was inclined to think that it was true. Anyway, Duviquet, who flattered himself with having made the best portraits of the century, knew that celebrated men seldom resemble the ideas one forms of them.

M. Daniel Salomon observed that the fine mask about which Duviquet talked, the plaster cast taken from the inanimate face of the Emperor, and brought to Europe by Dr. Antommarchi, had been moulded in bronze and sold by subscription for the first time in 1833, under Louis Philippe, and had then inspired surprise and mistrust. People suspected the Italian chemist, who was a sort of buffoon, always talkative and famished, of having tried to make fun of people. Disciples of Dr. Gall, whose system was then in favor, regarded the mask as suspicious. They did not find in it the bumps of genius; and the forehead, examined in accordance with the master's theories, presented nothing remarkable in its formation.

"Precisely," said Princess Seniavine. "Napoleon was remarkable only for having kicked Volney in the stomach and stealing a snuffbox ornamented with diamonds. Monsieur Garain has just taught us."

"And yet," said Madame Martin, "nobody is sure that he kicked Volney."

"Everything becomes known in the end," replied the Princess, gaily. "Napoleon did nothing at all. He did not even kick Volney, and his head was that of an idiot."

General Lariviere felt that he should say something. He hurled this phrase:

"Napoleon — his campaign of 1813 is much discussed."

The General wished to please Garain, and he had no other idea. However, he succeeded, after an effort, in formulating a judgment:

"Napoleon committed faults; in his situation he should not have committed any." And he stopped abruptly, very red.

Madame Martin asked:

"And you, Monsieur Vence, what do you think of Napoleon?"

"Madame, I have not much love for sword-bearers, and conquerors seem to me to be dangerous fools. But in spite of everything, that figure of the Emperor interests me as it interests the public. I find character and life in it. There is no poem or novel that is worth the Memoirs of Saint Helena, although it is written in ridiculous fashion. What I think of Napoleon, if you wish to know, is that, made for glory, he had the brilliant simplicity of the hero of an epic poem. A hero must be human. Napoleon was human."

"Oh, oh!" every one exclaimed.

But Paul Vence continued:

"He was violent and frivolous; therefore profoundly human. I mean, similar to everybody. He desired, with singular force, all that most men esteem and desire. He had illusions, which he gave to the people. This was his power and his weakness; it was his beauty. He believed in glory. He had of life and of the world the same opinion as any one of his grenadiers. He retained always the infantile gravity which finds pleasure in playing with swords and drums, and the sort of innocence which makes good military men. He esteemed force sincerely. He was a man among men, the flesh of human flesh. He had not a thought that was not in action, and all his actions were grand yet common. It is this vulgar grandeur which makes heroes. And Napoleon is the perfect hero. His brain never surpassed his hand — that hand, small and beautiful, which grasped the world. He never had, for a moment, the least care for what he could not reach."

"Then," said Garain, "according to you, he was not an intellectual genius. I am of your opinion."

"Surely," continued Paul Vence, "he had enough genius to be brilliant in the civil and military arena of the world. But he had not speculative genius. That genius is another pair of sleeves, as Buffon says. We have a collection of his writings and speeches. His style has movement and imagination. And in this mass of thoughts one can not find a philosophic curiosity, not one expression of anxiety about the unknowable, not an expression of fear of the mystery which surrounds destiny. At Saint Helena, when he talks of God and of the soul, he seems to be a little fourteen-year-old school-boy. Thrown upon the world, his mind found itself fit for the world, and embraced it all. Nothing of that mind was lost in the infinite. Himself a poet, he knew only the poetry of action. He limited to the earth his powerful dream of life. In his terrible and touching naiveté he believed that a man could be great, and neither time nor misfortune made him lose that idea. His youth, or rather his sublime adolescence, lasted as long as he lived, because life never brought him a real maturity. Such is the abnormal state of men of action. They live entirely in the present, and their genius concentrates on one point. The hours of their existence are not connected by a chain of grave and disinterested meditations. They succeed themselves in a series of acts. They lack interior life. This defect is particularly visible in Napoleon, who never lived within himself. From this is derived the frivolity of temperament which made him support easily the enormous load of his evils and of his faults. His mind was born anew every day. He had, more than any other person, a capacity for diversion. The first day that he saw the sun rise on his funereal rock at Saint Helena, he jumped from his bed, whistling a romantic air. It was the peace of a mind superior to fortune; it was the frivolity of a mind prompt in resurrection. He lived from the outside."

Garain, who did not like Paul Vence's ingenious turn of wit and language, tried to hasten the conclusion:

"In a word," he said, "there was something of the monster in the man."

"There are no monsters," replied Paul Vence; "and men who pass for monsters inspire horror. Napoleon was loved by an entire people. He had the power to win the love of men. The joy of his soldiers was to die for him."

Countess Martin would have wished Dechartre to give his opinion. But he excused himself with a sort of fright.

"Do you know," said Schmoll again, "the parable of the three rings, sublime inspiration of a Portuguese Jew."

Garain, while complimenting Paul Vence on his brilliant paradox, regretted that wit should be exercised at the expense of morality and justice.

"One great principle," he said, "is that men should be judged by their acts."

"And women?" asked Princess Seniavine, brusquely; "do you judge them by their acts? And how do you know what they do?"

The sound of voices was mingled with the clear tintinnabulation of silverware. A warm air bathed the room. The roses shed their leaves on the cloth. More ardent thoughts mounted to the brain.

General Lariviere fell into dreams.

"When public clamor has split my ears," he said to his neighbor, "I shall go to live at Tours. I shall cultivate flowers."

He flattered himself on being a good gardener; his name had been given to a rose. This pleased him highly.

Schmoll asked again if they knew the parable of the three rings.

The Princess rallied the Deputy.

"Then you do not know, Monsieur Garain, that one does the same things for very different reasons?"

Montessuy said she was right.

"It is very true, as you say, Madame, that actions prove nothing. This thought is striking in an episode in the life of Don Juan, which was known neither to Moliere nor to Mozart, but which is revealed in an English legend, a knowledge of which I owe to my friend James Russell Lowell of London. One learns from it that the great seducer lost his time with three women. One was a bourgeoise: she was in love with her husband; the other was a nun: she would not consent to violate her vows; the third, who had for a long time led a life of debauchery, had become ugly, and was a servant in a den. After what she had done, after what she had seen, love signified nothing to her. These three women behaved alike for very different reasons. An action proves nothing. It is the mass of actions, their weight, their sum total, which makes the value of the human being."

"Some of our actions," said Madame Martin, "have our look, our face: they are our daughters. Others do not resemble us at all."

She rose and took the General's arm.

On the way to the drawing-room the Princess said:

"Therese is right. Some actions do not express our real selves at all. They are like the things we do in nightmares."

The nymphs of the tapestries smiled vainly in their faded beauty at the guests, who did not see them.

Madame Martin served the coffee with her young cousin, Madame Belleme de Saint-Nom. She complimented Paul Vence on what he had said at the table.

"You talked of Napoleon with a freedom of mind that is rare in the conversations I hear. I have noticed that children, when they are handsome, look, when they pout, like Napoleon at Waterloo. You have made me feel the profound reasons for this similarity."

Then, turning toward Dechartre:

"Do you like Napoleon?"

"Madame, I do not like the Revolution. And Napoleon is the Revolution in boots."

"Monsieur Dechartre, why did you not say this at dinner? But I see you prefer to be witty only in tête-à-têtes."

Count Martin-Belleme escorted the men to the smoking-room. Paul Vence alone remained with the women. Princess Seniavine asked him if he had finished his novel, and what was the subject of it. It was a study in which he tried to reach the truth through a series of plausible conditions.

"Thus," he said, "the novel acquires a moral force which history, in its heavy frivolity, never had."

She inquired whether the book was written for women. He said it was not.

"You are wrong, Monsieur Vence, not to write for women. A superior man can do nothing else for them."

He wished to know what gave her that idea.

"Because I see that all the intelligent women love fools."

"Who bore them."

"Certainly! But superior men would weary them more. They would have more resources to employ in boring them. But tell me the subject of your novel."

"Do you insist?"

"Oh, I insist upon nothing."

"Well, I will tell you. It is a study of popular manners; the history of a young workman, sober and chaste, as handsome as a girl, with the mind of a virgin, a sensitive soul. He is a carver, and works well. At night, near his mother, whom he loves, he studies, he reads books. In his mind, simple and receptive, ideas lodge themselves like bullets in a wall. He has no desires. He has neither the passions nor the vices that attach us to life. He is solitary and pure. Endowed with strong virtues, he becomes conceited. He lives among miserable people. He sees suffering. He has devotion without humanity. He has that sort of cold charity which is called altruism. He is not human because he is not sensual."

"Oh! One must be sensual to be human?"

"Certainly, Madame. True pity, like tenderness, comes from the heart. He is not intelligent enough to doubt. He believes what he has read. And he has read that to establish universal happiness society must be destroyed. Thirst for martyrdom devours him. One morning, having kissed his mother, he goes out; he watches for the socialist deputy of his district, sees him, throws himself on him, and buries a poniard in his breast. Long live anarchy! He is arrested, measured, photographed, questioned, judged, condemned to death, and guillotined. That is my novel."

"It is not very amusing," said the Princess; "but that is not your fault. Your anarchists are as timid and moderate as other Frenchmen. The Russians have more audacity and more imagination."

Countess Martin asked Paul Vence whether he knew a silent, timid-looking man among the guests. Her husband had invited him. She knew nothing of him, not even his name. Paul Vence could only say that he was a senator. He had seen him one day by chance in the Luxembourg, in the gallery that served as a library.

"I went there to look at the cupola, where Delacroix has painted, in a wood of bluish myrtles, heroes and sages of antiquity. That gentleman was there, with the same wretched and pitiful air. His coat was damp and he was warming himself. He was talking with old colleagues and saying, while rubbing his hands: 'The proof that the Republic is the best of governments is that in 1871 it could kill in a week sixty thousand insurgents without becoming unpopular. After such a repression any other regime would have been impossible.'"

"He is a very wicked man," said Madame Martin. "And to think that I was pitying him!"

Madame Garain, her chin softly dropped on her chest, slept in the peace of her housewifely mind, and dreamed of her vegetable garden on the banks of the Loire, where singing-societies came to serenade her.

Joseph Schmoll and General Lariviere came out of the smoking-room. The General took a seat between Princess Seniavine and Madame Martin.

"I met this morning, in the park, Baronne Warburg, mounted on a magnificent horse. She said, 'General, how do you manage to have such fine horses?' I replied: Madame, to have fine horses, you must be either very wealthy or very clever.'"

He was so well satisfied with his reply that he repeated it twice.

Paul Vence came near Countess Martin:

"I know that senator's name: it is Lyer. He is the vice-president of a political society, and author of a book entitled, The Crime of December Second."

The General continued:

"The weather was horrible. I went into a hut and found Le Menil there. I was in a bad humor. He was making fun of me, I saw, because I sought shelter. He imagines that because I am a general I must like wind and snow. He said that he liked bad weather, and that he was to go foxhunting with friends next week."

There was a pause; the General continued:

"I wish him much joy, but I don't envy him. Foxhunting is not agreeable."

"But it is useful," said Montessuy.

The General shrugged his shoulders.

"Foxes are dangerous for chicken-coops in the spring when the fowls have to feed their families."

"Foxes are sly poachers, who do less harm to farmers than to hunters. I know something of this."

Therese was not listening to the Princess, who was talking to her. She was thinking:

"He did not tell me that he was going away!"

"Of what are you thinking, dear?" inquired the Princess.

"Of nothing interesting," Therese replied.

CHAPTER IV
THE END OF A DREAM

In the little shadowy room, where sound was deadened by curtains, portieres, cushions, bearskins, and carpets from the Orient, the firelight shone on glittering swords hanging among the faded favors of the cotillions of three winters. The rosewood chiffonier was surmounted by a silver cup, a prize from some sporting club. On a porcelain plaque, in the centre of the table, stood a crystal vase which held branches of white lilacs; and lights palpitated in the warm shadows. Therese and Robert, their eyes accustomed to obscurity, moved easily among these familiar objects. He lighted a cigarette while she arranged her hair, standing before the mirror, in a corner so dim she could hardly see herself. She took pins from the little Bohemian glass cup standing on the table, where she had kept it for three years. He looked at her, passing her light fingers quickly through the gold ripples of her hair, while her face, hardened and bronzed by the shadow, took on a mysterious expression. She did not speak.

He said to her:

"You are not cross now, my dear?"

And, as he insisted upon having an answer, she said:

"What do you wish me to say, my friend? I can only repeat what I said at first. I think it strange that I have to learn of your projects from General Lariviere."

He knew very well that she had not forgiven him; that she had remained cold and reserved toward him. But he affected to think that she only pouted.

"My dear, I have explained it to you. I have told you that when I met Lariviere I had just received a letter from Caumont, recalling my promise to hunt the fox in his woods, and I replied by return post. I meant to tell you about it to-day. I am sorry that General Lariviere told you first, but there was no significance in that."

Her arms were lifted like the handles of a vase. She turned toward him a glance from her tranquil eyes, which he did not understand.

"Then you are going?"

"Next week, Tuesday or Wednesday. I shall be away only ten days at most."

She put on her sealskin toque, ornamented with a branch of holly.

"Is it something that you can not postpone?"

"Oh, yes. Fox-skins would not be worth anything in a month. Moreover, Caumont has invited good friends of mine, who would regret my absence."

Fixing her toque on her head with a long pin, she frowned.

"Is fox-hunting interesting?"

"Oh, yes, very. The fox has stratagems that one must fathom. The intelligence of that animal is really marvellous. I have observed at night a fox hunting a rabbit. He had organized a real hunt. I assure you it is not easy to dislodge a fox. Caumont has an excellent cellar. I do not care for it, but it is generally appreciated. I will bring you half a dozen skins."

"What do you wish me to do with them?"

"Oh, you can make rugs of them."

"And you will be hunting eight days?"

"Not all the time. I shall visit my aunt, who expects me. Last year at this time there was a delightful reunion at her house. She had with her her two daughters and her three nieces with their husbands. All five women are pretty, gay, charming, and irreproachable. I shall probably find them at the beginning of next month, assembled for my aunt's birthday, and I shall remain there two days."

"My friend, stay as long as it may please you. I should be inconsolable if you shortened on my account a sojourn which is so agreeable."

"But you, Therese?"

"I, my friend? I can take care of myself."

378

The fire was languishing. The shadows were deepening between them. She said, in a dreamy tone:

"It is true, however, that it is never prudent to leave a woman alone."

He went near her, trying to see her eyes in the darkness. He took her hand.

"You love me?" he said.

"Oh, I assure you that I do not love another but — "

"What do you mean?"

"Nothing. I am thinking — I am thinking that we are separated all through the summer; that in winter you live with your parents and your friends half the time; and that, if we are to see so little of each other, it is better not to see each other at all."

He lighted the candelabra. His frank, hard face was illuminated. He looked at her with a confidence that came less from the conceit common to all lovers than from his natural lack of dignity. He believed in her through force of education and simplicity of intelligence.

"Therese, I love you, and you love me, I know. Why do you torment me? Sometimes you are painfully harsh."

She shook her little head brusquely.

"What will you have? I am harsh and obstinate. It is in the blood. I take it from my father. You know Joinville; you have seen the castle, the ceilings, the tapestries, the gardens, the park, the hunting-grounds, you have said that none better were in France; but you have not seen my father's workshop — a white wooden table and a mahogany bureau. Everything about me has its origin there. On that table my father made figures for forty years; at first in a little room, then in the apartment where I was born. We were not very wealthy then. I am a parvenu's daughter, or a conqueror's daughter, it's all the same. We are people of material interests. My father wanted to earn money, to possess what he could buy — that is, everything. I wish to earn and keep — what? I do not know — the happiness that I have — or that I have not. I have my own way of being exacting. I long for dreams and illusions. Oh, I know very well that all this is not worth the trouble that a woman takes in giving herself to a man; but it is a trouble that is worth something, because my trouble is myself, my life. I like to enjoy what I like, or think what I like. I do not wish to lose. I am like papa: I demand what is due to me. And then — "

She lowered her voice:

"And then, I have — impulses! Now, my dear, I bore you. What will you have? You shouldn't have loved me."

This language, to which she had accustomed him, often spoiled his pleasure. But it did not alarm him. He was sensitive to all that she did, but not at all to what she said; and he attached no importance to a woman's words. Talking little himself, he could not imagine that often words are the same as actions.

Although he loved her, or, rather, because he loved her with strength and confidence, he thought it his duty to resist her whims, which he judged absurd. Whenever he played the master, he succeeded with her; and, naively, he always ended by playing it.

"You know very well, Therese, that I wish to do nothing except to be agreeable to you. Don't be capricious with me."

"And why should I not be capricious? If I gave myself to you, it was not because I was logical, nor because I thought I must. It was because I was capricious."

He looked at her, astonished and saddened.

"The word is not pleasant to you, my friend? Well let us say that it was love. Truly it was, with all my heart, and because I felt that you loved me. But love must be a pleasure, and if I do not find in it the satisfaction of what you call my capriciousness, but which is really my desire, my life, my love, I do not want it; I prefer to live alone. You are astonishing! My caprices! Is there anything else in life? Your foxhunt, isn't that capricious?"

He replied, very sincerely:

"If I had not promised, I swear to you, Therese, that I would sacrifice that small pleasure with great joy."

She felt that he spoke the truth. She knew how exact he was in filling the most trifling engagements, yet realized that if she insisted he would not go. But it was too late: she did not wish to win. She would seek hereafter only the violent pleasure of losing. She pretended to take his reason seriously, and said:

"Ah, you have promised!"

And she affected to yield.

Surprised at first, he congratulated himself at last on having made her listen to reason. He was grateful to her for not having been stubborn. He put his arm around her waist and kissed her on the neck and eyelids as a reward. He said:

"We may meet three or four times before I go, and more, if you wish. I will wait for you as often as you wish to come. Will you meet me here to-morrow?"

She gave herself the satisfaction of saying that she could not come the next day nor any other day.

Softly she mentioned the things that prevented her.

The obstacles seemed light; calls, a gown to be tried on, a charity fair, exhibitions. As she dilated upon the difficulties they seemed to increase. The calls could not be postponed; there were three fairs; the exhibitions would soon close. In fine, it was impossible for her to see him again before his departure.

As he was well accustomed to making excuses of that sort, he failed to observe that it was not natural for Therese to offer them. Embarrassed by this tissue of social obligations, he did not persist, but remained silent and unhappy.

With her left arm she raised the portiere, placed her right hand on the key of the door; and, standing against the rich background of the sapphire and ruby-colored folds of the Oriental draperies, she turned her head toward the friend she was leaving, and said, a little mockingly, yet with a touch of tragic emotion:

"Good-by, Robert. Enjoy yourself. My calls, my errands, your little visits are nothing. Life is made up of just such trifles. Good-by!"

She went out. He would have liked to accompany her, but he made it a point not to show himself with her in the street, unless she absolutely forced him to do so.

In the street, Therese felt suddenly that she was alone in the world, without joy and without pain. She returned to her house on foot, as was her habit. It was night; the air was frozen, clear, and tranquil. But the avenues through which she walked, in shadows studded with lights, enveloped her with that mild atmosphere of the queen of cities, so agreeable to its inhabitants, which makes itself felt even in the cold of winter. She walked between the lines of huts and old houses, remains of the field-days of Auteuil, which tall houses interrupted here and there. These small shops, these monotonous windows, were nothing to her. Yet she felt that she was under the mysterious spell of the friendship of inanimate things; and it seemed to her that the stones, the doors of houses, the lights behind the windowpanes, looked kindly upon her. She was alone, and she wished to be alone. The steps she was taking between the two houses wherein her habits were almost equal, the steps she had taken so often, to-day seemed to her irrevocable. Why? What had that day brought? Not exactly a quarrel. And yet the words spoken that day had left a subtle, strange, persistent sting, which would never leave her. What had happened? Nothing. And that nothing had effaced everything. She had a sort of obscure certainty that she would never return to that room which had so recently enclosed the most secret and dearest phases of her life. She had loved Robert with the seriousness of a necessary joy. Made to be loved, and very reasonable, she had not lost in the abandonment of herself that instinct of reflection, that necessity for security, which was so strong in her. She had not chosen: one seldom chooses. She had not allowed herself to be taken at random and by surprise. She had done what she had wished to do, as much as one ever does what one wishes to do in such cases. She had nothing to regret. He had been to her what it was his duty to be. She felt, in spite of everything, that all was at an end. She thought, with dry sadness, that three years of her life had been given to an honest man who had loved her and whom she had loved. "For I loved him. I must have loved him in order to give myself to him." But she could not feel again the sentiments of early days, the movements of her

382

mind when she had yielded. She recalled small and insignificant circumstances: the flowers on the wall-paper and the pictures in the room. She recalled the words, a little ridiculous and almost touching, that he had said to her. But it seemed to her that the adventure had occurred to another woman, to a stranger whom she did not like and whom she hardly understood. And what had happened only a moment ago seemed far distant now. The room, the lilacs in the crystal vase, the little cup of Bohemian glass where she found her pins — she saw all these things as if through a window that one passes in the street. She was without bitterness, and even without sadness. She had nothing to forgive, alas! This absence for a week was not a betrayal, it was not a fault against her; it was nothing, yet it was everything. It was the end. She knew it. She wished to cease. It was the consent of all the forces of her being. She said to herself: "I have no reason to love him less. Do I love him no more? Did I ever love him?" She did not know and she did not care to know. Three years, during which there had been months when they had seen each other every day — was all this nothing? Life is not a great thing. And what one puts in it, how little that is!

In fine, she had nothing of which to complain. But it was better to end it all. All these reflections brought her back to that point. It was not a resolution; resolutions may be changed. It was graver: it was a state of the body and of the mind.

When she arrived at the square, in the centre of which is a fountain, and on one side of which stands a church of rustic style, showing its bell in an open belfry, she recalled the little bouquet of violets that he had given to her one night on the bridge near Notre Dame. They had loved each other that day — perhaps more than usual. Her heart softened at that reminiscence. But the little bouquet remained alone, a poor little flower skeleton, in her memory.

While she was thinking, passers-by, deceived by the simplicity of her dress, followed her. One of them made propositions to her: a dinner and the theatre. It amused her. She was not at all disturbed; this was not a crisis. She thought: "How do other women manage such things? And I, who promised myself not to spoil my life. What is life worth?"

Opposite the Greek lantern of the Musee des Religions she found the soil disturbed by workmen. There were paving-stones crossed by a bridge made of a narrow flexible plank. She had stepped on it, when she saw at the other end, in front of her, a man who was waiting for her. He recognized her and bowed. It was Dechartre. She saw that he was happy to meet her; she thanked him with a smile. He asked her permission to walk a few steps with her, and they entered into the large and airy space. In this place the tall houses, set somewhat back, efface themselves, and reveal a glimpse of the sky.

He told her that he had recognized her from a distance by the rhythm of her figure and her movements, which were hers exclusively.

"Graceful movements," he added, "are like music for the eyes."

She replied that she liked to walk; it was her pleasure, and the cause of her good health.

He, too, liked to walk in populous towns and beautiful fields. The mystery of highways tempted him. He liked to travel. Although voyages had become common and easy, they retained for him their powerful charm. He had seen golden days and crystalline nights, Greece, Egypt, and the Bosporus; but it was to Italy that he returned always, as to the mother country of his mind.

"I shall go there next week," he said. "I long to see again Ravenna asleep among the black pines of its sterile shore. Have you seen Ravenna, Madame? It is an enchanted tomb where sparkling phantoms appear. The magic of death lies there. The mosaic works of Saint Vitale, with their barbarous angels and their aureolated empresses, make one feel the monstrous delights of the Orient. Despoiled to-day of its silver lamels, the grave of Galla Placidia is frightful under its crypt, luminous yet gloomy. When one looks through an opening in the sarcophagus, it seems as if one saw the daughter of Theodosius, seated on her golden

384

chair, erect in her gown studded with stones and embroidered with scenes from the Old Testament; her beautiful, cruel face preserved hard and black with aromatic plants, and her ebony hands immovable on her knees. For thirteen centuries she retained this funereal majesty, until one day a child passed a candle through the opening of the grave and burned the body."

Madame Martin-Belleme asked what that dead woman, so obstinate in her conceit, had done during her life.

"Twice a slave," said Dechartre, "she became twice an empress."

"She must have been beautiful," said Madame Martin. "You have made me see her too vividly in her tomb. She frightens me. Shall you go to Venice, Monsieur Dechartre? Or are you tired of gondolas, of canals bordered by palaces, and of the pigeons of Saint Mark? I confess that I still like Venice, after being there three times."

He said she was right. He, too, liked Venice.

Whenever he went there, from a sculptor he became a painter, and made studies. He would like to paint its atmosphere.

"Elsewhere," he said, "even in Florence, the sky is too high. At Venice it is everywhere; it caresses the earth and the water. It envelops lovingly the leaden domes and the marble facades, and throws into the iridescent atmosphere its pearls and its crystals. The beauty of Venice is in its sky and its women. What pretty creatures the Venetian women are! Their forms are so slender and supple under their black shawls. If nothing remained of these women except a bone, one would find in that bone the charm of their exquisite structure. Sundays, at church, they form laughing groups, agitated, with hips a little pointed, elegant necks, flowery smiles, and inflaming glances. And all bend, with the suppleness of young animals, at the passage of a priest whose head resembles that of Vitellius, and who carries the chalice, preceded by two choir-boys."

He walked with unequal step, following the rhythm of his ideas, sometimes quick, sometimes slow. She walked more regularly, and almost outstripped him. He looked at her sidewise, and liked her firm and supple carriage. He observed the little shake which at moments her obstinate head gave to the holly on her toque.

Without expecting it, he felt a charm in that meeting, almost intimate, with a young woman almost unknown.

They had reached the place where the large avenue unfolds its four rows of trees. They were following the stone parapet surmounted by a hedge of boxwood, which entirely hides the ugliness of the buildings on the quay. One felt the presence of the river by the milky atmosphere which in misty days seems to rest on the water. The sky was clear. The lights of the city were mingled with the stars. At the south shone the three golden nails of the Orion belt. Dechartre continued:

"Last year, at Venice, every morning as I went out of my house, I saw at her door, raised by three steps above the canal, a charming girl, with small head, neck round and strong, and graceful hips. She was there, in the sun and surrounded by vermin, as pure as an amphora, fragrant as a flower. She smiled. What a mouth! The richest jewel in the most beautiful light. I realized in time that this smile was addressed to a butcher standing behind me with his basket on his head."

At the corner of the short street which goes to the quay, between two lines of small gardens, Madame Martin walked more slowly.

"It is true that at Venice," she said, "all women are pretty."

"They are almost all pretty, Madame. I speak of the common girls — the cigar-girls, the girls among the glass-workers. The others are commonplace enough."

"By others you mean society women; and you don't like these?"

"Society women? Oh, some of them are charming. As for loving them, that's a different affair."

"Do you think so?"

She extended her hand to him, and suddenly turned the corner.

CHAPTER V
A DINNER 'EN FAMILLE'

She dined that night alone with her husband. The narrow table had not the basket with golden eagles and winged Victorys. The candelabra did not light Oudry's paintings. While he talked of the events of the day, she fell into a sad reverie. It seemed to her that she floated in a mist. It was a peaceful and almost sweet suffering. She saw vaguely through the clouds the little room of the Rue Spontini transported by angels to one of the summits of the Himalaya Mountains, and Robert Le Menil — in the quaking of a sort of world's end — had disappeared while putting on his gloves. She felt her pulse to see whether she were feverish. A rattle of silverware on the table awoke her. She heard her husband saying:

"My dear friend Gavaut delivered to-day, in the Chamber, an excellent speech on the question of the reserve funds. It's extraordinary how his ideas have become healthy and just. Oh, he has improved a great deal."

She could not refrain from smiling.

"But Gavaut, my friend, is a poor devil who never thought of anything except escaping from the crowd of those who are dying of hunger. Gavaut never had any ideas except at his elbows. Does anybody take him seriously in the political world? You may be sure that he never gave an illusion to any woman, not even his wife. And yet to produce that sort of illusion a man does not need much." She added, brusquely:

"You know Miss Bell has invited me to spend a month with her at Fiesole. I have accepted; I am going."

Less astonished than discontented, he asked her with whom she was going.

At once she answered:

"With Madame Marmet."

There was no objection to make. Madame Marmet was a proper companion, and it was appropriate for her to visit Italy, where her husband had made some excavations. He asked only:

387

"Have you invited her? When are you going?"

"Next week."

He had the wisdom not to make any objection, judging that opposition would only make her capriciousness firmer, and fearing to give impetus to that foolish idea. He said:

"Surely, to travel is an agreeable pastime. I thought that we might in the spring visit the Caucasus and Turkestan. There is an interesting country. General Annenkoff will place at our disposal carriages, trains, and everything else on his railway. He is a friend of mine; he is quite charmed with you. He will provide us with an escort of Cossacks."

He persisted in trying to flatter her vanity, unable to realize that her mind was not worldly. She replied, negligently, that it might be a pleasant trip. Then he praised the mountains, the ancient cities, the bazaars, the costumes, the armor.

He added:

"We shall take some friends with us — Princess Seniavine, General Lariviere, perhaps Vence or Le Menil."

She replied, with a little dry laugh, that they had time to select their guests.

He became attentive to her wants.

"You are not eating. You will injure your health."

Without yet believing in this prompt departure, he felt some anxiety about it. Each had regained freedom, but he did not like to be alone. He felt that he was himself only when his wife was there. And then, he had decided to give two or three political dinners during the session. He saw his party growing. This was the moment to assert himself, to make a dazzling show. He said, mysteriously:

"Something might happen requiring the aid of all our friends. You have not followed the march of events, Therese?"

"No, my dear."

"I am sorry. You have judgment, liberality of mind. If you had followed the march of events you would have been struck by the current that is leading the country back to moderate opinions. The country is tired of exaggerations. It rejects the men

388

compromised by radical politics and religious persecution. Some day or other it will be necessary to make over a Casimir-Perier ministry with other men, and that day — "

He stopped: really she listened too inattentively.

She was thinking, sad and disenchanted. It seemed to her that the pretty woman, who, among the warm shadows of a closed room, placed her bare feet in the fur of the brown bear rug, and to whom her lover gave kisses while she twisted her hair in front of a glass, was not herself, was not even a woman that she knew well, or that she desired to know, but a person whose affairs were of no interest to her. A pin badly set in her hair, one of the pins from the Bohemian glass cup, fell on her neck. She shivered.

"Yet we really must give three or four dinners to our good political friends," said M. Martin-Belleme. "We shall invite some of the ancient radicals to meet the people of our circle. It will be well to find some pretty women. We might invite Madame Berard de la Malle; there has been no gossip about her for two years. What do you think of it?"

"But, my dear, since I am to go next week — "

This filled him with consternation.

They went, both silent and moody, into the drawing-room, where Paul Vence was waiting. He often came in the evening.

She extended her hand to him.

"I am very glad to see you. I am going out of town. Paris is cold and bleak. This weather tires and saddens me. I am going to Florence, for six weeks, to visit Miss Bell."

M. Martin-Belleme then lifted his eyes to heaven.

Vence asked whether she had been in Italy often.

"Three times; but I saw nothing. This time I wish to see, to throw myself into things. From Florence I shall take walks into Tuscany, into Umbria. And, finally, I shall go to Venice."

"You will do well. Venice suggests the peace of the Sabbath-day in the grand week of creative and divine Italy."

"Your friend Dechartre talked very prettily to me of Venice, of the atmosphere of Venice, which sows pearls."

"Yes, at Venice the sky is a colorist. Florence inspires the mind. An old author has said: 'The sky of Florence is light and subtle, and feeds the beautiful ideas of men.' I have lived delicious days in Tuscany. I wish I could live them again."

"Come and see me there."

He sighed.

The newspaper, books, and his daily work prevented him.

M. Martin-Belleme said everyone should bow before such reasons, and that one was too happy to read the articles and the fine books written by M. Paul Vence to have any wish to take him from his work.

"Oh, my books! One never says in a book what one wishes to say. It is impossible to express one's self. I know how to talk with my pen as well as any other person; but, after all, to talk or to write, what futile occupations! How wretchedly inadequate are the little signs which form syllables, words, and phrases. What becomes of the idea, the beautiful idea, which these miserable hieroglyphics hide? What does the reader make of my writing? A series of false sense, of counter sense, and of nonsense. To read, to hear, is to translate. There are beautiful translations, perhaps. There are no faithful translations. Why should I care for the admiration which they give to my books, since it is what they themselves see in them that they admire? Every reader substitutes his visions in the place of ours. We furnish him with the means to quicken his imagination. It is a horrible thing to be a cause of such exercises. It is an infamous profession."

"You are jesting," said M. Martin-Belleme.

"I do not think so," said Therese. "He recognizes that one mind is impenetrable to another mind, and he suffers from this. He feels that he is alone when he is thinking, alone when he is writing. Whatever one may do, one is always alone in the world. That is what he wishes to say. He is right. You may always explain: you never are understood."

"There are signs — " said Paul Vence.

"Don't you think, Monsieur Vence, that signs also are a form of hieroglyphics? Give me news of Monsieur Choulette. I do not see him any more."

Vence replied that Choulette was very busy in forming the Third Order of Saint Francis.

"The idea, Madame, came to him in a marvellous fashion one day when he had gone to call on his Maria in the street where she lives, behind the public hospital — a street always damp, the houses on which are tottering. You must know that he considers Maria the saint and martyr who is responsible for the sins of the people.

"He pulled the bell-rope, made greasy by two centuries of visitors. Either because the martyr was at the wine-shop, where she is familiarly known, or because she was busy in her room, she did not open the door. Choulette rang for a long time, and so violently that the bell rope remained in his hand. Skilful at understanding symbols and the hidden meaning of things, he understood at once that this rope had not been detached without the permission of spiritual powers. He made of it a belt, and realized that he had been chosen to lead back into its primitive purity the Third Order of Saint Francis. He renounced the beauty of women, the delights of poetry, the brightness of glory, and studied the life and the doctrine of Saint Francis. However, he has sold to his editor a book entitled 'Les Blandices', which contains, he says, the description of all sorts of loves. He flatters himself that in it he has shown himself a criminal with some elegance. But far from harming his mystic undertakings, this book favors them in this sense, that, corrected by his later work, he will become honest and exemplary; and the gold that he has received in payment, which would not have been paid to him for a more chaste volume, will serve for a pilgrimage to Assisi."

Madame Martin asked how much of this story was really true. Vence replied that she must not try to learn.

He confessed that he was the idealist historian of the poet, and that the adventures which he related of him were not to be taken in the literal and Judaic sense.

He affirmed that at least Choulette was publishing Les Blandices, and desired to visit the cell and the grave of St. Francis.

"Then," exclaimed Madame Martin, "I will take him to Italy with me. Find him, Monsieur Vence, and bring him to me. I am going next week."

M. Martin then excused himself, not being able to remain longer. He had to finish a report which was to be laid before the Chamber the next day.

Madame Martin said that nobody interested her so much as Choulette. Paul Vence said that he was a singular specimen of humanity.

"He is not very different from the saints of whose extraordinary lives we read. He is as sincere as they. He has an exquisite delicacy of sentiment and a terrible violence of mind. If he shocks one by many of his acts, the reason is that he is weaker, less supported, or perhaps less closely observed. And then there are unworthy saints, just as there are bad angels: Choulette is a worldly saint, that is all. But his poems are true poems, and much finer than those written by the bishops of the seventeenth century."

She interrupted him:

"While I think of it, I wish to congratulate you on your friend Dechartre. He has a charming mind."

She added:

"Perhaps he is a little too timid."

Vence reminded her that he had told her she would find Dechartre interesting.

"I know him by heart; he has been my friend since our childhood."

"You knew his parents?"

"Yes. He is the only son of Philippe Dechartre."

"The architect?"

"The architect who, under Napoleon III, restored so many castles and churches in Touraine and the Orleanais. He had taste and knowledge. Solitary and quiet in his life, he had the imprudence to attack Viollet-le-Duc, then all-powerful. He reproached him with trying to reestablish buildings in their primitive plan, as they had been, or as they might have been, at the beginning. Philippe Dechartre, on the contrary, wished that everything which the lapse of centuries had added to a church, an abbey, or a castle should be respected. To abolish anachronisms and restore a building to its primitive unity, seemed to him to be a scientific barbarity as culpable as that of ignorance. He said: 'It is a crime to efface the successive imprints made in stone by the hands of our ancestors. New stones cut in old style are false witnesses.' He wished to limit the task of the archaeological architect to that of supporting and consolidating walls. He was right. Everybody said that he was wrong. He achieved his ruin by dying young, while his rival triumphed. He bequeathed an honest fortune to his widow and his son. Jacques Dechartre was brought up by his mother, who adored him. I do not think that maternal tenderness ever was more impetuous. Jacques is a charming fellow; but he is a spoiled child."

"Yet he appears so indifferent, so easy to understand, so distant from everything."

"Do not rely on this. He has a tormented and tormenting imagination."

"Does he like women?"

"Why do you ask?"

"Oh, it isn't with any idea of match-making."

"Yes, he likes them. I told you that he was an egoist. Only selfish men really love women. After the death of his mother, he had a long liaison with a well-known actress, Jeanne Tancrede."

Madame Martin remembered Jeanne Tancrede; not very pretty, but graceful with a certain slowness of action in playing romantic roles.

"They lived almost together in a little house at Auteuil," Paul Vence continued. "I often called on them. I found him lost in his dreams, forgetting to model a figure drying under its cloths, alone with himself, pursuing his idea, absolutely incapable of listening to anybody; she, studying her roles, her complexion burned by rouge, her eyes tender, pretty because of her intelligence and her activity. She complained to me that he was inattentive, cross, and unreasonable. She loved him and deceived him only to obtain roles. And when she deceived him, it was done on the spur of the moment. Afterward she never thought of it. A typical woman! But she was imprudent; she smiled upon Joseph Springer in the hope that he would make her a member of the Comedie Francaise. Dechartre left her. Now she finds it more practical to live with her managers, and Jacques finds it more agreeable to travel."

"Does he regret her?"

"How can one know the things that agitate a mind anxious and mobile, selfish and passionate, desirous to surrender itself, prompt in disengaging itself, liking itself most of all among the beautiful things that it finds in the world?"

Brusquely she changed the subject.

"And your novel, Monsieur Vence?"

"I have reached the last chapter, Madame. My little workingman has been guillotined. He died with that indifference of virgins without desire, who never have felt on their lips the warm taste of life. The journals and the public approve the act of justice which has just been accomplished. But in another garret, another workingman, sober, sad, and a chemist, swears to himself that he will commit an expiatory murder."

He rose and said good-night.

She called him back.

"Monsieur Vence, you know that I was serious. Bring Choulette to me."

When she went up to her room, her husband was waiting for her, in his red-brown plush robe, with a sort of doge's cap framing his pale and hollow face. He had an air of gravity. Behind him, by the open door of his workroom, appeared under the lamp a mass of documents bound in blue, a collection of the annual budgets. Before she could reach her room he motioned that he wished to speak to her.

"My dear, I can not understand you. You are very inconsequential. It does you a great deal of harm. You intend to leave your home without any reason, without even a pretext. And you wish to run through Europe with whom? With a Bohemian, a drunkard — that man Choulette."

She replied that she should travel with Madame Marmet, in which there could be nothing objectionable.

"But you announce your going to everybody, yet you do not even know whether Madame Marmet can accompany you."

"Oh, Madame Marmet will soon pack her boxes. Nothing keeps her in Paris except her dog. She will leave it to you; you may take care of it."

"Does your father know of your project?"

It was his last resource to invoke the authority of Montessuy. He knew that his wife feared to displease her father. He insisted:

"Your father is full of sense and tact. I have been happy to find him agreeing with me several times in the advices which I have permitted myself to give you. He thinks as I do, that Madame Meillan's house is not a fit place for you to visit. The company that meets there is mixed, and the mistress of the house favors intrigue. You are wrong, I must say, not to take account of what people think. I am mistaken if your father does not think it singular that you should go away with so much frivolity, and the absence will be the more remarked, my dear, since circumstances have made me eminent in the course of this legislature. My merit has nothing to do with the case, surely. But if you had consented to listen to me at dinner I should have demonstrated to you that the group of politicians to which I belong has almost reached power. In such a moment you should not renounce your duties as mistress of the house. You must understand this yourself."

She replied "You annoy me." And, turning her back to him, she shut the door of her room between them. That night in her bed she opened a book, as she always did before going to sleep. It was a novel. She was turning the leaves with indifference, when her eyes fell on these lines:

"Love is like devotion: it comes late. A woman is hardly in love or devout at twenty, unless she has a special disposition to be either, a sort of native sanctity. Women who are predestined to love, themselves struggle a long time against that grace of love which is more terrible than the thunderbolt that fell on the road to Damascus. A woman oftenest yields to the passion of love only when age or solitude does not frighten her. Passion is an arid and burning desert. Passion is profane asceticism, as harsh as religious asceticism. Great woman lovers are as rare as great penitent women. Those who know life well know that women do not easily bind themselves in the chains of real love. They know that nothing is less common than sacrifice among them. And consider how much a worldly woman must sacrifice when she is in love — liberty, quietness, the charming play of a free mind, coquetry, amusement, pleasure — she loses everything.

"Coquetry is permissible. One may conciliate that with all the exigencies of fashionable life. Not so love. Love is the least mundane of passions, the most anti-social, the most savage, the most barbarous. So the world judges it more severely than mere gallantry or looseness of manners. In one sense the world is right. A woman in love betrays her nature and fails in her function, which is to be admired by all men, like a work of art. A woman is a work of art, the most marvellous that man's industry ever has produced. A woman is a wonderful artifice, due to the concourse of all the arts mechanical and of all the arts liberal. She is the work of everybody, she belongs to the world."

Therese closed the book and thought that these ideas were only the dreams of novelists who did not know life. She knew very well that there was in reality neither a Carmel of passion nor a chain of love, nor a beautiful and terrible vocation against which the predestined one resisted in vain; she knew very well that love was only a brief intoxication from which one recovered a little sadder. And yet, perhaps, she did not know everything; perhaps there were loves in which one was deliciously lost. She put out her lamp. The dreams of her first youth came back to her.

CHAPTER VI
A DISTINGUISHED RELICT

It was raining. Madame Martin-Belleme saw confusedly through the glass of her coupe the multitude of passing umbrellas, like black turtles under the watery skies. She was thinking. Her thoughts were gray and indistinct, like the aspect of the streets and the squares.

She no longer knew why the idea had come to her to spend a month with Miss Bell. Truly, she never had known. The idea had been like a spring, at first hidden by leaves, and now forming the current of a deep and rapid stream. She remembered that Tuesday night at dinner she had said suddenly that she wished to go, but she could not remember the first flush of that desire. It was not the wish to act toward Robert Le Menil as he was acting toward her. Doubtless she thought it excellent to go traveling in Italy while he went fox-hunting. This seemed to her a fair arrangement. Robert, who was always pleased to see her when he came back, would not find her on his return. She thought this would be right. She had not thought of it at first. And since then she had thought little of it, and really she was not going for the pleasure of making him grieve. She had against him a thought less piquant, and more harsh. She did not wish to see him soon. He had become to her almost a stranger. He seemed to her a man like others — better than most others — good-looking, estimable, and who did not displease her; but he did not preoccupy her. Suddenly he had gone out of her life. She could not remember how he had become mingled with it. The idea of belonging to him shocked her. The thought that they might meet again in the small apartment of the Rue Spontini was so painful to her that she discarded it at once. She preferred to think that an unforeseen event would prevent their meeting again — the end of the world, for example. M. Lagrange, member of the Academie des Sciences, had told her the day before of a comet which some day might meet the earth, envelop it with its flaming hair, imbue animals and plants with unknown poisons, and make all men die in a frenzy of laughter. She expected that this, or something else, would happen next month. It was not inexplicable that she wished to go. But that her desire to go should contain a vague joy, that she should feel the charm of what she was to find, was inexplicable to her.

Her carriage left her at the corner of a street.

There, under the roof of a tall house, behind five windows, in a small, neat apartment, Madame Marmet had lived since the death of her husband.

Countess Martin found her in her modest drawing-room, opposite M. Lagrange, half asleep in a deep armchair. This worldly old savant had remained ever faithful to her. He it was who, the day after M. Marmet's funeral, had conveyed to the unfortunate widow the poisoned speech delivered by Schmoll. She had fainted in his arms. Madame Marmet thought that he lacked judgment, but he was her best friend. They dined together often with rich friends.

Madame Martin, slender and erect in her zibeline corsage opening on a flood of lace, awakened with the charming brightness of her gray eyes the good man, who was susceptible to the graces of women. He had told her the day before how the world would come to an end. He asked her whether she had not been frightened at night by pictures of the earth devoured by flames or frozen to a mass of ice. While he talked to her with affected gallantry, she looked at the mahogany bookcase. There were not many books in it, but on one of the shelves was a skeleton in armor. It amazed one to see in this good lady's house that Etruscan warrior wearing a green bronze helmet and a cuirass. He slept among boxes of bonbons, vases of gilded porcelain, and carved images of the Virgin, picked up at Lucerne and on the Righi. Madame Marmet, in her widowhood, had sold the books which her husband had left. Of all the ancient objects collected by the archaeologist, she had retained nothing except the Etruscan. Many persons had tried to sell it for her. Paul Vence had obtained from the administration a promise to buy it for the Louvre, but the good widow would not part with it. It seemed to her that if she lost that warrior with his green bronze helmet she would lose the name that she wore worthily, and would cease to be the widow of Louis Marmet of the Academie des Inscriptions.

"Do not be afraid, Madame; a comet will not soon strike the earth. Such a phenomenon is very improbable."

Madame Martin replied that she knew no serious reason why the earth and humanity should not be annihilated at once.

Old Lagrange exclaimed with profound sincerity that he hoped the cataclysm would come as late as possible.

She looked at him. His bald head could boast only a few hairs dyed black. His eyelids fell like rags over eyes still smiling; his cheeks hung in loose folds, and one divined that his body was equally withered. She thought, "And even he likes life!"

Madame Marmet hoped, too, that the end of the world was not near at hand.

"Monsieur Lagrange," said Madame Martin, "you live, do you not, in a pretty little house, the windows of which overlook the Botanical Gardens? It seems to me it must be a joy to live in that garden, which makes me think of the Noah's Ark of my infancy, and of the terrestrial paradises in the old Bibles."

But he was not at all charmed with his house. It was small, unimproved, infested with rats.

She acknowledged that one seldom felt at home anywhere, and that rats were found everywhere, either real or symbolical, legions of pests that torment us. Yet she liked the Botanical Gardens; she had always wished to go there, yet never had gone. There was also the museum, which she was curious to visit.

Smiling, happy, he offered to escort her there. He considered it his house. He would show her rare specimens, some of which were superb.

She did not know what a bolide was. She recalled that some one had said to her that at the museum were bones carved by primitive men, and plaques of ivory on which were engraved pictures of animals, which were long ago extinct. She asked whether that were true. Lagrange ceased to smile. He replied indifferently that such objects concerned one of his colleagues.

"Ah!" said Madame Martin, "then they are not in your showcase."

She observed that learned men were not curious, and that it is indiscreet to question them on things that are not in their own showcases. It is true that Lagrange had made a scientific fortune in studying meteors. This had led him to study comets. But he was wise. For twenty years he had been preoccupied by nothing except dining out.

When he had left, Countess Martin told Madame Marmet what she expected of her.

"I am going next week to Fiesole, to visit Miss Bell, and you are coming with me."

The good Madame Marmet, with placid brow yet searching eyes, was silent for a moment; then she refused gently, but finally consented.

CHAPTER VII
MADAME HAS HER WAY

The Marseilles express was ready on the quay, where the postmen ran, and the carriages rolled amid smoke and noise, under the light that fell from the windows. Through the open doors travelers in long cloaks came and went. At the end of the station, blinding with soot and dust, a small rainbow could be discerned, not larger than one's hand. Countess Martin and the good Madame Marniet were already in their carriage, under the rack loaded with bags, among newspapers thrown on the cushions. Choulette had not appeared, and Madame Martin expected him no longer. Yet he had promised to be at the station. He had made his arrangements to go, and had received from his publisher the price of Les Blandices. Paul Vence had brought him one evening to Madame Martin's house. He had been sweet, polished, full of witty gayety and naive joy. She had promised herself much pleasure in traveling with a man of genius, original, picturesquely ugly, with an amusing simplicity; like a child prematurely old and abandoned, full of vices, yet with a certain degree of innocence. The doors closed. She expected him no longer. She should not have counted on his impulsive and vagabondish mind. At the moment when the engine began to breathe hoarsely, Madame Marmet, who was looking out of the window, said, quietly:

"I think that Monsieur Choulette is coming."

He was walking along the quay, limping, with his hat on the back of his head, his beard unkempt, and dragging an old carpet-bag. He was almost repulsive; yet, in spite of his fifty years of age, he looked young, so clear and lustrous were his eyes, so much ingenuous audacity had been retained in his yellow, hollow face, so vividly did this old man express the eternal adolescence of the poet and artist. When she saw him, Therese regretted having invited so strange a companion. He walked along, throwing a hasty glance into every carriage — a glance which, little by little, became sullen and distrustful. But when he recognized Madame

Martin, he smiled so sweetly and said good-morning to her in so caressing a voice that nothing was left of the ferocious old vagabond walking on the quay, nothing except the old carpet-bag, the handles of which were half broken.

He placed it in the rack with great care, among the elegant bags enveloped with gray cloth, beside which it looked conspicuously sordid. It was studded with yellow flowers on a blood-colored background.

He was soon perfectly at ease, and complimented Madame Martin on the elegance of her traveling attire.

"Excuse me, ladies," he added, "I was afraid I should be late. I went to six o'clock mass at Saint Severin, my parish, in the Virgin Chapel, under those pretty, but absurd columns that point toward heaven though frail as reeds-like us, poor sinners that we are."

"Ah," said Madame Martin, "you are pious to-day."

And she asked him whether he wore the cordon of the order which he was founding. He assumed a grave and penitent air.

"I am afraid, Madame, that Monsieur Paul Vence has told you many absurd stories about me. I have heard that he goes about circulating rumors that my ribbon is a bell-rope — and of what a bell! I should be pained if anybody believed so wretched a story. My ribbon, Madame, is a symbolical ribbon. It is represented by a simple thread, which one wears under one's clothes after a pauper has touched it, as a sign that poverty is holy, and that it will save the world. There is nothing good except in poverty; and since I have received the price of Les Blandices, I feel that I am unjust and harsh. It is a good thing that I have placed in my bag several of these mystic ribbons."

And, pointing to the horrible carpet-bag:

"I have also placed in it a host which a bad priest gave to me, the works of Monsieur de Maistre, shirts, and several other things."

Madame Martin lifted her eyebrows, a little ill at ease. But the good Madame Marmet retained her habitual placidity.

As the train rolled through the homely scenes of the outskirts, that black fringe which makes an unlovely border to the city, Choulette took from his pocket an old book which he began to fumble. The writer, hidden under the vagabond, revealed himself. Choulette, without wishing to appear to be careful of his papers, was very orderly about them. He assured himself that he had not lost the pieces of paper on which he noted at the coffeehouse his ideas for poems, nor the dozen of flattering letters which, soiled and spotted, he carried with him continually, to read them to his newly-made companions at night. After assuring himself that nothing was missing, he took from the book a letter folded in an open envelope. He waved it for a while, with an air of mysterious impudence, then handed it to the Countess Martin. It was a letter of introduction from the Marquise de Rieu to a princess of the House of France, a near relative of the Comte de Chambord, who, old and a widow, lived in retirement near the gates of Florence. Having enjoyed the effect which he expected to produce, he said that he should perhaps visit the Princess; that she was a good person, and pious.

"A truly great lady," he added, "who does not show her magnificence in gowns and hats. She wears her chemises for six weeks, and sometimes longer. The gentlemen of her train have seen her wear very dirty white stockings, which fell around her heels. The virtues of the great queens of Spain are revived in her. Oh, those soiled stockings, what real glory there is in them!"

He took the letter and put it back in his book. Then, arming himself with a horn-handled knife, he began, with its point, to finish a figure sketched in the handle of his stick. He complimented himself on it:

"I am skilful in all the arts of beggars and vagabonds. I know how to open locks with a nail, and how to carve wood with a bad knife."

The head began to appear. It was the head of a thin woman, weeping.

Choulette wished to express in it human misery, not simple and touching, such as men of other times may have felt it in a

403

world of mingled harshness and kindness; but hideous, and reflecting the state of ugliness created by the free-thinking bourgeois and the military patriots of the French Revolution. According to him the present regime embodied only hypocrisy and brutality.

"Their barracks are a hideous invention of modern times. They date from the seventeenth century. Before that time there were only guard-houses where the soldiers played cards and told tales. Louis XIV was a precursor of Bonaparte. But the evil has attained its plenitude since the monstrous institution of the obligatory enlistment. The shame of emperors and of republics is to have made it an obligation for men to kill. In the ages called barbarous, cities and princes entrusted their defence to mercenaries, who fought prudently. In a great battle only five or six men were killed. And when knights went to the wars, at least they were not forced to do it; they died for their pleasure. They were good for nothing else. Nobody in the time of Saint Louis would have thought of sending to battle a man of learning. And the laborer was not torn from the soil to be killed. Nowadays it is a duty for a poor peasant to be a soldier. He is exiled from his house, the roof of which smokes in the silence of night; from the fat prairies where the oxen graze; from the fields and the paternal woods. He is taught how to kill men; he is threatened, insulted, put in prison and told that it is an honor; and, if he does not care for that sort of honor, he is fusilladed. He obeys because he is terrorized, and is of all domestic animals the gentlest and most docile. We are warlike in France, and we are citizens. Another reason to be proud, this being a citizen! For the poor it consists in sustaining and preserving the wealthy in their power and their laziness. The poor must work for this, in presence of the majestic quality of the law which prohibits the wealthy as well as the poor from sleeping under the bridges, from begging in the streets, and from stealing bread. That is one of the good effects of the Revolution. As this Revolution was made by fools and idiots for the benefit of those who acquired national lands, and resulted in nothing but making the fortune of crafty peasants and financiering bourgeois, the Revolution only made stronger, under the pretence of making all men equal, the empire of wealth. It has betrayed France into the hands of the men of wealth. They are masters and lords. The apparent government, composed of poor devils, is in the pay of the financiers. For one hundred years, in this poisoned country, whoever has loved the poor has been considered a traitor to society. A man is called dangerous when he says that there are wretched people. There are laws against indignation and pity, and what I say here could not go into print."

Choulette became excited and waved his knife, while under the wintry sunlight passed fields of brown earth, trees despoiled by winter, and curtains of poplars beside silvery rivers.

He looked with tenderness at the figure carved on his stick.

"Here you are," he said, "poor humanity, thin and weeping, stupid with shame and misery, as you were made by your masters — soldiers and men of wealth."

The good Madame Marmet, whose nephew was a captain in the artillery, was shocked at the violence with which Choulette attacked the army. Madame Martin saw in this only an amusing fantasy. Choulette's ideas did not frighten her. She was afraid of nothing. But she thought they were a little absurd. She did not think that the past had ever been better than the present.

"I believe, Monsieur Choulette, that men were always as they are to-day, selfish, avaricious, and pitiless. I believe that laws and manners were always harsh and cruel to the unfortunate."

Between La Roche and Dijon they took breakfast in the dining-car, and left Choulette in it, alone with his pipe, his glass of benedictine, and his irritation.

In the carriage, Madame Marmet talked with peaceful tenderness of the husband she had lost. He had married her for love; he had written admirable verses to her, which she had kept, and never shown to any one. He was lively and very gay. One would not have thought it who had seen him later, tired by work and weakened by illness. He studied until the last moment. Two hours before he died he was trying to read again. He was

405

affectionate and kind. Even in suffering he retained all his sweetness. Madame Martin said to her:

"You have had long years of happiness; you have kept the reminiscence of them; that is a share of happiness in this world."

But good Madame Marmet sighed; a cloud passed over her quiet brow.

"Yes," she said, "Louis was the best of men and the best of husbands. Yet he made me very miserable. He had only one fault, but I suffered from it cruelly. He was jealous. Good, kind, tender, and generous as he was, this horrible passion made him unjust, ironical, and violent. I can assure you that my behavior gave not the least cause for suspicion. I was not a coquette. But I was young, fresh; I passed for beautiful. That was enough. He would not let me go out alone, and would not let me receive calls in his absence. Whenever we went to a reception, I trembled in advance with the fear of the scene which he would make later in the carriage."

And the good Madame Marmet added, with a sigh:

"It is true that I liked to dance. But I had to renounce going to balls; it made him suffer too much."

Countess Martin expressed astonishment. She had always imagined Marmet as an old man, timid, and absorbed by his thoughts; a little ridiculous, between his wife, plump, white, and amiable, and the skeleton wearing a helmet of bronze and gold. But the excellent widow confided to her that, at fifty-five years of age, when she was fifty-three, Louis was just as jealous as on the first day of their marriage.

And Therese thought that Robert had never tormented her with jealousy. Was it on his part a proof of tact and good taste, a mark of confidence, or was it that he did not love her enough to make her suffer? She did not know, and she did not have the heart to try to know. She would have to look through recesses of her mind which she preferred not to open.

She murmured carelessly:

"We long to be loved, and when we are loved we are tormented or worried."

The day was finished in reading and thinking. Choulette did not reappear. Night covered little by little with its gray clouds the mulberry-trees of the Dauphine. Madame Marmet went to sleep peacefully, resting on herself as on a mass of pillows. Therese looked at her and thought:

"She is happy, since she likes to remember."

The sadness of night penetrated her heart. And when the moon rose on the fields of olive-trees, seeing the soft lines of plains and of hills pass, Therese, in this landscape wherein everything spoke of peace and oblivion, and nothing spoke of her, regretted the Seine, the Arc de Triomphe with its radiating avenues, and the alleys of the park where, at least, the trees and the stones knew her.

Suddenly Choulette threw himself into the carriage. Armed with his knotty stick, his face and head enveloped in red wool and a fur cap, he almost frightened her. It was what he wished to do. His violent attitudes and his savage dress were studied. Always seeking to produce effects, it pleased him to seem frightful.

He was a coward himself, and was glad to inspire the fears he often felt. A moment before, as he was smoking his pipe, he had felt, while seeing the moon swallowed up by the clouds, one of those childish frights that tormented his light mind. He had come near the Countess to be reassured.

"Arles," he said. "Do you know Arles? It is a place of pure beauty. I have seen, in the cloister, doves resting on the shoulders of statues, and I have seen the little gray lizards warming themselves in the sun on the tombs. The tombs are now in two rows on the road that leads to the church. They are formed like cisterns, and serve as beds for the poor at night. One night, when I was walking among them, I met a good old woman who was placing dried herbs in the tomb of an old maid who had died on her wedding-day. We said goodnight to her. She replied: 'May God hear-you! but fate wills that this tomb should open on the side of the northwest wind. If only it were open on the other side, I should be lying as comfortably as Queen Jeanne.'"

Therese made no answer. She was dozing. And Choulette shivered in the cold of the night, in the fear of death.

CHAPTER VIII
THE LADY OF THE BELLS

In her English cart, which she drove herself, Miss Bell had brought over the hills, from the railway station at Florence, the Countess Martin-Belleme and Madame Marmet to her pink-tinted house at Fiesole, which, crowned with a long balustrade, overlooked the incomparable city. The maid followed with the luggage. Choulette, lodged, by Miss Bell's attention, in the house of a sacristan's widow, in the shadow of the cathedral of Fiesole, was not expected until dinner. Plain and gentle, wearing short hair, a waistcoat, a man's shirt on a chest like a boy's, almost graceful, with small hips, the poetess was doing for her French friends the honors of the house, which reflected the ardent delicacy of her taste. On the walls of the drawing-room were pale Virgins, with long hands, reigning peacefully among angels, patriarchs, and saints in beautiful gilded frames. On a pedestal stood a Magdalena, clothed only with her hair, frightful with thinness and old age, some beggar of the road to Pistoia, burned by the suns and the snows, whom some unknown precursor of Donatello had moulded. And everywhere were Miss Bell's chosen arms-bells and cymbals. The largest lifted their bronze clappers at the angles of the room; others formed a chain at the foot of the walls. Smaller ones ran along the cornices. There were bells over the hearth, on the cabinets, and on the chairs. The shelves were full of silver and golden bells. There were big bronze bells marked with the Florentine lily; bells of the Renaissance, representing a lady wearing a white gown; bells of the dead, decorated with tears and bones; bells covered with symbolical animals and leaves, which had rung in the churches in the time of St. Louis; table-bells of the seventeenth century, having a statuette for a handle; the flat, clear cow-bells of the Ruth Valley; Hindu bells; Chinese bells formed like cylinders — they had come from all countries and all times, at the magic call of little Miss Bell.

"You look at my speaking arms," she said to Madame Martin. "I think that all these Misses Bell are pleased to be here, and I should not be astonished if some day they all began to sing together. But you must not admire them all equally. Reserve your purest and most fervent praise for this one."

And striking with her finger a dark, bare bell which gave a faint sound:

"This one," she said, "is a holy village-bell of the fifth century. She is a spiritual daughter of Saint Paulin de Nole, who was the first to make the sky sing over our heads. The metal is rare. Soon I will show to you a gentle Florentine, the queen of bells. She is coming. But I bore you, darling, with my babble. And I bore, too, the good Madame Marmet. It is wrong."

She escorted them to their rooms.

An hour later, Madame Martin, rested, fresh, in a gown of foulard and lace, went on the terrace where Miss Bell was waiting for her. The humid air, warmed by the sun, exhaled the restless sweetness of spring. Therese, resting on the balustrade, bathed her eyes in the light. At her feet, the cypress-trees raised their black distaffs, and the olive-trees looked like sheep on the hills. In the valley, Florence extended its domes, its towers, and the multitudes of its red roofs, through which the Arno showed its undulating line. Beyond were the soft blue hills.

She tried to recognize the Boboli Gardens, where she had walked at her first visit; the Cascine, which she did not like; the Pitti Palace. Then the charming infinity of the sky attracted her. She looked at the forms in the clouds.

After a long silence, Vivian Bell extended her hand toward the horizon.

"Darling, I do not know how to say what I wish. But look, darling, look again. What you see there is unique in the world. Nature is nowhere else so subtle, elegant, and fine. The god who made the hills of Florence was an artist. Oh, he was a jeweler, an engraver, a sculptor, a bronze-founder, and a painter; he was a Florentine. He did nothing else in the world, darling. The rest was made by a hand less delicate, whose work was less perfect. How can you think that that violet hill of San Miniato, so firm and so pure in relief, was made by the author of Mont Blanc? It is not possible. This landscape has the beauty of an antique medal and of a precious painting. It is a perfect and measured work of art. And here is another thing that I do not know how to say, that I can not even understand, but which is a real thing. In this country I feel — and you will feel as I do, darling — half alive and half dead; in a condition which is sad, noble, and very sweet. Look, look again; you will realize the melancholy of those hills that surround Florence, and see a delicious sadness ascend from the land of the dead."

The sun was low over the horizon. The bright points of the mountain-peaks faded one by one, while the clouds inflamed the sky. Madame Marmet sneezed.

Miss Bell sent for some shawls, and warned the French women that the evenings were fresh and that the night-air was dangerous.

Then suddenly she said:

"Darling, you know Monsieur Jacques Dechartre? Well, he wrote to me that he would be at Florence next week. I am glad Monsieur Jacques Dechartre is to meet you in our city. He will accompany us to the churches and to the museums, and he will be a good guide. He understands beautiful things, because he loves them. And he has an exquisite talent as a sculptor. His figures in medallions are admired more in England than in France. Oh, I am so glad Monsieur Jacques Dechartre and you are to meet at Florence, darling!"

CHAPTER IX
CHOULETTE FINDS A NEW FRIEND

She next day, as they were traversing the square where are planted, in imitation of antique amphitheatres, two marble pillars, Madame Marmet said to the Countess Martin:

"I think I see Monsieur Choulette."

Seated in a shoemaker's shop, his pipe in his hand, Choulette was making rhythmic gestures, and appeared to be reciting verses. The Florentine cobbler listened with a kind smile. He was a little, bald man, and represented one of the types familiar to Flemish painters. On a table, among wooden lasts, nails, leather, and wax, a basilic plant displayed its round green head. A sparrow, lacking a leg, which had been replaced by a match, hopped on the old man's shoulder and head.

Madame Martin, amused by this spectacle, called Choulette from the threshold. He was softly humming a tune, and she asked him why he had not gone with her to visit the Spanish chapel.

He arose and replied:

"Madame, you are preoccupied by vain images; but I live in life and in truth."

He shook the cobbler's hand and followed the two ladies.

"While going to church," he said, "I saw this old man, who, bending over his work, and pressing a last between his knees as in a vise, was sewing coarse shoes. I felt that he was simple and kind. I said to him, in Italian: 'My father, will you drink with me a glass of Chianti?' He consented. He went for a flagon and some glasses, and I kept the shop."

And Choulette pointed to two glasses and a flagon placed on a stove.

"When he came back we drank together; I said vague but kind things to him, and I charmed him by the sweetness of sounds. I will go again to his shop; I will learn from him how to make shoes, and how to live without desire. After which, I shall not be sad again. For desire and idleness alone make us sad."

The Countess Martin smiled.

"Monsieur Choulette, I desire nothing, and, nevertheless, I am not joyful. Must I make shoes, too?"

Choulette replied, gravely:

"It is not yet time for that."

When they reached the gardens of the Oricellari, Madame Marmet sank on a bench. She had examined at Santa Maria-Novella the frescoes of Ghirlandajo, the stalls of the choir, the Virgin of Cimabue, the paintings in the cloister. She had done this carefully, in memory of her husband, who had greatly liked Italian art. She was tired. Choulette sat by her and said:

"Madame, could you tell me whether it is true that the Pope's gowns are made by Worth?"

Madame Marmet thought not. Nevertheless, Choulette had heard people say this in cafes. Madame Marmet was astonished that Choulette, a Catholic and a socialist, should speak so disrespectfully of a pope friendly to the republic. But he did not like Leo XIII.

"The wisdom of princes is shortsighted," he said; "the salvation of the Church must come from the Italian republic, as Leo XIII believes and wishes; but the Church will not be saved in the manner which this pious Machiavelli thinks. The revolution will make the Pope lose his last sou, with the rest of his patrimony. And it will be salvation. The Pope, destitute and poor, will then become powerful. He will agitate the world. We shall see again Peter, Lin, Clet, Anaclet, and Clement; the humble, the ignorant; men like the early saints will change the face of the earth. If to-morrow, in the chair of Peter, came to sit a real bishop, a real Christian, I would go to him, and say: 'Do not be an old man buried alive in a golden tomb; quit your noble guards and your cardinals; quit your court and its simulacrums of power. Take my arm and come with me to beg for your bread among the nations. Covered with rags, poor, ill, dying, go on the highways, showing in yourself the image of Jesus. Say, "I am begging my bread for the condemnation of the wealthy." Go into the cities, and shout from door to door, with a sublime stupidity, "Be humble, be gentle, be poor!" Announce peace and charity to the cities, to the dens, and to the barracks. You will be disdained; the mob will throw stones at you. Policemen will drag you into prison. You shall be for the humble as for the powerful, for the poor as for the rich, a subject of laughter, an object of disgust and of pity. Your priests will dethrone you, and elevate against you an anti-pope, or will say that you are crazy. And it is necessary that they should tell the truth; it is necessary that you should be crazy; the lunatics have saved the world. Men will give to you the crown of thorns and the reed sceptre, and they will spit in your face, and it is by that sign that you will appear as Christ and true king; and it is by such means that you will establish Christian socialism, which is the kingdom of God on earth.'"

Having spoken in this way, Choulette lighted one of those long and tortuous Italian cigars, which are pierced with a straw. He drew from it several puffs of infectious vapor, then he continued, tranquilly:

"And it would be practical. You may refuse to acknowledge any quality in me except my clear view of situations. Ah, Madame Marmet, you will never know how true it is that the great works of this world were always achieved by madmen. Do you think, Madame Martin, that if Saint Francis of Assisi had been reasonable, he would have poured upon the earth, for the refreshment of peoples, the living water of charity and all the perfumes of love?"

"I do not know," replied Madame Martin; "but reasonable people have always seemed to me to be bores. I can say this to you, Monsieur Choulette."

They returned to Fiesole by the steam tramway which goes up the hill. The rain fell. Madame Marmet went to sleep and Choulette complained. All his ills came to attack him at once: the humidity in the air gave him a pain in the knee, and he could not bend his leg; his carpet-bag, lost the day before in the trip from the station to Fiesole, had not been found, and it was an irreparable disaster; a Paris review had just published one of his poems, with typographical errors as glaring as Aphrodite's shell.

He accused men and things of being hostile to him. He became puerile, absurd, odious. Madame Martin, whom Choulette and the rain saddened, thought the trip would never end. When she reached the house she found Miss Bell in the drawing-room, copying with gold ink on a leaf of parchment, in a handwriting formed after the Aldine italics, verses which she had composed in the night. At her friend's coming she raised her little face, plain but illuminated by splendid eyes.

"Darling, permit me to introduce to you the Prince Albertinelli."

The Prince possessed a certain youthful, godlike beauty, that his black beard intensified. He bowed.

"Madame, you would make one love France, if that sentiment were not already in our hearts."

The Countess and Choulette asked Miss Bell to read to them the verses she was writing. She excused herself from reciting her uncertain cadence to the French poet, whom she liked best after Francois Villon. Then she recited in her pretty, hissing, birdlike voice.

"That is very pretty," said Choulette, "and bears the mark of Italy softly veiled by the mists of Thule."

"Yes," said the Countess Martin, "that is pretty. But why, dear Vivian, did your two beautiful innocents wish to die?"

"Oh, darling, because they felt as happy as possible, and desired nothing more. It was discouraging, darling, discouraging. How is it that you do not understand that?"

"And do you think that if we live the reason is that we hope?"

"Oh, yes. We live in the hope of what to-morrow, tomorrow, king of the land of fairies, will bring in his black mantle studded with stars, flowers, and tears. Oh, bright king, To-morrow!"

BOOK 2
CHAPTER X
DECHARTRE ARRIVES IN FLORENCE

They had dressed for dinner. In the drawing-room Miss Bell was sketching monsters in imitation of Leonard. She created them, to know what they would say afterward, sure that they would speak and express rare ideas in odd rhythms, and that she would listen to them. It was in this way that she often found her inspiration.

Prince Albertinelli strummed on the piano the Sicilian 'O Lola'! His soft fingers hardly touched the keys.

Choulette, even harsher than was his habit, asked for thread and needles that he might mend his clothes. He grumbled because he had lost a needle-case which he had carried for thirty years in his pocket, and which was dear to him for the sweetness of the reminiscences and the strength of the good advice that he had received from it. He thought he had lost it in the hall devoted to historic subjects in the Pitti Palace; and he blamed for this loss the Medicis and all the Italian painters.

Looking at Miss Bell with an evil eye, he said:

"I compose verses while mending my clothes. I like to work with my hands. I sing songs to myself while sweeping my room; that is the reason why my songs have gone to the hearts of men, like the old songs of the farmers and artisans, which are even more beautiful than mine, but not more natural. I have pride enough not to want any other servant than myself. The sacristan's widow offered to repair my clothes. I would not permit her to do it. It is wrong to make others do servilely for us work which we can do ourselves with noble pride."

The Prince was nonchalantly playing his nonchalant music. Therese, who for eight days had been running to churches and museums in the company of Madame Marmet, was thinking of the annoyance which her companion caused her by discovering in the faces of the old painters resemblances to persons she knew. In the morning, at the Ricardi Palace, on the frescoes of Gozzoli, she had recognized M. Gamin, M. Lagrange, M. Schmoll, the Princess Seniavine as a page, and M. Renan on horseback. She was terrified at finding M. Renan everywhere. She led all her ideas back to her little circle of academicians and fashionable people, by an easy turn, which irritated her friend. She recalled in her soft voice the public meetings at the Institute, the lectures at the Sorbonne, the evening receptions where shone the worldly and the spiritualist philosophers. As for the women, they were all charming and irreproachable. She dined with all of them. And Therese thought: "She is too prudent. She bores me." And she thought of leaving her at Fiesole and visiting the churches alone. Employing a word that Le Menil had taught her, she said to herself:

"I will 'plant' Madame Marmet."

A lithe old man came into the parlor. His waxed moustache and his white imperial made him look like an old soldier; but his glance betrayed, under his glasses, the fine softness of eyes worn by science and voluptuousness. He was a Florentine, a friend of Miss Bell and of the Prince, Professor Arrighi, formerly adored by women, and now celebrated in Tuscany for his studies of agriculture. He pleased the Countess Martin at once. She questioned him on his methods, and on the results he obtained from them. He said that he worked with prudent energy. "The earth," he said, "is like women. The earth does not wish one to treat it with either timidity or brutality." The Ave Maria rang in all the campaniles, seeming to make of the sky an immense instrument of religious music. "Darling," said Miss Bell, "do you observe that the air of Florence is made sonorous and silvery at night by the sound of the bells?"

"It is singular," said Choulette, "we have the air of people who are waiting for something."

Vivian Bell replied that they were waiting for M. Dechartre. He was a little late; she feared he had missed the train.

Choulette approached Madame Marmet, and said, gravely "Madame Marmet, is it possible for you to look at a door — a simple, painted, wooden door like yours, I suppose, or like mine, or like this one, or like any other — without being terror-stricken at the thought of the visitor who might, at any moment, come in? The door of one's room, Madame Marmet, opens on the infinite. Have you ever thought of that? Does one ever know the true name of the man or woman, who, under a human guise, with a known face, in ordinary clothes, comes into one's house?"

He added that when he was closeted in his room he could not look at the door without feeling his hair stand on end. But Madame Marmet saw the doors of her rooms open without fear. She knew the name of every one who came to see her — charming persons.

Choulette looked at her sadly, and said, shaking his head: "Madame Marmet, those whom you call by their terrestrial names have other names which you do not know, and which are their real names."

Madame Martin asked Choulette if he thought that misfortune needed to cross the threshold in order to enter one's life.

"Misfortune is ingenious and subtle. It comes by the window, it goes through walls. It does not always show itself, but it is always there. The poor doors are innocent of the coming of that unwelcome visitor."

Choulette warned Madame Martin severely that she should not call misfortune an unwelcome visitor.

"Misfortune is our greatest master and our best friend. Misfortune teaches us the meaning of life. Madame, when you suffer, you know what you must know; you believe what you must believe; you do what you must do; you are what you must be. And you shall have joy, which pleasure expels. True joy is timid, and does not find pleasure among a multitude."

Prince Albertinelli said that Miss Bell and her French friends did not need to be unfortunate in order to be perfect, and that the doctrine of perfection reached by suffering was a barbarous cruelty, held in horror under the beautiful sky of Italy. When the conversation languished, he prudently sought again at the piano the phrases of the graceful and banal Sicilian air, fearing

418

to slip into an air of Trovatore, which was written in the same manner.

Vivian Bell questioned the monsters she had created, and complained of their absurd replies.

"At this moment," she said, "I should like to hear speak only figures on tapestries which should say tender things, ancient and precious as themselves."

And the handsome Prince, carried away by the flood of melody, sang. His voice displayed itself like a peacock's plumage, and died in spasms of "ohs" and "ahs."

The good Madame Marmet, her eyes fixed on the door, said:

"I think that Monsieur Dechartre is coming."

He came in, animated, with joy on his usually grave face.

Miss Bell welcomed him with birdlike cries.

"Monsieur Dechartre, we were impatient to see you. Monsieur Choulette was talking evil of doors — yes, of doors of houses; and he was saying also that misfortune is a very obliging old gentleman. You have lost all these beautiful things. You have made us wait very long, Monsieur Dechartre. Why?"

He apologized; he had taken only the time to go to his hotel and change his dress. He had not even gone to bow to his old friend the bronze San Marco, so imposing in his niche on the San Michele wall. He praised the poetess and saluted the Countess Martin with joy hardly concealed.

"Before quitting Paris I went to your house, where I was told you had gone to wait for spring at Fiesole, with Miss Bell. I then had the hope of finding you in this country, which I love now more than ever."

She asked him whether he had gone to Venice, and whether he had seen again at Ravenna the empresses wearing aureolas, and the phantoms that had formerly dazzled him.

No, he had not stopped anywhere.

She said nothing. Her eyes remained fixed on the corner of the wall, on the St. Paulin bell.

He said to her:

"You are looking at the Nolette."

Vivian Bell laid aside her papers and her pencils.

"You shall soon see a marvel, Monsieur Dechartre. I have found the queen of small bells. I found it at Rimini, in an old building in ruins, which is used as a warehouse. I bought it and packed it myself. I am waiting for it. You shall see. It bears a Christ on a cross, between the Virgin and Saint John, the date of 1400, and the arms of Malatesta — Monsieur Dechartre, you are not listening enough. Listen to me attentively. In 1400 Lorenzo Ghiberti, fleeing from war and the plague, took refuge at Rimini, at Paola Malatesta's house. It was he that modelled the figures of my bell. And you shall see here, next week, Ghiberti's work."

The servant announced that dinner was served.

Miss Bell apologized for serving to them Italian dishes. Her cook was a poet of Fiesole.

At table, before the fiascani enveloped with corn straw, they talked of the fifteenth century, which they loved. Prince Albertinelli praised the artists of that epoch for their universality, for the fervent love they gave to their art, and for the genius that devoured them. He talked with emphasis, in a caressing voice.

Dechartre admired them. But he admired them in another way.

"To praise in a becoming manner," he said, "those men, who worked so heartily, the praise should be modest and just. They should be placed in their workshops, in the shops where they worked as artisans. It is there that one may admire their simplicity and their genius. They were ignorant and rude. They had read little and seen little. The hills that surround Florence were the boundary of their horizon. They knew only their city, the Holy Scriptures, and some fragments of antique sculptures, studied and caressed lovingly."

"You are right," said Professor Arrighi. "They had no other care than to use the best processes. Their minds bent only on preparing varnish and mixing colors. The one who first thought of pasting a canvas on a panel, in order that the painting should not be broken when the wood was split, passed for a marvellous man. Every master had his secret formulae."

"Happy time," said Dechartre, "when nobody troubled himself about that originality for which we are so avidly seeking to-day. The apprentice tried to work like the master. He had no other ambition than to resemble him, and it was without trying to be that he was different from the others. They worked not for glory, but to live."

"They were right," said Choulette. "Nothing is better than to work for a living."

"The desire to attain fame," continued Dechartre, "did not trouble them. As they did not know the past, they did not conceive the future; and their dream did not go beyond their lives. They exercised a powerful will in working well. Being simple, they made few mistakes, and saw the truth which our intelligence conceals from us."

Choulette began to relate to Madame Marmet the incidents of a call he had made during the day on the Princess of the House of France to whom the Marquise de Rieu had given him a letter of introduction. He liked to impress upon people the fact that he, the Bohemian and vagabond, had been received by that royal Princess, at whose house neither Miss Bell nor the Countess Martin would have been admitted, and whom Prince Albertinelli prided himself on having met one day at some ceremony.

"She devotes herself," said the Prince, "to the practices of piety."

"She is admirable for her nobility, and her simplicity," said Choulette. "In her house, surrounded by her gentlemen and her ladies, she causes the most rigorous etiquette to be observed, so that her grandeur is almost a penance, and every morning she scrubs the pavement of the church. It is a village church, where the chickens roam, while the 'cure' plays briscola with the sacristan."

And Choulette, bending over the table, imitated, with his napkin, a servant scrubbing; then, raising his head, he said, gravely:

"After waiting in consecutive anterooms, I was at last permitted to kiss her hand."

And he stopped.

Madame Martin asked, impatiently:

"What did she say to you, that Princess so admirable for her nobility and her simplicity?"

"She said to me: 'Have you visited Florence? I am told that recently new and handsome shops have been opened which are lighted at night.' She said also 'We have a good chemist here. The Austrian chemists are not better. He placed on my leg, six months ago, a porous plaster which has not yet come off.' Such are the words that Maria Therese deigned to address to me. O simple grandeur! O Christian virtue! O daughter of Saint Louis! O marvellous echo of your voice, holy Elizabeth of Hungary!"

Madame Martin smiled. She thought that Choulette was mocking. But he denied the charge, indignantly, and Miss Bell said that Madame Martin was wrong. It was a fault of the French, she said, to think that people were always jesting.

Then they reverted to the subject of art, which in that country is inhaled with the air.

"As for me," said the Countess Martin, "I am not learned enough to admire Giotto and his school. What strikes me is the sensuality of that art of the fifteenth century which is said to be Christian. I have seen piety and purity only in the images of Fra Angelico, although they are very pretty. The rest, those figures of Virgins and angels, are voluptuous, caressing, and at times perversely ingenuous. What is there religious in those young Magian kings, handsome as women; in that Saint Sebastian, brilliant with youth, who seems merely the dolorous Bacchus of Christianity?"

Dechartre replied that he thought as she did, and that they must be right, she and he; since Savonarola was of the same opinion, and, finding no piety in any work of art, wished to burn them all.

"There were at Florence, in the time of the superb Manfred, who was half a Moslem, men who were said to be of the sect of

Epicurus, and who sought for arguments against the existence of God. Guido Cavalcanti disdained the ignorant folk who believed in the immortality of the soul. The following phrase by him was quoted: 'The death of man is exactly similar to that of brutes.' Later, when antique beauty was excavated from ruins, the Christian style of art seemed sad. The painters that worked in the churches and cloisters were neither devout nor chaste. Perugino was an atheist, and did not conceal it."

"Yes," said Miss Bell; "but it was said that his head was hard, and that celestial truths, could not penetrate his thick cranium. He was harsh and avaricious, and quite embedded in material interests. He thought only of buying houses."

Professor Arrighi defended Pietro Vanucci of Perugia.

"He was," he said, "an honest man. And the prior of the Gesuati of Florence was wrong to mistrust him. That monk practiced the art of manufacturing ultramarine blue by crushing stones of burned lapis-lazuli. Ultramarine was then worth its weight in gold; and the prior, who doubtless had a secret, esteemed it more precious than rubies or sapphires. He asked Pietro Vanucci to decorate the two cloisters of his convent, and he expected marvels, less from the skillfulness of the master than from the beauty of that ultramarine in the skies. During all the time that the painter worked in the cloisters at the history of Jesus Christ, the prior kept by his side and presented to him the precious powder in a bag which he never quitted. Pietro took from it, under the saintly man's eyes, the quantity he needed, and dipped his brush, loaded with color, in a cupful of water, before rubbing the wall with it. He used in that manner a great quantity of the powder. And the good father, seeing his bag getting thinner, sighed: 'Jesus! How that lime devours the ultramarine!' When the frescoes were finished, and Perugino had received from the monk the agreed price, he placed in his hand a package of blue powder: 'This is for you, father. Your ultramarine which I took with my brush fell to the bottom of my cup, whence I gathered it every day. I return it to you. Learn to trust honest people.'"

"Oh," said Therese, "there is nothing extraordinary in the fact that Perugino was avaricious yet honest. Interested people are not always the least scrupulous. There are many misers who are honest."

"Naturally, darling," said Miss Bell. "Misers do not wish to owe anything, and prodigal people can bear to have debts. They do not think of the money they have, and they think less of the money they owe. I did not say that Pietro Vanucci of Perugia was a man without property. I said that he had a hard business head and that he bought houses. I am very glad to hear that he returned the ultramarine to the prior of the Gesuati."

"Since your Pietro was rich," said Choulette, "it was his duty to return the ultramarine. The rich are morally bound to be honest; the poor are not."

At this moment, Choulette, to whom the waiter was presenting a silver bowl, extended his hands for the perfumed water. It came from a vase which Miss Bell passed to her guests, in accordance with antique usage, after meals.

"I wash my hands," he said, "of the evil that Madame Martin does or may do by her speech, or otherwise."

And he rose, awkwardly, after Miss Bell, who took the arm of Professor Arrighi.

In the drawing-room she said, while serving the coffee:

"Monsieur Choulette, why do you condemn us to the savage sadness of equality? Why, Daphnis's flute would not be melodious if it were made of seven equal reeds. You wish to destroy the beautiful harmonies between masters and servants, aristocrats and artisans. Oh, I fear you are a sad barbarian, Monsieur Choulette. You are full of pity for those who are in need, and you have no pity for divine beauty, which you exile from this world. You expel beauty, Monsieur Choulette; you repudiate her, nude and in tears. Be certain of this: she will not remain on earth when the poor little men shall all be weak, delicate, and ignorant. Believe me, to abolish the ingenious grouping which men of diverse conditions form in society, the humble with the magnificent, is to be the enemy of the poor and of the rich, is to be the enemy of the human race."

"Enemies of the human race!" replied Choulette, while stirring his coffee. "That is the phrase the harsh Roman applied to the Christians who talked of divine love to him."

Dechartre, seated near Madame Martin, questioned her on her tastes about art and beauty, sustained, led, animated her admirations, at times prompted her with caressing brusquerie, wished her to see all that he had seen, to love all that he loved.

He wished that she should go in the gardens at the first flush of spring. He contemplated her in advance on the noble terraces; he saw already the light playing on her neck and in her hair; the shadow of laurel-trees falling on her eyes. For him the land and the sky of Florence had nothing more to do than to serve as an adornment to this young woman.

He praised the simplicity with which she dressed, the characteristics of her form and of her grace, the charming frankness of the lines which every one of her movements created. He liked, he said, the animated and living, subtle, and free gowns which one sees so rarely, which one never forgets.

Although she had been much lauded, she had never heard praise which had pleased her more. She knew she dressed well, with bold and sure taste. But no man except her father had made to her on the subject the compliments of an expert. She thought that men were capable of feeling only the effect of a gown, without understanding the ingenious details of it. Some men who knew gowns disgusted her by their effeminate air. She was resigned to the appreciation of women only, and these had in their appreciation narrowness of mind, malignity, and envy. The artistic admiration of Dechartre astonished and pleased her. She received agreeably the praise he gave her, without thinking that perhaps it was too intimate and almost indiscreet.

"So you look at gowns, Monsieur Dechartre?"

No, he seldom looked at them. There were so few women well dressed, even now, when women dress as well as, and even better, than ever. He found no pleasure in seeing packages of dry-goods walk. But if a woman having rhythm and line passed before him, he blessed her.

He continued, in a tone a little more elevated:

"I can not think of a woman who takes care to deck herself every day, without meditating on the great lesson which she gives to artists. She dresses for a few hours, and the care she has taken is not lost. We must, like her, ornament life without thinking of the future. To paint, carve, or write for posterity is only the silliness of conceit."

"Monsieur Dechartre," asked Prince Albertinelli, "how do you think a mauve waist studded with silver flowers would become Miss Bell?"

"I think," said Choulette, "so little of a terrestrial future, that I have written my finest poems on cigarette paper. They vanished easily, leaving to my verses only a sort of metaphysical existence."

He had an air of negligence for which he posed. In fact, he had never lost a line of his writing. Dechartre was more sincere. He was not desirous of immortality. Miss Bell reproached him for this.

"Monsieur Dechartre, that life may be great and complete, one must put into it the past and the future. Our works of poetry and of art must be accomplished in honor of the dead and with the thought of those who are to come after us. Thus we shall participate in what has been, in what is, and in what shall be. You do not wish to be immortal, Monsieur Dechartre? Beware, for God may hear you."

Dechartre replied:

"It would be enough for me to live one moment more."

And he said good-night, promising to return the next day to escort Madame Martin to the Brancacci chapel.

An hour later, in the aesthetic room hung with tapestry, whereon citron-trees loaded with golden fruit formed a fairy forest, Therese, her head on the pillow, and her handsome bare arms folded under her head, was thinking, seeing float confusedly before her the images of her new life: Vivian Bell and her bells, her pre-Raphaelite figures, light as shadows, ladies, isolated knights, indifferent among pious scenes, a little sad, and looking to see who was coming; she thought also of the Prince Albertinelli, Professor Arrighi, Choulette, with his odd play of ideas, and Dechartre, with youthful eyes in a careworn face.

She thought he had a charming imagination, a mind richer than all those that had been revealed to her, and an attraction which she no longer tried to resist. She had always recognized his gift to please. She discovered now that he had the will to please. This idea was delightful to her; she closed her eyes to retain it. Then, suddenly, she shuddered. She had felt a deep blow struck within her in the depth of her being. She had a sudden vision of Robert, his gun under his arm, in the woods. He walked with firm and regular step in the shadowy thicket. She could not see his face, and that troubled her. She bore him no ill-will. She was not discontented with him, but with herself. Robert went straight on, without turning his head, far, and still farther, until he was only a black point in the desolate wood. She thought that perhaps she had been capricious and harsh in leaving him without a word of farewell, without even a letter. He was her lover and her only friend. She never had had another. "I do not wish him to be unfortunate because of me," she thought.

Little by little she was reassured. He loved her, doubtless; but he was not susceptible, not ingenious, happily, in tormenting himself. She said to herself:

"He is hunting and enjoying the sport. He is with his aunt, whom he admires." She calmed her fears and returned to the charming gayety of Florence. She had seen casually, at the Offices, a picture that Dechartre liked. It was a decapitated head of the Medusa, a work wherein Leonardo, the sculptor said, had expressed the minute profundity and tragic refinement of his genius. She wished to see it again, regretting that she had not seen it better at first. She extinguished her lamp and went to sleep.

She dreamed that she met in a deserted church Robert Le Menil enveloped in furs which she had never seen him wear. He was waiting for her, but a crowd of priests had separated them.

She did not know what had become of him. She had not seen his face, and that frightened her. She awoke and heard at the open window a sad, monotonous cry, and saw a humming-bird darting about in the light of early dawn. Then, without cause, she began to weep in a passion of self-pity, and with the abandon of a child.

CHAPTER XI
"THE DAWN OF FAITH AND LOVE"

She took pleasure in dressing early, with delicate and subtle taste. Her dressing-room, an aesthetic fantasy of Vivian Bell, with its coarsely varnished pottery, its tall copper pitchers, and its faience pavement, like a chess-board, resembled a fairy's kitchen. It was rustic and marvellous, and the Countess Martin could have in it the agreeable surprise of mistaking herself for a fairy. While her maid was dressing her hair, she heard Dechartre and Choulette talking under her windows. She rearranged all the work Pauline had done, and uncovered the line of her nape, which was fine and pure. She looked at herself in the glass, and went into the garden.

Dechartre was there, reciting verses of Dante, and looking at Florence: "At the hour when our mind, a greater stranger to the flesh. . ."

Near him, Choulette, seated on the balustrade of the terrace, his legs hanging, and his nose in his beard, was still at work on the figure of Misery on his stick.

Dechartre resumed the rhymes of the canticle: "At the hour when our mind, a greater stranger to the flesh; and less under the obsession of thoughts, is almost divine in its visions, ..."

She approached beside the boxwood hedge, holding a parasol and dressed in a straw-colored gown. The faint sunlight of winter enveloped her in pale gold.

Dechartre greeted her joyfully.

She said:

"You are reciting verses that I do not know. I know only Metastasio. My teacher liked only Metastasio. What is the hour when the mind has divine visions?"

"Madame, that hour is the dawn of the day. It may be also the dawn of faith and of love."

Choulette doubted that the poet meant dreams of the morning, which leave at awakening vivid and painful impressions, and which are not altogether strangers to the flesh. But Dechartre

429

had quoted these verses in the pleasure of the glorious dawn which he had seen that morning on the golden hills. He had been, for a long time, troubled about the images that one sees in sleep, and he believed that these images were not related to the object that preoccupies one the most, but, on the contrary, to ideas abandoned during the day.

Therese recalled her morning dream, the hunter lost in the thicket.

"Yes," said Dechartre, "the things we see at night are unfortunate remains of what we have neglected the day before. Dreams avenge things one has disdained. They are reproaches of abandoned friends. Hence their sadness."

She was lost in dreams for a moment, then she said:

"That is perhaps true."

Then, quickly, she asked Choulette if he had finished the portrait of Misery on his stick. Misery had now become a figure of Piety, and Choulette recognized the Virgin in it. He had even composed a quatrain which he was to write on it in spiral form — a didactic and moral quatrain. He would cease to write, except in the style of the commandments of God rendered into French verses. The four lines expressed simplicity and goodness. He consented to recite them.

Therese rested on the balustrade of the terrace and sought in the distance, in the depth of the sea of light, the peaks of Vallambrosa, almost as blue as the sky. Jacques Dechartre looked at her. It seemed to him that he saw her for the first time, such was the delicacy that he discovered in her face, which tenderness and intelligence had invested with thoughtfulness without altering its young, fresh grace. The daylight which she liked, was indulgent to her. And truly she was pretty, bathed in that light of Florence, which caresses beautiful forms and feeds noble thoughts. A fine, pink color rose to her well-rounded cheeks; her eyes, bluish-gray, laughed; and when she talked, the brilliancy of her teeth set off her lips of ardent sweetness. His look embraced her supple bust, her full hips, and the bold attitude of her waist. She held her parasol with her left hand, the other hand played with violets. Dechartre had a mania for beautiful hands. Hands presented to his eyes a physiognomy as striking as the face — a character, a soul. These hands enchanted him. They were exquisite. He adored their slender fingers, their pink nails, their palms soft and tender, traversed by lines as elegant as arabesques, and rising at the base of the fingers in harmonious mounts. He examined them with charmed attention until she closed them on the handle of her umbrella. Then, standing behind her, he looked at her again. Her bust and arms, graceful and pure in line, her beautiful form, which was like that of a living amphora, pleased him.

"Monsieur Dechartre, that black spot over there is the Boboli Gardens, is it not? I saw the gardens three years ago. There were not many flowers in them. Nevertheless, I liked their tall, sombre trees."

It astonished him that she talked, that she thought. The clear sound of her voice amazed him, as if he never had heard it.

He replied at random. He was awkward. She feigned not to notice it, but felt a deep inward joy. His low voice, which was veiled and softened, seemed to caress her. She said ordinary things:

"That view is beautiful, The weather is fine."

431

CHAPTER XII
HEARTS AWAKENED

In the morning, her head on the embroidered pillow, Therese was thinking of the walks of the day before; of the Virgins, framed with angels; of the innumerable children, painted or carved, all beautiful, all happy, who sing ingenuously the Alleluia of grace and of beauty. In the illustrious chapel of the Brancacci, before those frescoes, pale and resplendent as a divine dawn, he had talked to her of Masaccio, in language so vivid that it had seemed to her as if she had seen him, the adolescent master of the masters, his mouth half open, his eyes dark and blue, dying, enchanted. And she had liked these marvels of a morning more charming than a day. Dechartre was for her the soul of those magnificent forms, the mind of those noble things. It was by him, it was through him, that she understood art and life. She took no interest in things that did not interest him. How had this affection come to her? She had no precise remembrance of it. In the first place, when Paul Vence wished to introduce him to her, she had no desire to know him, no presentiment that he would please her. She recalled elegant bronze statuettes, fine waxworks signed with his name, that she had remarked at the Champ de Mars salon or at Durand-Ruel's. But she did not imagine that he could be agreeable to her, or more seductive than many artists and lovers of art at whom she laughed with her friends. When she saw him, he pleased her; she had a desire to attract him, to see him often. The night he dined at her house she realized that she had for him a noble and elevating affection. But soon after he irritated her a little; it made her impatient to see him closeted within himself and too little preoccupied by her. She would have liked to disturb him. She was in that state of impatience when she met him one evening, in front of the grille of the Musee des Religions, and he talked to her of Ravenna and of the Empress seated on a gold chair in her tomb. She had found him serious and charming, his voice warm, his eyes soft in the shadow of the night, but too much a stranger, too far from her, too unknown. She had felt a

432

sort of uneasiness, and she did not know, when she walked along the boxwood bordering the terrace, whether she desired to see him every day or never to see him again.

Since then, at Florence, her only pleasure was to feel that he was near her, to hear him. He made life for her charming, diverse, animated, new. He revealed to her delicate joys and a delightful sadness; he awakened in her a voluptuousness which had been always dormant. Now she was determined never to give him up. But how? She foresaw difficulties; her lucid mind and her temperament presented them all to her. For a moment she tried to deceive herself; she reflected that perhaps he, a dreamer, exalted, lost in his studies of art, might remain assiduous without being exacting. But she did not wish to reassure herself with that idea. If Dechartre were not a lover, he lost all his charm. She did not dare to think of the future. She lived in the present, happy, anxious, and closing her eyes.

She was dreaming thus, in the shade traversed by arrows of light, when Pauline brought to her some letters with the morning tea. On an envelope marked with the monogram of the Rue Royale Club she recognized the handwriting of Le Menil. She had expected that letter. She was only astonished that what was sure to come had come, as in her childhood, when the infallible clock struck the hour of her piano lesson.

In his letter Robert made reasonable reproaches. Why did she go without saying anything, without leaving a word of farewell? Since his return to Paris he had expected every morning a letter which had not come. He was happier the year before, when he had received in the morning, two or three times a week, letters so gentle and so well written that he regretted not being able to print them. Anxious, he had gone to her house.

"I was astounded to hear of your departure. Your husband received me. He said that, yielding to his advice, you had gone to finish the winter at Florence with Miss Bell. He said that for some time you had looked pale and thin. He thought a change of air would do you good. You had not wished to go, but, as you suffered more and more, he succeeded in persuading you.

"I had not noticed that you were thin. It seemed to me, on the contrary, that your health was good. And then Florence is not a good winter resort. I cannot understand your departure. I am much tormented by it. Reassure me at once, I pray you.

"Do you think it is agreeable for me to get news of you from your husband and to receive his confidences? He is sorry you are not here; it annoys him that the obligations of public life compel him to remain in Paris. I heard at the club that he had chances to become a minister. This astonishes me, because ministers are not usually chosen among fashionable people."

Then he related hunting tales to her. He had brought for her three fox-skins, one of which was very beautiful; the skin of a brave animal which he had pulled by the tail, and which had bitten his hand.

In Paris he was worried. His cousin had been presented at the club. He feared he might be blackballed. His candidacy had been posted. Under these conditions he did not dare advise him to withdraw; it would be taking too great a responsibility. If he were blackballed it would be very disagreeable. He finished by praying her to write and to return soon.

Having read this letter, she tore it up gently, threw it in the fire, and calmly watched it burn.

Doubtless, he was right. He had said what he had to say; he had complained, as it was his duty to complain. What could she answer? Should she continue her quarrel? The subject of it had become so indifferent to her that it needed reflection to recall it. Oh, no; she had no desire to be tormented. She felt, on the contrary, very gentle toward him! Seeing that he loved her with confidence, in stubborn tranquility, she became sad and frightened. He had not changed. He was the same man he had been before. She was not the same woman. They were separated now by imperceptible yet strong influences, like essences in the air that make one live or die. When her maid came to dress her, she had not begun to write an answer.

Anxious, she thought: "He trusts me. He suspects nothing." This made her more impatient than anything. It irritated her to think that there were simple people who doubt neither themselves nor others.

She went into the parlor, where she found Vivian Bell writing. The latter said:

"Do you wish to know, darling, what I was doing while waiting for you? Nothing and everything. Verses. Oh, darling, poetry must be our souls naturally expressed."

Therese kissed Miss Bell, rested her head on her friend's shoulder, and said:

"May I look?"

"Look if you wish, dear. They are verses made on the model of the popular songs of your country."

"Is it a symbol, Vivian? Explain it to me."

"Oh, darling, why explain, why? A poetic image must have several meanings. The one that you find is the real one. But there is a very clear meaning in them, my love; that is, that one should not lightly disengage one's self from what one has taken into the heart."

The horses were harnessed. They went, as had been agreed, to visit the Albertinelli gallery. The Prince was waiting for them, and Dechartre was to meet them in the palace. On the way, while the carriage rolled along the wide highway, Vivian Bell talked with her usual transcendentalism. As they were descending among houses pink and white, gardens and terraces ornamented with statues and fountains, she showed to her friend the villa, hidden under bluish pines, where the ladies and the cavaliers of the Decameron took refuge from the plague that ravaged Florence, and diverted one another with tales frivolous, facetious, or tragic. Then she confessed the thought which had come to her the day before.

"You had gone, darling, to Carmine with Monsieur Dechartre, and you had left at Fiesole Madame Marmet, who is an agreeable person, a moderate and polished woman. She knows many anecdotes about persons of distinction who live in Paris. And when she tells them, she does as my cook Pompaloni does when he serves eggs: he does not put salt in them, but he puts the salt-cellar next to them. Madame Marmet's tongue is very sweet, but the salt is near it, in her eyes. Her conversation is like Pompaloni's dish, my love — each one seasons to his taste. Oh, I like Madame Marmet a great deal. Yesterday, after you had gone, I found her alone and sad in a corner of the drawing-room. She was thinking mournfully of her husband. I said to her: 'Do you wish me to think of your husband, too? I will think of him with you. I have been told that he was a learned man, a member of the Royal Society of Paris. Madame Marmet, talk to me of him.' She replied that he had devoted himself to the Etruscans, and that he had given to them his entire life. Oh, darling, I cherished at once the memory of that Monsieur Marmet, who lived for the Etruscans. And then a good idea came to me. I said to Madame Marmet, 'We have at Fiesole, in the Pretorio Palace, a modest little Etruscan museum. Come and visit it with me. Will you?' She replied it was what she most desired to see in Italy. We went to the Pretorio Palace; we saw a lioness and a great many little bronze figures, grotesque, very fat or very thin. The Etruscans were a seriously gay people. They made bronze caricatures. But the monkeys — some afflicted with big stomachs, others astonished to show their bones — Madame Marmet looked at them with reluctant admiration. She contemplated them like — there is a beautiful French word that escapes me — like the monuments and the trophies of Monsieur Marmet."

Madame Martin smiled. But she was restless. She thought the sky dull, the streets ugly, the passers-by common.

"Oh, darling, the Prince will be very glad to receive you in his palace."

"I do not think so."

"Why, darling, why?"

"Because I do not please him much."

Vivian Bell declared that the Prince, on the contrary, was a great admirer of the Countess Martin.

The horses stopped before the Albertinelli palace. On the sombre facade were sealed those bronze rings which formerly, on festival nights, held rosin torches. These bronze rings mark, in

Florence, the palaces of the most illustrious families. The palace had an air of lofty pride. The Prince hastened to meet them, and led them through the empty salons into the gallery. He, apologized for showing canvases which perhaps had not an attractive aspect. The gallery had been formed by Cardinal Giulio Albertinelli at a time when the taste for Guido and Caraccio, now fallen, had predominated. His ancestor had taken pleasure in gathering the works of the school of Bologna. But he would show to Madame Martin several paintings which had not displeased Miss Bell, among others a Mantegna.

The Countess Martin recognized at once a banal and doubtful collection; she felt bored among the multitude of little Parrocels, showing in the darkness a bit of armor and a white horse.

A valet presented a card.

The Prince read aloud the name of Jacques Dechartre. At that moment he was turning his back on the two visitors. His face wore the expression of cruel displeasure one finds on the marble busts of Roman emperors. Dechartre was on the staircase.

The Prince went toward him with a languid smile. He was no longer Nero, but Antinous.

"I invited Monsieur Dechartre to come to the Albertinelli palace," said Miss Bell. "I knew it would please you. He wished to see your gallery."

And it is true that Dechartre had wished to be there with Madame Martin. Now all four walked among the Guidos and the Albanos.

Miss Bell babbled to the Prince — her usual prattle about those old men and those Virgins whose blue mantles were agitated by an immovable tempest. Dechartre, pale, enervated, approached Therese, and said to her, in a low tone:

"This gallery is a warehouse where picture dealers of the entire world hang the things they can not sell. And the Prince sells here things that Jews could not sell."

He led her to a Holy Family exhibited on an easel draped with green velvet, and bearing on the border the name of Michael-Angelo.

"I have seen that Holy Family in the shops of picture-dealers of London, of Basle, and of Paris. As they could not get the twenty-five louis that it is worth, they have commissioned the last of the Albertinellis to sell it for fifty thousand francs."

The Prince, divining what they were saying, approached them gracefully.

"There is a copy of this picture almost everywhere. I do not affirm that this is the original. But it has always been in the family, and old inventories attribute it to Michael-Angelo. That is all I can say about it."

And the Prince turned toward Miss Bell, who was trying to find pictures by the pre-Raphaelites.

Dechartre felt uneasy. Since the day before he had thought of Therese. He had all night dreamed and yearned over her image. He saw her again, delightful, but in another manner, and even more desirable than he had imagined in his insomnia; less visionary, of a more vivid piquancy, and also of a mind more mysteriously impenetrable. She was sad; she seemed cold and indifferent. He said to himself that he was nothing to her; that he was becoming importunate and ridiculous. This irritated him. He murmured bitterly in her ear: "I have reflected. I did not wish to come. Why did I come?" She understood at once what he meant, that he feared her now, and that he was impatient, timid, and awkward. It pleased her that he was thus, and she was grateful to him for the trouble and the desires he inspired in her. Her heart throbbed faster. But, affecting to understand that he regretted having disturbed himself to come and look at bad paintings, she replied that in truth this gallery was not interesting. Already, under the terror of displeasing her, he felt reassured, and believed that, really indifferent, she had not perceived the accent nor the significance of what he had said. He said "No, nothing interesting." The Prince, who had invited the two visitors to breakfast, asked their friend to remain with them. Dechartre

438

excused himself. He was about to depart when, in the large empty salon, he found himself alone with Madame Martin. He had had the idea of running away from her. He had no other wish now than to see her again. He recalled to her that she was the next morning to visit the Bargello. "You have permitted me to accompany you." She asked him if he had not found her moody and tiresome. Oh, no; he had not thought her tiresome, but he feared she was sad.

"Alas," he added, "your sadness, your joys, I have not the right to know them." She turned toward him a glance almost harsh. "You do not think that I shall take you for a confidante, do you?" And she walked away brusquely.

CHAPTER XIII
"YOU MUST TAKE ME WITH MY OWN SOUL!"

After dinner, in the salon of the bells, under the lamps from which the great shades permitted only an obscure light to filter, good Madame Marmet was warming herself by the hearth, with a white cat on her knees. The evening was cool. Madame Martin, her eyes reminiscent of the golden light, the violet peaks, and the ancient trees of Florence, smiled with happy fatigue. She had gone with Miss Bell, Dechartre, and Madame Marmet to the Chartrist convent of Ema. And now, in the intoxication of her visions, she forgot the care of the day before, the importunate letters, the distant reproaches, and thought of nothing in the world but cloisters chiseled and painted, villages with red roofs, and roads where she saw the first blush of spring. Dechartre had modelled for Miss Bell a waxen figure of Beatrice. Vivian was painting angels. Softly bent over her, Prince Albertinelli caressed his beard and threw around him glances that appeared to seek admiration.

Replying to a reflection of Vivian Bell on marriage and love:

"A woman must choose," he said. "With a man whom women love her heart is not quiet. With a man whom the women do not love she is not happy."

"Darling," asked Miss Bell, "what would you wish for a friend dear to you?"

"I should wish, Vivian, that my friend were happy. I should wish also that she were quiet. She should be quiet in hatred of treason, humiliating suspicions, and mistrust."

"But, darling, since the Prince has said that a woman can not have at the same time happiness and security, tell me what your friend should choose."

"One never chooses, Vivian; one never chooses. Do not make me say what I think of marriage."

At this moment Choulette appeared, wearing the magnificent air of those beggars of whom small towns are proud. He had played briscola with peasants in a coffeehouse of Fiesole.

"Here is Monsieur Choulette," said Miss Bell. "He will teach what we are to think of marriage. I am inclined to listen to him as to an oracle. He does not see the things that we see, and he sees things that we do not see. Monsieur Choulette, what do you think of marriage?"

He took a seat and lifted in the air a Socratic finger:

"Are you speaking, Mademoiselle, of the solemn union between man and woman? In this sense, marriage is a sacrament. But sometimes, alas! it is almost a sacrilege. As for civil marriage, it is a formality. The importance given to it in our society is an idiotic thing which would have made the women of other times laugh. We owe this prejudice, like many others, to the bourgeois, to the mad performances of a lot of financiers which have been called the Revolution, and which seem admirable to those that have profited by it. Civil marriage is, in reality, only registry, like many others which the State exacts in order to be sure of the condition of persons: in every well organized state everybody must be indexed. Morally, this registry in a big ledger has not even the virtue of inducing a wife to take a lover. Who ever thinks of betraying an oath taken before a mayor? In order to find joy in adultery, one must be pious."

"But, Monsieur," said Therese, "we were married at the church."

Then, with an accent of sincerity:

"I can not understand how a man ever makes up his mind to marry; nor how a woman, after she has reached an age when she knows what she is doing, can commit that folly."

The Prince looked at her with distrust. He was clever, but he was incapable of conceiving that one might talk without an object, disinterestedly, and to express general ideas. He imagined that Countess Martin-Belleme was suggesting to him projects that she wished him to consider. And as he was thinking of defending himself and also avenging himself, he made velvet eyes at her and talked with tender gallantry:

"You display, Madame, the pride of the beautiful and intelligent French women whom subjection irritates. French women love liberty, and none of them is as worthy of liberty as you. I have lived in France a little. I have known and admired the elegant society of Paris, the salons, the festivals, the conversations, the plays. But in our mountains, under our olive-trees, we become rustic again. We assume golden-age manners, and marriage is for us an idyll full of freshness."

Vivian Bell examined the statuette which Dechartre had left on the table.

"Oh! it was thus that Beatrice looked, I am sure. And do you know, Monsieur Dechartre, there are wicked men who say that Beatrice never existed?"

Choulette declared he wished to be counted among those wicked men. He did not believe that Beatrice had any more reality than other ladies through whom ancient poets who sang of love represented some scholastic idea, ridiculously subtle.

Impatient at praise which was not destined for himself, jealous of Dante as of the universe, a refined man of letters, Choulette continued:

"I suspect that the little sister of the angels never lived, except in the imagination of the poet. It seems a pure allegory, or, rather, an exercise in arithmetic or a theme of astrology. Dante, who was a good doctor of Bologna and had many moons in his head, under his pointed cap — Dante believed in the virtue of numbers. That inflamed mathematician dreamed of figures, and his Beatrice is the flower of arithmetic, that is all."

And he lighted his pipe.

Vivian Bell exclaimed:

"Oh, do not talk in that way, Monsieur Choulette. You grieve me much, and if our friend Monsieur Gebhart heard you, he would not be pleased with you. To punish you, Prince Albertinelli will read to you the canticle in which Beatrice explains the spots on the moon. Take the Divine Comedy, Eusebio. It is the white book which you see on the table. Open it and read it."

During the Prince's reading, Dechartre, seated on the couch near Countess Martin, talked of Dante with enthusiasm as the best sculptor among the poets. He recalled to Therese the painting they had seen together two days before, on the door of the Servi, a fresco almost obliterated, where one hardly divined the presence of the poet wearing a laurel wreath, Florence, and the seven circles. This was enough to exalt the artist. But she had distinguished nothing, she had not been moved. And then she confessed that Dante did not attract her. Dechartre, accustomed to her sharing all his ideas of art and poetry, felt astonishment and some discontent. He said, aloud:

"There are many grand and strong things which you do not feel."

Miss Bell, lifting her head, asked what were these things that "darling" did not feel; and when she learned that it was the genius of Dante, she exclaimed, in mock anger:

"Oh, do you not honor the father, the master worthy of all praise, the god? I do not love you any more, darling. I detest you."

And, as a reproach to Choulette and to the Countess Martin, she recalled the piety of that citizen of Florence who took from the altar the candles that had been lighted in honor of Christ, and placed them before the bust of Dante.

The Prince resumed his interrupted reading. Dechartre persisted in trying to make Therese admire what she did not know. Certainly he would have easily sacrificed Dante and all the poets of the universe for her. But near him, tranquil, and an object of desire, she irritated him, almost without his realizing it, by the charm of her laughing beauty. He persisted in imposing on her his ideas, his artistic passions, even his fantasy, and his capriciousness. He insisted in a low tone, in phrases concise and quarrelsome. She said:

"Oh, how violent you are!"

Then he bent to her ear, and in an ardent voice, which he tried to soften:

"You must take me with my own soul!"

Therese felt a shiver of fear mingled with joy.

CHAPTER XIV
THE AVOWAL

She next day she said to herself that she would reply to Robert. It was raining. She listened languidly to the drops falling on the terrace. Vivian Bell, careful and refined, had placed on the table artistic stationery, sheets imitating the vellum of missals, others of pale violet powdered with silver dust; celluloid pens, white and light, which one had to manage like brushes; an iris ink which, on a page, spread a mist of azure and gold. Therese did not like such delicacy. It seemed to her not appropriate for letters which she wished to make simple and modest. When she saw that the name of "friend," given to Robert on the first line, placed on the silvery paper, tinted itself like mother-of-pearl, a half smile came to her lips. The first phrases were hard to write. She hurried the rest, said a great deal of Vivian Bell and of Prince Albertinelli, a little of Choulette, and that she had seen Dechartre at Florence. She praised some pictures of the museums, but without discrimination, and only to fill the pages. She knew that Robert had no appreciation of painting; that he admired nothing except a little cuirassier by Detaille, bought at Goupil's.

She saw again in her mind this cuirassier, which he had shown to her one day, with pride, in his bedroom, near the mirror, under family portraits. All this, at a distance, seemed to her petty and tiresome. She finished her letter with words of friendship, the sweetness of which was not feigned. Truly, she had never felt more peaceful and gentle toward her lover. In four pages she had said little and explained less. She announced only that she should stay a month in Florence, the air of which did her good. Then she wrote to her father, to her husband, and to Princess Seniavine. She went down the stairway with the letters in her hand. In the hall she threw three of them on the silver tray destined to receive papers for the post-office. Mistrusting Madame Marmet, she slipped into her pocket the letter to Le Menil, counting on chance to throw it into a post-box.

Almost at the same time Dechartre came to accompany the three friends in a walk through the city. As he was waiting he saw the letters on the tray.

Without believing that characters could be divined through penmanship, he was susceptible to the form of letters as to elegance of drawing. The writing of Therese charmed him, and he liked its openness, the bold and simple turn of its lines. He looked at the addresses without reading them, with an artist's admiration.

They visited, that morning, Santa Maria Novella, where the Countess Martin had already gone with Madame Marmet. But Miss Bell had reproached them for not observing the beautiful Ginevra of Benci on a fresco of the choir. "You must visit that figure of the morning in a morning light," said Vivian. While the poetess and Therese were talking together, Dechartre listened patiently to Madame Marmet's conversation, filled with anecdotes, wherein academicians dined with elegant women, and shared the anxiety of that lady, much preoccupied for several days by the necessity to buy a tulle veil. She could find none to her taste in the shops of Florence.

As they came out of the church they passed the cobbler's shop. The good man was mending rustic shoes. Madame Martin asked the old man whether he was well, whether he had enough work for a living, whether he was happy. To all these questions he replied with the charming affirmative of Italy, the musical si, which sounded melodious even in his toothless mouth. She made him tell his sparrow's story. The poor bird had once dipped its leg in burning wax.

"I have made for my little companion a wooden leg out of a match, and he hops upon my shoulder as formerly," said the cobbler.

"It is this good old man," said Miss Bell, "who teaches wisdom to Monsieur Choulette. There was at Athens a cobbler named Simon, who wrote books on philosophy, and who was the friend of Socrates. I have always thought that Monsieur Choulette resembled Socrates."

Therese asked the cobbler to tell his name and his history. His name was Serafino Stoppini, and he was a native of Stia. He was old. He had had much trouble in his life.

He lifted his spectacles to his forehead, uncovering blue eyes, very soft, and almost extinguished under their red lids.

"I have had a wife and children; I have none now. I have known things which I know no more."

Miss Bell and Madame Marmet went to look for a veil.

"He has nothing in the world," thought Therese, "but his tools, a handful of nails, the tub wherein he dips his leather, and a pot of basilic, yet he is happy."

She said to him:

"This plant is fragrant, and it will soon be in bloom."

He replied:

"If the poor little plant comes into bloom it will die."

Therese, when she left him, placed a coin on the table.

Dechartre was near her. Gravely, almost severely, he said to her:

"You know . . . "

She looked at him and waited.

He finished his phrase:

" . . . that I love you?"

She continued to fix on him, silently, the gaze of her clear eyes, the lids of which were trembling. Then she made a motion with her head that meant Yes. And, without his trying to stop her, she rejoined Miss Bell and Madame Marmet, who were waiting for her at the corner.

CHAPTER XV
THE MYSTERIOUS LETTER

Therese, after quitting Dechartre, took breakfast with her friend and Madame Marmet at the house of an old Florentine lady whom Victor Emmanuel had loved when he was Duke of Savoy. For thirty years she had not once gone out of her palace on the Arno, where, she painted, and wearing a wig, she played the guitar in her spacious white salon. She received the best society of Florence, and Miss Bell often called on her. At table this recluse, eighty-seven years of age, questioned the Countess Martin on the fashionable world of Paris, whose movement was familiar to her through the journals. Solitary, she retained respect and a sort of devotion for the world of pleasure.

As they came out of the palazzo, in order to avoid the wind which was blowing on the river, Miss Bell led her friends into the old streets with black stone houses and a view of the distant horizon, where, in the pure air, stands a hill with three slender trees. They walked; and Vivian showed to her friend, on facades where red rags were hanging, some marble masterpiece — a Virgin, a lily, a St. Catherine. They walked through these alleys of the antique city to the church of Or San Michele, where it had been agreed that Dechartre should meet them. Therese was thinking of him now with deepest interest. Madame Marmet was thinking of buying a veil; she hoped to find one on the Corso. This affair recalled to her M. Lagrange, who, at his regular lecture one day, took from his pocket a veil with gold dots and wiped his forehead with it, thinking it was his handkerchief. The audience was astonished, and whispered to one another. It was a veil that had been confided to him the day before by his niece, Mademoiselle Jeanne Michot, whom he had accompanied to the theatre, and Madame Marmet explained how, finding it in the pocket of his overcoat, he had taken it to return it to his niece.

At Lagrange's name, Therese recalled the flaming comet announced by the savant, and said to herself, with mocking sadness, that it was time for that comet to put an end to the world and take her out of her trouble. But above the walls of the old church she saw the sky, which, cleared of clouds by the wind from the sea, shone pale blue and cold. Miss Bell showed to her one of the bronze statues which, in their chiseled niches, ornament the facade of the church.

"See, darling, how young and proud is Saint George. Saint George was formerly the cavalier about whom young girls dreamed."

But "darling" said that he looked precise, tiresome, and stubborn. At this moment she recalled suddenly the letter that was still in her pocket.

"Ah! here comes Monsieur Dechartre," said the good Madame Marmet.

He had looked for them in the church, before the tabernacle. He should have recalled the irresistible attraction which Donatello's St. George held for Miss Bell. He too admired that famous figure. But he retained a particular friendship for St. Mark, rustic and frank, whom they could see in his niche at the left.

When Therese approached the statue which he was pointing out to her, she saw a post-box against the wall of the narrow street opposite the saint. Dechartre, placed at the most convenient point of view, talked of his St. Mark with abundant friendship.

"It is to him I make my first visit when I come to Florence. I failed to do this only once. He will forgive me; he is an excellent man. He is not appreciated by the crowd, and does not attract attention. I take pleasure in his society, however. He is vivid. I understand that Donatello, after giving a soul to him, exclaimed: 'Mark, why do you not speak?'"

Madame Marmet, tired of admiring St. Mark, and feeling on her face the burning wind, dragged Miss Bell toward Calzaioli Street in search of a veil.

Therese and Dechartre remained.

"I like him," continued the sculptor; "I like Saint Mark because I feel in him, much more than in the Saint George, the hand and mind of Donatello, who was a good workman. I like him even more to-day, because he recalls to me, in his venerable and touching candor, the old cobbler to whom you were speaking so kindly this morning."

"Ah," she said, "I have forgotten his name. When we talk with Monsieur Choulette we call him Quentin Matsys, because he resembles the old men of that painter."

As they were turning the corner of the church to see the facade, she found herself before the post-box, which was so dusty and rusty that it seemed as if the postman never came near it. She put her letter in it under the ingenuous gaze of St. Mark.

Dechartre saw her, and felt as if a heavy blow had been struck at his heart. He tried to speak, to smile; but the gloved hand which had dropped the letter remained before his eyes. He recalled having seen in the morning Therese's letters on the hall tray. Why had she not put that one with the others? The reason was not hard to guess. He remained immovable, dreamy, and gazed without seeing. He tried to be reassured; perhaps it was an insignificant letter which she was trying to hide from the tiresome curiosity of Madame Marmet.

"Monsieur Dechartre, it is time to rejoin our friends at the dressmaker's."

Perhaps it was a letter to Madame Schmoll, who was not a friend of Madame Marmet, but immediately he realized that this idea was foolish.

All was clear. She had a lover. She was writing to him. Perhaps she was saying to him: "I saw Dechartre to-day; the poor fellow is deeply in love with me." But whether she wrote that or something else, she had a lover. He had not thought of that. To know that she belonged to another made him suffer profoundly. And that hand, that little hand dropping the letter, remained in his eyes and made them burn.

She did not know why he had become suddenly dumb and sombre. When she saw him throw an anxious glance back at the post-box, she guessed the reason. She thought it odd that he should be jealous without having the right to be jealous; but this did not displease her.

When they reached the Corso, they saw Miss Bell and Madame Marmet coming out of the dressmaker's shop.

Dechartre said to Therese, in an imperious and supplicating voice:

"I must speak to you. I must see you alone tomorrow; meet me at six o'clock at the Lungarno Acciaoli."

She made no reply.

CHAPTER XVI
"TO-MORROW?"

When, in her Carmelite mantle, she came to the Lungarno Acciaoli, at about half-past six, Dechartre greeted her with a humble look that moved her. The setting sun made the Arno purple. They remained silent for a moment. While they were walking past the monotonous line of palaces to the old bridge, she was the first to speak.

"You see, I have come. I thought I ought to come. I do not think I am altogether innocent of what has happened. I know: I have done what was my fate in order that you should be to me what you are now. My attitude has put thoughts into your head which you would not have had otherwise."

He looked as if he did not understand. She continued:

"I was selfish, I was imprudent. You were agreeable to me; I liked your wit; I could not get along without you. I have done what I could to attract you, to retain you. I was a coquette — not coldly, nor perfidiously, but a coquette."

He shook his head, denying that he ever had seen a sign of this.

"Yes, I was a coquette. Yet it was not my habit. But I was a coquette with you. I do not say that you have tried to take advantage of it, as you had the right to do, nor that you are vain about it. I have not remarked vanity in you. It may be possible that you had not noticed. Superior men sometimes lack cleverness. But I know very well that I was not as I should have been, and I beg your pardon. That is the reason why I came. Let us be good friends, since there is yet time."

He repeated, with sombre softness, that he loved her. The first hours of that love had been easy and delightful. He had only desired to see her, and to see her again. But soon she had troubled him. The evil had come suddenly and violently one day on the terrace of Fiesole. And now he had not the courage to suffer and say nothing. He had not come with a fixed design. If he spoke of his passion he spoke by force and in spite of himself; in the

451

strong necessity of talking of her to herself, since she was for him the only being in the world. His life was no longer in himself, it was in her. She should know it, then, that he was in love with her, not with vague tenderness, but with cruel ardor. Alas! his imagination was exact and precise. He saw her continually, and she tortured him.

And then it seemed to him that they might have joys which should make life worth living. Their existence might be a work of art, beautiful and hidden. They would think, comprehend, and feel together. It would be a marvellous world of emotions and ideas.

"We could make of life a delightful garden."

She feigned to think that the dream was innocent.

"You know very well that I am susceptible to the charm of your mind. It has become a necessity to see you and hear you. I have allowed this to be only too plain to you. Count upon my friendship and do not torment yourself." She extended her hand to him. He did not take it, but replied, brusquely:

"I do not desire your friendship. I will not have it. I must have you entirely or never see you again. You know that very well. Why do you extend your hand to me with derisive phrases? Whether you wished it or not, you have made me desperately in love with you. You have become my evil, my suffering, my torture, and you ask me to be an agreeable friend. Now you are coquettish and cruel. If you can not love me, let me go; I will go, I do not know where, to forget and hate you. For I have against you a latent feeling of hatred and anger. Oh, I love you, I love you!"

She believed what he was saying, feared that he might go, and feared the sadness of living without him. She replied:

"I found you in my path. I do not wish to lose you. No, I do not wish to lose you."

Timid yet violent, he stammered; the words were stifled in his throat. Twilight descended from the far-off mountains, and the last reflections of the sun became pallid in the east. She said:

"If you knew my life, if you had seen how empty it was before I knew you, you would know what you are to me, and would not think of abandoning me."

But, with the tranquil tone of her voice and with the rustle of her skirts on the pavement, she irritated him.

He told her how he suffered. He knew now the divine malady of love.

"The grace of your thoughts, your magnificent courage, your superb pride, I inhale them like a perfume. It seems to me when you speak that your mind is floating on your lips. Your mind is for me only the odor of your beauty. I have retained the instincts of a primitive man; you have reawakened them. I feel that I love you with savage simplicity."

She looked at him softly and said nothing. They saw the lights of evening, and heard lugubrious songs coming toward them. And then, like spectres chased by the wind, appeared the black penitents. The crucifix was before them. They were Brothers of Mercy, holding torches, singing psalms on the way to the cemetery. In accordance with the Italian custom, the cortege marched quickly. The crosses, the coffin, the banners, seemed to leap on the deserted quay. Jacques and Therese stood against the wall in order that the funeral train might pass.

The black avalanche had disappeared. There were women weeping behind the coffin carried by the black phantoms, who wore heavy shoes.

Therese sighed:

"What will be the use of having tormented ourselves in this world?"

He looked as if he had not heard, and said:

"Before I knew you I was not unhappy. I liked life. I was retained in it by dreams. I liked forms, and the mind in forms, the appearances that caress and flatter. I had the joy of seeing and of dreaming. I enjoyed everything and depended upon nothing. My desires, abundant and light, I gratified without fatigue. I was interested in everything and wished for nothing. One suffers only through the will. Without knowing it, I was happy. Oh, it was not much, it was only enough to live. Now I have no joy in life. My pleasures, the interest that I took in the images of life and of art, the vivid amusement of creating with my hands the figures of my dreams — you have made me lose everything and have not left me even regret. I do not want my liberty and tranquility again. It seems to me that before I knew you I did not live; and now that I feel that I am living, I can not live either far from you or near you. I am more wretched than the beggars we saw on the road to Ema. They had air to breathe, and I can breathe only you, whom I have not. Yet I am glad to have known you. That alone counts in my existence. A moment ago I thought I hated you. I was wrong; I adore you, and I bless you for the harm you have done me. I love all that comes to me from you."

They were nearing the black trees at the entrance to San Niccola bridge. On the other side of the river the vague fields displayed their sadness, intensified by night. Seeing that he was calm and full of a soft languor, she thought that his love, all imagination, had fled in words, and that his desires had become only a reverie. She had not expected so prompt a resignation. It almost disappointed her to escape the danger she had feared.

She extended her hand to him, more boldly this time than before.

"Then, let us be friends. It is late. Let us return. Take me to my carriage. I shall be what I have been to you, an excellent friend. You have not displeased me."

But he led her to the fields, in the growing solitude of the shore.

"No, I will not let you go without having told you what I wish to say. But I know no longer how to speak; I can not find the words. I love you. I wish to know that you are mine. I swear to you that I will not live another night in the horror of doubting it."

He pressed her in his arms; and seeking the light of her eyes through the obscurity of her veil, said "You must love me. I desire you to love me, and it is your fault, for you have desired it too. Say that you are mine. Say it."

Having gently disengaged herself, she replied, faintly and slowly "I can not! I can not! You see I am acting frankly with you. I said to you a moment ago that you had not displeased me. But I can not do as you wish."

And recalling to her thought the absent one who was waiting for her, she repeated: "I can not!" Bending over her he anxiously questioned her eyes, the double stars that trembled and veiled themselves. "Why? You love me, I feel it, I see it. You love me. Why will you do me this wrong?"

He drew her to him, wishing to lay his soul, with his lips, on her veiled lips. She escaped him swiftly, saying: "I can not. Do not ask more. I can not be yours."

His lips trembled, his face was convulsed. He exclaimed "You have a lover, and you love him. Why do you mock me?"

"I swear to you I have no desire to mock you, and that if I loved any one in the world it would be you." But he was not listening to her.

"Leave me, leave me!" And he ran toward the dark fields. The Arno formed lagoons, upon which the moon, half veiled, shone fitfully. He walked through the water and the mud, with a step rapid, blind, like that of one intoxicated. She took fright and shouted. She called him. But he did not turn his head and made no answer. He fled with alarming recklessness. She ran after him. Her feet were hurt by the stones, and her skirt was heavy with water, but soon she overtook him.

"What were you about to do?"

He looked at her, and saw her fright in her eyes. "Do not be afraid," he said. "I did not see where I was going. I assure you I did not intend to kill myself. I am desperate, but I am calm. I was only trying to escape from you. I beg your pardon. But I could not see you any longer. Leave me, I pray you. Farewell!"

She replied, agitated and trembling: "Come! We shall do what we can."

He remained sombre and made no reply. She repeated "Come!"

She took his arm. The living warmth of her hand animated him. He said:

"Do you wish it?"

"I can not leave you."

"You promise?"

"I must."

And, in her anxiety and anguish, she almost smiled, in thinking that he had succeeded so quickly by his folly.

"To-morrow?" said he, inquiringly.

She replied quickly, with a defensive instinct:

"Oh, no; not to-morrow!"

"You do not love me; you regret that you have promised."

"No, I do not regret, but — "

He implored, he supplicated her. She looked at him for a moment, turned her head, hesitated, and said, in a low tone:

"Saturday."

CHAPTER XVII
MISS BELL ASKS A QUESTION

After dinner, Miss Bell was sketching in the drawing-room. She was tracing, on canvas, profiles of bearded Etruscans for a cushion which Madame Marmet was to embroider. Prince Albertinelli was selecting the wool with an almost feminine knowledge of shades. It was late when Choulette, having, as was his habit, played briscola with the cook at the caterer's, appeared, as joyful as if he possessed the mind of a god. He took a seat on a sofa, beside Madame Martin, and looked at her tenderly. Voluptuousness shone in his green eyes. He enveloped her, while talking to her, with poetic and picturesque phrases. It was like the sketch of a love song that he was improvising for her. In oddly involved sentences, he told her of the charm that she exhaled.

"He, too!" said she to herself.

She amused herself by teasing him. She asked whether he had not found in Florence, in the low quarters, one of the kind of women whom he liked to visit. His preferences were known. He could deny it as much as he wished: no one was ignorant of the door where he had found the cordon of his Third Order. His friends had met him on the boulevard. His taste for unfortunate women was evident in his most beautiful poems.

"Oh, Monsieur Choulette, so far as I am able to judge, you like very bad women."

He replied with solemnity:

"Madame, you may collect the grain of calumny sown by Monsieur Paul Vence and throw handfuls of it at me. I will not try to avoid it. It is not necessary you should know that I am chaste and that my mind is pure. But do not judge lightly those whom you call unfortunate, and who should be sacred to you, since they are unfortunate. The disdained and lost girl is the docile clay under the finger of the Divine Potter: she is the victim and the altar of the holocaust. The unfortunates are nearer God than the honest women: they have lost conceit. They do not glorify themselves with the untried virtue the matron prides

457

herself on. They possess humility, which is the cornerstone of virtues agreeable to heaven. A short repentance will be sufficient for them to be the first in heaven; for their sins, without malice and without joy, contain their own forgiveness. Their faults, which are pains, participate in the merits attached to pain; slaves to brutal passion, they are deprived of all voluptuousness, and in this they are like the men who practice continence for the kingdom of God. They are like us, culprits; but shame falls on their crime like a balm, suffering purifies it like fire. That is the reason why God will listen to the first voice which they shall send to him. A throne is prepared for them at the right hand of the Father. In the kingdom of God, the queen and the empress will be happy to sit at the feet of the unfortunate; for you must not think that the celestial house is built on a human plan. Far from it, Madame."

Nevertheless, he conceded that more than one road led to salvation. One could follow the road of love.

"Man's love is earthly," he said, "but it rises by painful degrees, and finally leads to God."

The Prince had risen. Kissing Miss Bell's hand, he said: "Saturday."

"Yes, the day after to-morrow, Saturday," replied Vivian.

Therese started. Saturday! They were talking of Saturday quietly, as of an ordinary day. Until then she had not wished to think that Saturday would come so soon or so naturally.

The guests had been gone for half an hour. Therese, tired, was thinking in her bed, when she heard a knock at the door of her room. The panel opened, and Vivian's little head appeared.

"I am not intruding, darling? You are not sleepy?"

No, Therese had no desire to sleep. She rose on her elbow. Vivian sat on the bed, so light that she made no impression on it.

"Darling, I am sure you have a great deal of reason. Oh, I am sure of it. You are reasonable in the same way that Monsieur Sadler is a violinist. He plays a little out of tune when he wishes. And you, too, when you are not quite logical, it is for your own pleasure. Oh, darling, you have a great deal of reason and of judgment, and I come to ask your advice."

Astonished, and a little anxious, Therese denied that she was logical. She denied this very sincerely. But Vivian would not listen to her.

"I have read Francois Rabelais a great deal, my love. It is in Rabelais and in Villon that I studied French. They are good old masters of language. But, darling, do you know the 'Pantagruel?' 'Pantagruel' is like a beautiful and noble city, full of palaces, in the resplendent dawn, before the street-sweepers of Paris have come. The sweepers have not taken out the dirt, and the maids have not washed the marble steps. And I have seen that French women do not read the 'Pantagruel.' You do not know it? Well, it is not necessary. In the 'Pantagruel,' Panurge asks whether he must marry, and he covers himself with ridicule, my love. Well, I am quite as laughable as he, since I am asking the same question of you."

Therese replied with an uneasiness she did not try to conceal:

"As for that, my dear, do not ask me. I have already told you my opinion."

"But, darling, you have said that only men are wrong to marry. I can not take that advice for myself."

Madame Martin looked at the little boyish face and head of Miss Bell, which oddly expressed tenderness and modesty.

Then she embraced her, saying:

"Dear, there is not a man in the world exquisite and delicate enough for you."

She added, with an expression of affectionate gravity:

"You are not a child. If some one loves you, and you love him, do what you think you ought to do, without mingling interests and combinations that have nothing to do with sentiment. This is the advice of a friend."

Miss Bell hesitated a moment. Then she blushed and arose. She had been a little shocked.

CHAPTER XVIII
"I KISS YOUR FEET BECAUSE THEY HAVE COME!"

Saturday, at four o'clock, Therese went, as she had promised, to the gate of the English cemetery. There she found Dechartre. He was serious and agitated; he spoke little. She was glad he did not display his joy. He led her by the deserted walls of the gardens to a narrow street which she did not know. She read on a signboard: Via Alfieri. After they had taken fifty steps, he stopped before a sombre alley:

"It is in there," he said.

She looked at him with infinite sadness.

"You wish me to go in?"

She saw he was resolute, and followed him without saying a word, into the humid shadow of the alley. He traversed a courtyard where the grass grew among the stones. In the back was a pavilion with three windows, with columns and a front ornamented with goats and nymphs. On the moss-covered steps he turned in the lock a key that creaked and resisted. He murmured,

"It is rusty."

She replied, without thought "All the keys are rusty in this country."

They went up a stairway so silent that it seemed to have forgotten the sound of footsteps. He pushed open a door and made Therese enter the room. She went straight to a window opening on the cemetery. Above the wall rose the tops of pine-trees, which are not funereal in this land where mourning is mingled with joy without troubling it, where the sweetness of living extends to the city of the dead. He took her hand and led her to an armchair. He remained standing, and looked at the room which he had prepared so that she would not find herself lost in it. Panels of old print cloth, with figures of Comedy, gave to the walls the sadness of past gayeties. He had placed in a corner a dim pastel which they had seen together at an antiquary's, and which, for its shadowy grace, she called the shade

460

of Rosalba. There was a grandmother's armchair; white chairs; and on the table painted cups and Venetian glasses. In all the corners were screens of colored paper, whereon were masks, grotesque figures, the light soul of Florence, of Bologna, and of Venice in the time of the Grand Dukes and of the last Doges. A mirror and a carpet completed the furnishings.

He closed the window and lighted the fire. She sat in the armchair, and as she remained in it erect, he knelt before her, took her hands, kissed them, and looked at her with a wondering expression, timorous and proud. Then he pressed his lips to the tip of her boot.

"What are you doing?"

"I kiss your feet because they have come."

He rose, drew her to him softly, and placed a long kiss on her lips. She remained inert, her head thrown back, her eyes closed. Her toque fell, her hair dropped on her shoulders.

Two hours later, when the setting sun made immeasurably longer the shadows on the stones, Therese, who had wished to walk alone in the city, found herself in front of the two obelisks of Santa Maria Novella without knowing how she had reached there. She saw at the corner of the square the old cobbler drawing his string with his eternal gesture. He smiled, bearing his sparrow on his shoulder.

She went into the shop, and sat on a chair. She said in French:

"Quentin Matsys, my friend, what have I done, and what will become of me?"

He looked at her quietly, with laughing kindness, not understanding nor caring. Nothing astonished him. She shook her head.

"What I did, my good Quentin, I did because he was suffering, and because I loved him. I regret nothing."

He replied, as was his habit, with the sonorous syllable of Italy:

"Si! si!"

"Is it not so, Quentin? I have not done wrong? But, my God! what will happen now?"

She prepared to go. He made her understand that he wished her to wait. He culled carefully a bit of basilic and offered it to her.

"For its fragrance, signora!"

CHAPTER XIX
CHOULETTE TAKES A JOURNEY

It was the next day.

Having carefully placed on the drawing-room table his knotty stick, his pipe, and his antique carpet-bag, Choulette bowed to Madame Martin, who was reading at the window. He was going to Assisi. He wore a sheepskin coat, and resembled the old shepherds in pictures of the Nativity.

"Farewell, Madame. I am quitting Fiesole, you, Dechartre, the too handsome Prince Albertinelli, and that gentle ogress, Miss Bell. I am going to visit the Assisi mountain, which the poet says must be named no longer Assisi, but the Orient, because it is there that the sun of love rose. I am going to kneel before the happy crypt where Saint Francis is resting in a stone manger, with a stone for a pillow. For he would not even take out of this world a shroud — out of this world where he left the revelation of all joy and of all kindness."

"Farewell, Monsieur Choulette. Bring me a medal of Saint Clara. I like Saint Clara a great deal."

"You are right, Madame; she was a woman of strength and prudence. When Saint Francis, ill and almost blind, came to spend a few days at Saint Damien, near his friend, she built with her own hands a hut for him in the garden. Pain, languor, and burning eyelids deprived him of sleep. Enormous rats came to attack him at night. Then he composed a joyous canticle in praise of our splendid brother the Sun, and our sister the Water, chaste, useful, and pure. My most beautiful verses have less charm and splendor. And it is just that it should be thus, for Saint Francis's soul was more beautiful than his mind. I am better than all my contemporaries whom I have known, yet I am worth nothing. When Saint Francis had composed his Song of the Sun he rejoiced. He thought: 'We shall go, my brothers and I, into the cities, and stand in the public squares, with a lute, on the market-day. Good people will come near us, and we shall say to them: "We are the jugglers of God, and we shall sing a lay to you. If you are pleased, you will reward us." They will promise, and when we shall have sung, we shall recall their promise to them. We shall say to them: "You owe a reward to us. And the one that we ask of you is that you love one another." Doubtless, to keep their word and not injure God's poor jugglers, they will avoid doing ill to others.'"

Madame Martin thought St. Francis was the most amiable of the saints.

"His work," replied Choulette, "was destroyed while he lived. Yet he died happy, because in him was joy with humility. He was, in fact, God's sweet singer. And it is right that another poor poet should take his task and teach the world true religion and true joy. I shall be that poet, Madame, if I can despoil myself of reason and of conceit. For all moral beauty is achieved in this world through the inconceivable wisdom that comes from God and resembles folly."

"I shall not discourage you, Monsieur Choulette. But I am anxious about the fate which you reserve for the poor women in your new society. You will imprison them all in convents."

"I confess," replied Choulette, "that they embarrass me a great deal in my project of reform. The violence with which one loves them is harsh and injurious. The pleasure they give is not peaceful, and does not lead to joy. I have committed for them, in my life, two or three abominable crimes of which no one knows. I doubt whether I shall ever invite you to supper, Madame, in the new Saint Mary of the Angels." He took his pipe, his carpet-bag, and his stick:

"The crimes of love shall be forgiven. Or, rather, one can not do evil when one loves purely. But sensual love is formed of hatred, selfishness, and anger as much as of passion. Because I found you beautiful one night, on this sofa, I was assailed by a cloud of violent thoughts. I had come from the Albergo, where I had heard Miss Bell's cook improvise magnificently twelve hundred verses on Spring. I was inundated by a celestial joy which the sight of you made me lose. It must be that a profound truth is enclosed in the curse of Eve. For, near you, I felt reckless and wicked. I had soft words on my lips. They were lies. I felt that I was your adversary and your enemy; I hated you. When I saw you smile, I felt a desire to kill you."

"Truly?"

"Oh, Madame, it is a very natural sentiment, which you must have inspired more than once. But common people feel it without being conscious of it, while my vivid imagination represents me to myself incessantly. I contemplate my mind, at times splendid, often hideous. If you had been able to read my mind that night you would have screamed with fright."

Therese smiled:

"Farewell, Monsieur Choulette. Do not forget my medal of Saint Clara."

He placed his bag on the floor, raised his arm, and pointed his finger:

"You have nothing to fear from me. But the one whom you will love and who will love you will harm you. Farewell, Madame."

He took his luggage and went out. She saw his long, rustic form disappear behind the bushes of the garden.

In the afternoon she went to San Marco, where Dechartre was waiting for her. She desired yet she feared to see him again so soon. She felt an anguish which an unknown sentiment, profoundly soft, appeased. She did not feel the stupor of the first time that she had yielded for love; she did not feel the brusque vision of the irreparable. She was under influences slower, more vague, and more powerful. This time a charming reverie bathed the reminiscence of the caresses which she had received. She was full of trouble and anxiety, but she felt no regret. She had acted less through her will than through a force which she divined to be higher. She absolved herself because of her disinterestedness. She counted on nothing, having calculated nothing.

Doubtless, she had been wrong to yield, since she was not free; but she had exacted nothing. Perhaps she was for him only a violent caprice. She did not know him. She had not one of those vivid imaginations that surpass immensely, in good as in evil, common mediocrity. If he went away from her and disappeared she would not reproach him for it; at least, she thought not. She would keep the reminiscence and the imprint of the rarest and most precious thing one may find in the world. Perhaps he was incapable of real attachment. He thought he loved her. He had loved her for an hour. She dared not wish for more, in the embarrassment of the false situation which irritated her frankness and her pride, and which troubled the lucidity of her intelligence. While the carriage was carrying her to San Marco, she persuaded herself that he would say nothing to her of the day before, and that the room from which one could see the pines rise to the sky would leave to them only the dream of a dream.

He extended his hand to her. Before he had spoken she saw in his look that he loved her as much now as before, and she perceived at the same time that she wished him to be thus.

"You — " he said, "I have been here since noon. I was waiting, knowing that you would not come so soon, but able to live only at the place where I was to see you. It is you! Talk; let me see and hear you."

"Then you still love me?"

"It is now that I love you. I thought I loved you when you were only a phantom. Now, you are the being in whose hands I have put my soul. It is true that you are mine! What have I done to obtain the greatest, the only, good of this world? And those men with whom the earth is covered think they are living! I alone live! Tell me, what have I done to obtain you?"

"Oh, what had to be done, I did. I say this to you frankly. If we have reached that point, the fault is mine. You see, women do not always confess it, but it is always their fault. So, whatever may happen, I never will reproach you for anything."

An agile troupe of yelling beggars, guides, and coachmen surrounded them with an importunity wherein was mingled the gracefulness which Italians never lose. Their subtlety made them divine that these were lovers, and they knew that lovers are prodigal. Dechartre threw coin to them, and they all returned to their happy laziness.

A municipal guard received the visitors. Madame Martin regretted that there was no monk. The white gown of the Dominicans was so beautiful under the arcades of the cloister!

They visited the cells where, on the bare plaster, Fra Angelico, aided by his brother Benedetto, painted innocent pictures for his companions.

"Do you recall the winter night when, meeting you before the Guimet Museum, I accompanied you to the narrow street bordered by small gardens which leads to the Billy Quay? Before separating we stopped a moment on the parapet along which runs a thin boxwood hedge. You looked at that boxwood, dried by winter. And when you went away I looked at it for a long time."

They were in the cell wherein Savonarola lived. The guide showed to them the portrait and the relics of the martyr.

"What could there have been in me that you liked that day? It was dark."

"I saw you walk. It is in movements that forms speak. Each one of your steps told me the secrets of your charming beauty. Oh! my imagination was never discreet in anything that concerned you. I did not dare to speak to you. When I saw you, it frightened me. It frightened me because you could do everything for me. When you were present, I adored you tremblingly. When you were far from me, I felt all the impieties of desire."

"I did not suspect this. But do you recall the first time we saw each other, when Paul Vence introduced you? You were seated near a screen. You were looking at the miniatures. You said to me: 'This lady, painted by Siccardi, resembles Andre Chenier's mother.' I replied to you: 'She is my husband's great-grandmother. How did Andre Chenier's mother look?' And you said: 'There is a portrait of her: a faded Levantine.'"

He excused himself and thought that he had not spoken so impertinently.

"You did. My memory is better than yours."

They were walking in the white silence of the convent. They saw the cell which Angelico had ornamented with the loveliest painting. And there, before the Virgin who, in the pale sky, receives from God the Father the immortal crown, he took Therese in his arms and placed a kiss on her lips, almost in view of two Englishwomen who were walking through the corridors, consulting their Baedeker. She said to him:

"We must not forget Saint Anthony's cell."

"Therese, I am suffering in my happiness from everything that is yours and that escapes me. I am suffering because you do not live for me alone. I wish to have you wholly, and to have had you in the past."

She shrugged her shoulders a little.

"Oh, the past!"

"The past is the only human reality. Everything that is, is past."

She raised toward him her eyes, which resembled bits of blue sky full of mingled sun and rain.

"Well, I may say this to you: I never have felt that I lived except with you."

When she returned to Fiesole, she found a brief and threatening letter from Le Menil. He could not understand, her prolonged absence, her silence. If she did not announce at once her return, he would go to Florence for her.

She read without astonishment, but was annoyed to see that everything disagreeable that could happen was happening, and that nothing would be spared to her of what she had feared. She could still calm him and reassure him: she had only to say to him that she loved him; that she would soon return to Paris; that he should renounce the foolish idea of rejoining her here; that Florence was a village where they would be watched at once. But she would have to write: "I love you." She must quiet him with caressing phrases.

She had not the courage to do it. She would let him guess the truth. She accused herself in veiled terms. She wrote obscurely of souls carried away by the flood of life, and of the atom one is on the moving ocean of events. She asked him, with affectionate sadness, to keep of her a fond reminiscence in a corner of his soul.

She took the letter to the post-office box on the Fiesole square. Children were playing in the twilight. She looked from the top of the hill to the beautiful cup which carried beautiful Florence like a jewel. And the peace of night made her shiver. She dropped the letter into the box. Then only she had the clear vision of what she had done and of what the result would be.

CHAPTER XX
WHAT IS FRANKNESS?

In the square, where the spring sun scattered its yellow roses, the bells at noon dispersed the rustic crowd of grain-merchants assembled to sell their wares. At the foot of the Lanzi, before the statues, the venders of ices had placed, on tables covered with red cotton, small castles bearing the inscription: 'Bibite ghiacciate'. And joy descended from heaven to earth. Therese and Jacques, returning from an early promenade in the Boboli Gardens, were passing before the illustrious loggia. Therese looked at the Sabine by John of Bologna with that interested curiosity of a woman examining another woman. But Dechartre looked at Therese only. He said to her:

"It is marvellous how the vivid light of day flatters your beauty, loves you, and caresses the mother-of-pearl on your cheeks."

"Yes," she said. "Candle-light hardens my features. I have observed this. I am not an evening woman, unfortunately. It is at night that women have a chance to show themselves and to please. At night, Princess Seniavine has a fine blond complexion; in the sun she is as yellow as a lemon. It must be owned that she does not care. She is not a coquette."

"And you are?"

"Oh, yes. Formerly I was a coquette for myself, now I am a coquette for you."

She looked at the Sabine woman, who with her waving arms, long and robust, tried to avoid the Roman's embraces.

"To be beautiful, must a woman have that thin form and that length of limb? I am not shaped in that way."

He took pains to reassure her. But she was not disturbed about it. She was looking now at the little castle of the ice-vender. A sudden desire had come to her to eat an ice standing there, as the working-girls of the city stood.

"Wait a moment," said Dechartre.

He ran toward the street that follows the left side of the Lanzi, and disappeared.

After a moment he came back, and gave her a little gold spoon, the handle of which was finished in a lily of Florence, with its chalice enameled in red.

"You must eat your ice with this. The man does not give a spoon with his ices. You would have had to put out your tongue. It would have been pretty, but you are not accustomed to it."

She recognized the spoon, a jewel which she had remarked the day before in the showcase of an antiquarian.

They were happy; they disseminated their joy, which was full and simple, in light words which had no sense. And they laughed when the Florentine repeated to them passages of the old Italian writers. She enjoyed the play of his face, which was antique in style and jovial in expression. But she did not always understand what he said. She asked Jacques:

"What did he say?"

"Do you really wish to know?"

Yes, she wished to know.

"Well, he said he should be happy if the fleas in his bed were shaped like you!"

When she had eaten the ice, he asked her to return to San Michele. It was so near! They would cross the square and at once discover the masterpiece in stone. They went. They looked at the St. George and at the bronze St. Mark. Dechartre saw again on the wall the post-box, and he recalled with painful exactitude the little gloved hand that had dropped the letter. He thought it hideous, that copper mouth which had swallowed Therese's secret. He could not turn his eyes away from it. All his gayety had fled. She admired the rude statue of the Evangelist.

"It is true that he looks honest and frank, and it seems that, if he spoke, nothing but words of truth would come out of his mouth."

He replied bitterly:

"It is not a woman's mouth."

She understood his thought, and said, in her soft tone:

471

"My friend, why do you say this to me? I am frank."

"What do you call frank? You know that a woman is obliged to lie."

She hesitated. Then she said:

"A woman is frank when she does not lie uselessly."

CHAPTER XXI
"I NEVER HAVE LOVED ANY ONE BUT YOU!"

Therese was dressed in sombre gray. The bushes on the border of the terrace were covered with silver stars and on the hillsides the laurel-trees threw their odoriferous flame. The cup of Florence was in bloom.

Vivian Bell walked, arrayed in white, in the fragrant garden.

"You see, darling, Florence is truly the city of flowers, and it is not inappropriate that she should have a red lily for her emblem. It is a festival to-day, darling."

"A festival, to-day?"

"Darling, do you not know this is the first day of May? You did not wake this morning in a charming fairy spectacle? Do you not celebrate the Festival of Flowers? Do you not feel joyful, you who love flowers? For you love them, my love, I know it: you are very good to them. You said to me that they feel joy and pain; that they suffer as we do."

"Ah! I said that they suffer as we do?"

"Yes, you said it. It is their festival to-day. We must celebrate it with the rites consecrated by old painters."

Therese heard without understanding. She was crumpling under her glove a letter which she had just received, bearing the Italian postage-stamp, and containing only these two lines:

"I am staying at the Great Britain Hotel, Lungarno Acciaoli. I shall expect you to-morrow morning. No. 18."

"Darling, do you not know it is the custom of Florence to celebrate spring on the first day of May every year? Then you did not understand the meaning of Botticelli's picture consecrated to the Festival of Flowers. Formerly, darling, on the first day of May the entire city gave itself up to joy. Young girls, crowned with sweetbrier and other flowers, made a long cortege through the Corso, under arches, and sang choruses on the new grass. We shall do as they did. We shall dance in the garden."

"Ah, we shall dance in the garden?"

"Yes, darling; and I will teach you Tuscan steps of the fifteenth century which have been found in a manuscript by Mr. Morrison, the oldest librarian in London. Come back soon, my love; we shall put on flower hats and dance."

"Yes, dear, we shall dance," said Therese.

And opening the gate, she ran through the little pathway that hid its stones under rose-bushes. She threw herself into the first carriage she found. The coachman wore forget-me-nots on his hat and on the handle of his whip:

"Great Britain Hotel, Lungarno Acciaoli."

She knew where that was, Lungarno Acciaoli. She had gone there at sunset, and she had seen the rays of the sun on the agitated surface of the river. Then night had come, the murmur of the waters in the silence, the words and the looks that had troubled her, the first kiss of her lover, the beginning of incomparable love. Oh, yes, she recalled Lungarno Acciaoli and the river-side beyond the old bridge — Great Britain Hotel — she knew: a big stone facade on the quay. It was fortunate, since he would come, that he had gone there. He might as easily have gone to the Hotel de la Ville, where Dechartre was. It was fortunate they were not side by side in the same corridor. Lungarno Acciaoli! The dead body which they had seen pass was at peace somewhere in the little flowery cemetery.

"Number 18."

It was a bare hotel room, with a stove in the Italian fashion, a set of brushes displayed on the table, and a time-table. Not a book, not a journal. He was there; she saw suffering on his bony face, a look of fever. This produced on her a sad impression. He waited a moment for a word, a gesture; but she dared do nothing. He offered a chair. She refused it and remained standing.

"Therese, something has happened of which I do not know. Speak."

After a moment of silence, she replied, with painful slowness:

"My friend, when I was in Paris, why did you go away from me?"

By the sadness of her accent he believed, he wished to believe, in the expression of an affectionate reproach. His face colored. He replied, ardently:

"Ah, if I could have foreseen! That hunting party — I cared little for it, as you may think! But you — your letter, that of the twenty-seventh" — he had a gift for dates — "has thrown me into a horrible anxiety. Something has happened. Tell me everything."

"My friend, I believed you had ceased to love me."

"But now that you know the contrary?"

"Now — "

She paused, her arms fell before her and her hands were joined.

Then, with affected tranquility, she continued:

"Well, my friend, we took each other without knowing. One never knows. You are young; younger than I, since we are of the same age. You have, doubtless, projects for the future."

He looked at her proudly. She continued:

"Your family, your mother, your aunts, your uncle the General, have projects for you. That is natural. I might have become an obstacle. It is better that I should disappear from your life. We shall keep a fond remembrance of each other."

She extended her gloved hand. He folded his arms:

"Then, you do not want me? You have made me happy, as no other man ever was, and you think now to brush me aside? Truly, you seem to think you have finished with me. What have you come to say to me? That it was a liaison, which is easily broken? That people take each other, quit each other — well, no! You are not a person whom one can easily quit."

"Yes," said Therese, "you had perhaps given me more of your heart than one does ordinarily in such 180 cases. I was more than an amusement for you. But, if I am not the woman you thought I was, if I have deceived you, if I am frivolous — you know people have said so — well, if I have not been to you what I should have been — "

She hesitated, and continued in a brave tone, contrasting with what she said:

"If, while I was yours, I have been led astray; if I have been curious; if I say to you that I was not made for serious sentiment — "

He interrupted her:

"You are not telling the truth."

"No, I am not telling the truth. And I do not know how to lie. I wished to spoil our past. I was wrong. It was — you know what it was. But — "

"But?"

"I have always told you I was not sure of myself. There are women, it is said, who are sure of themselves. I warned you that I was not like them."

He shook his head violently, like an irritated animal.

"What do you mean? I do not understand. I understand nothing. Speak clearly. There is something between us. I do not know what. I demand to know what it is. What is it?"

"There is the fact that I am not a woman sure of herself, and that you should not rely on me. No, you should not rely on me. I had promised nothing — and then, if I had promised, what are words?"

"You do not love me. Oh, you love me no more! I can see it. But it is so much the worse for you! I love you. You should not have given yourself to me. Do not think that you can take yourself back. I love you and I shall keep you. So you thought you could get out of it very quietly? Listen a moment. You have done everything to make me love you, to attach me to you, to make it impossible for me to live without you.

"Six weeks ago you asked for nothing better. You were everything for me, I was everything for you. And now you desire suddenly that I should know you no longer; that you should be to me a stranger, a lady whom one meets in society. Ah, you have a fine audacity! Have I dreamed? All the past is a dream? I invented it all? Oh, there can be no doubt of it. You loved me. I feel it still. Well, I have not changed. I am what I was; you have nothing to complain of. I have not betrayed you for other women. It isn't credit that I claim. I could not have done it. When one has known you, one finds the prettiest women insipid. I never have had the idea of deceiving you. I have always acted well toward you. Why should you not love me? Answer! Speak! Say you love me still. Say it, since it is true. Come, Therese, you will feel at once that you love as you loved me formerly in the little nest where we were so happy. Come!"

He approached her ardently. She, her eyes full of fright, pushed him away with a kind of horror.

He understood, stopped, and said:

"You have a lover."

She bent her head, then lifted it, grave and dumb.

Then he made a gesture as if to strike her, and at once recoiled in shame. He lowered his eyes and was silent. His fingers to his lips, and biting his nails, he saw that his hand had been pricked by a pin on her waist, and bled. He threw himself in an armchair, drew his handkerchief to wipe off the blood, and remained indifferent and without thought.

She, with her back to the door, her face calm and pale, her look vague, arranged her hat with instinctive care. At the noise, formerly delicious, that the rustle of her skirts made, he started, looked at her, and asked furiously:

"Who is he? I will know."

She did not move. She replied with soft firmness:

"I have told you all I can. Do not ask more; it would be useless."

He looked at her with a cruel expression which she had never seen before.

"Oh, do not tell me his name. It will not be difficult for me to find it."

She said not a word, saddened for him, anxious for another, full of anguish and fear, and yet without regret, without bitterness, because her real soul was elsewhere.

He had a vague sensation of what passed in her mind. In his anger to see her so sweet and so serene, to find her beautiful, and beautiful for another, he felt a desire to kill her, and he shouted at her:

"Go!"

Then, weakened by this effort of hatred, which was not natural to him, he buried his head in his hands and sobbed.

His pain touched her, gave her the hope of quieting him. She thought she might perhaps console him for her loss. Amicably and comfortably she seated herself beside him.

"My friend, blame me. I am to blame, but more to be pitied. Disdain me, if you wish, if one can disdain an unfortunate creature who is the plaything of life. In fine, judge me as you wish. But keep for me a little friendship in your anger, a little bitter-sweet reminiscence, something like those days of autumn when there is sunlight and strong wind. That is what I deserve. Do not be harsh to the agreeable but frivolous visitor who passed through your life. Bid good-by to me as to a traveler who goes one knows not where, and who is sad. There is so much sadness in separation! You were irritated against me a moment ago. Oh, I do not reproach you for it. I only suffer for it. Reserve a little sympathy for me. Who knows? The future is always unknown. It is very gray and obscure before me. Let me say to myself that I have been kind, simple, frank with you, and that you have not forgotten it. In time you will understand, you will forgive; to-day have a little pity."

He was not listening to her words. He was appeased simply by the caress of her voice, of which the tone was limpid and clear. He exclaimed:

"You do not love him. I am the one whom you love. Then — "

She hesitated:

"Ah, to say whom one loves or loves not is not an easy thing for a woman, or at least for me. I do not know how other women do. But life is not good to me. I am tossed to and fro by force of circumstances."

He looked at her calmly. An idea came to him. He had taken a resolution; he forgave, he forgot, provided she returned to him at once.

"Therese, you do not love him. It was an error, a moment of forgetfulness, a horrible and stupid thing that you did through weakness, through surprise, perhaps in spite. Swear to me that you never will see him again."

He took her arm:

"Swear to me!"

She said not a word, her teeth were set, her face was sombre. He wrenched her wrist. She exclaimed:

"You hurt me!"

However, he followed his idea; he led her to the table, on which, near the brushes, were an ink-stand, and several leaves of letter-paper ornamented with a large blue vignette, representing the facade of the hotel, with innumerable windows.

"Write what I am about to dictate to you. I will call somebody to take the letter."

And as she resisted, he made her fall on her knees. Proud and determined, she said:

"I can not, I will not."

"Why?"

"Because — do you wish to know? — because I love him."

Brusquely he released her. If he had had his revolver at hand, perhaps he would have killed her. But almost at once his anger was dampened by sadness; and now, desperate, he was the one who wished to die.

"Is what you say true? Is it possible?"

"How do I know? Can I say? Do I understand? Have I an idea, a sentiment, about anything?"

With an effort she added:

"Am I at this moment aware of anything except my sadness and your despair?"

"You love him, you love him! What is he, who is he, that you should love him?"

His surprise made him stupid; he was in an abyss of astonishment. But what she had said separated them. He dared not complain. He only repeated:

"You love him, you love him! But what has he done to you, what has he said, to make you love him? I know you. I have not told you every time your ideas shocked me. I would wager he is not even a man in society. And you believe he loves you? You believe it? Well, you are deceiving yourself. He does not love you. You flatter him, simply. He will quit you at the first opportunity. When he shall have compromised you, he will abandon you. Next year people will say of you: 'She is not at all exclusive.' I am sorry for your father; he is one of my friends, and will know of your behavior. You can not expect to deceive him."

She listened, humiliated but consoled, thinking how she would have suffered had she found him generous.

In his simplicity he sincerely disdained her. This disdain relieved him.

"How did the thing happen? You can tell me."

She shrugged her shoulders with so much pity that he dared not continue. He became contemptuous again.

"Do you imagine that I shall aid you in saving appearances, that I shall return to your house, that I shall continue to call on your husband?"

"I think you will continue to do what a gentleman should. I ask nothing of you. I should have liked to preserve of you the reminiscence of an excellent friend. I thought you might be indulgent and kind to, me, but it is not possible. I see that lovers never separate kindly. Later, you will judge me better. Farewell!"

He looked at her. Now his face expressed more pain than anger. She never had seen his eyes so dry and so black. It seemed as if he had grown old in an hour.

"I prefer to tell you in advance. It will be impossible for me to see you again. You are not a woman whom one may meet after one has been loved by her. You are not like others. You have a poison of your own, which you have given to me, and which I feel in me, in my veins. Why have I known you?"

She looked at him kindly.

"Farewell! Say to yourself that I am not worthy of being regretted so much."

Then, when he saw that she placed her hand on the latch of the door, when he felt at that gesture that he was to lose her, that he should never have her again, he shouted. He forgot everything. There remained in him only the dazed feeling of a great misfortune accomplished, of an irreparable calamity. And from the depth of his stupor a desire ascended. He desired to possess again the woman who was leaving him and who would never return. He drew her to him. He desired her, with all the strength of his animal nature. She resisted with all the force of her will, which was free and on the alert. She disengaged herself, crumpled, torn, without even having been afraid.

He understood that everything was useless; he realized she was no longer for him, because she belonged to another. As his suffering returned, he pushed her out of the door.

She remained a moment in the corridor, proudly waiting for a word.

But he shouted again, "Go!" and shut the door violently.

On the Via Alfieri, she saw again the pavilion in the rear of the courtyard where pale grasses grew. She found it silent and tranquil, faithful, with its goats and nymphs, to the lovers of the time of the Grand Duchess Eliza. She felt at once freed from the painful, brutal world, and transported to ages wherein she had not known the sadness of life. At the foot of the stairs, the steps of which were covered with roses, Dechartre was waiting. She threw herself in his arms. He carried her inert, like a precious trophy before which he had become pallid and trembling. She enjoyed, her eyelids half closed, the superb humiliation of being a beautiful prey. Her fatigue, her sadness, her disgust with the day, the reminiscence of violence, her regained liberty, the need of forgetting, remains of fright, everything vivified, awakened her tenderness. She threw her arms around the neck of her lover.

They were as gay as children. They laughed, said tender nothings, played, ate lemons, oranges, and other fruits piled up near-them on painted plates. Her lips, half-open, showed her brilliant teeth. She asked, with coquettish anxiety, if he were not disillusioned after the beautiful dream he had made of her.

In the caressing light of the day, for the enjoyment of which he had arranged, he contemplated her with youthful joy. He lavished praise and kisses upon her. They forgot themselves in caresses, in friendly quarrels, in happy glances.

He asked her how a little red mark on her temple had come there. She replied that she had forgotten; that it was nothing. She hardly lied; she had really forgotten.

They recalled to each other their short but beautiful history, all their life, which began upon the day when they had met.

"You know, on the terrace, the day after your arrival, you said vague things to me. I guessed that you loved me."

"I was afraid to seem stupid to you."

"You were, a little. It was my triumph. It made me impatient to see you so little troubled near me. I loved you before you loved me. Oh, I do not blush for it!"

He gave her a glass of Asti. But there was a bottle of Trasimene. She wished to taste it, in memory of the lake which she had seen silent and beautiful at night in its opal cup. That was when she had first visited Italy, six years before.

He chided her for having discovered the beauty of things without his aid.

She said:

"Without you, I did not know how to see anything. Why did you not come to me before?"

He closed her lips with a kiss. Then she said:

"Yes, I love you! Yes, I never have loved any one but you!"

CHAPTER XXII
A MEETING AT THE STATION

Le Menil had written: "I leave tomorrow evening at seven o'clock. Meet me at the station."

She had gone to meet him. She saw him in long coat and cape, precise and calm, in front of the hotel stages. He said only:

"Ah, you have come."

"But, my friend, you called me."

He did not confess that he had written in the absurd hope that she would love him again and that the rest would be forgotten, or that she would say to him: "It was only a trial of your love."

If she had said so he would have believed her, however.

Astonished because she did not speak, he said, dryly:

"What have you to say to me? It is not for me to speak, but for you. I have no explanations to give you. I have not to justify a betrayal."

"My friend, do not be cruel, do not be ungrateful. This is what I had to say to you. And I must repeat that I leave you with the sadness of a real friend."

"Is that all? Go and say this to the other man. It will interest him more than it interests me."

"You called me, and I came; do not make me regret it."

"I am sorry to have disturbed you. You could doubtless find a better employment for your time. I will not detain you. Rejoin him, since you are longing to do so."

At the thought that his unhappy words expressed a moment of eternal human pain, and that tragedy had illustrated many similar griefs, she felt all the sadness and irony of the situation, which a curl of her lips betrayed. He thought she was laughing.

"Do not laugh; listen to me. The other day, at the hotel, I wanted to kill you. I came so near doing it that now I know what I escaped. I will not do it. You may rest secure. What would be the use? As I wish to keep up appearances, I shall call on you in Paris. It will grieve me to learn that you can not receive me. I shall see your husband, I shall see your father also. It will be to say good-by to them, as I intend to go on a long voyage. Farewell, Madame!"

At the moment when he turned his back to her, Therese saw Miss Bell and Prince Albertinelli coming out of the freight-station toward her. The Prince was very handsome. Vivian was walking by his side with the lightness of chaste joy.

"Oh, darling, what a pleasant surprise to find you here! The Prince, and I have seen, at the customhouse, the new bell, which has just come."

"Ah, the bell has come?"

"It is here, darling, the Ghiberti bell. I saw it in its wooden cage. It did not ring, because it was a prisoner. But it will have a campanile in my Fiesole house.

"When it feels the air of Florence, it will be happy to let its silvery voice be heard. Visited by the doves, it will ring for all our joys and all our sufferings. It will ring for you, for me, for the Prince, for good Madame Marmet, for Monsieur Choulette, for all our friends."

"Dear, bells never ring for real joys and for real sufferings. Bells are honest functionaries, who know only official sentiments."

"Oh, darling, you are much mistaken. Bells know the secrets of souls; they know everything. But I am very glad to find you here. I know, my love, why you came to the station. Your maid betrayed you. She told me you were waiting for a pink gown which was delayed in coming and that you were very impatient. But do not let that trouble you. You are always beautiful, my love."

She made Madame Martin enter her wagon.

"Come, quick, darling; Monsieur Jacques Dechartre dines at the house to-night, and I should not like to make him wait."

And while they were driving through the silence of the night, through the pathways full of the fresh perfume of wildflowers, she said:

"Do you see over there, darling, the black distaffs of the Fates, the cypresses of the cemetery? It is there I wish to sleep."

But Therese thought anxiously: "They saw him. Did they recognize him? I think not. The place was dark, and had only little blinding lights. Did she know him? I do not recall whether she saw him at my house last year."

What made her anxious was a sly smile on the Prince's face.

"Darling, do you wish a place near me in that rustic cemetery? Shall we rest side by side under a little earth and a great deal of sky? But I do wrong to extend to you an invitation which you can not accept. It will not be permitted to you to sleep your eternal sleep at the foot of the hill of Fiesole, my love. You must rest in Paris, in a handsome tomb, by the side of Count Martin-Belleme."

"Why? Do you think, dear, that the wife must be united to her husband even after death?"

"Certainly she must, darling. Marriage is for time and for eternity. Do you not know the history of a young pair who loved each other in the province of Auvergne? They died almost at the same time, and were placed in two tombs separated by a road. But every night a sweetbrier bush threw from one tomb to the other its flowery branches. The two coffins had to be buried together."

When they had passed the Badia, they saw a procession coming up the side of the hill. The wind blew on the candles borne in gilded wooden candlesticks. The girls of the societies, dressed in white and blue, carried painted banners. Then came a little St. John, blond, curly-haired, nude, under a lamb's fleece which showed his arms and shoulders; and a St. Mary Magdalene, seven years old, crowned only with her waving golden hair. The people of Fiesole followed. Countess Martin recognized Choulette among them. With a candle in one hand, a book in the other, and blue spectacles on the end of his nose, he was singing. His unkempt beard moved up and down with the rhythm of the song. In the harshness of light and shade that worked in his face, he had an air that suggested a solitary monk capable of accomplishing a century of penance.

"How amusing he is!" said Therese. "He is making a spectacle of himself for himself. He is a great artist."

"Darling, why will you insist that Monsieur Choulette is not a pious man? Why? There is much joy and much beauty in faith. Poets know this. If Monsieur Choulette had not faith, he could not write the admirable verses that he does."

"And you, dear, have you faith?"

"Oh, yes; I believe in God and in the word of Christ."

Now the banners and the white veils had disappeared down the road. But one could see on the bald cranium of Choulette the flame of the candle reflected in rays of gold.

Dechartre, however, was waiting alone in the garden. Therese found him resting on the balcony of the terrace where he had felt the first sufferings of love. While Miss Bell and the Prince were trying to fix upon a suitable place for the campanile, Dechartre led his beloved under the trees.

"You promised me that you would be in the garden when I came. I have been waiting for you an hour, which seemed eternal. You were not to go out. Your absence has surprised and grieved me."

She replied vaguely that she had been compelled to go to the station, and that Miss Bell had brought her back in the wagon.

He begged her pardon for his anxiety, but everything alarmed him. His happiness made him afraid.

They were already at table when Choulette appeared, with the face of an antique satyr. A terrible joy shone in his phosphorous eyes. Since his return from Assisi, he lived only among paupers, drank chianti all day with girls and artisans to whom he taught the beauty of joy and innocence, the advent of Jesus Christ, and the imminent abolition of taxes and military service. At the beginning of the procession he had gathered vagabonds in the ruins of the Roman theatre, and had delivered to them in a macaronic language, half French and half Tuscan, a sermon, which he took pleasure in repeating:

"Kings, senators, and judges have said: 'The life of nations is in us.' Well, they lie; and they are the coffin saying: 'I am the cradle.'

"The life of nations is in the crops of the fields yellowing under the eye of the Lord. It is in the vines, and in the smiles and tears with which the sky bathes the fruits on the trees.

"The life of nations is not in the laws, which were made by the rich and powerful for the preservation of riches and power.

"The chiefs of kingdoms and of republics have said in their books that the right of peoples is the right of war, and they have glorified violence. And they render honors unto conquerors, and they raise in the public squares statues to the victorious man and horse. But one has not the right to kill; that is the reason why the just man will not draw from the urn a number that will send him to the war. The right is not to pamper the folly and crimes of a prince raised over a kingdom or over a republic; and that is the reason why the just man will not pay taxes and will not give money to the publicans. He will enjoy in peace the fruit of his work, and he will make bread with the wheat that he has sown, and he will eat the fruits of the trees that he has cut."

"Ah, Monsieur Choulette," said Prince Albertinelli, gravely, "you are right to take interest in the state of our unfortunate fields, which taxes exhaust. What fruit can be drawn from a soil taxed to thirty-three per cent. of its net income? The master and the servants are the prey of the publicans."

Dechartre and Madame Martin were struck by the unexpected sincerity of his accent.

He added:

"I like the King. I am sure of my loyalty, but the misfortunes of the peasants move me."

The truth was, he pursued with obstinacy a single aim: to reestablish the domain of Casentino that his father, Prince Carlo, an officer of Victor Emmanuel, had left devoured by usurers. His affected gentleness concealed his stubbornness. He had only useful vices. It was to become a great Tuscan landowner that he had dealt in pictures, sold the famous ceilings of his palace, made

487

love to rich old women, and, finally, sought the hand of Miss Bell, whom he knew to be skilful at earning money and practiced in the art of housekeeping. He really liked peasants. The ardent praises of Choulette, which he understood vaguely, awakened this affection in him. He forgot himself enough to express his mind:

"In a country where master and servants form one family, the fate of the one depends on that of the others. Taxes despoil us. How good are our farmers! They are the best men in the world to till the soil."

Madame Martin confessed that she should not have believed it. The country of Lombardy alone seemed to her to be well cultivated. Tuscany appeared a beautiful, wild orchard.

The Prince replied, smilingly, that perhaps she would not speak in that way if she had done him the honor of visiting his farms of Casentino, although these had suffered from long and ruinous lawsuits. She would have seen there what an Italian landscape really is.

"I take a great deal of care of my domain. I was coming from it to-night when I had the double pleasure of finding at the station Miss Bell, who had gone there to find her Ghiberti bell, and you, Madame, who were talking with a friend from Paris."

He had the idea that it would be disagreeable to her to hear him speak of that meeting. He looked around the table, and saw the expression of anxious surprise which Dechartre could not restrain. He insisted:

"Forgive, Madame, in a rustic, a certain pretension to knowing something about the world. In the man who was talking to you I recognized a Parisian, because he had an English air; and while he affected stiffness, he showed perfect ease and particular vivacity."

"Oh," said Therese, negligently, "I have not seen him for a long time. I was much surprised to meet him at Florence at the moment of his departure."

She looked at Dechartre, who affected not to listen.

"I know that gentleman," said Miss Bell. "It is Monsieur Le Menil. I dined with him twice at Madame Martin's, and he talked to me very well. He said he liked football; that he introduced the game in France, and that now football is quite the fashion. He also related to me his hunting adventures. He likes animals. I have observed that hunters like animals. I assure you, darling, that Monsieur Le Menil talks admirably about hares. He knows their habits. He said to me it was a pleasure to look at them dancing in the moonlight on the plains. He assured me that they were very intelligent, and that he had seen an old hare, pursued by dogs, force another hare to get out of the trail so as to deceive the hunters. Darling, did Monsieur Le Menil ever talk to you about hares?"

Therese replied she did not know, and that she thought hunters were tiresome.

Miss Bell exclaimed. She did not think M. Le Menil was ever tiresome when talking of the hares that danced in the moonlight on the plains and among the vines. She would like to raise a hare, like Phanion.

"Darling, you do not know Phanion. Oh, I am sure that Monsieur Dechartre knows her. She was beautiful, and dear to poets. She lived in the Island of Cos, beside a dell which, covered with lemon-trees, descended to the blue sea. And they say that she looked at the blue waves. I related Phanion's history to Monsieur Le Menil, and he was very glad to hear it. She had received from some hunter a little hare with long ears. She held it on her knees and fed it on spring flowers. It loved Phanion and forgot its mother. It died before having eaten too many flowers. Phanion lamented over its loss. She buried it in the lemon-grove, in a grave which she could see from her bed. And the shade of the little hare was consoled by the songs of the poets."

The good Madame Marmet said that M. Le Menil pleased by his elegant and discreet manners, which young men no longer practice. She would have liked to see him. She wanted him to do something for her.

"Or, rather, for my nephew," she said. "He is a captain in the artillery, and his chiefs like him. His colonel was for a long time under orders of Monsieur Le Menil's uncle, General La

Briche. If Monsieur Le Menil would ask his uncle to write to Colonel Faure in favor of my nephew I should be grateful to him. My nephew is not a stranger to Monsieur Le Menil. They met last year at the masked ball which Captain de Lassay gave at the hotel at Caen."

Madame Marmet cast down her eyes and added:

"The invited guests, naturally, were not society women. But it is said some of them were very pretty. They came from Paris. My nephew, who gave these details to me, was dressed as a coachman. Monsieur Le Menil was dressed as a Hussar of Death, and he had much success."

Miss Bell said that she was sorry not to have known that M. Le Menil was in Florence. Certainly, she should have invited him to come to Fiesole.

Dechartre remained sombre and distant during the rest of the dinner: and when, at the moment of leaving, Therese extended her hand to him, she felt that he avoided pressing it in his.

BOOK 3
CHAPTER XXIII
"ONE IS NEVER KIND WHEN ONE IS IN LOVE"

The next day, in the hidden pavilion of the Via Alfieri, she found him preoccupied. She tried to distract him with ardent gayety, with the sweetness of pressing intimacy, with superb humility. But he remained sombre. He had all night meditated, labored over, and recognized his sadness. He had found reasons for suffering. His thought had brought together the hand that dropped a letter in the post-box before the bronze San Marco and the dreadful unknown who had been seen at the station. Now Jacques Dechartre gave a face and a name to the cause of his suffering. In the grandmother's armchair where Therese had been seated on the day of her welcome, and which she had this time offered to him, he was assailed by painful images; while she, bent over one of his arms, enveloped him with her warm embrace and her loving heart. She divined too well what he was suffering to ask it of him simply.

In order to bring him back to pleasanter ideas, she recalled the secrets of the room where they were and reminiscences of their walks through the city. She was gracefully familiar.

"The little spoon you gave me, the little red lily spoon, I use for my tea in the morning. And I know by the pleasure I feel at seeing it when I wake how much I love you."

Then, as he replied only in sentences sad and evasive, she said:

"I am near you, but you do not care for me. You are preoccupied by some idea that I do not fathom. Yet I am alive, and an idea is nothing."

"An idea is nothing? Do you think so? One may be wretched or happy for an idea; one may live and one may die for an idea. Well, I am thinking."

"Of what are you thinking?"

"Why do you ask? You know very well I am thinking of what I heard last night, which you had concealed from me. I am

491

thinking of your meeting at the station, which was not due to chance, but which a letter had caused, a letter dropped — remember! — in the postbox of San Michele. Oh, I do not reproach you for it. I have not the right. But why did you give yourself to me if you were not free?"

She thought she must tell an untruth.

"You mean some one whom I met at the station yesterday? I assure you it was the most ordinary meeting in the world."

He was painfully impressed with the fact that she did not dare to name the one she spoke of. He, too, avoided pronouncing that name.

"Therese, he had not come for you? You did not know he was in Florence? He is nothing more to you than a man whom you meet socially? He is not the one who, when absent, made you say to me, 'I can not?' He is nothing to you?"

She replied resolutely:

"He comes to my house at times. He was introduced to me by General Lariviere. I have nothing more to say to you about him. I assure you he is of no interest to me, and I can not conceive what may be in your mind about him."

She felt a sort of satisfaction at repudiating the man who had insisted against her; with so much harshness and violence, upon his rights of ownership. But she was in haste to get out of her tortuous path. She rose and looked at her lover, with beautiful, tender, and grave eyes.

"Listen to me: the day when I gave my heart to you, my life was yours wholly. If a doubt or a suspicion comes to you, question me. The present is yours, and you know well there is only you, you alone, in it. As for my past, if you knew what nothingness it was you would be glad. I do not think another woman made as I was, to love, would have brought to you a mind newer to love than is mine. That I swear to you. The years that were spent without you — I did not live! Let us not talk of them. There is nothing in them of which I should be ashamed. To regret them is another thing. I regret to have known you so late. Why did you not come sooner? You could have known me five years ago as easily as to-day. But, believe me, we should not tire ourselves with speaking of time that has gone. Remember Lohengrin. If you love me, I am for you like the swan's knight. I have asked nothing of you. I have wanted to know nothing. I have not chided you about Mademoiselle Jeanne Tancrede. I saw you loved me, that you were suffering, and it was enough — because I loved you."

"A woman can not be jealous in the same manner as a man, nor feel what makes us suffer."

"I do not know that. Why can not she?"

"Why? Because there is not in the blood, in the flesh of a woman that absurd and generous fury for ownership, that primitive instinct of which man has made a right. Man is the god who wants his mate to himself. Since time immemorial woman is accustomed to sharing men's love. It is the past, the obscure past, that determines our passions. We are already so old when we are born! Jealousy, for a woman, is only a wound to her own self-love. For a man it is a torture as profound as moral suffering, as continuous as physical suffering. You ask the reason why? Because, in spite of my submission and of my respect, in spite of the alarm you cause me, you are matter and I am the idea; you are the thing and I am the mind; you are the clay and I am the artisan. Do not complain of this. Near the perfect amphora, surrounded with garlands, what is the rude and humble potter? The amphora is tranquil and beautiful; he is wretched; he is tormented; he wills; he suffers; for to will is to suffer. Yes, I am jealous. I know what there is in my jealousy. When I examine it, I find in it hereditary prejudices, savage conceit, sickly susceptibility, a mingling of rudest violence and cruel feebleness, imbecile and wicked revolt against the laws of life and of society. But it does not matter that I know it for what it is: it exists and it torments me. I am the chemist who, studying the properties of an acid which he has drunk, knows how it was combined and what salts form it. Nevertheless the acid burns him, and will burn him to the bone."

"My love, you are absurd."

493

"Yes, I am absurd. I feel it better than you feel it yourself. To desire a woman in all the brilliancy of her beauty and her wit, mistress of herself, who knows and who dares; more beautiful in that and more desirable, and whose choice is free, voluntary, deliberate; to desire her, to love her for what she is, and to suffer because she is not puerile candor nor pale innocence, which would be shocking in her if it were possible to find them there; to ask her at the same time that she be herself and not be herself; to adore her as life has made her, and regret bitterly that life, which has made her so beautiful, has touched her — Oh, this is absurd! I love you! I love you with all that you bring to me of sensations, of habits, with all that comes of your experiences, with all that comes from him-perhaps, from them-how do I know? These things are my delight and they are my torture. There must be a profound sense in the public idiocy which says that love like ours is guilty. Joy is guilty when it is immense. That is the reason why I suffer, my beloved."

She knelt before him, took his hands, and drew him to her.

"I do not wish you to suffer; I will not have it. It would be folly. I love you, and never have loved any one but you. You may believe me; I do not lie."

He kissed her forehead.

"If you deceived me, my dear, I should not reproach you for that; on the contrary, I should be grateful to you. Nothing is so legitimate, so human, as to deceive pain. What would become of us if women had not for us the pity of untruth? Lie, my beloved, lie for the sake of charity. Give me the dream that colors black sorrow. Lie; have no scruples. You will only add another illusion to the illusion of love and beauty."

He sighed:

"Oh, common-sense, common wisdom!"

She asked him what he meant, and what common wisdom was. He said it was a sensible proverb, but brutal, which it was better not to repeat.

"Repeat it all the same."

"You wish me to say it to you: 'Kissed lips do not lose their freshness.'"

And he added:

"It is true that love preserves beauty, and that the beauty of women is fed on caresses as bees are fed on flowers."

She placed on his lips a pledge in a kiss.

"I swear to you I never loved any one but you. Oh, no, it is not caresses that have preserved the few charms which I am happy to have in order to offer them to you. I love you! I love you!"

But he still remembered the letter dropped in the post-box, and the unknown person met at the station.

"If you loved me truly, you would love only me."

She rose, indignant:

"Then you believe I love another? What you are saying is monstrous. Is that what you think of me? And you say you love me! I pity you, because you are insane."

"True, I am insane."

She, kneeling, with the supple palms of her hands enveloped his temples and his cheeks. He said again that he was mad to be anxious about a chance and commonplace meeting. She forced him to believe her, or, rather, to forget. He no longer saw or knew anything. His vanished bitterness and anger left him nothing but the harsh desire to forget everything, to make her forget everything.

She asked him why he was sad.

"You were happy a moment ago. Why are you not happy now?"

And as he shook his head and said nothing:

"Speak! I like your complaints better than your silence."

Then he said:

"You wish to know? Do not be angry. I suffer now more than ever, because I know now what you are capable of giving."

She withdrew brusquely from his arms and, with eyes full of pain and reproach, said:

"You can believe that I ever was to another what I am to you! You wound me in my most susceptible sentiment, in my love

495

for you. I do not forgive you for this. I love you! I never have loved any one except you. I never have suffered except through you. Be content. You do me a great deal of harm. How can you be so unkind?"

"Therese, one is never kind when one is in love."

She remained for a long time immovable and dreamy. Her face flushed, and a tear rose to her eyes.

"Therese, you are weeping!"

"Forgive me, my heart, it is the first time that I have loved and that I have been really loved. I am afraid."

CHAPTER XXIV
CHOULETTE'S AMBITION

While the rolling of arriving boxes filled the Bell villa; while Pauline, loaded with parcels, lightly came down the steps; while good Madame Marmet, with tranquil vigilance, supervised everything; and while Miss Bell finished dressing in her room, Therese, dressed in gray, resting on the terrace, looked once again at the Flower City.

She had decided to return home. Her husband recalled her in every one of his letters. If, as he asked her to do, she returned to Paris in the first days of May, they might give two or three dinners, followed by receptions. His political group was supported by public opinion. The tide was pushing him along, and Garain thought the Countess Martin's drawing-room might exercise an excellent influence on the future of the country. These reasons moved her not; but she felt a desire to be agreeable to her husband. She had received the day before a letter from her father, Monsieur Montessuy, who, without sharing the political views of his son-in-law and without giving any advice to his daughter, insinuated that society was beginning to gossip of the Countess Martin's mysterious sojourn at Florence among poets and artists. The Bell villa took, from a distance, an air of sentimental fantasy. She felt herself that she was too closely observed at Resole. Madame Marmet annoyed her. Prince Albertinelli disquieted her. The meetings in the pavilion of the Via Alfieri had become difficult and dangerous. Professor Arrighi, whom the Prince often met, had seen her one night as she was walking through the deserted streets leaning on Dechartre. Professor Arrighi, author of a treatise on agriculture, was the most amiable of wise men. He had turned his beautiful, heroic face, and said, only the next day, to the young woman "Formerly, I could discern from a long distance the coming of a beautiful woman. Now that I have gone beyond the age to be viewed favorably by women, heaven has pity on me. Heaven prevents my seeing them. My eyes are very bad. The most charming face I can no longer recognize." She had understood, and heeded the warning. She wished now to conceal her joy in the vastness of Paris.

Vivian, to whom she had announced her departure, had asked her to remain a few days longer. But Therese suspected that her friend was still shocked by the advice she had received one night in the lemon-decorated room; that, at least, she did not enjoy herself entirely in the familiarity of a confidante who disapproved of her choice, and whom the Prince had represented to her as a coquette, and perhaps worse. The date of her departure had been fixed for May 5th.

The day shone brilliant, pure, and charming on the Arno valley. Therese, dreamy, saw from the terrace the immense morning rose placed in the blue cup of Florence. She leaned forward to discover, at the foot of the flowery hills, the imperceptible point where she had known infinite joys. There the cemetery garden made a small, sombre spot near which she divined the Via Alfieri. She saw herself again in the room wherein, doubtless, she never would enter again. The hours there passed had for her the sadness of a dream. She felt her eyes becoming veiled, her knees weaken, and her soul shudder. It seemed to her that life was no longer in her, and that she had left it in that corner where she saw the black pines raise their immovable summits. She reproached herself for feeling anxiety without reason, when, on the contrary, she should be reassured and joyful. She knew she would meet Jacques Dechartre in Paris. They would have liked to arrive there at the same time, or, rather, to go there together. They had thought it indispensable that he should remain three or four days longer in Florence, but their meeting would not be retarded beyond that. They had appointed a rendezvous, and she rejoiced in the thought of it. She wore her love mingled with her being and running in her blood. Still, a part of herself remained in the pavilion decorated with goats and nymphs a part of herself which never would return to her. In the full ardor of life, she was dying for things infinitely delicate and precious. She recalled that Dechartre had said to her: "Love likes charms. I gathered from the terrace the leaves of a tree that you had admired." Why had she not thought of taking a stone of the pavilion wherein she had forgotten the world?

A shout from Pauline drew her from her thoughts. Choulette, jumping from a bush, had suddenly kissed the maid, who was carrying overcoats and bags into the carriage. Now he was running through the alleys, joyful, his ears standing out like horns. He bowed to the Countess Martin.

"I have, then, to say farewell to you, Madame."

He intended to remain in Italy. A lady was calling him, he said: it was Rome. He wanted to see the cardinals. One of them, whom people praised as an old man full of sense, would perhaps share the ideas of the socialist and revolutionary church. Choulette had his aim: to plant on the ruins of an unjust and cruel civilization the Cross of Calvary, not dead and bare, but vivid, and with its flowery arms embracing the world. He was founding with that design an order and a newspaper. Madame Martin knew the order. The newspaper was to be sold for one cent, and to be written in rhythmic phrases. It was a newspaper to be sung. Verse, simple, violent, or joyful, was the only language that suited the people. Prose pleased only people whose intelligence was very subtle. He had seen anarchists in the taverns of the Rue Saint Jacques. They spent their evenings reciting and listening to romances.

And he added:

"A newspaper which shall be at the same time a song-book will touch the soul of the people. People say I have genius. I do not know whether they are right. But it must be admitted that I have a practical mind."

Miss Bell came down the steps, putting on her gloves:

"Oh, darling, the city and the mountains and the sky wish you to lament your departure. They make themselves beautiful to-day in order to make you regret quitting them and desire to see them again."

But Choulette, whom the dryness of the Tuscan climate tired, regretted green Umbria and its humid sky. He recalled Assisi. He said:

"There are woods and rocks, a fair sky and white clouds. I have walked there in the footsteps of good Saint Francis, and I transcribed his canticle to the sun in old French rhymes, simple and poor."

Madame Martin said she would like to hear it. Miss Bell was already listening, and her face wore the fervent expression of an angel sculptured by Mino.

Choulette told them it was a rustic and artless work. The verses were not trying to be beautiful. They were simple, although uneven, for the sake of lightness. Then, in a slow and monotonous voice, he recited the canticle.

"Oh, Monsieur Choulette," said Miss Bell, "this canticle goes up to heaven, like the hermit in the Campo Santo of Pisa, whom some one saw going up the mountain that the goats liked. I will tell you. The old hermit went up, leaning on the staff of faith, and his step was unequal because the crutch, being on one side, gave one of his feet an advantage over the other. That is the reason why your verses are unequal. I have understood it."

The poet accepted this praise, persuaded that he had unwittingly deserved it.

"You have faith, Monsieur Choulette," said Therese. "Of what use is it to you if not to write beautiful verses?"

"Faith serves me to commit sin, Madame."

"Oh, we commit sins without that."

Madame Marmet appeared, equipped for the journey, in the tranquil joy of returning to her pretty apartment, her little dog Toby, her old friend Lagrange, and to see again, after the Etruscans of Fiesole, the skeleton warrior who, among the bonbon boxes, looked out of the window.

Miss Bell escorted her friends to the station in her carriage.

CHAPTER XXV
"WE ARE ROBBING LIFE"

Dechartre came to the carriage to salute the two travelers. Separated from him, Therese felt what he was to her: he had given to her a new taste of life, delicious and so vivid, so real, that she felt it on her lips. She lived under a charm in the dream of seeing him again, and was surprised when Madame Marmet, along the journey, said: "I think we are passing the frontier," or "Rose-bushes are in bloom by the seaside." She was joyful when, after a night at the hotel in Marseilles, she saw the gray olive-trees in the stony fields, then the mulberry-trees and the distant profile of Mount Pilate, and the Rhone, and Lyons, and then the familiar landscapes, the trees raising their summits into bouquets clothed in tender green, and the lines of poplars beside the rivers. She enjoyed the plenitude of the hours she lived and the astonishment of profound joys. And it was with the smile of a sleeper suddenly awakened that, at the station in Paris, in the light of the station, she greeted her husband, who was glad to see her. When she kissed Madame Marmet, she told her that she thanked her with all her heart. And truly she was grateful to all things, like M. Choulette's St. Francis.

In the coupe, which followed the quays in the luminous dust of the setting sun, she listened without impatience to her husband confiding to her his successes as an orator, the intentions of his parliamentary groups, his projects, his hopes, and the necessity to give two or three political dinners. She closed her eyes in order to think better. She said to herself: "I shall have a letter to-morrow, and shall see him again within eight days." When the coupe passed on the bridge, she looked at the water, which seemed to roll flames; at the smoky arches; at the rows of trees; at the heads of the chestnut-trees in bloom on the Cours-la-Reine; all these familiar aspects seemed to be clothed for her in novel magnificence. It seemed to her that her love had given a new color to the universe. And she asked herself whether the trees and the stones recognized her. She was thinking; "How is it that my silence, my eyes, and heaven and earth do not tell my dear secret?"

M. Martin-Belleme, thinking she was a little tired, advised her to rest. And at night, closeted in her room, in the silence wherein she heard the palpitations of her heart, she wrote to the absent one a letter full of these words, which are similar to flowers in their perpetual novelty: "I love you. I am waiting for you. I am happy. I feel you are near me. There is nobody except you and me in the world. I see from my window a blue star which trembles, and I look at it, thinking that you see it in Florence. I have put on my table the little red lily spoon. Come! Come!" And she found thus, fresh in her mind, the eternal sensations and images.

For a week she lived an inward life, feeling within her the soft warmth which remained of the days passed in the Via Alfieri, breathing the kisses which she had received, and loving herself for being loved. She took delicate care and displayed attentive taste in new gowns. It was to herself, too, that she was pleasing. Madly anxious when there was nothing for her at the post office, trembling and joyful when she received through the small window a letter wherein she recognized the large handwriting of her beloved, she devoured her reminiscences, her desires, and her hopes. Thus the hours passed quickly.

The morning of the day when he was to arrive seemed to her to be odiously long. She was at the station before the train arrived. A delay had been signaled. It weighed heavily upon her. Optimist in her projects, and placing by force, like her father, faith on the side of her will, that delay which she had not foreseen seemed to her to be treason. The gray light, which the three-quarters of an hour filtered through the window-panes of the station, fell on her like the rays of an immense hour-glass which measured for her the minutes of happiness lost. She was lamenting her fate, when, in the red light of the sun, she saw the locomotive of the express stop, monstrous and docile, on the quay, and, in the crowd of travelers coming out of the carriages, Jacques approached her. He was looking at her with that sort of sombre and violent joy which she had often observed in him. He said:

"At last, here you are. I feared to die before seeing you again. You do not know, I did not know myself, what torture it is to live a week away from you. I have returned to the little pavilion of the Via Alfieri. In the room you know, in front of the old pastel, I have wept for love and rage."

She looked at him tenderly.

"And I, do you not think that I called you, that I wanted you, that when alone I extended my arms toward you? I had hidden your letters in the chiffonier where my jewels are. I read them at night: it was delicious, but it was imprudent. Your letters were yourself — too much and not enough."

They traversed the court where fiacres rolled away loaded with boxes. She asked whether they were to take a carriage.

He made no answer. He seemed not to hear. She said:

"I went to see your house; I did not dare go in. I looked through the grille and saw windows hidden in rose-bushes in the rear of a yard, behind a tree, and I said: 'It is there!' I never have been so moved."

He was not listening to her nor looking at her. He walked quickly with her along the paved street, and through a narrow stairway reached a deserted street near the station. There, between wood and coal yards, was a hotel with a restaurant on the first floor and tables on the sidewalk. Under the painted sign were white curtains at the windows. Dechartre stopped before the small door and pushed Therese into the obscure alley. She asked:

"Where are you leading me? What is the time? I must be home at half-past seven. We are mad."

When they left the house, she said:

"Jacques, my darling, we are too happy; we are robbing life."

CHAPTER XXVI
IN DECHARTRE'S STUDIO

A fiacre brought her, the next day, to a populous street, half sad, half gay, with walls of gardens in the intervals of new houses, and stopped at the point where the sidewalk passes under the arcade of a mansion of the Regency, covered now with dust and oblivion, and fantastically placed across the street. Here and there green branches lent gayety to that city corner. Therese, while ringing at the door, saw in the limited perspective of the houses a pulley at a window and a gilt key, the sign of a locksmith. Her eyes were full of this picture, which was new to her. Pigeons flew above her head; she heard chickens cackle. A servant with a military look opened the door. She found herself in a yard covered with sand, shaded by a tree, where, at the left, was the janitor's box with bird-cages at the windows. On that side rose, under a green trellis, the mansard of the neighboring house. A sculptor's studio backed on it its glass-covered roof, which showed plaster figures asleep in the dust. At the right, the wall that closed the yard bore debris of monuments, broken bases of columnettes. In the rear, the house, not very large, showed the six windows of its facade, half hidden by vines and rosebushes.

Philippe Dechartre, infatuated with the architecture of the fifteenth century in France, had reproduced there very cleverly the characteristics of a private house of the time of Louis XII. That house, begun in the middle of the Second Empire, had not been finished. The builder of so many castles died without being able to finish his own house. It was better thus. Conceived in a manner which had then its distinction and its value, but which seems to-day banal and outlandish, having lost little by little its large frame of gardens, cramped now between the walls of the tall buildings, Philippe Dechartre's little house, by the roughness of its stones, by the naive heaviness of its windows, by the simplicity of the roof, which the architect's widow had caused to be covered with little expense, by all the lucky accidents of the unfinished and unpremeditated, corrected the lack of grace of its new and affected antiquity and archeological romanticism, and harmonized with the humbleness of a district made ugly by progress of population.

In fine, notwithstanding its appearance of ruin and its green drapery, that little house had its charm. Suddenly and instinctively, Therese discovered in it other harmonies. In the elegant negligence which extended from the walls covered with vines to the darkened panes of the studio, and even in the bent tree, the bark of which studded with its shells the wild grass of the courtyard, she divined the mind of the master, nonchalant, not skilful in preserving, living in the long solitude of passionate men. She had in her joy a sort of grief at observing this careless state in which her lover left things around him. She found in it a sort of grace and nobility, but also a spirit of indifference contrary to her own nature, opposite to the interested and careful mind of the Montessuys. At once she thought that, without spoiling the pensive softness of that rough corner, she would bring to it her well-ordered activity; she would have sand thrown in the alley, and in the angle wherein a little sunlight came she would put the gayety of flowers. She looked sympathetically at a statue which had come there from some park, a Flora, lying on the earth, eaten by black moss, her two arms lying by her sides. She thought of raising her soon, of making of her a centrepiece for a fountain. Dechartre, who for an hour had been watching for her coming, joyful, anxious, trembling in his agitated happiness, descended the steps. In the fresh shade of the vestibule, wherein she divined confusedly the severe splendor of bronze and marble statues, she stopped, troubled by the beatings of her heart, which throbbed with all its might in her chest. He pressed her in his arms and kissed her. She heard him, through the tumult of her temples, recalling to her the short delights of the day before. She saw again the lion of the Atlas on the carpet, and returned to Jacques his kisses with delicious slowness. He led her, by a wooden stairway, into the vast hall which had served formerly as a workshop, where he designed and modelled his figures, and, above all, read; he liked reading as if it were opium.

505

Pale-tinted Gothic tapestries, which let one perceive in a marvellous forest a lady at the feet of whom a unicorn lay on the grass, extended above cabinets to the painted beams of the ceiling. He led her to a large and low divan, loaded with cushions covered with sumptuous fragments of Spanish and Byzantine cloaks; but she sat in an armchair. "You are here! You are here! The world may come to an end."

She replied "Formerly I thought of the end of the world, but I was not afraid of it. Monsieur Lagrange had promised it to me, and I was waiting for it. When I did not know you, I felt so lonely." She looked at the tables loaded with vases and statuettes, the tapestries, the confused and splendid mass of weapons, the animals, the marbles, the paintings, the ancient books. "You have beautiful things."

"Most of them come from my father, who lived in the golden age of collectors. These histories of the unicorn, the complete series of which is at Cluny, were found by my father in 1851 in an inn."

But, curious and disappointed, she said: "I see nothing that you have done; not a statue, not one of those wax figures which are prized so highly in England, not a figurine nor a plaque nor a medal."

"If you think I could find any pleasure in living among my works! I know my figures too well — they weary me. Whatever is without secret lacks charm." She looked at him with affected spite.

"You had not told me that one had lost all charm when one had no more secrets."

He put his arm around her waist.

"Ah! The things that live are only too mysterious; and you remain for me, my beloved, an enigma, the unknown sense of which contains the light of life. Do not fear to give yourself to me. I shall desire you always, but I never shall know you. Does one ever possess what one loves? Are kisses, caresses, anything else than the effort of a delightful despair? When I embrace you, I am still searching for you, and I never have you; since I want you

506

always, since in you I expect the impossible and the infinite. What you are, the devil knows if I shall ever know! Because I have modelled a few bad figures I am not a sculptor; I am rather a sort of poet and philosopher who seeks for subjects of anxiety and torment in nature. The sentiment of form is not sufficient for me. My colleagues laugh at me because I have not their simplicity. They are right. And that brute Choulette is right too, when he says we ought to live without thinking and without desiring. Our friend the cobbler of Santa Maria Novella, who knows nothing of what might make him unjust and unfortunate, is a master of the art of living. I ought to love you naively, without that sort of metaphysics which is passional and makes me absurd and wicked. There is nothing good except to ignore and to forget. Come, come, I have thought of you too cruelly in the tortures of your absence; come, my beloved! I must forget you with you. It is with you only that I can forget you and lose myself."

He took her in his arms and, lifting her veil, kissed her on the lips.

A little frightened in that vast, unknown hall, embarrassed by the look of strange things, she drew the black tulle to her chin.

"Here! You can not think of it."

He said they were alone.

"Alone? And the man with terrible moustaches who opened the door?"

He smiled:

"That is Fusellier, my father's former servant. He and his wife take charge of the house. Do not be afraid. They remain in their box. You shall see Madame Fusellier; she is inclined to familiarity. I warn you."

"My friend, why has Monsieur Fusellier, a janitor, moustaches like a Tartar?"

"My dear, nature gave them to him. I am not sorry that he has the air of a sergeant-major and gives me the illusion of being a country neighbor."

Seated on the corner of the divan, he drew her to his knees and gave to her kisses which she returned.

She rose quickly.

"Show me the other rooms. I am curious. I wish to see everything."

He escorted her to the second story. Aquarelles by Philippe Dechartre covered the walls of the corridor. He opened the door and made her enter a room furnished with white mahogany:

It was his mother's room. He kept it intact in its past. Uninhabited for nine years, the, room had not the air of being resigned to its solitude. The mirror waited for the old lady's glance, and on the onyx clock a pensive Sappho was lonely because she did not hear the noise of the pendulum.

There were two portraits on the walls. One by Ricard represented Philippe Dechartre, very pale, with rumpled hair, and eyes lost in a romantic dream. The other showed a middle-aged woman, almost beautiful in her ardent slightness. It was Madame Philippe Dechartre.

"My poor mother's room is like me," said Jacques; "it remembers."

"You resemble your mother," said Therese; "you have her eyes. Paul Vence told me she adored you."

"Yes," he replied, smilingly. "My mother was excellent, intelligent, exquisite, marvelously absurd. Her madness was maternal love. She did not give me a moment of rest. She tormented herself and tormented me."

Therese looked at a bronze figure by Carpeaux, placed on the chiffonier.

"You recognize," said Dechartre, "the Prince Imperial by his ears, which are like the wings of a zephyr, and which enliven his cold visage. This bronze is a gift of Napoleon III. My parents went to Compiegne. My father, while the court was at Fontainebleau, made the plan of the castle, and designed the gallery. In the morning the Emperor would come, in his frock-coat, and smoking his meerschaum pipe, to sit near him like a penguin on a rock. At that time I went to day-school. I listened to his stories at table, and I have not forgotten them. The Emperor stayed there, peaceful and quiet, interrupting his long silence with few words smothered under his big moustache; then he roused himself a little and explained his ideas of machinery. He was an inventor. He would draw a pencil from his pocket and make drawings on my father's designs. He spoiled in that way two or three studies a week. He liked my father a great deal, and promised works and honors to him which never came. The Emperor was kind, but he had no influence, as mamma said. At that time I was a little boy. Since then a vague sympathy has remained in me for that man, who was lacking in genius, but whose mind was affectionate and beautiful, and who carried through great adventures a simple courage and a gentle fatalism. Then he is sympathetic to me because he has been combated and insulted by people who were eager to take his place, and who had not, as he had, in the depths of their souls, a love for the people. We have seen them in power since then. Heavens, how ugly they are! Senator Loyer, for instance, who at your house, in the smoking-room, filled his pockets with cigars, and invited me to do likewise. That Loyer is a bad man, harsh to the unfortunate, to the weak, and to the humble. And Garain, don't you think his mind is disgusting? Do you remember the first time I dined at your house and we talked of Napoleon? Your hair, twisted above your neck, and shot through by a diamond arrow, was adorable. Paul Vence said subtle things. Garain did not understand. You asked for my opinion."

"It was to make you shine. I was already conceited for you."

"Oh, I never could say a single phrase before people who are so serious. Yet I had a great desire to say that Napoleon III pleased me more than Napoleon I; that I thought him more touching; but perhaps that idea would have produced a bad effect. But I am not so destitute of talent as to care about politics."

He looked around the room, and at the furniture with familiar tenderness. He opened a drawer:

"Here are mamma's eye-glasses. How she searched for these eye-glasses! Now I will show you my room. If it is not in order you must excuse Madame Fusellier, who is trained to respect my disorder."

The curtains at the windows were down. He did not lift them. After an hour she drew back the red satin draperies; rays of light dazzled her eyes and fell on her floating hair. She looked for a mirror and found only a looking-glass of Venice, dull in its wide ebony border. Rising on the tips of her toes to see herself in it, she said:

"Is that sombre and far-away spectre I? The women who have looked at themselves in this glass can not have complimented you on it."

As she was taking pins from the table she noticed a little bronze figure which she had not yet seen. It was an old Italian work of Flemish taste: a nude woman, with short legs and heavy stomach, who apparently ran with an arm extended. She thought the figure had a droll air. She asked what she was doing.

"She is doing what Madame Mundanity does on the portal of the cathedral at Basle."

But Therese, who had been at Basle, did not know Madame Mundanity. She looked at the figure again, did not understand, and asked:

"Is it something very bad? How can a thing shown on the portal of a church be so difficult to tell here?"

Suddenly an anxiety came to her:

"What will Monsieur and Madame Fusellier think of me?"

Then, discovering on the wall a medallion wherein Dechartre had modelled the profile of a girl, amusing and vicious:

"What is that?"

"That is Clara, a newspaper girl. She brought the Figaro to me every morning. She had dimples in her cheeks, nests for kisses. One day I said to her: 'I will make your portrait.' She came, one summer morning, with earrings and rings which she had bought at the Neuilly fair. I never saw her again. I do not know what has become of her. She was too instinctive to become a fashionable demi-mondaine. Shall I take it out?"

"No; it looks very well in that corner. I am not jealous of Clara."

It was time to return home, and she could not decide to go. She put her arms around her lover's neck.

"Oh, I love you! And then, you have been to-day good-natured and gay. Gayety becomes you so well. I should like to make you gay always. I need joy almost as much as love; and who will give me joy if you do not?"

CHAPTER XXVII
THE PRIMROSE PATH

After her return to Paris, for six weeks Therese lived in the ardent half sleep of happiness, and prolonged delightfully her thoughtless dream. She went to see Jacques every day in the little house shaded by a tree; and when they had at last parted at night, she took away with her adored reminiscences. They had the same tastes; they yielded to the same fantasies. The same capricious thoughts carried them away. They found pleasure in running to the suburbs that border the city, the streets where the wine-shops are shaded by acacia, the stony roads where the grass grows at the foot of walls, the little woods and the fields over which extended the blue sky striped by the smoke of manufactories. She was happy to feel him near her in this region where she did not know herself, and where she gave to herself the illusion of being lost with him.

One day they had taken the boat that she had seen pass so often under her windows. She was not afraid of being recognized. Her danger was not great, and, since she was in love, she had lost prudence. They saw shores which little by little grew gay, escaping the dusty aridity of the suburbs; they went by islands with bouquets of trees shading taverns, and innumerable boats tied under willows. They debarked at Bas-Meudon. As she said she was warm and thirsty, he made her enter a wine-shop. It was a building with wooden galleries, which solitude made to appear larger, and which slept in rustic peace, waiting for Sunday to fill it with the laughter of girls, the cries of boatmen, the odor of fried fish, and the smoke of stews.

They went up the creaking stairway, shaped like a ladder, and in a first-story room a maid servant brought wine and biscuits to them. On the mantelpiece, at one of the corners of the room, was an oval mirror in a flower-covered frame. Through the open window one saw the Seine, its green shores, and the hills in the distance bathed with warm air. The trembling peace of a summer evening filled the sky, the earth, and the water.

512

Therese looked at the running river. The boat passed on the water, and when the wake which it left reached the shore it seemed as if the house rocked like a vessel.

"I like the water," said Therese. "How happy I am!"

Their lips met.

Lost in the enchanted despair of love, time was not marked for them except by the cool plash of the water, which at intervals broke under the half-open window. To the caressing praise of her lover she replied:

"It is true I was made for love. I love myself because you love me."

Certainly, he loved her; and it was not possible for him to explain to himself why he loved her with ardent piety, with a sort of sacred fury. It was not because of her beauty, although it was rare and infinitely precious. She had exquisite lines, but lines follow movement, and escape incessantly; they are lost and found again; they cause aesthetic joys and despair. A beautiful line is the lightning which deliciously wounds the eyes. One admires and one is surprised. What makes one love is a soft and terrible force, more powerful than beauty. One finds one woman among a thousand whom one wants always. Therese was that woman whom one can not leave or betray.

She exclaimed, joyfully:

"I never shall be forsaken?"

She asked why he did not make her bust, since he thought her beautiful.

"Why? Because I am an ordinary sculptor, and I know it; which is not the faculty of an ordinary mind. But if you wish to think that I am a great artist, I will give you other reasons. To create a figure that will live, one must take the model like common material from which one will extract the beauty, press it, crush it, and obtain its essence. There is nothing in you that is not precious to me. If I made your bust I should be servilely attached to these things which are everything to me because they are something of you. I should stubbornly attach myself to the details, and should not succeed in composing a finished figure."

She looked at him astonished.

He continued:

"From memory I might. I tried a pencil sketch." As she wished to see it, he showed it to her. It was on an album leaf, a very simple sketch. She did not recognize herself in it, and thought he had represented her with a kind of soul that she did not have.

"Ah, is that the way in which you see me? Is that the way in which you love me?"

He closed the album.

"No; this is only a note. But I think the note is just. It is probable you do not see yourself exactly as I see you. Every human creature is a different being for every one that looks at it."

He added, with a sort of gayety:

"In that sense one may say one woman never belonged to two men. That is one of Paul Vence's ideas."

"I think it is true," said Therese.

It was seven o'clock. She said she must go. Every day she returned home later. Her husband had noticed it. He had said: "We are the last to arrive at all the dinners; there is a fatality about it!" But, detained every day in the Chamber of Deputies, where the budget was being discussed, and absorbed by the work of a subcommittee of which he was the chairman, state reasons excused Therese's lack of punctuality. She recalled smilingly a night when she had arrived at Madame Garain's at half-past eight. She had feared to cause a scandal. But it was a day of great affairs. Her husband came from the Chamber at nine o'clock only, with Garain. They dined in morning dress. They had saved the Ministry.

Then she fell into a dream.

"When the Chamber shall be adjourned, my friend, I shall not have a pretext to remain in Paris. My father does not understand my devotion to my husband which makes me stay in Paris. In a week I shall have to go to Dinard. What will become of me without you?"

514

She clasped her hands and looked at him with a sadness infinitely tender. But he, more sombre, said:

"It is I, Therese, it is I who must ask anxiously, What will become of me without you? When you leave me alone I am assailed by painful thoughts; black ideas come and sit in a circle around me."

She asked him what those ideas were.

He replied:

"My beloved, I have already told you: I have to forget you with you. When you are gone, your memory will torment me. I have to pay for the happiness you give me."

CHAPTER XXVIII
NEWS OF LE MENIL

The blue sea, studded with pink shoals, threw its silvery fringe softly on the fine sand of the beach, along the amphitheatre terminated by two golden horns. The beauty of the day threw a ray of sunlight on the tomb of Chateaubriand. In a room where a balcony looked out upon the beach, the ocean, the islands, and the promontories, Therese was reading the letters which she had found in the morning at the St. Malo post-office, and which she had not opened in the boat, loaded with passengers. At once, after breakfast, she had closeted herself in her room, and there, her letters unfolded on her knees, she relished hastily her furtive joy. She was to drive at two o'clock on the mall with her father, her husband, the Princess Seniavine; Madame Berthier-d'Eyzelles, the wife of the Deputy, and Madame Raymond, the wife of the Academician. She had two letters that day. The first one she read exhaled a tender aroma of love. Jacques had never displayed more simplicity, more happiness, and more charm.

Since he had been in love with her, he said, he had walked so lightly and was supported by such joy that his feet did not touch the earth. He had only one fear, which was that he might be dreaming, and might awake unknown to her. Doubtless he was only dreaming. And what a dream! He was like one intoxicated and singing. He had not his reason, happily. Absent, he saw her continually. "Yes, I see you near me; I see your lashes shading eyes the gray of which is more delicious than all the blue of the sky and the flowers; your lips, which have the taste of a marvellous fruit; your cheeks, where laughter puts two adorable dimples; I see you beautiful and desired, but fleeing and gliding away; and when I open my arms, you have gone; and I see you afar on the long, long beach, not taller than a fairy, in your pink gown, under your parasol. Oh, so small! — small as you were one day when I saw you from the height of the Campanile in the square at Florence. And I say to myself, as I said that day: 'A bit of grass would suffice to hide her from me, yet she is for me the infinite of joy and of pain.'"

He complained of the torments of absence. And he mingled with his complaints the smiles of fortunate love. He threatened jokingly to surprise her at Dinard. "Do not be afraid. They will not recognize me. I shall be disguised as a vender of plaster images. It will not be a lie. Dressed in gray tunic and trousers, my beard and face covered with white dust, I shall ring the bell of the Montessuy villa. You may recognize me, Therese, by the statuettes on the plank placed on my head. They will all be cupids. There will be faithful Love, jealous Love, tender Love, vivid Love; there will be many vivid Loves. And I shall shout in the rude and sonorous language of the artisans of Pisa or of Florence: 'Tutti gli Amori per la Signora Teersinal!'"

The last page of this letter was tender and grave. There were pious effusions in it which reminded Therese of the prayer-books she read when a child. "I love you, and I love everything in you: the earth that carries you, on which you weigh so lightly, and which you embellish; the light that allows me to see you; the air you breathe. I like the bent tree of my yard because you have seen it. I have walked tonight on the avenue where I met you one winter night. I have culled a branch of the boxwood at which you looked. In this city, where you are not, I see only you."

He said at the end of his letter that he was to dine out. In the absence of Madame Fusellier, who had gone to the country, he should go to a wine-shop of the Rue Royale where he was known. And there, in the indistinct crowd, he should be alone with her.

Therese, made languid by the softness of invisible caresses, closed her eyes and threw back her head on the armchair. When she heard the noise of the carriage coming near the house, she opened the second letter. As soon as she saw the altered handwriting of it, the lines precipitate and uneven, the distracted look of the address, she was troubled.

Its obscure beginning indicated sudden anguish and black suspicion: "Therese, Therese, why did you give yourself to me if you were not giving yourself to me wholly? How does it serve me that you have deceived me, now that I know what I did not wish to know?"

She stopped; a veil came over her eyes. She thought:

"We were so happy a moment ago. What has happened? And I was so pleased at his joy, when it had already gone; it would be better not to write, since letters show only vanished sentiments and effaced ideas."

She read further. And seeing that he was full of jealousy, she felt discouraged.

"If I have not proved to him that I love him with all my strength, that I love him with all there is in me, how am I ever to persuade him of it?"

And she was impatient to discover the cause of his folly. Jacques told it. While taking breakfast in the Rue Royale he had met a former companion who had just returned from the seaside. They had talked together; chance made that man speak of the Countess Martin, whom he knew. And at once, interrupting the narration, Jacques exclaimed: "Therese, Therese, why did you lie to me, since I was sure to learn some day that of which I alone was ignorant? But the error is mine more than yours. The letter which you put into the San Michele post-box, your meeting at the Florence station, would have enlightened me if I had not obstinately retained my illusions and disdained evidence.

"I did not know; I wished to remain ignorant. I did not ask you anything, from fear that you might not be able to continue to lie; I was prudent; and it has happened that an idiot suddenly, brutally, at a restaurant table, has opened my eyes and forced me to know. Oh, now that I know, now that I can not doubt, it seems to me that to doubt would be delicious! He gave the name — the name which I heard at Fiesole from Miss Bell, and he added: 'Everybody knows about that.'

"So you loved him. You love him still! He is near you, doubtless. He goes every year to the Dinard races. I have been told so. I see him. I see everything. If you knew the images that worry me, you would say, 'He is mad,' and you would take pity on me. Oh, how I should like to forget you and everything! But I can not. You know very well I can not forget you except with you. I see you incessantly with him. It is torture. I thought I was unfortunate that night on the banks of the Arno. But I did not know then what it is to suffer. To-day I know."

As she finished reading that letter, Therese thought: "A word thrown haphazard has placed him in that condition, a word has made him despairing and mad." She tried to think who might be the wretched fellow who could have talked in that way. She suspected two or three young men whom Le Menil had introduced to her once, warning her not to trust them. And with one of the white and cold fits of anger she had inherited from her father she said to herself: "I must know who he is." In the meanwhile what was she to do? Her lover in despair, mad, ill, she could not run to him, embrace him, and throw herself on him with such an abandonment that he would feel how entirely she was his, and be forced to believe in her. Should she write? How much better it would be to go to him, to fall upon his heart and say to him: "Dare to believe I am not yours only!" But she could only write. She had hardly begun her letter when she heard voices and laughter in the garden. Therese went down, tranquil and smiling; her large straw hat threw on her face a transparent shadow wherein her gray eyes shone.

"How beautiful she is!" exclaimed Princess Seniavine. "What a pity it is we never see her! In the morning she is promenading in the alleys of Saint Malo, in the afternoon she is closeted in her room. She runs away from us."

The coach turned around the large circle of the beach at the foot of the villas and gardens on the hillside. And they saw at the left the ramparts and the steeple of St. Malo rise from the blue sea. Then the coach went into a road bordered by hedges, along which walked Dinard women, erect under their wide headdresses.

"Unfortunately," said Madame Raymond, seated on the box by Montessuy's side, "old costumes are dying out. The fault is with the railways."

"It is true," said Montessuy, "that if it were not for the railways the peasants would still wear their picturesque costumes of other times. But we should not see them."

"What does it matter?" replied Madame Raymond. "We could imagine them."

"But," asked the Princess Seniavine, "do you ever see interesting things? I never do."

Madame Raymond, who had taken from her husband's books a vague tint of philosophy, declared that things were nothing, and that the idea was everything.

Without looking at Madame Berthier-d'Eyzelles, seated at her right, the Countess Martin murmured:

"Oh, yes, people see only their ideas; they follow only their ideas. They go along, blind and deaf. One can not stop them."

"But, my dear," said Count Martin, placed in front of her, by the Princess's side, "without leading ideas one would go haphazard. Have you read, Montessuy, the speech delivered by Loyer at the unveiling of the Cadet-Gassicourt statue? The beginning is remarkable. Loyer is not lacking in political sense."

The carriage, having traversed the fields bordered with willows, went up a hill and advanced on a vast, wooded plateau. For a long time it skirted the walls of the park.

"Is it the Guerric?" asked the Princess Seniavine.

Suddenly, between two stone pillars surmounted by lions, appeared the closed gate. At the end of a long alley stood the gray stones of a castle.

"Yes," said Montessuy, "it is the Guerric."

And, addressing Therese:

"You knew the Marquis de Re? At sixty-five he had retained his strength and his youth. He set the fashion and was loved. Young men copied his frockcoat, his monocle, his gestures, his exquisite insolence, his amusing fads. Suddenly he abandoned society, closed his house, sold his stable, ceased to show himself. Do you remember, Therese, his sudden disappearance? You had been married a short time. He called on you often. One fine day people learned that he had quitted Paris. This is the place where he had come in winter. People tried to find a reason for his sudden retreat; some thought he had run away under the influence of sorrow or humiliation, or from fear that the world might see him grow old. He was afraid of old age more than of anything else. For seven years he has lived in retirement from society; he has not gone out of the castle once. He receives at the Guerric two or three old men who were his companions in youth. This gate is opened for them only. Since his retirement no one has seen him; no one ever will see him. He shows the same care to conceal himself that he had formerly to show himself. He has not suffered from his decline. He exists in a sort of living death."

And Therese, recalling the amiable old man who had wished to finish gloriously with her his life of gallantry, turned her head and looked at the Guerric lifting its four towers above the gray summits of oaks.

On their return she said she had a headache and that she would not take dinner. She locked herself in her room and drew from her jewel casket the lamentable letter. She read over the last page.

"The thought that you belong to another burns me. And then, I did not wish that man to be the one."

It was a fixed idea. He had written three times on the same leaf these words: "I did not wish that man to be the one."

She, too, had only one idea: not to lose him. Not to lose him, she would have said anything, she would have done anything. She went to her table and wrote, under the spur of a tender, and plaintive violence, a letter wherein she repeated like a groan: "I love you, I love you! I never have loved any one but you. You are alone, alone — do you hear? — in my mind, in me. Do not think of what that wretched man said. Listen to me! I never loved any one, I swear, any one, before you."

As she was writing, the soft sigh of the sea accompanied her own sigh. She wished to say, she believed she was saying, real things; and all that she was saying was true of the truth of her love. She heard the heavy step of her father on the stairway. She hid her letter and opened the door. Montessuy asked her whether she felt better.

"I came," he said, "to say good-night to you, and to ask you something. It is probable that I shall meet Le Menil at the races. He goes there every year. If I meet him, darling, would you have any objection to my inviting him to come here for a few days? Your husband thinks he would be agreeable company for you. We might give him the blue room."

"As you wish. But I should prefer that you keep the blue room for Paul Vence, who wishes to come. It is possible, too, that Choulette may come without warning. It is his habit. We shall see him some morning ringing like a beggar at the gate. You know my husband is mistaken when he thinks Le Menil pleases me. And then I must go to Paris next week for two or three days."

CHAPTER XXIX
JEALOUSY

Twenty-four hours after writing her letter, Therese went from Dinard to the little house in the Ternes. It had not been difficult for her to find a pretext to go to Paris. She had made the trip with her husband, who wanted to see his electors whom the Socialists were working over. She surprised Jacques in the morning, at the studio, while he was sketching a tall figure of Florence weeping on the shore of the Arno.

The model, seated on a very high stool, kept her pose. She was a long, dark girl. The harsh light which fell from the skylight gave precision to the pure lines of her hip and thighs, accentuated her harsh visage, her dark neck, her marble chest, the lines of her knees and feet, the toes of which were set one over the other. Therese looked at her curiously, divining her exquisite form under the miseries of her flesh, poorly fed and badly cared for.

Dechartre came toward Therese with an air of painful tenderness which moved her. Then, placing his clay and the instrument near the easel, and covering the figure with a wet cloth, he said to the model:

"That is enough for to-day."

She rose, picked up awkwardly her clothing, a handful of dark wool and soiled linen, and went to dress behind the screen.

Meanwhile the sculptor, having dipped in the water of a green bowl his hands, which the tenacious clay made white, went out of the studio with Therese.

They passed under the tree which studded the sand of the courtyard with the shells of its flayed bark. She said:

"You have no more faith, have you?"

He led her to his room.

The letter written from Dinard had already softened his painful impressions. She had come at the moment when, tired of suffering, he felt the need of calm and of tenderness. A few lines of handwriting had appeased his mind, fed on images, less susceptible to things than to the signs of things; but he felt a pain in his heart.

In the room where everything spoke of her, where the furniture, the curtains, and the carpets told of their love, she murmured soft words:

"You could believe — do you not know what you are? — it was folly! How can a woman who has known you care for another after you?"

"But before?"

"Before, I was waiting for you."

"And he did not attend the races at Dinard?"

She did not think he had, and it was very certain she did not attend them herself. Horses and horsy men bored her.

"Jacques, fear no one, since you are not comparable to any one."

He knew, on the contrary, how insignificant he was and how insignificant every one is in this world where beings, agitated like grains in a van, are mixed and separated by a shake of the rustic or of the god. This idea of the agricultural or mystical van represented measure and order too well to be exactly applied to life. It seemed to him that men were grains in a coffee-mill. He had had a vivid sensation of this the day before, when he saw Madame Fusellier grinding coffee in her mill.

Therese said to him:

"Why are you not conceited?"

She added few words, but she spoke with her eyes, her arms, the breath that made her bosom rise.

In the happy surprise of seeing and hearing her, he permitted himself to be convinced.

She asked who had said so odious a thing.

He had no reason to conceal his name from her. It was Daniel Salomon.

She was not surprised. Daniel Salomon, who passed for not having been the lover of any woman, wished at least to be in the confidence of all and know their secrets. She guessed the reason why he had talked.

"Jacques, do not be cross at what I say to you. You are not skilful in concealing your sentiments. He suspected you were in love with me, and he wished to be sure of it. I am persuaded that now he has no doubt of our relations. But that is indifferent to me. On the contrary, if you knew better how to dissimulate, I should be less happy. I should think you did not love me enough."

For fear of disquieting him, she turned to other thoughts:

"I have not told you how much I like your sketch. It is Florence on the Arno. Then it is we?"

"Yes, I have placed in that figure the emotion of my love. It is sad, and I wish it were beautiful. You see, Therese, beauty is painful. That is why, since life is beautiful, I suffer."

He took out of his flannel coat his cigarette-holder, but she told him to dress. She would take him to breakfast with her. They would not quit each other that day. It would be delightful.

She looked at him with childish joy. Then she became sad, thinking she would have to return to Dinard at the end of the week, later go to Joinville, and that during that time they would be separated.

At Joinville, at her father's, she would cause him to be invited for a few days. But they would not be free and alone there, as they were in Paris.

"It is true," he said, "that Paris is good to us in its confused immensity."

And he added:

"Even in your absence I can not quit Paris. It would be terrible for me to live in countries that do not know you. A sky, mountains, trees, fountains, statues which do not know how to talk of you would have nothing to say to me."

While he was dressing she turned the leaves of a book which she had found on the table. It was The Arabian Nights. Romantic engravings displayed here and there in the text grand viziers, sultanas, black tunics, bazaars, and caravans.

She asked:

"The Arabian Nights-does that amuse you?"

"A great deal," he replied, tying his cravat. "I believe as much as I wish in these Arabian princes whose legs become black marble, and in these women of the harem who wander at night in cemeteries. These tales give me pleasant dreams which make me forget life. Last night I went to bed in sadness and read the history of the Three Calendars."

She said, with a little bitterness:

"You are trying to forget. I would not consent for anything in the world to lose the memory of a pain which came to me from you."

They went down together to the street. She was to take a carriage a little farther on and precede him at her house by a few minutes.

"My husband expects you to breakfast."

They talked, on the way, of insignificant things, which their love made great and charming. They arranged their afternoon in advance in order to put into it the infinity of profound joy and of ingenious pleasure. She consulted him about her gowns. She could not decide to leave him, happy to walk with him in the streets, which the sun and the gayety of noon filled. When they reached the Avenue des Ternes they saw before them, on the avenue, shops displaying side by side a magnificent abundance of food. There were chains of chickens at the caterer's, and at the fruiterer's boxes of apricots and peaches, baskets of grapes, piles of pears. Wagons filled with fruits and flowers bordered the sidewalk. Under the awning of a restaurant men and women were taking breakfast. Therese recognized among them, alone, at a small table against a laurel-tree in a box, Choulette lighting his pipe.

Having seen her, he threw superbly a five-franc piece on the table, rose, and bowed. He was grave; his long frock-coat gave him an air of decency and austerity.

He said he should have liked to call on Madame Martin at Dinard, but he had been detained in the Vendee by the Marquise de Rieu. However, he had issued a new edition of the Jardin Clos, augmented by the Verger de Sainte-Claire. He had moved souls which were thought to be insensible, and had made springs come out of rocks.

"So," he said, "I was, in a fashion, a Moses."

He fumbled in his pocket and drew from a book a letter, worn and spotted.

"This is what Madame Raymond, the Academician's wife, writes me. I publish what she says, because it is creditable to her."

And, unfolding the thin leaves, he read:

"I have made your book known to my husband, who exclaimed: 'It is pure spiritualism. Here is a closed garden, which on the side of the lilies and white roses has, I imagine, a small gate opening on the road to the Academie.'"

Choulette relished these phrases, mingled in his mouth with the perfume of whiskey, and replaced carefully the letter in its book.

Madame Martin congratulated the poet on being Madame Raymond's candidate.

"You should be mine, Monsieur Choulette, if I were interested in Academic elections. But does the Institute excite your envy?"

He kept for a few moments a solemn silence, then:

"I am going now, Madame, to confer with divers notable persons of the political and religious worlds who reside at Neuilly. The Marquise de Rieu wishes me to be a candidate, in her country, for a senatorial seat which has become vacant by the death of an old man, who was, they say, a general during his illusory life. I shall consult with priests, women and children — oh, eternal wisdom! — of the Bineau Boulevard. The constituency whose suffrages I shall attempt to obtain inhabits an undulated and wooded land wherein willows frame the fields. And it is not a rare thing to find in the hollow of one of these old willows the skeleton of a Chouan pressing his gun against his breast and holding his beads in his fleshless fingers. I shall have my program posted on the bark of oaks. I shall say 'Peace to presbyteries! Let the day come when bishops, holding in their hands the wooden crook, shall make themselves similar to the poorest servant of the poorest parish! It was the bishops who crucified Jesus Christ. Their names were Anne and Caiph. And they still retain these names before the Son of God. While they were nailing Him to the cross, I was the good thief hanged by His side.'"

He lifted his stick and pointed toward Neuilly:

"Dechartre, my friend, do you not think the Bineau Boulevard is the dusty one over there, at the right?"

"Farewell, Monsieur Choulette," said Therese. "Remember me when you are a senator."

"Madame, I do not forget you in any of my prayers, morning and evening. And I say to God: 'Since, in your anger, you gave to her riches and beauty, regard her, Lord, with kindness, and treat her in accordance with your sovereign mercy.'"

And he went erect, and dragging his leg, along the populous avenue.

CHAPTER XXX
A LETTER FROM ROBERT

Enveloped in a mantle of pink broad cloth, Therese went down the steps with Dechartre. He had come in the morning to Joinville. She had made him join the circle of her intimate friends, before the hunting-party to which she feared Le Menil had been invited, as was the custom. The light air of September agitated the curls of her hair, and the sun made golden darts shine in the profound gray of her eyes. Behind them, the facade of the palace displayed above the three arcades of the first story, in the intervals of the windows, on long tables, busts of Roman emperors. The house was placed between two tall pavilions which their great slate roofs made higher, over pillars of the Ionic order. This style betrayed the art of the architect Leveau, who had constructed, in 1650, the castle of Joinville-sur-Oise for that rich Mareuilles, creature of Mazarin, and fortunate accomplice of Fouquet.

Therese and Jacques saw before them the flower-beds designed by Le Notre, the green carpet, the fountain; then the grotto with its five rustic arcades crowned by the tall trees on which autumn had already begun to spread its golden mantle.

"This green geometry is beautiful," said Dechartre.

"Yes," said Therese. "But I think of the tree bent in the small courtyard where grass grows among the stones. We shall build a beautiful fountain in it, shall we not, and put flowers in it?"

Leaning against one of the stone lions with almost human faces, that guarded the steps, she turned her head toward the castle, and, looking at one of the windows, said:

"There is your room; I went into it last night. On the same floor, on the other side, at the other end, is my father's office. A white wooden table, a mahogany portfolio, a decanter on the mantelpiece: his office when he was a young man. Our entire fortune came from that place."

Through the sand-covered paths between the flowerbeds they walked to the boxwood hedge which bordered the park on the southern side. They passed before the orange-grove, the monumental door of which was surmounted by the Lorraine cross of Mareuilles, and then passed under the linden-trees which formed an alley on the lawn. Statues of nymphs shivered in the damp shade studded with pale lights. A pigeon, posed on the shoulder of one of the white women, fled. From time to time a breath of wind detached a dried leaf which fell, a shell of red gold, where remained a drop of rain. Therese pointed to the nymph and said:

"She saw me when I was a girl and wishing to die. I suffered from dreams and from fright. I was waiting for you. But you were so far away!"

The linden alley stopped near the large basin, in the centre of which was a group of tritons blowing in their shells to form, when the waters played, a liquid diadem with flowers of foam.

"It is the Joinville crown," she said.

She pointed to a pathway which, starting from the basin, lost itself in the fields, in the direction of the rising sun.

"This is my pathway. How often I walked in it sadly! I was sad when I did not know you."

They found the alley which, with other lindens and other nymphs, went beyond. And they followed it to the grottoes. There was, in the rear of the park, a semicircle of five large niches of rocks surmounted by balustrades and separated by gigantic Terminus gods. One of these gods, at a corner of the monument, dominated all the others by his monstrous nudity, and lowered on them his stony look.

"When my father bought Joinville," she said, "the grottoes were only ruins, full of grass and vipers. A thousand rabbits had made holes in them. He restored the Terminus gods and the arcades in accordance with prints by Perrelle, which are preserved at the Bibliotheque Nationale. He was his own architect."

A desire for shade and mystery led them toward the arbor near the grottoes. But the noise of footsteps which they heard, coming from the covered alley, made them stop for a moment, and they saw, through the leaves, Montessuy, with his arm around the Princess Seniavine's waist. Quietly they were walking toward the palace. Jacques and Therese, hiding behind the enormous Terminus god, waited until they had passed.

Then she said to Dechartre, who was looking at her silently:

"That is amazing! I understand now why the Princess Seniavine, this winter, asked my father to advise her about buying horses."

Yet Therese admired her father for having conquered that beautiful woman, who passed for being hard to please, and who was known to be wealthy, in spite of the embarrassments which her mad disorder had caused her. She asked Jacques whether he did not think the Princess was beautiful. He said she had elegance. She was beautiful, doubtless.

Therese led Jacques to the moss-covered steps which, ascending behind the grottoes, led to the Gerbe-de-l'Oise, formed of leaden reeds in the midst of a great pink marble vase. Tall trees closed the park's perspective and stood at the beginning of the forest. They walked under them. They were silent under the faint moan of the leaves.

He pressed her in his arms and placed kisses on her eyelids. Night was descending, the first stars were trembling among the branches. In the damp grass sighed the frog's flutes. They went no farther.

When she took with him, in darkness, the road to the palace, the taste of kisses and of mint remained on her lips, and in her eyes was the image of her lover. She smiled under the lindens at the nymphs who had seen the tears of her childhood. The Swan lifted in the sky its cross of stars, and the moon mirrored its slender horn in the basin of the crown. Insects in the grass uttered appeals to love. At the last turn of the boxwood hedge, Therese and Jacques saw the triple black mass of the castle, and through the wide bay-windows of the first story distinguished moving forms in the red light. The bell rang.

Therese exclaimed:

"I have hardly time to dress for dinner."

And she passed swiftly between the stone lions, leaving her lover under the impression of a fairy-tale vision.

In the drawing-room, after dinner, M. Berthier d'Eyzelles read the newspaper, and the Princess Seniavine played solitaire. Therese sat, her eyes half closed over a book.

The Princess asked whether she found what she was reading amusing.

"I do not know. I was reading and thinking. Paul Vence is right: 'We find only ourselves in books.'"

Through the hangings came from the billiard-room the voices of the players and the click of the balls.

"I have it!" exclaimed the Princess, throwing down the cards.

She had wagered a big sum on a horse which was running that day at the Chantilly races.

Therese said she had received a letter from Fiesole. Miss Bell announced her forthcoming marriage with Prince Eusebia Albertinelli della Spina.

The Princess laughed:

"There's a man who will render a service to her."

"What service?" asked Therese.

"He will disgust her with men, of course."

Montessuy came into the parlor joyfully. He had won the game.

He sat beside Berthier-d'Eyzelles, and, taking a newspaper from the sofa, said:

"The Minister of Finance announces that he will propose, when the Chamber reassembles, his savings-bank bill."

This bill was to give to savings-banks the authority to lend money to communes, a proceeding which would take from Montessuy's business houses their best customers.

"Berthier," asked the financier, "are you resolutely hostile to that bill?"

Berthier nodded.

Montessuy rose, placed his hand on the Deputy's shoulder, and said:

"My dear Berthier, I have an idea that the Cabinet will fall at the beginning of the session."

He approached his daughter.

"I have received an odd letter from Le Menil."

Therese rose and closed the door that separated the parlor from the billiard-room.

She was afraid of draughts, she said.

"A singular letter," continued Montessuy. "Le Menil will not come to Joinville. He has bought the yacht Rosebud. He is on the Mediterranean, and can not live except on the water. It is a pity. He is the only one who knows how to manage a hunt."

At this instant Dechartre came into the room with Count Martin, who, after beating him at billiards, had acquired a great affection for him and was explaining to him the dangers of a personal tax based on the number of servants one kept.

CHAPTER XXXI
AN UNWELCOME APPARITION

A pale winter sun piercing the mists of the Seine, illuminated the dogs painted by Oudry on the doors of the dining room.

Madame Martin had at her right Garain the Deputy, formerly Chancellor, also President of the Council, and at her left Senator Loyer. At Count Martin-Belleme's right was Monsieur Berthier-d'Eyzelles. It was an intimate and serious business gathering. In conformity with Montessuy's prediction, the Cabinet had fallen four days before. Called to the Elysee the same morning, Garain had accepted the task of forming a cabinet. He was preparing, while taking breakfast, the combination which was to be submitted in the evening to the President. And, while they were discussing names, Therese was reviewing within herself the images of her intimate life.

She had returned to Paris with Count Martin at the opening of the parliamentary session, and since that moment had led an enchanted life.

Jacques loved her; he loved her with a delicious mingling of passion and tenderness, of learned experience and curious ingenuity. He was nervous, irritable, anxious. But the uncertainty of his humor made his gayety more charming. That artistic gayety, bursting out suddenly like a flame, caressed love without offending it. And the playful wit of her lover made Therese marvel. She never could have imagined the infallible taste which he exercised naturally in joyful caprice and in familiar fantasy. At first he had displayed only the monotony of passionate ardor. That alone had captured her. But since then she had discovered in him a gay mind, well stored and diverse, as well as the gift of agreeable flattery.

"To assemble a homogeneous ministry," exclaimed Garain, "is easily said. Yet one must be guided by the tendencies of the various factions of the Chamber."

He was uneasy. He saw himself surrounded by as many snares as those which he had laid. Even his collaborators became hostile to him.

Count Martin wished the new ministry to satisfy the aspirations of the new men.

"Your list is formed of personalities essentially different in origin and in tendency," he said. "Yet the most important fact in the political history of recent years is the possibility, I should say the necessity, to introduce unity of views in the government of the republic. These are ideas which you, my dear Garin, have expressed with rare eloquence."

M. Berthier-d'Eyzelles kept silence.

Senator Loyer rolled crumbs with his fingers. He had been formerly a frequenter of beer-halls, and while moulding crumbs or cutting corks he found ideas. He raised his red face. And, looking at Garain with wrinkled eyes wherein red fire sparkled, he said:

"I said it, and nobody would believe it. The annihilation of the monarchical Right was for the chiefs of the Republican party an irreparable misfortune. We governed formerly against it. The real support of a government is the Opposition. The Empire governed against the Orleanists and against us; MacMahon governed against the Republicans. More fortunate, we governed against the Right. The Right — what a magnificent Opposition it was! It threatened, was candid, powerless, great, honest, unpopular! We should have nursed it. We did not know how to do that. And then, of course, everything wears out. Yet it is always necessary to govern against something. There are to-day only Socialists to give us the support which the Right lent us fifteen years ago with so constant a generosity. But they are too weak. We should reinforce them, make of them a political party. To do this at the present hour is the first duty of a State minister."

Garain, who was not cynical, made no answer.

"Garain, do you not yet know," asked Count Martin, "whether with the Premiership you are to take the Seals or the Interior?"

Garain replied that his decision would depend on the choice which some one else would make. The presence of that personage in the Cabinet was necessary, and he hesitated between two portfolios. Garain sacrificed his personal convenience to superior interests.

Senator Loyer made a wry face. He wanted the Seals. It was a long-cherished desire. A teacher of law under the Empire, he gave, in cafes, lessons that were appreciated. He had the sense of chicanery. Having begun his political fortune with articles skillfully written in order to attract to himself prosecution, suits, and several weeks of imprisonment, he had considered the press as a weapon of opposition which every good government should break. Since September 4, 1870, he had had the ambition to become Keeper of the Seals, so that everybody might see how the old Bohemian who formerly explained the code while dining on sauerkraut, would appear as supreme chief of the magistracy.

Idiots by the dozen had climbed over his back. Now having become aged in the ordinary honors of the Senate, unpolished, married to a brewery girl, poor, lazy, disillusioned, his old Jacobin spirit and his sincere contempt for the people surviving his ambition, made of him a good man for the Government. This time, as a part of the Garain combination, he imagined he held the Department of Justice. And his protector, who would not give it to him, was an unfortunate rival. He laughed, while moulding a dog from a piece of bread.

M. Berthier-d'Eyzelles, calm and grave, caressed his handsome white beard.

"Do you not think, Monsieur Garain, that it would be well to give a place in the Cabinet to the men who have followed from the beginning the political principles toward which we are directing ourselves to-day?"

"They lost themselves in doing it," replied Garam, impatiently. "The politician never should be in advance of circumstances. It is an error to be in the right too soon. Thinkers are not men of business. And then — let us talk frankly — if you want a Ministry of the Left Centre variety, say so: I will retire. But I warn you that neither the Chamber nor the country will sustain you."

"It is evident," said Count Martin, "that we must be sure of a majority."

"With my list, we have a majority," said Garain. "It is the minority which sustained the Ministry against us. Gentlemen, I appeal to your devotion."

And the laborious distribution of the portfolios began again. Count Martin received, in the first place, the Public Works, which he refused, for lack of competency, and afterward the Foreign Affairs, which he accepted without objection.

But M. Berthier-d'Eyzelles, to whom Garain offered Commerce and Agriculture, reserved his decision.

Loyer got the Colonies. He seemed very busy trying to make his bread dog stand on the cloth. Yet he was looking out of the corners of his little wrinkled eyelids at the Countess Martin and thinking that she was desirable. He vaguely thought of the pleasure of meeting her again.

Leaving Garain to his combination, he was preoccupied by his fair hostess, trying to divine her tastes and her habits, asking her whether she went to the theatre, and if she ever went at night to the coffee-house with her husband. And Therese was beginning to think he was more interesting than the others, with his apparent ignorance of her world and his superb cynicism.

Gamin arose. He had to see several persons before submitting his list to the President of the Republic. Count Martin offered his carriage, but Garain had one.

"Do you not think," asked Count Martin, "that the President might object to some names?"

"The President," replied Garain, "will be inspired by the necessities of the situation."

He had already gone out of the door when he struck his forehead with his hand.

"We have forgotten the Ministry of War."

"We shall easily find somebody for it among the generals," said Count Martin.

"Ah," exclaimed Garain, "you believe the choice of a minister of war is easy. It is clear you have not, like me, been a member of three cabinets and President of the Council. In my cabinets, and during my presidency the greatest difficulties came from the Ministry of War. Generals are all alike. You know the one I chose for the cabinet that I formed. When we took him, he knew nothing of affairs. He hardly knew there were two Chambers. We had to explain to him all the wheels of parliamentary machinery; we had to teach him that there were an army committee, finance committee, subcommittees, presidents of committees, a budget. He asked that all this information be written for him on a piece of paper. His ignorance of men and of things amazed and alarmed us. In a fortnight he knew the most subtle tricks of the trade; he knew personally all the senators and all the deputies, and was intriguing with them against us. If it had not been for President Grevy's help, he would have overthrown us. And he was a very ordinary general, a general like any other. Oh, no; do not think that the portfolio of war may be given hastily, without reflection."

And Garain still shivered at the thought of his former colleague.

Therese rose. Senator Loyer offered his arm to her, with the graceful attitude that he had learned forty years before at Bullier's dancing-hall. She left the politicians in the drawing-room, and hastened to meet Dechartre.

A rosy mist covered the Seine, the stone quays, and the gilded trees. The red sun threw into the cloudy sky the last glories of the year. Therese, as she went out, relished the sharpness of the air and the dying splendor of the day. Since her return to Paris, happy, she found pleasure every morning in the changes of the weather. It seemed to her, in her generous selfishness, that it was for her the wind blew in the trees, or the fine, gray rain wet the horizon of the avenues; for her, so that she might say, as she entered the little house of the Ternes, "It is windy; it is raining; the weather is pleasant;" mingling thus the ocean of things in the intimacy of her love. And every day was beautiful for her, since each one brought her to the arms of her beloved.

While on her way that day to the little house of the Ternes she thought of her unexpected happiness, so full and so secure. She walked in the last glory of the sun already touched by winter, and said to herself:

"He loves me; I believe he loves me entirely. To love is easier and more natural for him than for other men. They have in life ideas they think superior to love — faith, habits, interests. They believe in God, or in duties, or in themselves. He believes in me only. I am his God, his duty, and his life."

Then she thought:

"It is true, too, that he needs nobody, not even me. His thoughts alone are a magnificent world in which he could easily live by himself. But I can not live without him. What would become of me if I did not have him?"

She was not alarmed by the violent passion that he had for her. She recalled that she had said to him one day: "Your love for me is only sensual. I do not complain of it; it is perhaps the only true love." And he had replied: "It is also the only grand and strong love. It has its measure and its weapons. It is full of meaning and of images. It is violent and mysterious. It attaches itself to the flesh and to the soul of the flesh. The rest is only illusion and untruth." She was almost tranquil in her joy. Suspicions and anxieties had fled like the mists of a summer storm. The worst weather of their love had come when they had been separated from each other. One should never leave the one whom one loves.

At the corner of the Avenue Marceau and of the Rue Galilee, she divined rather than recognized a shadow that had passed by her, a forgotten form. She thought, she wished to think, she was mistaken. The one whom she thought she had seen existed no longer, never had existed. It was a spectre seen in the limbo of another world, in the darkness of a half light. And she continued to walk, retaining of this ill-defined meeting an impression of coldness, of vague embarrassment, and of pain in the heart.

As she proceeded along the avenue she saw coming toward her newspaper carriers holding the evening sheets announcing the new Cabinet. She traversed the square; her steps followed the happy impatience of her desire. She had visions of Jacques waiting for her at the foot of the stairway, among the marble figures; taking her in his arms and carrying her, trembling from kisses, to that room full of shadows and of delights, where the sweetness of life made her forget life.

But in the solitude of the Avenue MacMahon, the shadow which she had seen at the corner of the Rue Galilee came near her with a directness that was unmistakable.

She recognized Robert Le Menil, who, having followed her from the quay, was stopping her at the most quiet and secure place.

His air, his attitude, expressed the simplicity of motive which had formerly pleased Therese. His face, naturally harsh, darkened by sunburn, somewhat hollowed, but calm, expressed profound suffering.

"I must speak to you."

She slackened her pace. He walked by her side.

"I have tried to forget you. After what had happened it was natural, was it not? I have done all I could. It was better to forget you, surely; but I could not. So I bought a boat, and I have been traveling for six months. You know, perhaps?"

She made a sign that she knew.

He continued:

"The Rosebud, a beautiful yacht. There were six men in the crew. I manoeuvred with them. It was a pastime."

He paused. She was walking slowly, saddened, and, above all, annoyed. It seemed to her an absurd and painful thing, beyond all expression, to have to listen to such words from a stranger.

He continued:

"What I suffered on that boat I should be ashamed to tell you."

She felt he spoke the truth.

"Oh, I forgive you — I have reflected alone a great deal. I passed many nights and days on the divan of the deckhouse, turning always the same ideas in my mind. For six months I have thought more than I ever did in my life. Do not laugh. There is nothing like suffering to enlarge the mind. I understand that if I have lost you the fault is mine. I should have known how to keep you. And I said to myself: 'I did not know. Oh; if I could only begin again!' By dint of thinking and of suffering, I understand. I know now that I did not sufficiently share your tastes and your ideas. You are a superior woman. I did not notice it before, because it was not for that that I loved you. Without suspecting it, I irritated you."

She shook her head. He insisted.

"Yes, yes, I often wounded your feelings. I did not consider your delicacy. There were misunderstandings between us. The reason was, we have not the same temperament. And then, I did not know how to amuse you. I did not know how to give you the amusement you need. I did not procure for you the pleasures that a woman as intelligent as you requires."

So simple and so true was he in his regrets and in his pain, she found him worthy of sympathy. She said to him, softly:

"My friend, I never had reason to complain of you."

He continued:

"All I have said to you is true. I understood this when I was alone in my boat. I have spent hours on it to which I would not condemn my worst enemy. Often I felt like throwing myself into the water. I did not do it. Was it because I have religious principles or family sentiments, or because I have no courage? I do not know. The reason is, perhaps, that from a distance you held me to life. I was attracted by you, since I am here. For two days I have been watching you. I did not wish to reappear at your house. I should not have found you alone; I should not have been able to talk to you. And then you would have been forced to receive me. I thought it better to speak to you in the street. The idea came to me on the boat. I said to myself: 'In the street she will listen to me only if she wishes, as she wished four years ago in the park of Joinville, you know, under the statues, near the crown.'"

He continued, with a sigh:

"Yes, as at Joinville, since all is to be begun again. For two days I have been watching you. Yesterday it was raining; you went out in a carriage. I might have followed you and learned where you were going if I wished to do it. I did not do it. I do not wish to do what would displease you."

She extended her hand to him.

"I thank you. I knew I should not regret the trust I have placed in you."

Alarmed, impatient, fearing what more he might say, she tried to escape him.

"Farewell! You have all life before you. You should be happy. Appreciate it, and do not torment yourself about things that are not worth the trouble."

He stopped her with a look. His face had changed to the violent and resolute expression which she knew.

"I have told you I must speak to you. Listen to me for a minute."

She was thinking of Jacques, who was waiting for her. An occasional passer-by looked at her and went on his way. She stopped under the black branches of a tree, and waited with pity and fright in her soul.

He said:

"I forgive you and forget everything. Take me back. I will promise never to say a word of the past."

She shuddered, and made a movement of surprise and distaste so natural that he stopped. Then, after a moment of reflection:

"My proposition to you is not an ordinary one, I know it well. But I have reflected. I have thought of everything. It is the only possible thing. Think of it, Therese, and do not reply at once."

"It would be wrong to deceive you. I can not, I will not do what you say; and you know the reason why."

A cab was passing slowly near them. She made a sign to the coachman to stop. Le Menil kept her a moment longer.

"I knew you would say this to me, and that is the reason why I say to you, do not reply at once."

Her fingers on the handle of the door, she turned on him the glance of her gray eyes.

It was a painful moment for him. He recalled the time when he saw those charming gray eyes gleam under half-closed lids. He smothered a sob, and murmured:

"Listen; I can not live without you. I love you. It is now that I love you. Formerly I did not know."

And while she gave to the coachman, haphazard, the address of a tailor, Le Menil went away.

The meeting gave her much uneasiness and anxiety. Since she was forced to meet him again, she would have preferred to see him violent and brutal, as he had been at Florence. At the corner of the avenue she said to the coachman:

"To the Ternes."

CHAPTER XXXII
THE RED LILY

It was Friday, at the opera. The curtain had fallen on Faust's laboratory. From the orchestra, opera-glasses were raised in a surveying of the gold and purple theatre. The sombre drapery of the boxes framed the dazzling heads and bare shoulders of women. The amphitheatre bent above the parquette its garland of diamonds, hair, gauze, and satin. In the proscenium boxes were the wife of the Austrian Ambassador and the Duchess Gladwin; in the amphitheatre Berthe d'Osigny and Jane Tulle, the latter made famous the day before by the suicide of one of her lovers; in the boxes, Madame Berard de La Malle, her eyes lowered, her long eyelashes shading her pure cheeks; Princess Seniavine, who, looking superb, concealed under her fan panther — like yawnings; Madame de Morlaine, between two young women whom she was training in the elegances of the mind; Madame Meillan, resting assured on thirty years of sovereign beauty; Madame Berthier d'Eyzelles, erect under iron-gray hair sparkling with diamonds. The bloom of her cheeks heightened the austere dignity of her attitude. She was attracting much notice. It had been learned in the morning that, after the failure of Garain's latest combination, M. Berthier-d'Eyzelles had, undertaken the task of forming a Ministry. The papers published lists with the name of Martin-Belleme for the treasury, and the opera-glasses were turned toward the still empty box of the Countess Martin.

A murmur of voices filled the hall. In the third rank of the parquette, General Lariviere, standing at his place, was talking with General de La Briche.

"I will do as you do, my old comrade, I will go and plant cabbages in Touraine."

He was in one of his moments of melancholy, when nothingness appeared to him to be the end of life. He had flattered Garain, and Garain, thinking him too clever, had preferred for Minister of War a shortsighted and national artillery general. At least, the General relished the pleasure of seeing Garain abandoned, betrayed by his friends Berthier-d'Eyzelles and Martin-Belleme. It made him laugh even to the wrinkles of his small eyes. He laughed in profile. Weary of a long life of dissimulation, he gave to himself suddenly the joy of expressing his thoughts.

"You see, my good La Briche, they make fools of us with their civil army, which costs a great deal, and is worth nothing. Small armies are the only good ones. This was the opinion of Napoleon I, who knew."

"It is true, it is very true," sighed General de La Briche, with tears in his eyes.

Montessuy passed before them; Lariviere extended his hand to him.

"They say, Montessuy, that you are the one who checked Garain. Accept my compliments."

Montessuy denied that he had exercised any political influence. He was not a senator nor a deputy, nor a councilor-general. And, looking through his glasses at the hall:

"See, Lariviere, in that box at the right, a very beautiful woman, a brunette."

And he took his seat quietly, relishing the sweets of power.

However, in the hall, in the corridors, the names of the new Ministers went from mouth to mouth in the midst of profound indifference: President of the Council and Minister of the Interior, Berthier-d'Eyzelles; justice and Religions, Loyer; Treasury, Martin-Belleme. All the ministers were known except those of Commerce, War, and the Navy, who were not yet designated.

The curtain was raised on the wine-shop of Bacchus. The students were singing their second chorus when Madame Martin appeared in her box. Her white gown had sleeves like wings, and on the drapery of her corsage, at the left breast, shone a large ruby lily.

Miss Bell sat near her, in a green velvet Queen Anne gown. Betrothed to Prince Eusebio Albertinelli della Spina, she had come to Paris to order her trousseau.

In the movement and the noise of the kermess she said:

"Darling, you have left at Florence a friend who retains the charm of your memory. It is Professor Arrighi. He reserves for you the praise-which he says is the most beautiful. He says you are a musical creature. But how could Professor Arrighi forget you, darling, since the trees in the garden have not forgotten you? Their unleaved branches lament your absence. Even they regret you, darling."

"Tell them," said Therese, "that I have of Fiesole a delightful reminiscence, which I shall always keep."

In the rear of the opera-box M. Martin-Belleme was explaining in a low voice his ideas to Joseph Springer and to Duviquet. He was saying: "France's signature is the best in the world." He was inclined to prudence in financial matters.

And Miss Bell said:

"Darling, I will tell the trees of Fiesole that you regret them and that you will soon come to visit them on their hills. But I ask you, do you see Monsieur Dechartre in Paris? I should like to see him very much. I like him because his mind is graceful. Darling, the mind of Monsieur Dechartre is full of grace and elegance."

Therese replied M. Jacques Dechartre was doubtless in the theatre, and that he would not fail to come and salute Miss Bell.

The curtain fell on the gayety of the waltz scene. Visitors crowded the foyers. Financiers, artists, deputies met in the anteroom adjoining the box. They surrounded M. Martin-Belleme, murmured polite congratulations, made graceful gestures to him, and crowded one another in order to shake his hand. Joseph Schmoll, coughing, complaining, blind and deaf, made his way through the throng and reached Madame Martin. He took her hand and said:

"They say your husband is appointed Minister. Is it true?"

She knew they were talking of it, but she did not think he had been appointed yet. Her husband was there, why not ask him? Sensitive to literal truths only, Schmoll said:

"Your husband is not yet a Minister? When he is appointed, I will ask you for an interview. It is an affair of the highest importance."

He paused, throwing from his gold spectacles the glances of a blind man and of a visionary, which kept him, despite the brutal exactitude of his temperament, in a sort of mystical state of mind. He asked, brusquely:

"Were you in Italy this year, Madame?"

And, without giving her time to answer:

"I know, I know. You went to Rome. You have looked at the arch of the infamous Titus, that execrable monument, where one may see the seven-branched candlestick among the spoils of the Jews. Well, Madame, it is a shame to the world that that monument remains standing in the city of Rome, where the Popes have subsisted only through the art of the Jews, financiers and money-changers. The Jews brought to Italy the science of Greece and of the Orient. The Renaissance, Madame, is the work of Israel. That is the truth, certain but misunderstood."

And he went through the crowd of visitors, crushing hats as he passed.

Princess Seniavine looked at her friend from her box with the curiosity that the beauty of women at times excited in her. She made a sign to Paul Vence who was near her:

"Do you not think Madame Martin is extraordinarily beautiful this year?"

In the lobby, full of light and gold, General de La Briche asked Lariviere:

"Did you see my nephew?"

"Your nephew, Le Menil?"

"Yes — Robert. He was in the theatre a moment ago."

La Briche remained pensive for a moment. Then he said:

"He came this summer to Semanville. I thought him odd. A charming fellow, frank and intelligent. But he ought to have some occupation, some aim in life."

547

The bell which announced the end of an intermission between the acts had hushed. In the foyer the two old men were walking alone.

"An aim in life," repeated La Briche, tall, thin, and bent, while his companion, lightened and rejuvenated, hastened within, fearing to miss a scene.

Marguerite, in the garden, was spinning and singing. When she had finished, Miss Bell said to Madame Martin:

"Darling, Monsieur Choulette has written me a perfectly beautiful letter. He has told me that he is very celebrated. And I am glad to know it. He said also: 'The glory of other poets reposes in myrrh and aromatic plants. Mine bleeds and moans under a rain of stones and of oyster-shells.' Do the French, my love, really throw stones at Monsieur Choulette?"

While Therese reassured Miss Bell, Loyer, imperious and somewhat noisy, caused the door of the box to be opened. He appeared wet and spattered with mud.

"I come from the Elysee," he said.

He had the gallantry to announce to Madame Martin, first, the good news he was bringing:

"The decrees are signed. Your husband has the Finances. It is a good portfolio."

"The President of the Republic," inquired M. Martin — Belleme, "made no objection when my name was pronounced?"

"No; Berthier praised the hereditary property of the Martins, your caution, and the links with which you are attached to certain personalities in the financial world whose concurrence may be useful to the government. And the President, in accordance with Garain's happy expression, was inspired by the necessities of the situation. He has signed."

On Count Martin's yellowed face two or three wrinkles appeared. He was smiling.

"The decree," continued Loyer, "will be published tomorrow. I accompanied myself the clerk who took it to the printer. It was surer. In Grevy's time, and Grevy was not an idiot, decrees were intercepted in the journey from the Elysee to the Quai Voltaire."

And Loyer threw himself on a chair. There, enjoying the view of Madame Martin, he continued:

"People will not say, as they did in the time of my poor friend Gambetta, that the republic is lacking in women. You will give us fine festivals, Madame, in the salons of the Ministry."

Marguerite, looking at herself in the mirror, with her necklace and earrings, was singing the jewel song.

"We shall have to compose the declaration," said Count Martin. "I have thought of it. For my department I have found, I think, a fine formula."

Loyer shrugged his shoulders.

"My dear Martin, we have nothing essential to change in the declaration of the preceding Cabinet; the situation is unchanged."

He struck his forehead with his hand.

"Oh, I had forgotten. We have made your friend, old Lariviere, Minister of War, without consulting him. I have to warn him."

He thought he could find him in the boulevard cafe, where military men go. But Count Martin knew the General was in the theatre.

"I must find him," said Loyer.

Bowing to Therese, he said:

"You permit me, Countess, to take your husband?"

They had just gone out when Jacques Dechartre and Paul Vence came into the box.

"I congratulate you, Madame," said Paul Vence.

But she turned toward Dechartre:

"I hope you have not come to congratulate me, too."

Paul Vence asked her if she would move into the apartments of the Ministry.

"Oh, no," she replied.

"At least, Madame," said Paul Vence, "you will go to the balls at the Elysees, and we shall admire the art with which you retain your mysterious charm."

"Changes in cabinets," said Madame Martin, "inspire you, Monsieur Vence, with very frivolous reflections."

"Madame," continued Paul Vence, "I shall not say like Renan, my beloved master: 'What does Sirius care?' because somebody would reply with reason 'What does little Earth care for big Sirius?' But I am always surprised when people who are adult, and even old, let themselves be deluded by the illusion of power, as if hunger, love, and death, all the ignoble or sublime necessities of life, did not exercise on men an empire too sovereign to leave them anything other than power written on paper and an empire of words. And, what is still more marvellous, people imagine they have other chiefs of state and other ministers than their miseries, their desires, and their imbecility. He was a wise man who said: 'Let us give to men irony and pity as witnesses and judges.'"

"But, Monsieur Vence," said Madame Martin, laughingly, "you are the man who wrote that. I read it."

The two Ministers looked vainly in the theatre and in the corridors for the General. On the advice of the ushers, they went behind the scenes.

Two ballet-dancers were standing sadly, with a foot on the bar placed against the wall. Here and there men in evening dress and women in gauze formed groups almost silent.

Loyer and Martin-Belleme, when they entered, took off their hats. They saw, in the rear of the hall, Lariviere with a pretty girl whose pink tunic, held by a gold belt, was open at the hips.

She held in her hand a gilt pasteboard cup. When they were near her, they heard her say to the General:

"You are old, to be sure, but I think you do as much as he does."

And she was pointing disdainfully to a grinning young man, with a gardenia in his button-hole, who stood near them.

Loyer motioned to the General that he wished to speak to him, and, pushing him against the bar, said:

"I have the pleasure to announce to you that you have been appointed Minister of War."

Lariviere, distrustful, said nothing. That badly dressed man with long hair, who, under his dusty coat, resembled a clown, inspired so little confidence in him that he suspected a snare, perhaps a bad joke.

"Monsieur Loyer is Keeper of the Seals," said Count Martin.

"General, you cannot refuse," Loyer said. "I have said you will accept. If you hesitate, it will be favoring the offensive return of Garain. He is a traitor."

"My dear colleague, you exaggerate," said Count Martin; "but Garain, perhaps, is lacking a little in frankness. And the General's support is urgent."

"The Fatherland before everything," replied Lariviere with emotion.

"You know, General," continued Loyer, "the existing laws are to be applied with moderation."

He looked at the two dancers who were extending their short and muscular legs on the bar.

Lariviere murmured:

"The army's patriotism is excellent; the good-will of the chiefs is at the height of the most critical circumstances."

Loyer tapped his shoulder.

"My dear colleague, there is some use in having big armies."

"I believe as you do," replied Lariviere; "the present army fills the superior necessities of national defence."

"The use of big armies," continued Loyer, "is to make war impossible. One would be crazy to engage in a war these immeasurable forces, the management of which surpasses all human faculty. Is not this your opinion, General?"

General Lariviere winked.

"The situation," he said, "exacts circumspection. We are facing a perilous unknown."

Then Loyer, looking at his war colleague with cynical contempt, said:

"In the very improbable case of a war, don't you think, my dear colleague, that the real generals would be the station-masters?"

The three Ministers went out by the private stairway. The President of the Council was waiting for them.

The last act had begun; Madame Martin had in her box only Dechartre and Miss Bell. Miss Bell was saying:

"I rejoice, darling, I am exalted, at the thought that you wear on your heart the red lily of Florence. Monsieur Dechartre, whose soul is artistic, must be very glad, too, to see at your corsage that charming jewel.

"I should like to know the jeweler that made it, darling. This lily is lithe and supple like an iris. Oh, it is elegant, magnificent, and cruel. Have you noticed, my love, that beautiful jewels have an air of magnificent cruelty?"

"My jeweler," said Therese, "is here, and you have named him; it is Monsieur Dechartre who designed this jewel."

The door of the box was opened. Therese half turned her head and saw in the shadow Le Menil, who was bowing to her with his brusque suppleness.

"Transmit, I pray you, Madame, my congratulations to your husband."

He complimented her on her fine appearance. He spoke to Miss Bell a few courteous and precise words.

Therese listened anxiously, her mouth half open in the painful effort to say insignificant things in reply. He asked her whether she had had a good season at Joinville. He would have liked to go in the hunting time, but could not. He had gone to the Mediterranean, then he had hunted at Semanville.

"Oh, Monsieur Le Menil," said Miss Bell, "you have wandered on the blue sea. Have you seen sirens?"

No, he had not seen sirens, but for three days a dolphin had swum in the yacht's wake.

Miss Bell asked him if that dolphin liked music.

He thought not.

"Dolphins," he said, "are very ordinary fish that sailors call sea-geese, because they have goose-shaped heads."

But Miss Bell would not believe that the monster which had earned the poet Arion had a goose-shaped head.

"Monsieur Le Menil, if next year a dolphin comes to swim near your boat, I pray you play to him on the flute the Delphic Hymn to Apollo. Do you like the sea, Monsieur Le Menil?"

"I prefer the woods."

Self-contained, simple, he talked quietly.

"Oh, Monsieur Le Menil, I know you like woods where the hares dance in the moonlight."

Dechartre, pale, rose and went out.

The church scene was on. Marguerite, kneeling, was wringing her hands, and her head drooped with the weight of her long tresses. The voices of the organ and the chorus sang the death-song.

"Oh, darling, do you know that that death-song, which is sung only in the Catholic churches, comes from a Franciscan hermitage? It sounds like the wind which blows in winter in the trees on the summit of the Alverno."

Therese did not hear. Her soul had followed Dechartre through the door of her box.

In the anteroom was a noise of overthrown chairs. It was Schmoll coming back. He had learned that M. Martin-Belleme had recently been appointed Minister. At once he claimed the cross of Commander of the Legion of Honor and a larger apartment at the Institute. His apartment was small, narrow, insufficient for his wife and his five daughters. He had been forced to put his workshop under the roof. He made long complaints, and consented to go only after Madame Martin had promised that she would speak to her husband.

"Monsieur Le Menil," asked Miss Bell, "shall you go yachting next year?"

Le Menil thought not. He did not intend to keep the Rosebud. The water was tiresome.

And calm, energetic, determined, he looked at Therese.

On the stage, in Marguerite's prison, Mephistopheles sang, and the orchestra imitated the gallop of horses. Therese murmured:

"I have a headache. It is too warm here."

Le Menil opened the door.

The clear phrase of Marguerite calling the angels ascended to heaven in white sparks.

"Darling, I will tell you that poor Marguerite does not wish to be saved according to the flesh, and for that reason she is saved in spirit and in truth. I believe one thing, darling, I believe firmly we shall all be saved. Oh, yes, I believe in the final purification of sinners."

Therese rose, tall and white, with the red flower at her breast. Miss Bell, immovable, listened to the music. Le Menil, in the anteroom, took Madame Martin's cloak, and, while he held it unfolded, she traversed the box, the anteroom, and stopped before the mirror of the half-open door. He placed on her bare shoulders the cape of red velvet embroidered with gold and lined with ermine, and said, in a low tone, but distinctly:

"Therese, I love you. Remember what I asked you the day before yesterday. I shall be every day, at three o'clock, at our home, in the Rue Spontini."

At this moment, as she made a motion with her head to receive the cloak, she saw Dechartre with his hand on the knob of the door. He had heard. He looked at her with all the reproach and suffering that human eyes can contain. Then he went into the dim corridor. She felt hammers of fire beating in her chest and remained immovable on the threshold.

"You were waiting for me?" said Montessuy. "You are left alone to-day. I will escort you and Miss Bell."

554

CHAPTER XXXIII
A WHITE NIGHT

In the carriage, and in her room, she saw again the look of her lover, that cruel and dolorous look. She knew with what facility he fell into despair, the promptness of his will not to will. She had seen him run away thus on the shore of the Arno. Happy then in her sadness and in her anguish, she could run after him and say, "Come." Now, again surrounded, watched, she should have found something to say, and not have let him go from her dumb and desolate. She had remained surprised, stunned. The accident had been so absurd and so rapid! She had against Le Menil the sentiment of simple anger which malicious things cause. She reproached herself bitterly for having permitted her lover to go without a word, without a glance, wherein she could have placed her soul.

While Pauline waited to undress her, Therese walked to and fro impatiently. Then she stopped suddenly. In the obscure mirrors, wherein the reflections of the candles were drowned, she saw the corridor of the playhouse, and her beloved flying from her through it.

Where was he now? What was he saying to himself alone? It was torture for her not to be able to rejoin him and see him again at once.

She pressed her heart with her hands; she was smothering.

Pauline uttered a cry. She saw drops of blood on the white corsage of her mistress.

Therese, without knowing it, had pricked her hand with the red lily.

She detached the emblematic jewel which she had worn before all as the dazzling secret of her heart, and, holding it in her fingers, contemplated it for a long time. Then she saw again the days of Florence — the cell of San Marco, where her lover's kiss weighed delicately on her mouth, while, through her lowered lashes, she vaguely perceived again the angels and the sky painted on the wall, and the dazzling fountain of the ice-vender against the bright cloth; the pavilion of the Via Alfieri, its nymphs, its goats, and the room where the shepherds and the masks on the screens listened to her sighs and noted her long silences.

No, all these things were not shadows of the past, spectres of ancient hours. They were the present reality of her love. And a word stupidly cast by a stranger would destroy these beautiful things! Happily, it was not possible. Her love, her lover, did not depend on such insignificant matters. If only she could run to his house! She would find him before the fire, his elbows on his knees, his head in his hands, sad. Then she would run her fingers through his hair, force him to lift his head, to see that she loved him, that she was his treasure, palpitating with joy and love.

She had dismissed her maid. In her bed she thought of only one thing.

It was an accident, an absurd accident. He would understand it; he would know that their love had nothing to do with anything so stupid. What folly for him to care about another! As if there were other men in the world!

M. Martin-Belleme half opened the bedroom door. Seeing a light he went in.

"You are not asleep, Therese?"

He had been at a conference with his colleagues. He wanted advice from his wife on certain points. He needed to hear sincere words.

"It is done," he said. "You will help me, I am sure, in my situation, which is much envied, but very difficult and even perilous. I owe it to you somewhat, since it came to me through the powerful influence of your father."

He consulted her on the choice of a Chief of Cabinet.

She advised him as best she could. She thought he was sensible, calm, and not sillier than many others.

He lost himself in reflections.

"I have to defend before the Senate the budget voted by the Chamber of Deputies. The budget contains innovations which I did not approve. When I was a deputy I fought against them. Now that I am a minister I must support them. I saw things from the outside formerly. I see them from the inside now, and their aspect is changed. And, then, I am free no longer."

He sighed:

"Ah, if the people only knew the little that we can do when we are powerful!"

He told her his impressions. Berthier was reserved. The others were impenetrable. Loyer alone was excessively authoritative.

She listened to him without attention and without impatience. His pale face and voice marked for her like a clock the minutes that passed with intolerable slowness.

Loyer had odd sallies of wit. Immediately after he had declared his strict adhesion to the Concordat, he said: "Bishops are spiritual prefects. I will protect them since they belong to me. And through them I shall hold the guardians of souls, curates."

He recalled to her that she would have to meet people who were not of her class and who would shock her by their vulgarity. But his situation demanded that he should not disdain anybody. At all events, he counted on her tact and on her devotion.

She looked at him, a little astonished.

"There is no hurry, my dear. We shall see later."

He was tired. He said good-night and advised her to sleep. She was ruining her health by reading all night. He left her.

She heard the noise of his footsteps, heavier than usual, while he traversed the library, encumbered with blue books and journals, to reach his room, where he would perhaps sleep. Then she felt the weight on her of the night's silence. She looked at her watch. It was half-past one.

She said to herself: "He, too, is suffering. He looked at me with so much despair and anger."

She was courageous and ardent. She was impatient at being a prisoner. When daylight came, she would go, she would see him, she would explain everything to him. It was so clear! In the painful monotony of her thought, she listened to the rolling of wagons which at long intervals passed on the quay. That noise preoccupied, almost interested her. She listened to the rumble, at first faint and distant, then louder, in which she could distinguish the rolling of the wheels, the creaking of the axles, the shock of horses' shoes, which, decreasing little by little, ended in an imperceptible murmur.

And when silence returned, she fell again into her reverie.

He would understand that she loved him, that she had never loved any one except him. It was unfortunate that the night was so long. She did not dare to look at her watch for fear of seeing in it the immobility of time.

She rose, went to the window, and drew the curtains. There was a pale light in the clouded sky. She thought it might be the beginning of dawn. She looked at her watch. It was half-past three.

She returned to the window. The sombre infinity outdoors attracted her. She looked. The sidewalks shone under the gas-jets. A gentle rain was falling. Suddenly a voice ascended in the silence; acute, and then grave, it seemed to be made of several voices replying to one another. It — was a drunkard disputing with the beings of his dream, to whom he generously gave utterance, and whom he confounded afterward with great gestures and in furious sentences. Therese could see the poor man walk along the parapet in his white blouse, and she could hear words recurring incessantly: "That is what I say to the government."

Chilled, she returned to her bed. She thought, "He is jealous, he is madly jealous. It is a question of nerves and of blood. But his love, too, is an affair of blood and of nerves. His love and his jealousy are one and the same thing. Another would understand. It would be sufficient to please his self-love." But he was jealous from the depth of his soul. She knew this; she knew that in him jealousy was a physical torture, a wound enlarged by imagination. She knew how profound the evil was. She had seen him grow pale before the bronze St. Mark when she had thrown the letter in the box on the wall of the old Florentine house at a time when she was his only in dreams.

She recalled his smothered complaints, his sudden fits of sadness, and the painful mystery of the words which he repeated frequently: "I can forget you only when I am with you." She saw again the Dinard letter and his furious despair at a word overheard at a wine-shop table. She felt that the blow had been struck accidentally at the most sensitive point, at the bleeding wound. But she did not lose courage. She would tell everything, she would confess everything, and all her avowals would say to him: "I love you. I have never loved any one except you!" She had not betrayed him. She would tell him nothing that he had not guessed. She had lied so little, as little as possible, and then only not to give him pain. How could he not understand? It was better he should know everything, since everything meant nothing. She represented to herself incessantly the same ideas, repeated to herself the same words.

Her lamp gave only a smoky light. She lighted candles. It was six o'clock. She realized that she had slept. She ran to the window. The sky was black, and mingled with the earth in a chaos of thick darkness. Then she was curious to know exactly at what hour the sun would rise. She had had no idea of this. She thought only that nights were long in December. She did not think of looking at the calendar. The heavy step of workmen walking in squads, the noise of wagons of milkmen and marketmen, came to her ear like sounds of good augury. She shuddered at this first awakening of the city.

CHAPTER XXXIV
"I SEE THE OTHER WITH YOU ALWAYS!"

At nine o'clock, in the yard of the little house, she observed M. Fusellier sweeping, in the rain, while smoking his pipe. Madame Fusellier came out of her box. Both looked embarrassed. Madame Fusellier was the first to speak:

"Monsieur Jacques is not at home." And, as Therese remained silent, immovable, Fusellier came near her with his broom, hiding with his left hand his pipe behind his back —

"Monsieur Jacques has not yet come home."

"I will wait for him," said Therese.

Madame Fusellier led her to the parlor, where she lighted the fire. As the wood smoked and would not flame, she remained bent, with her hands on her knees.

"It is the rain," she said, "which causes the smoke."

Madame Martin said it was not worth while to make a fire, that she did not feel cold.

She saw herself in the glass.

She was livid, with glowing spots on her cheeks. Then only she felt that her feet were frozen. She approached the fire. Madame Fusellier, seeing her anxious, spoke softly to her:

"Monsieur Jacques will come soon. Let Madame warm herself while waiting for him."

A dim light fell with the rain on the glass ceiling.

Upon the wall, the lady with the unicorn was not beautiful among the cavaliers in a forest full of flowers and birds. Therese was repeating to herself the words: "He has not yet come home." And by dint of saying this she lost the meaning of it. With burning eyes she looked at the door.

She remained thus without a movement, without a thought, for a time the duration of which she did not know; perhaps half an hour. The noise of a footstep came to her, the door was opened. He came in. She saw that he was wet with rain and mud, and burning with fever.

560

She fixed on him a look so sincere and so frank that it struck him. But almost at once he recalled within himself all his sufferings.

He said to her:

"What do you want of me? You have done me all the harm you could do me."

Fatigue gave him an air of gentleness. It frightened her.

"Jacques, listen to me!"

He motioned to her that he wished to hear nothing from her.

"Jacques, listen to me. I have not deceived you. Oh, no, I have not deceived you. Was it possible? Was it — "

He interrupted her:

"Have some pity for me. Do not make me suffer again. Leave me, I pray you. If you knew the night I have passed, you would not have the courage to torment me again."

He let himself fall on the divan. He had walked all night. Not to suffer too much, he had tried to find diversions. On the Bercy Quay he had looked at the moon floating in the clouds. For an hour he had seen it veil itself and reappear. Then he had counted the windows of houses with minute care. The rain began to fall. He had gone to the market and had drunk whiskey in a wine-room. A big girl who squinted had said to him, "You don't look happy." He had fallen half asleep on the leather bench. It had been a moment of oblivion. The images of that painful night passed before his eyes. He said: "I recalled the night of the Arno. You have spoiled for me all the joy and beauty in the world." He asked her to leave him alone. In his lassitude he had a great pity for himself. He would have liked to sleep — not to die; he held death in horror — but to sleep and never to wake again. Yet, before him, as desirable as formerly, despite the painful fixity of her dry eyes, and more mysterious than ever, he saw her. His hatred was vivified by suffering.

She extended her arms to him. "Listen to me, Jacques." He motioned to her that it was useless for her to speak. Yet he wished to listen to her, and already he was listening with avidity.

He detested and rejected in advance what she would say, but nothing else in the world interested him.

She said:

"You may have believed I was betraying you, that I was not living for you alone. But can you not understand anything? You do not see that if that man were my lover it would not have been necessary for him to talk to me at the play-house in that box; he would have a thousand other ways of meeting me. Oh, no, my friend, I assure you that since the day when I had the happiness to meet you, I have been yours entirely. Could I have been another's? What you imagine is monstrous. But I love you, I love you! I love only you. I never have loved any one except you."

He replied slowly, with cruel heaviness:

"'I shall be every day, at three o'clock, at our home, in the Rue Spontini.' It was not a lover, your lover, who said these things? No! it was a stranger, an unknown person."

She straightened herself, and with painful gravity said:

"Yes, I had been his. You knew it. I have denied it, I have told an untruth, not to irritate or grieve you. I saw you so anxious. But I lied so little and so badly. You knew. Do not reproach me for it. You knew; you often spoke to me of the past, and then one day somebody told you at the restaurant — and you imagined much more than ever happened. While telling an untruth, I was not deceiving you. If you knew the little that he was in my life! There! I did not know you. I did not know you were to come. I was lonely."

She fell on her knees.

"I was wrong. I should have waited for you. But if you knew how slight a matter that was in my life!"

And with her voice modulated to a soft and singing complaint she said:

"Why did you not come sooner, why?"

She dragged herself to him, tried to take his hands. He repelled her.

"I was stupid. I did not think. I did not know. I did not wish to know."

He rose and exclaimed, in an explosion of hatred:

"I did not wish him to be that man."

She sat in the place which he had left, and there, plaintively, in a low voice, she explained the past. In that time she lived in a world horribly commonplace. She had yielded, but she had regretted at once. If he but knew the sadness of her life he would not be jealous. He would pity her. She shook her head and said, looking at him through the falling locks of her hair:

"I am talking to you of another woman. There is nothing in common between that woman and me. I exist only since I have known you, since I have belonged to you."

He walked about the room madly. He laughed painfully.

"Yes; but while you loved me, the other woman — the one who was not you?"

She looked at him indignantly:

"Can you believe — "

"Did you not see him again at Florence? Did you not accompany him to the station?"

She told him that he had come to Italy to find her; that she had seen him; that she had broken with him; that he had gone, irritated, and that since then he was trying to win her back; but that she had not even paid any attention to him.

"My beloved, I see, I know, only you in the world." He shook his head.

"I do not believe you."

She revolted.

"I have told you everything. Accuse me, condemn me, but do not offend me in my love for you."

He shook his head.

"Leave me. You have harmed me too much. I have loved you so much that all the pain which you could have given me I would have taken, kept, loved; but this is too hideous. I hate it. Leave me. I am suffering too much. Farewell!"

She stood erect.

"I have come. It is my happiness, it is my life, I am fighting for. I will not go."

And she said again all that she had already said. Violent and sincere, sure of herself, she explained how she had broken the tie which was already loose and irritated her; how since the day when she had loved him she had been his only, without regret, without a wandering look or thought. But in speaking to him of another she irritated him. And he shouted at her:

"I do not believe you."

She only repeated her declarations.

And suddenly, instinctively, she looked at her watch:

"Oh, it is noon!"

She had often given that cry of alarm when the farewell hour had surprised them. And Jacques shuddered at the phrase which was so familiar, so painful, and was this time so desperate. For a few minutes more she said ardent words and shed tears. Then she left him; she had gained nothing.

At her house she found in the waiting-room the marketwoman, who had come to present a bouquet to her. She remembered that her husband was a State minister. There were telegrams, visiting-cards and letters, congratulations and solicitations. Madame Marmet wrote to recommend her nephew to General Lariviere.

She went into the dining-room and fell in a chair. M. Martin-Belleme was just finishing his breakfast. He was expected at the Cabinet Council and at the former Finance Minister's, to whom he owed a call.

"Do not forget, my dear friend, to call on Madame Berthier d'Eyzelles. You know how sensitive she is."

She made no answer. While he was dipping his fingers in the glass bowl, he saw she was so tired that he dared not say any more. He found himself in the presence of a secret which he did not wish to know; in presence of an intimate suffering which one word would reveal. He felt anxiety, fear, and a certain respect.

He threw down his napkin.

"Excuse me, dear."

He went out.

She tried to eat, but could swallow nothing.

At two o'clock she returned to the little house of the Ternes. She found Jacques in his room. He was smoking a wooden pipe. A cup of coffee almost empty was on the table. He looked at her with a harshness that chilled her. She dared not talk, feeling that everything that she could say would offend and irritate him, and yet she knew that in remaining discreet and dumb she intensified his anger. He knew that she would return; he had waited for her with impatience. A sudden light came to her, and she saw that she had done wrong to come; that if she had been absent he would have desired, wanted, called for her, perhaps. But it was too late; and, at all events, she was not trying to be crafty.

She said to him:

"You see I have returned. I could not do otherwise. And then it was natural, since I love you. And you know it."

She knew very well that all she could say would only irritate him. He asked her whether that was the way she spoke in the Rue Spontini.

She looked at him with sadness.

"Jacques, you have often told me that there were hatred and anger in your heart against me. You like to make me suffer. I can see it."

With ardent patience, at length, she told him her entire life, the little that she had put into it; the sadness of the past; and how, since he had known her, she had lived only through him and in him.

The words fell as limpid as her look. She sat near him. He listened to her with bitter avidity. Cruel with himself, he wished to know everything about her last meetings with the other. She reported faithfully the events of the Great Britain Hotel; but she changed the scene to the outside, in an alley of the Casino, from fear that the image of their sad interview in a closed room should irritate her lover. Then she explained the meeting at the station. She had not wished to cause despair to a suffering man who was so violent. But since then she had had no news from him until the day when he spoke to her on the street. She repeated what she had replied to him. Two days later she had seen him at the opera, in her box. Certainly, she had not encouraged him to come. It was the truth.

It was the truth. But the old poison, slowly accumulating in his mind, burned him. She made the past, the irreparable past, present to him, by her avowals. He saw images of it which tortured him. He said:

"I do not believe you."

And he added:

"And if I believed you, I could not see you again, because of the idea that you have loved that man. I have told you, I have written to you, you remember, that I did not wish him to be that man. And since — "

He stopped.

She said:

"You know very well that since then nothing has happened."

He replied, with violence:

"Since then I have seen him."

They remained silent for a long time. Then she said, surprised and plaintive:

"But, my friend, you should have thought that a woman such as I, married as I was — every day one sees women bring to their lovers a past darker than mine and yet they inspire love. Ah, my past — if you knew how insignificant it was!"

"I know what you can give. One can not forgive to you what one may forgive to another."

"But, my friend, I am like others."

"No, you are not like others. To you one can not forgive anything."

He talked with set teeth. His eyes, which she had seen so large, glowing with tenderness, were now dry, harsh, narrowed between wrinkled lids and cast a new glance at her. He frightened her. She went to the rear of the room, sat on a chair, and there she remained, trembling, for a long time, smothered by her sobs. Then she broke into tears.

He sighed:

"Why did I ever know you?"

She replied, weeping:

"I do not regret having known you. I am dying of it, and I do not regret it. I have loved."

He stubbornly continued to make her suffer. He felt that he was playing an odious part, but he could not stop.

"It is possible, after all, that you have loved me too."

She answered, with soft bitterness:

"But I have loved only you. I have loved you too much. And it is for that you are punishing me. Oh, can you think that I was to another what I have been to you?"

"Why not?"

She looked at him without force and without courage.

"It is true that you do not believe me."

She added softly:

"If I killed myself would you believe me?"

"No, I would not believe you."

She wiped her cheeks with her handkerchief; then, lifting her eyes, shining through her tears, she said:

"Then, all is at an end!"

She rose, saw again in the room the thousand things with which she had lived in laughing intimacy, which she had regarded as hers, now suddenly become nothing to her, and confronting her as a stranger and an enemy. She saw again the nude woman who made, while running, the gesture which had not been explained to her; the Florentine models which recalled to her Fiesole and the enchanted hours of Italy; the profile sketch by Dechartre of the girl who laughed in her pretty pathetic thinness. She stopped a moment sympathetically in front of that little newspaper girl who had come there too, and had disappeared, carried away in the irresistible current of life and of events.

She repeated:

"Then all is at an end?"

He remained silent.

The twilight made the room dim.

"What will become of me?" she asked.

"And what will become of me?" he replied.

They looked at each other with sympathy, because each was moved with self-pity.

Therese said again:

"And I, who feared to grow old in your eyes, for fear our beautiful love should end! It would have been better if it had never come. Yes, it would be better if I had not been born. What a presentiment was that which came to me, when a child, under the lindens of Joinville, before the marble nymphs! I wished to die then."

Her arms fell, and clasping her hands she lifted her eyes; her wet glance threw a light in the shadows.

"Is there not a way of my making you feel that what I am saying to you is true? That never since I have been yours, never — But how could I? The very idea of it seems horrible, absurd. Do you know me so little?"

He shook his head sadly. "I do not know you."

She questioned once more with her eyes all the objects in the room.

"But then, what we have been to each other was vain, useless. Men and women break themselves against one another; they do not mingle."

She revolted. It was not possible that he should not feel what he was to her. And, in the ardor of her love, she threw herself on him and smothered him with kisses and tears. He forgot everything, and took her in his arms — sobbing, weak, yet happy — and clasped her close with the fierceness of desire. With her head leaning back against the pillow, she smiled through her tears. Then, brusquely he disengaged himself.

"I do not see you alone. I see the other with you always." She looked at him, dumb, indignant, desperate. Then, feeling that all was indeed at an end, she cast around her a surprised glance of her unseeing eyes, and went slowly away.

www.ingramcontent.com/pod-product-compliance
Lightning Source LLC
Chambersburg PA
CBHW070349030726
47504CB00001B/115